Branches of Heaven
A History of the Imperial Clan of Sung China

Harvard East Asian Monographs, 183

Branches of Heaven
A History of the Imperial Clan of Sung China

John W. Chaffee

Published by the Harvard University Asia Center
and distributed by Harvard University Press
Cambridge, Massachusetts, and London 1999

Printed in the United States of America

The Harvard University Asia Center publishes a monograph series and, in coordination with the Fairbank Center for East Asian Research, the Korea Institute, the Reischauer Institute of Japanese Studies, and other faculties and institutes, administers research projects designed to further scholarly understanding of China, Japan, Vietnam, Korea, and other Asian countries. The Center also sponsors projects addressing multidisciplinary and regional issues in Asia.

Library of Congress Cataloging-in-Publication Data
Chaffee, John W.
    Branches of heaven : a history of the imperial clan of Sung China
/ John W. Chaffee
        p.   cm. -- (Harvard East Asian monographs ; 183)
    Includes bibliographical references and index.
    ISBN 0-674-08049-1 (alk. paper)
    1. China--History--Sung dynasty, 960–1279.   2. China--Kings and rulers.   3. Nobility--China.   I. Title.   II. Title: History of the imperial clan of Sung China.   III. Series.
    DS 751.3.C35   1999
    951'.024--dc21   99-28564
                                                                    CIP

Index by the author

    ⊗ Printed on acid-free paper

Last figure below indicates year of this printing
09 08 07 06 05 04 03 02 01 00 99

To Barbara

Acknowledgments

This study began with a group. While working on the Sung examination system for *The Thorny Gates of Learning in Sung China*, I became curious about the imperial clansmen, for in the Southern Sung they occupy a highly visible position in the examinations. In 1256, for example, they accounted for 12.5 percent of the successful candidates for the *chin-shih* degree that year and had their own qualifying and even departmental examinations. I was also familiar with the statistics of Li Hsin-ch'uan, the Southern Sung historian, who documented both the spectacular growth of the imperial clan in the Northern Sung—from three brothers to over five thousand clansmen in six generations—and their imposing bureaucratic presence in 1203, when they constituted 3 percent of the civil service and 17 percent of the military service. Yet despite their obvious importance, they had virtually been ignored by past historians. Who, I wondered, were these people, and what role or roles did they play in Sung society and politics?

The ensuing research involved not only the standard documentary collections, histories, and essays by individual writers but also all the biographies of clansmen and clanswomen that I could find, including some two hundred epitaphs. As my knowledge of the clan deepened, my questions multiplied. What justified the enormous expenditures of the state to support the imperial clan, when its practical functions were often minimal? What happens when people are locked up in palaces amid great luxury but with little to do, as was the case with the imperial clan for much of the Northern Sung? What effect did their imperial status have on the many clansmen-officials in the Southern Sung? And what were the affinal connections of the clan?

Perhaps most important was my growing recognition that the imperial clan could be understood only in the context of emperorship. However much the clan came to assume its own institutional identity and the clan members a social identity, the clan was first and foremost a creation of emperors and an element in the broader institution of emperorship. Throughout the often dramatic history of the imperial clan during the three centuries of the dynasty, that fact remained paramount, even though the particulars of the clan's relationship to the emperor evolved considerably. These issues, moreover, were not simply of significance to Sung history. The Sung clan was an important model for the Ming and Ch'ing in deciding how to structure their imperial clans. In a more general sense, the treatment of imperial (or royal) kin is a critical issue for the comparative study of monarchy.

In the twelve years since this project's inception during a year's leave in Kyoto in 1986–87, the list of institutions and individuals that have provided me with assistance and advice has grown to an impressive length. The American Council of Learned Societies provided a fellowship that made my stay in Kyoto possible, and the American Philosophical Society a grant that made possible a research trip to China in 1996. Two years of sabbaticals and research semesters from Binghamton University gave me the time necessary for much of the research and writing. Research for the book was done primarily at the libraries of Kyoto, Cornell, Columbia, and Binghamton universities, but I also made important use of the Peking National Library and Hang-chou University library in China and the library of the Academia Sinica in Taiwan. To the ever courteous and helpful librarians at all these institutions, I extend my thanks.

I thank Kinugawa Tsuyoshi, both for his wonderful hospitality toward me and my family during our year in Kyoto and for his many suggestions and discussions concerning the Sung imperial clan during our year there; Huang Kailai and Huang Wanglai, for their research assistance in the early stages of the project; Li Hsin-feng (Li Xinfeng), for his assistance on a Chinese translation of my article on marriage patterns of the imperial clan; Li Yü-k'un (Li Yukun), for the photograph of the great Sung boat from Ch'üan-chou; Angela Schottenhammer, for the photograph of the stone inscription at Nine Day Mountain (Chiu-jih shan), also in Ch'üan-chou;

Valerie Hansen, for ascertaining that the fragments of Sung imperial gene-alogies were indeed still in the Peking National Library collection; Hugh Clark, for providing me with photographs of the contents of a unique Chao genealogy from rural Fu-chien; and Rick Shumaker, for rescuing half of Chapter 9 from the land of ruined computer disks. Li T'u-ch'ang (Li Tu-chang), Liu Ch'eng-fang (Liu Chengfang), and especially the archaeologist Li Hsi-p'eng (Li Xipeng) entertained me royally during my visit to the Sung naval site of Yai-shan in 1996. Evelyn Rawski, Christian de Pee, Mark Hal-perin, and Angela Leong sent me their own works in progress and thereby aided me appreciably. More generally I have benefited from my discussions with the late Teng Kuang-ming (Deng Guangming), Yang Wei-sheng (Yang Weisheng), Wang Tseng-yü (Wang Zengyu), Chang Hsi-ch'ing (Zhang Xiqing), Ch'en Chih-ch'ao (Chen Zhichao), Pao Wei-min (Bao Weimin), Fu Tsung-wen (Fu Zongwen), Wang Lien-mao (Wang Lian-mao), and Chang Fan-chih (Zhang Fanzhi) in China; Shiba Yoshinobu, Umehara Kaoru, Ihara Hiroshi, Kojima Tsuyoshi, Sugiyama Masaaki, and Yanagida Setsuko in Japan; Achim Mittag and Helmut Schmidt-Glintzer in Europe; and Patricia Ebrey, Robert Hymes, Thomas H. C. Lee, Conrad Schirokauer, Bettine Birge, Beverly Bossler, James Hargett, and Charles Hartman in the United States.

A few special thanks are also in order. Zu-yen Chen, my colleague at Binghamton University and an authority on T'ang literature, helped me with numerous linguistic challenges in Sung texts as well as problems with Chinese word-processing programs, and even translated one of my articles on the imperial clan into Chinese. My special gratitude goes to Gerald Ka-dish, Paul Smith, Rifa'at Abou-El-Haj, and Peter Bol, for their willingness to read and comment upon large portions—in some cases all—of my book manuscript. And John Ziemer has been a pleasure to work with as my edi-tor at Harvard. Although all of the above have enriched the final product in more ways than I can count, the problems and blemishes that remain are mine and mine alone.

I cannot close without a word of thanks to my family for their constant support over the years: my sons, Conrad, Philip and Timothy, who largely grew up while I worked on the book, and my wife, Barbara, whose love has carried me through the years of work and to whom I dedicate this book.

J.W.C.

Contents

Appendixes

Reference Matter

Tables, Maps, and Figures

Tables

Maps

Figures

The Sung Emperors and Their Reigns

T'ai-tsu 太祖, 960–76   Chao K'uang-yin 趙匡胤 (927–76)

T'ai-tsung 太宗, 976–97   Chao Kuei 趙炅 (originally K'uang-i 趙匡義; 939–97). Brother of T'ai-tsu.

Chen-tsung 眞宗, 997–1022   Chao Heng 趙恆 (968–1022). Son of T'ai-tsung.

Jen-tsung 仁宗, 1022–63   Chao Chen 趙禎 (1010–63). Son of Chen-tsung.

Ying-tsung 英宗, 1063–67   Chao Shu 趙曙 (originally Tsung-shih 宗實; 1032–67). Son of Chao Yun-jang 允讓 (BCB; 995–1059). Adopted and named Crown Prince in 1062.

Shen-tsung 神宗, 1067–85   Chao Hsu 趙頊 (1048–85). Son of Ying-tsung.

Che-tsung 哲宗, 1085–1100   Chao Hsu 趙煦 (1077–1100). Son of Shen-tsung.

Hui-tsung 徽宗, 1100–1126   Chao Chi 趙佶 (1082–1135). Brother of Che-tsung. Abdicated in favor of Ch'in-tsung. Captured by the Jurchen and died in captivity.

Ch'in-tsung 欽宗, 1126–27   Chao Huan 趙桓 (1100–1161). Son of Hui-tsung. Captured by the Jurchen and died in captivity.

Kao-tsung 高宗, 1127–62   Chao Kou 趙構 (1107–87). Brother of Ch'in-tsung. Reestablished the dynasty in the south. Abdicated in favor of Hsiao-tsung.

Hsiao-tsung 孝宗, 1162–89   Chao Shen 趙慎 (originally Po-ts'ung 伯琮, ABBACEAB; 1127–94). Adopted and named Crown Prince in 1153. Abdicated in favor of Kuang-tsung.

Kuang-tsung 光宗, 1189–94   Chao Tun 趙盾 (1147–1200). Son of Hsiao-tsung. Forced to abdicate in favor of Ning-tsung.

Ning-tsung 寧宗, 1192–1224   Chao K'uo 趙擴 (1168–1224). Son of Kuang-tsung.

Li-tsung 理宗, 1224–64   Chao Yun 趙昀 (originally Kuei-ch'eng 貴誠; 1205–64). Son of Chao Hsi-lu 趙希瓐 (AABDEAEABB). Adopted and made Crown Prince when Ning-tsung was on his death bed.

Tu-tsung 度宗, 1264–74   Chao Ch'i 趙祺 (originally Yü-jui, AABDEAEABBA; 1240–74). Nephew of Li-tsung. Adopted in 1253 and made Crown Prince in 1260.

Kung-tsung 恭宗, 1274–76   Chao Hsien 趙㬎 (1271–1323). Captured by the Mongols and died in captivity.

Tuan-tsung 端宗, 1276–78   Chao Shih 趙昰 (ca. 1268–78). Brother of Kung-tsung.

Ti-ping 帝昺, 1278–79   Chao Ping 趙昺 (1272–79). Brother of Kung-tsung and Tuan-tsung.

Abbreviations

For complete citations, see the Bibliography, pp. 371–91.

CCC	Yang Wan-li, *Ch'eng-chai chi*
CKWC	Ch'en Mi, *Fu-chai hsien-sheng Ch'en kung wen-chi*
CMC	*Ming-kung shu-k'an Ch'ing-ming chi*
CSTP	Chao Hsi-nien, *Chao-shih tsu-p'u*
CWCKWC	Chen Te-hsiu, *Hsi-shan hsien-sheng Chen wen-chung kung wen-chi*
CWKWC	Chu Hsi, *Chu wen-kung wen-chi*
CWTC	Mu-jung Yen-feng, *Ch'ih-wen t'ang-chi*
CYTC	Li Hsin-ch'uan, *Chien-yen i-lai ch'ao-yeh tsa-chi*
HCC	Yuan Hsieh, *Hsieh-chai chi*
HCLAC	Ch'ien Yueh-yu, *Hsien-ch'un Lin-an chih*
HCP	Li T'ao, *Hsu Tzu-chih t'ung-chien ch'ang-pien*
HNYL	Li Hsin-ch'uan, *Chien-yen i-lai hsi-nien yao-lu*
HTCTC	Pi Yuan, *Hsu Tzu-chih t'ung-chien*
HTHSTCC	Liu K'o-chuang, *Hou-ts'un hsien-sheng ta-ch'üan-chi*
HYC	Wang Kuei, *Hua-yang chi*
HYLP	Shih Hao, ed., *Hsien-yuan lei-p'u*
KKC	Lou Yueh, *Kung-k'uei chi*

KSC	Liu Ch'ang, *Kung-shih chi*
LCC	Chang Fang-p'ing, *Lo-ch'üan chi*
NWTYCSTP	Chao Shih-t'ung, ed., *Nan-wai t'ien-yuan Chao-shih tsu-p'u*
OYWCKWC	Ou-yang Hsiu, *Ou-yang wen-chung kung wen-chi*
SCHMCM	Liu Kuang-tsu, "Sung ch'eng-hsiang Chung-ting Chao kung mu-chih-ming," in Fu Tseng-hsiang, *Sung-tai Shu-wen chi-ts'un*
SHY:CJ	*Sung hui-yao chi-kao*, "Ch'ung-ju" section
SHY:CK	*Sung hui-yao*, "Chih-kuan" section
SHY:HC	*Sung hui-yao*, "Hsuan-chü" section
SHY:TH	*Sung hui-yao*, "Ti-hsi" section
SS	T'o T'o, *Sung shih*
TTSL	Wang Ch'eng, *Tung-tu shih-lueh*, Sung-shih tzu-liao ts'ui-pien (Taipei: Wen-hai ch'u-pan-she)
WCC	Chou Pi-ta, *Wen-chung chi*
WHTK	Ma Tuan-lin, *Wen-hsien t'ung-k'ao*
WWC	Yang Chieh, *Wu-wei chi*
YCC	Cheng Hsieh, *Yun-ch'i chi*
YSC	Yeh Shih, *Yeh Shih chi*

Note on the Genealogical Coding of Clansmen

The genealogy found in chapters 215–41 of the *Sung History* is a source of great value for the study of the imperial clan, containing as it does the names of some 20,000–30,000 clansmen and their precise location in the clan. But it is also bulky and difficult to use, since the search for a given individual can mean scanning thousands of pages of text to find him, and even then it is not easy to describe his location beyond providing the names of his patrilineal ancestors. In preparing this book, I have therefore coded all the individuals encountered in my research according to their position in the genealogy. The genealogy is ordered according to standard Chinese practice of providing generational rows, with the top row representing the first generation, the second row the second, and so forth, with all descendants of the first son listed before the second son is listed, and so forth. The coding uses alphabetical letters, with the number of letters representing the generational depth of the individual from the founding generation. The first letter delineates offspring of the three brothers who founded the clan: T'ai-tsu (A; 927–76), T'ai-tsung (B; 939–97), and Wei-wang (C; 947–84). Thereafter "A" indicates the first son, "B" the second son, "C" the third son, and so on. To give one example, Chao Chung-yuan (BCBFB; 1054–1123) was the second son of Tsung-hui (BCBF; 1024–94), who was the sixth son of Yun-jang (BCB; 995–1059), who was the second son of Yuan-fen (BC; 968–1004), who was the third son of T'ai-tsung (r. 976–97).

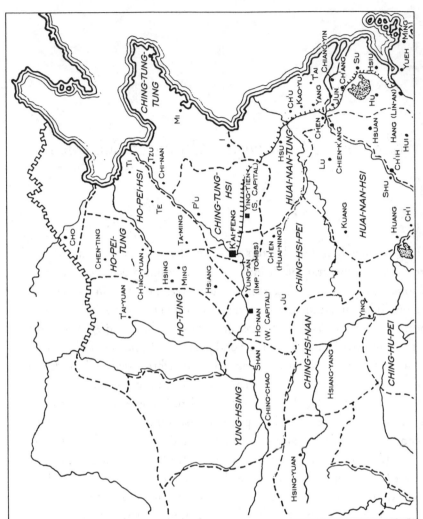

Map 1 North China in the Northern Sung

Map 2 Southeastern China in the Southern Sung

Branches of Heaven

A History of the Imperial Clan of Sung China

ONE

Introduction

Two Incidents

The emperor was touched. All seven of the young imperial clansmen who
had approached the throne were close to him in age and united in their zeal
to assist the dynasty. The year was 1038, and along the northwest border
with the Hsi Hsia the Sung was threatened by Chao Yüan-hao (1003–48)—
a border general, who despite his adopted imperial surname was most em-
phatically not an imperial kinsman—who had declared his independence
from the Sung, taking 22 prefectures with him.[1] The seven had devised plans
for subduing the rebel and proposed to lead an expedition against him. They
included Chao Ts'ung-shih (ABBB; 1007–71), Chao Shih-jung (AADAB;
1016–55), and most notably Chao Shih-yung (AABAA; 1010–68), who as a
youth had been a companion to the emperor, Jen-tsung (1010–63; r. 1022–
63), when the latter as crown prince was studying in the Hall of Natural
Goodness (Tzu-shan tien). But although he praised the clansmen for their
proposal and rewarded them for their initiative, Jen-tsung refused their
request. The general, for his part, was bought off with noble titles.[2]

Exactly two hundred years later, in 1238, the imperial clansman Chao I-fu
(CECBCCDAD; 1189–1256) was appointed coastal commissioner and prefect of Ch'ing-yüan fu (or Ming-chou, Liang-che)—the two offices were
often paired—one of the most important local postings in the empire.[3] But
upon his arrival at the prefectural capital, he found a city in turmoil. His
predecessor, Ch'en Kai, had left unpaid and restive troops in the city. His

temporary replacement, the clansman Chao Shan-hsiang (BCBGFCJA; d. 1242), had distributed grain and cash, but the troops had grown increasingly arrogant, plotting and resisting orders, and Shan-hsiang had fled into the mountains. I-fu arrived in a single carriage. The troops led him into the city and threw down their spears in welcome and homage. I-fu bought grain for the troops but made do, for himself, with the spoilage from the granary, and he sent Shan-hsiang a note inviting his return. But the situation remained critical, for the army supervisor, the clansman Chao Ch'ien-fu, acting on Shan-hsiang's authority, had summarily executed resisting troops, which had provoked other troops into planning an uprising. When some of the officers involved were arrested, I-fu had them sent in fetters to the Yin county magistrate, the clansman Chao Shih-ku, and after they were interrogated—one shudders to think of the methods employed—he obtained the names of all the plotters and learned that the uprising was scheduled for the third drum that night. I-fu ordered the third drum to be delayed while he played chess (*wei-ch'i*) with guests to demonstrate his lack of concern. Meanwhile a marine unit secretly entered the city and captured the rebels. By dawn all was secure, and the townspeople reassured. As for the rebels, over thirty were beheaded, one hundred or more were imprisoned, and the rest were released.[4]

These two stories would seem to have nothing in common except that both concern Sung imperial clansmen. Yet both are remarkable for what they leave unsaid. None of the biographers of the clansmen in the first incident mentions the reason for Jen-tsung's refusal, namely, that since the end of the tenth century all clansmen had been prohibited from holding substantive military or civil office, however august their titles. Liu K'o-chuang (1187–1269), the author of the second account, does not call attention to the fact that all four officials involved were imperial clansmen, for the simple reason that it was not remarkable; by the thirteenth century not only were clansmen allowed to hold office but thousands were doing so.

For us these incidents raise many questions. How did this dramatic change in the roles of imperial clansmen occur and why? What was an imperial clansman? Can the terms *imperial clan* and *clansmen* retain any real meaning in the face of such change? Answering these questions and others is the goal of this book.

Imperial Clans in Chinese History

At first glance, the idea of an imperial clan (as distinct from the imperial family) seems simple enough. After all, hereditary monarchs—be they emperors or kings—have kin, extended circles of relatives as well as immediate families. Yet to the best of my knowledge, an imperial clan in the Sung sense—a patrilineal kinship group unlimited in its generational depth, supported by the throne through allowances and privileges but also governed by state-imposed restrictions—is unique in world history. Even in China, which had a history of imperial clans, the Sung clan was unprecedented in its character and scope, although given the acute historical consciousness of the Sung emperors and their ministers, the earlier clans provided models both to be emulated and to be avoided. In particular, the practices of the Chou, Han, and T'ang dynasties loomed large in Sung eyes, not only because they were seen as the three greatest dynasties, but also because their longevity made it necessary to address the issue of an imperial clan.

During the Western Chou (1127–771 B.C.E.), royal kinsmen played a central role in the political order. With the conquest of the Shang, the Chou was suddenly transformed from a territorial state in the Wei River valley to a vast empire stretching across the north China plain. To rule it, the Chou created what Hsu Cho-yun has characterized as a "garrison system," with large numbers of royal princes and kinsmen—over fifty, according to historical accounts[5]—as well as allies from outside the royal family enfeoffed as feudal lords in the lower Yellow River valley.[6] Only around the capital in the west was rule exercised directly by the Chou kings, but through such mechanisms as investiture ceremonies for sons succeeding to their fathers' positions and punitive campaigns against rebellious lords, the Chou managed to maintain the system over a remarkably long period of time. This process of enfeoffment created a political structure that not only lasted throughout the Western Chou but also evolved into the multiple and contending states of the Eastern Chou (771–256 B.C.E.), when a central monarchy had become a thing of the past.

That royal princes, nephews, and cousins were invested with lands of their own is hardly remarkable, for historical examples of this solution to the problem of royal kin are common, especially from medieval Europe.[7] Like other feudal systems, the Chou state also drew heavily on patrimonial models and language. Thus, "the Chou kings habitually addressed dukes as uncles, either paternal or maternal, according to whether or not the addressee possessed the royal surname. Other feudal lords of the royal surname were usually called 'brother' by the kings. 'Now you brothers of my house come and meet seasonally.'"[8] More distinctive, perhaps, was the Chou reliance on a segmentary lineage system known as the *tsung-fa*, whereby the descent lines of eldest sons were favored in religious status and political power. Discussing the relation between the royal Chou and the ruling lords of the states of Lu, Chin, Wei, Yü, and others who shared the royal surname Chi, the anthropologist Chang Kuang-chih has noted: "Their relative political status, it is well known, was determined by the so-called *tsung-fa* system, at least in a normative sense. The *tsung-fa* system of Chou is characterized by the fact that the eldest son of each generation formed the main line of descent and political authority, whereas the younger brothers were moved out to establish new lineages of lesser authority. The farther removed, the lesser was the political authority."[9]

Whether the political and social realities of Chou society corresponded to the hierarchies of the *tsung-fa* is hard to glean from the sources, but for Sung scholars struggling to come to terms with a world in which kinship structures were in flux, the Chou model of a descent line (*tsung*) with its clear principles of organization was an attractive one, as we will see in Chapter 4. But as important as its organization was its inclusiveness, which provided an important precedent for the Sung imperial clan. Thus Wei Liao-weng (1178–1237) described the Chou royal *tsung* in highly idealistic terms: "All served in the ancestral temple, and in the temple the clansmen were all ordered according to the spirit tablets, and likewise ordered for the ritual libations. . . . Some were used provincially as feudal lords, some had salaries, and some served as great ministers, but since all were classed as relatives, people knew respect for the *tsung*; because the lineages (*tsu*) were differentiated, people avoided excessive covetousness."[10] The idealistic tone of this passage, which is taken from an epitaph for an imperial clansman, makes it of dubious value as historical description, but it is revealing of Sung attempts to invoke the golden age of antiquity to establish a precedent for the Sung imperial kin, especially since imperial clans from the imperial period (post-221 B.C.E.) were organized on far less inclusive principles.

When the Han dynasty (206 B.C.E.–220 C.E.) came to power following the demise of the short-lived Ch'in (221–206 B.C.E.), one of its key actions was to modify the system of commandaries into which the Ch'in had divided the empire by establishing vassal kingdoms (*kuo*) and marquisates under imperial princes and confederates of Liu Pang (Han Kao-ti, r. 206–195 B.C.E) whose support had been critical during the preceding civil war. This formal similarity to the Western Chou's treatment of royal princes, however, belied a very different reality, for the Han emperors were jealous of their power and worked at every turn to diminish the power of the kings (*wang*).[11] Indeed, within a half century of the founding of the Han, kings who were not members of the imperial family had been eliminated, usually to be replaced by imperial princes.[12] The imperial prince-kings were in turn curbed through a variety of measures. They were stripped of their autonomy, with the central government making all senior appointments and ruling the kingdoms through a chancellor and commandant who answered to the emperor. Moreover, rather than allowing the eldest son to inherit the title and kingdom, as was initially the case, Emperor Wu (r. 140–87 B.C.E.) mandated that each son of a deceased king receive a marquisate, with the kingdom's land divided for that purpose.[13]

The possession of kingdoms and marquisates thus became a central feature of the Han imperial kin and served to limit the support that kinsmen received from the government. The Sung philosopher Chu Hsi (1130–1200), a critic of unlimited government support of the imperial clan, described a process of rather rapid movement from royalty to peasantry, which he saw as characterizing the Han imperial clan.

According to Han law, the imperial clan (*tsung-shih*) simply [consisted of] sons of the Son of Heaven, who were enfeoffed as kings (*wang*) with land that had been divided up; among the sons of the kings, a son of the legal wife would inherit the title, and the others were ennobled as marquises (*hou*). A son of the marquis's legal wife would inherit his title, but the others would receive no titles. Thus after several generations, all [the descendents of the emperor] would become indistinguishable from the common people, and if they did not achieve power on their own, then life as a peasant would be unavoidable.[14]

If the Han policies toward imperial kin are judged by the simple criteria of whether they kept descendents of the imperial house from becoming a political problem and at the same time assured a supply of potential heirs when for some reason direct descendents of the emperor were not available, then they were successful. Over the course of the Western Han, large numbers of imperial descendents settled in the countryside as commoners, most notably in the Nan-yang region of southern Honan.[15] There, during the brief period of Wang Mang's Hsin dynasty (8–23 C.E.), they served as a focus of opposition, rebelling even on the eve of Wang's seizure of the throne in 8 C.E. and leading the widespread rebellions that broke out in the year 22. In this endeavor, the Nan-yang Lius were far from united. Although the defeat of Wang Mang was accomplished in 23 C.E. under Liu Hsuan, who became the Keng-shih emperor, his rule was disputed by Liu Hsiu— formerly a rice dealer—and in 25 C.E. Liu Hsiu, in concert with an army of the Red Eyebrow rebels, defeated Liu Hsuan in Ch'ang-an. Thus it is Liu Hsiu as the Kuang-tu emperor (r. 25–57 C.E.), not Liu Hsuan, who is recognized as the founder of the Later Han dynasty (25–220 C.E.).[16]

The restoration of the Han represented an isolated high point for the Han imperial kinsmen, for they were generally excluded from any meaningful political role. Although there were a few instances from both the Former and the Later Han of kinsmen serving as officials, their numbers were few, and the Kuang-wu emperor, who owed much to his relatives, was generous in providing them with noble titles but did not use them in government.[17] The imperial family was headed by a superintendent (*tsung-cheng*), one of the nine senior posts in the bureaucracy, and it was always filled by an imperial kinsman. But his main responsibility was to maintain the genealogical registers and on rare occasions to summon a kinsman to court when an heir to the throne was needed.[18] Moreover, the Han kinsmen's physical location outside the capital gave them little opportunity to participate in the politics of the "inner palace," which consisted of the groups most directly associated with the person of the emperor and used by him— not only in China but in many premodern bureaucratic empires—as a counterweight to the formal bureaucracy.[19] Thus while kinsmen were involved in some of the bloody succession struggles that punctuated Han history, their roles were minor, overshadowed by those of two groups far more active in the Han inner palace: the families of imperial consorts and eunuchs.[20]

In the four centuries between the Han and T'ang dynasties, the Han practice of sharply circumscribing the political power of imperial princes gave way to a far more active role for them. Beginning with the state of Wu (222–80 c.e.) in the Three Kingdoms period, and continuing with the Western Chin (265–316) and the Southern dynasties (317–589), imperial princes played vital roles both at court and in the military.[21] The early T'ang dynasty (618–907) was also marked by powerful princes, so much so that the first succession was decided by an internecine struggle in 626 in which Li Shih-min (T'ai-tsung) killed off his two adult brothers.

In a study of this incident, Andrew Eisenberg argues that Kao-tsu (r. 618–26), who was still emperor at the time, was following the practice of nomadic societies in letting his sons fight out the succession, and that he took care to ensure that the process did not get out of hand.[22] Whether this was in fact Kao-tsu's intention—some scholars remain unconvinced[23]—the contested succession had the virtue of producing tested, adult rulers, much as did the succession by combat practiced centuries later by the Ottoman emperors during the early years of their empire. According to Leslie Peirce, when the Ottoman empire was transformed from "an expansionist, military state to an administrative, bureaucratic one," imperial succession was also transformed, being determined thereafter by the seniority of princes. In the process the power of the women of the harem grew greatly.[24] Like the Ottoman, the T'ang also moved away from fratricidal conflict as a method of determining the succession. Although successions were frequently contested and violent and often involved impatient heirs apparent, the key players were generally eunuchs, palace women, and their families—as in the Han—but not the imperial family. Indeed, under the Empress Wu, who through ambition, ruthlessness, and talent moved from dominating the government as empress and empress dowager to ruling as an emperor in her own right (690–705), a rebellion led by members of the imperial family proved abortive and disastrous, and the great majority of clansmen and women were executed.[25] Although the clan survived and Empress Wu was eventually forced to yield power to the Lis once again, this outcome owed little to the kinsmen themselves.

The T'ang imperial kinsmen differed from their Han predecessors in several important respects. First, although the T'ang, like the Han, initially enfeoffed princes in the provinces,[26] in the early eighth century they and their descendents were moved to the capital, where they resided in ten princely houses (*wang-chai*) and 100 halls for grandsons (*sun-yuan*).[27] These were not long lived; according to one late T'ang report, the princely houses ceased to be maintained after the rebellion of An Lu-shan in the 750s,[28] but they created an important precedent for locating the imperial family in the capital. Second, in 670 the T'ang established the Court of the Imperial Clan (Tsung-cheng ssu), the first institution expressly established to oversee the affairs of the imperial kinsmen or clan.[29] Third, in contrast to Han imperial kin, who, if they did not inherit the noble title of king or marquis, became essentially indistinguishable from commoners, the T'ang created an elaborate hierarchy of five levels (*wu teng*) of imperial clan members under the authority of the Court of the Imperial Clan, which closely followed the five degrees of mourning (*wu-fu*), thus making the clan a more defined body and much deeper, genealogically, than had previously been the case.[30]

In all these ways, the T'ang paved the way for the Sung imperial clan, particularly during the Northern Sung. However, there were also some key differences. The T'ang, for one, seem to have construed clan membership rather broadly, and the five levels included some affinal kin, namely, the relatives of empresses.[31] Moreover, on several occasions T'ang Kao-tsu conferred the Li surname and with it inclusion in the imperial genealogy on particularly meritorious individuals.[32] At the same time, T'ang regulations clearly stated that "those who are beyond these five levels are not considered kin" (*kuo wu teng che pu wei ch'in*),[33] and although in 751 the emperor made an exception to this, ordering that some 300 individuals outside the five levels be given clan status,[34] there was no expansion in the definition of the imperial clan, as was to occur in the Sung.

Finally, the T'ang were unique in the history of imperial China in their willingness to use imperial kin not only widely in the government[35] but especially in the highest offices. Thus no fewer than eleven served as grand councilor, a fact that greatly interested Sung historians.[36] This was an ambiguous legacy, however, for although they were honored by the eleventh-century *New T'ang History* (*Hsin T'ang-shu*) with their own chapter of biographies titled "Clansmen Grand Councilors"—their number also included the infamous Li Lin-fu (d. 752), Hsuan-tsung's grand councilor, who was perceived in the Sung as responsible for the catastrophe of the An Lu-shan rebellion and whose biography is found in the section on "treasonous ministers."[37]

The T'ang treatment of imperial kin also had a profound impact in Japan during the late Nara and Heian periods. The Nara emperors modeled their system on that of the Sui and T'ang, and invoked the T'ang mourning rule. They removed imperial kin outside the fives degrees of mourning from the imperial household by giving them surnames of their own—either Minamoto or Taira—and as a rule sending them to the countryside. This practice had momentous long-term consequences, for in the eleventh and twelfth centuries the provincial Minamoto and Taira returned to dominate court and capital. But the system took on a life of its own, and in the Heian came to be used for kin within the five degrees of mourning as well, including even the sons and daughters of emperors.[38]

As historians have long noted, the Sung polity, in spite of great institutional continuities, differed greatly from the T'ang. One source of difference is the success of the founding emperors at reining in the military. Often expressed in the phrase "esteeming the civil and slighting the military" (*ch'ung-wen chien-wu*), this policy succeeded in ending the dominance of generals both at court and in local government, even though the price—many have argued—was chronic military weakness. The second explanation, first articulated by the Japanese scholar Naitō Torajirō and in fact often linked to the curbing of the military, is that the growth in imperial power in Sung times led to the rise of autocracy and thereby constituted the beginning of China's modern period of history.

Although these explanations have done much to further our understanding of the Sung state, they have also left unanswered questions. If the Sung military was truly curbed, then how do we explain the unprecedented size of the Sung army and navy, their technological innovations, and their success in the thirteenth century in withstanding Mongol attacks for decades? Perhaps more important, to what extent was Sung "weakness" caused not by internal factors but rather by the existence of well-established and powerful states in that arc of border regions from Tibet in the west to the

Liao in the northeast? As for the autocracy thesis, if in fact the emperor had evolved from first among equals to autocrat, then what do we make of the many powerful grand councilors who served under Sung emperors, especially of individuals like Shih Mi-yuan, the thirteenth-century grand councilor who—as we will see in Chapter 8—was able to countermand the decision of the dying Ning-tsung regarding his successor?

The issue of emperorship is particularly germane to this study, for as one of its most important creations, the imperial clan can be understood only in the context of the larger institution. In a recent review article on Ch'ing emperorship, Pamela Crossley takes issue with the current models of emperorship—such as the division into the inner and outer bureaucracies—not as wrong but as inadequate. In their place she proposes a multifaceted entity:

> The emperorship can be seen as an ensemble of instruments playing the dynamic role, or the ascribed dynamic role, in the governing process. This role itself can be interpreted as an organism incorporating not only the emperor personally but also his lineage; the rituals he performed; the offices for management of his education, health, sexual activity, wardrobe, properties, and daily schedule; the secretariats that functioned as extensions of his hearing in the form of intelligence gathering and expedited memoranda; the editorial boards that functioned as extensions of his speech in the generation of military commands, civil edicts, imperial prefaces to reprinted or newly commissioned works.[39]

Although Professor Crossley is specifically discussing the Ch'ing, her description works well for the Chinese imperium generally, especially for the Sung, when, I would argue, there was a concerted strengthening of emperorship.

The restraint of the military, which certainly occurred under Sung T'ai-tsu (r. 960–76) and T'ai-tsung (976–97), was hardly an isolated policy. Eunuchs and consort families, two groups that had played powerful and prominent roles throughout past imperial history, were remarkably docile during the Sung. The case of consort families is especially instructive, for the promise of marriage with imperial kin was one of the benefits that T'ai-tsu promised his generals even as he was taking away their power, and in fact, for the first century of the dynasty, imperial clan members married overwhelmingly with military families (see Chapter 2). However, Jennifer

Holmgren has astutely observed that this paired the imperial family with "spouses from elite families on the decline," thus depriving empresses of the kind of status that they had brought with themselves in the Han and T'ang.[40] But perhaps the most important example of growing imperial power is that of the scholar-officials who staffed the imperial bureaucracy. One effect of the dramatic expansion of the examination system under T'ai-tsung was to make examination success the predominant and normative route to office, thereby weakening methods of entry that depended on family connections, and this certainly worked to the benefit of the emperor, who oversaw the final palace examination and was thus the final arbiter of examination success.[41]

Although all these changes strengthened the Sung emperors vis-à-vis potential rivals, the real beneficiary was the institution of emperorship rather than the emperors themselves. The changes described above were systemic, institutional changes, and they constrained the emperor as well as those around him. As in Meiji and Showa Japan, the absolute powers theoretically vested in the emperor did not translate into the capacity to exercise power arbitrarily, and it was quite possible for powerful grand councilors, with the consent of compliant emperors, to use the powers of emperorship quite effectively.

Against this background, the imperial clan as it evolved over the first century of the Sung can be seen as an artifact of emperorship. The primary bargain—an affluent life in the capital for all imperial descendents but no political power—enabled the emperors to honor their ancestors and lavish support on their family even as they controlled potential rivals to the throne. What is most remarkable is that the imperial clan was an imperial creation that virtually had no function, save its ritual roles in ancestral sacrifices and ceremonies at court. It was also expensive. It is a tribute to the unparalleled wealth of the Sung state that the clan was maintained in this fashion for four to five generations. As shown in Chapter 4, the changes in the late eleventh century were forced both by the expense of maintaining an increasing number of people and the breaching of the limits of mourning relationships that had defined the clan. But in contrast to both the Han and the T'ang, the clan, although redefined and restructured, was also enlarged to include all patrilineal descendents of the Sung founders regardless of mourning relationship. As time went by, clan members were increasingly integrated into the bureaucracy and elite society, but until the dynasty's end they never lost their status as a group apart, an instrument and aspect of emperorship.

Historiography and Sources

In the seven centuries since the fall of the Sung, the Sung imperial clan has evoked little interest from historians. There has been no book or monograph dealing with it, and only a scattering of articles in Chinese, Japanese, and English.[42] Based on numerous conversations with colleagues, especially in East Asia, I would suggest that the reason for this neglect is that the imperial clan had generally been regarded as a not very significant historical curiosity. Confined to their palaces, as they were in the Northern Sung, separate from the emperor yet not one of the social categories that have been considered important—the scholar-officials, merchants, the military, and even eunuchs and palace women—imperial clansmen and women have simply not elicited the interest of scholars.

The irony of this modern neglect is that Sung writers documented the imperial clan, its institutions, history, and the lives of its members voluminously. Indeed, the volume and scope of the sources—all devoted to a single discrete kin group—make possible a multifaceted study of a sort that is rare in premodern history. The challenge has been to master the sources and decide what to use among the vast quantity of material available.

Although references to the imperial clan and its members can be found in virtually every genre of Sung writing, the research for this book is based primarily on institutional sources, contemporary histories, biographies, and genealogies. Sources treating the institutions of the imperial clan—particularly the Court of the Imperial Clan (*Tsung-cheng ssu*) and the Great Office of Imperial Clan Affairs (*Ta tsung-cheng ssu*)—include the institutional treatise section of the official *Sung History* (*Sung shih*),[43] and the compilations of individuals such as Li Hsin-ch'uan's *Chien-yen i-lai ch'ao-yeh tsa-chi* (Miscellaneous records from the court and countryside since the beginning of the Chien-yen period)[44] and Ma Tuan-lin's encyclopedia *Wen-hsien t'ung-k'ao* (General investigation on important writings).[45] Most important, several sections of the massive *Sung hui-yao chi-kao* (Drafts of Sung documents pertaining to matters of state) cover the Court and Great Office, clan schools and examinations, genealogical practices, and there is, as well, a six-chapter section of "miscellaneous records."[46] The "miscellaneous records," in particular, provide a wealth of information concerning the clan, for they deal with all aspects of the lives and activities of clansmen and women.

Histories are another essential group of sources for this project, for the evolution of the imperial clan is inextricably interwoven with the history of the dynasty, and this book is concerned first and foremost with the theme of change. Fortunately, the Sung period is blessed with two of the greatest period histories in the historiographical tradition: Li T'ao's *Hsu Tzu-chih t'ung-chien ch'ang-pien* (Collected data for a continuation of the *Comprehensive Mirror for Aid in Government*), which covers most of the Northern Sung, and Li Hsin-ch'uan's *Chien-yen i-lai Hsi-nien yao-lu* (A record of important affairs since the beginning of the Hsi-nien period), a history of the first 36 years of the Southern Sung. Together they cover most of the Sung. We are at a disadvantage in treating the years they do not cover—notably the last century of the Southern Sung, and have to make use of inferior, less informative histories, including the chronicle section of the *Sung History*, which is commonly acknowledged to be second-rate.

Although all existing studies of the Sung imperial clan have drawn from these sources, none has attempted to make systematic use of the large store of biographical records that exist for the imperial clan. Convinced that the human face of the imperial clan would never become visible without using them, I have attempted to read and analyze all the available biographies of clansmen and women and many biographies of the wives of clansmen as well. A great many of these are found in a five-chapter section of the *Sung History*—four devoted to clansmen and one to imperial princesses—that are noteworthy for the willingness of the authors to include material reflecting negatively on their subjects.[47] Biographies can also be found in local histories and later genealogies, although with some exceptions these tend to be short and rather mediocre. Finally, I have used over two hundred epitaphs (*mu-chih-ming*) for clansmen and clanswomen, drawn primarily from the collected writings (*wen-chi*) of their authors.[48]

The epitaphs call for some comment, for as compositions intended to praise the dead, they are naturally open to questions concerning their veracity and historical utility. In a careful analysis of Sung epitaphs, Angela Schottenhammer argues persuasively for the reliability of the information included in epitaphs and notes, too, the relative emphasis upon character description in Sung epitaphs compared with pre-Sung epitaphs.[49] Character description is in short supply in the imperial clan epitaphs of the eleventh century, when clan members were effectively segregated from the rest of society behind their palace walls. As shown in Chapter 3, court officials were commissioned to write epitaphs for clan members en masse, and the results are formulaic and of value primarily for vital statistics (birth and death dates) and information concerning ancestry and marriage ties. However, as clan members emerged from their isolation in the late Northern Sung, their epitaphs were increasingly written by scholars who knew them personally. Consequently they are fuller and far more useful—and thus far more like the epitaphs analyzed by Schottenhammer.

It would be difficult to overstate the value of these varied biographies for the project at hand; without them we would be confined largely to the realm of institutions and occasional individuals who appear in the historical records. However, we also need to recognize that the subjects of these biographies represent only a small fraction of all clan members, that various selection processes are behind the particular collection of biographies that we now possess, and therefore that we cannot assume the lives portrayed in them to be representative of the clan as a whole. We will confront this issue at various points in the chapters that follow, particularly in Chapter 6 when we consider changing patterns of marriage relations.

As is clear from the discussion of the Han and T'ang clans, the maintenance of an official genealogy was a central responsibility of clan officials, and this was also true of the Sung. The Office of the Jade Register (Yü-tieh suo) in the Court of the Imperial Clan was devoted specifically to keeping records on every clan member and to the compilation of a variety of genealogies relating to the ever-growing clan. The imperial clan genealogical sources available today are of two kinds: those drawn from or at least directly related to the clan's official genealogy, and more recent lineage genealogies of the

Chao descendents of the imperial clan. Among the former, we have a comprehensive but simplified genealogy in the *Sung History* and two extant Sung fragments of the clan's official genealogies.

The *Sung History* genealogy, which is found in chapters 215–41, is a massive document, covering almost 2,000 pages in the modern Chung-hua edition and containing on the order of 30,000 names. It is arranged on thirteen horizontal rows, the sons of T'ai-tsu and his two brothers (whose offspring constituted the imperial clan) occupying the uppermost row, and twelve generations of their descendents in the rows below them. The layout is such that one can trace father-son lines and thus place individuals genealogically with precision. Using an alphabetical coding system (see p. xxi for an explanation), I have located the great majority of clansmen whom I have encountered in my research and provide codes for their genealogical locations. Unfortunately, since this genealogy gives little beyond the names of individuals, its use is limited.[50]

Although the vast majority of the detailed genealogies produced by the Office of the Jade Register have been lost, the Peking National Library has fragments of two, namely, the *Tsung-fan ch'ing-hsi lu* (Records of princely branches; 22 chapters extant) and the *Hsien-yuan lei-p'u* (Classified genealogy of immortal origins; 30 chapters extant). The function of the former was reportedly "to distinguish the branches that emerged in the clan and to put in order the sons and grandsons and arrange them with their names and offices." By contrast, the latter focused upon affines, "to put in order the clan's men, women, wives, and the affinal families, and [to record] their offices, noble titles, achievements, punishments, births, and deaths."[51] Upon an examination of the two in 1991, I found the *Hsien-yuan lei-p'u* (hereafter HYLP) to be far more informative, for where the *Tsung-fan ch'ing-hsi lu* has only names and titular rank for each individual—little more than one finds in the *Sung History* genealogy—the HYLP has a wealth of information about the sons, daughters, and sons-in-law of the individual clansmen covered, in many cases giving birth and death dates as well. The chief limitation of the work is its fragmentary nature; the extant chapters treat portions of the sixth- and seventh-generation descendents of T'ai-tsu and T'ai-tsung. Nevertheless, these fragments provide cross-sections of the imperial clan with complete and reliable information about the individuals covered. The resulting data on the demography and affinal relations of the clan are essential for the analyses in Chapters 3 and 7.[52]

The lineage genealogies of Chao descendents are among the most problematic of the sources used in this book. I have found references to some two dozen of them scattered throughout libraries in Asia and the United States, and although I have not examined all of them, those that I have share a number of features. They are the genealogies of Ming and Ch'ing lineages that trace themselves back to the Sung imperial clan, specifically to an apical ancestor from the late Sung or early Yuan. They were largely produced in the late Ch'ing or even Republican eras, although in many cases they reproduce earlier prefaces dating to the Ming and even Yuan. Finally, although the greater part of these works is devoted to tracing the lineage's membership in the Ming and Ch'ing dynasties, they devote a good deal of space to the Sung emperors and imperial clan.

These sources must be used with care, not only because of their late date but also because of the obvious temptation for non-imperial Chao lineages to claim imperial ancestry, although I found no cases in which the lineage's claims are demonstrably false. But this is no reason to reject them out of hand. The best of the genealogies—for instance, the *Chao-shih tsu-p'u* from Kuang-tung compiled by Chao Hsi-nien at the beginning of the twentieth century, and the early Ch'ing *Nan-wai t'ien-yuan Chao-shih tsu-p'u* from Ch'üan-chou—contain a wealth of documents and information that are plausible in their detail and in some cases can be corroborated.[53] They provide unique material not found elsewhere, particularly on the subject of the fall of the Sung, about which most other sources are silent. Thus, so long as they are used with a measured skepticism and in conjunction with other sources, they help to round out our view of the imperial clan.

The Approach

Although the wide range of material relating to the Sung imperial clan is well suited to a topical organization—and in fact most of my articles on the imperial clan have been topical—the approach of this book is historical, focusing on the changes that the clan underwent during its three-century existence. Indeed, an understanding of its story—its evolution from a group of cloistered kin to a multitude of privileged officials, and their movement from capital to countryside—is essential for the proper appreciation of its institutions, educational and examination practices, political significance, social status, marital relations, and cultural activities, all of which will be examined.

The eight chapters that follow are evenly divided between the Northern (960–1126) and Southern Sung (1127–1279), but the sharply contrasting nature of the clan's experience in these two periods has required different approaches in these two sections. During the Northern Sung, the clan underwent a series of dramatic changes—driven both by its rapid demographic growth and by changes in government policy—hence, the next four chapters are arranged chronologically. Chapter 2 begins the coverage of the Northern Sung, treating the reigns of the founding emperors T'ai-tsu and T'ai-tsung, when there was no imperial clan, only the immediate families of the two emperors and their brother, the Prince of Wei (or Wei-wang, 947–84). These years were critical to the later evolution of the imperial clan. T'ai-tsu's vision of an imperial clan as a corporate body of great genealogical depth consisting of the offspring of the three brothers essentially set the parameters of the future clan. And T'ai-tsung's suspicions of his brother and nephews do much to explain the policy of rigorously excluding clansmen from any political power, especially since his own succession to the emperorship was considered suspicious. Chapter 3 traces the emergence of an identifiable clan, the establishment of its institutions, and clan life in the first half of the eleventh century under the emperors Chen-tsung and Jen-tsung (997–1063). In many respects this was the golden age of the imperial clan. All clan members were known to the emperor and lived lives of great luxury, even though they were segregated from the rest of society and had little to occupy themselves beyond ceremonial functions and personal avocations. In this period of palace life, the lifestyle and cultural orientation of the clan members came increasingly to resemble those of the civil elite, the primary difference being that, for clan youths, studies sometimes led to examinations but never to office.

In the late eleventh century, the imperial clan encountered its first major turning point, which is the subject of Chapter 4. With the clan mushroom-

ing in size, the court faced a crisis that was at once fiscal (the clan was increasingly expensive), social (the palaces were overflowing), and genealogical
(the appearance of a generation outside the five degrees of relationship to
the emperor). Of these, the third was most important, for by T'ang precedent they should not have been counted as clan members. For a time, it
seemed that the government would cut off these kin; it discontinued the
granting of names and titular office to non–mourning kin youths, allowing
them instead to take examinations for officeholding. But then it hedged,
instituting allowances for non-mourning kin and entering their names on
the Jade Register genealogies. These actions effectively repudiated a clan
identity based upon mourning relations in favor of a structure that was
genealogically open-ended. Then, as we shall see in Chapter 5, the emperor
Hui-tsung (r. 1101–26) consolidated this new definition by creating two vast
satellite residential complexes for non-mourning kin in the dynasty's western and southern capitals: Ho-nan fu (modern Loyang) and Ying-t'ien fu
(modern Shang-ch'iu), respectively. Still unclear, however, was what political role the new generations of clansmen would play, for although they had
begun entering the bureaucracy, they were largely confined to minor positions.

Chapter 6 covers the beginning of the Southern Sung: the Jurchen invasion of northern China, the fall of K'ai-feng, the capture of both the retired
and the sitting emperors as well as most of the imperial clan, the flight south
by remnants of the court and clan, and their reconstitution of the dynasty
to the south of the Yangtze. This was easily the most traumatic period of
the clan's existence—prior to the dynasty's later fall—as many tragic stories
bear witness. But it was also a time of unparalleled opportunity for those
clansmen who managed to elude capture, for the southern court under the
emperor Kao-tsung (r. 1127–62) was desperate for capable officials and made
use of clansmen in military as well as civil positions. Indeed, a number
played prominent roles in the war against the Jurchen.

The imperial clan in the early Southern Sung was therefore a strikingly
different entity from its Northern Sung predecessor. In Chapter 7, which
offers an overview of the clan through the first seventy years of the Southern

Sung, we see the basic elements of its new existence: the creation of several clan centers, the most important of which were not in the capital of Lin-an but in the Fu-chien prefectures of Ch'üan-chou and Fu-chou; the settlement of many clan families away from clan centers altogether; increasing integration into the local elites of the empire; and the creation of special channels for the examination and recruitment of clansmen. The approach of this chapter is notably less historical and more syncretic than the preceding chapters, for the constant changes of the earlier period dictated by the growth of the clan and government policies had no counterpart in the Southern Sung. As a result, its new structural elements, once in place, changed relatively little as the Southern Sung progressed.

Changes were more visible in the roles of clansmen in the government, especially in high office, which is the subject of Chapter 8. Using the biographical records of outstanding clansmen-officials from the mid-twelfth to mid-thirteenth centuries—the reigns of Hsiao-tsung, Ning-tsung, Kuang-tsung, and Li-tsung—the chapter examines their patterns of service and behavior, their ties (or claimed ties) to the emperor (two of whom were themselves clansmen selected to succeed heirless emperors), and especially the hotly contested issue of whether clansmen should hold high positions in the central government—a debate that became very real with the grand councillorship of Chao Ju-yü (BAAKFBDAA; 1140–96).

Finally, Chapter 9 looks at the imperial clan in its maturity and at its end. By the late Southern Sung, the clan was suffering from bloated numbers, problems with genealogical recordkeeping, contested claims to clan status, and difficulties in controlling clan members. These problems were especially evident in Ch'üan-chou, the largest of the clan centers. Special attention is given to the large Ch'üan-chou center and the influences—positive and negative—of the clan on the overseas commerce for which that city was justly famous. The chapter concludes by recounting the responses of clan members to the Mongol invasion, their role in the resistance movement, the massacre of clan members in Ch'üan-chou, and the strategies employed by surviving families for coping with a new regime when they were no longer a clan and no longer imperial.

Finally, Chapter 10 returns to the issue of the place of the imperial clan in Sung history and surveys the many contributions of clansmen, a testimony to their successful integration into the elite society and high culture of the Sung. This brief concluding chapter also considers the legacy of the clan, as a model for later dynasties and in the form of Chao lineages that arose in the Ming and Ch'ing and, in some cases, continue to flourish today.

TWO

A Royal Family

The glory days came later. Only in the middle of the Northern Sung did the imperial clan achieve its special brilliance. Yet the early history of the imperial family was crucial to its subsequent development. Chinese imperial clans were unlike any other kinship group in Chinese society; transforming an ordinary family into one was a complex and difficult process. The founding emperor Chao K'uang-yin (T'ai-tsu, 927–76; r. 960–76) and even more his brother and successor on the throne, K'uang-i (T'ai-tsung, 939–97; r. 976–97), were mindful of this process and of the need to create a long-lasting entity that would reflect their love and generosity toward their kinsmen, produce men of integrity and ability who could maintain the imperial line, and at the same time preserve the prerogatives of the emperor's power. They and their advisors were also students of history, well aware of the problems of past dynasties with their imperial kinsmen. Their decisions largely determined the nature of the imperial clan throughout most of the Northern Sung, and even when the clan subsequently metamorphosed in unexpected ways, the influence of the founding emperors remained great.

Family Origins

Despite later attempts to claim an eminent ancestry of ancient Taoist divinities for the Chaos,[1] the family's pre-imperial history was not especially distinguished. Their lineage can be traced with certainty only four generations back from T'ai-tsu, to Chao T'iao (828–74), a late T'ang official who held three magistracies in the vicinity of Cho-chou in northern Hopei, which was also the family's residence.[2] T'iao's second son, Chao T'ing (851–928), and his grandson Chao Ching (872–933; K'uang-yin's grandfather), both served as local officials in Hopei, the latter holding three prefectships, including Cho-chou. Then in a move that broke with the family tradition but was critical to his sons' success, K'uang-yin's father, Chao Hung-yin (posthumously Hsuan-tsu; 899–956), converted a passion for the military arts (his biography notes that he was well educated in literary studies too), success in the Later T'ang's military *chin-shih* examinations of 923, and the patronage of the military governor of Chen-chou, Wang Jung, into a general-ship.

Despite this record of local political service, contemporaries considered the Chao family of Cho-chou to be of humble status. A famous story concerning Hung-yin as a youth has him caught on the road in a snowstorm. Taking shelter in the gate of the illustrious Tu family, he was befriended by them and so impressed the master of the household—the military governor Tu Jang—that he was given the fourth Tu daughter in marriage, the future Empress Dowager Tu (899–961).[3] By the time that Chao K'uang-yin and his younger brothers, K'uang-i (T'ai-tsung) and K'uang-mei[4] (947–84), reached adulthood (two others had died in infancy), however, the family was well established as part of the military elite.

K'uang-yin, who had little patience for the classical education his father arranged for him and his brothers, joined the staff of the military governor Wang Yen-ch'ao and rose rapidly to become the Commander of the Palace Army in the Later Chou, a position of pre-eminent military power.[5] Thus when the capable Later Chou emperor Shih-tsung (r. 954–60) died unexpectedly, leaving a child as heir, K'uang-yin was poised to seize the throne himself, although the traditional account stresses that he did so with reluctance, at the demand of his mutinous troops.

T'ai-tsu's Definition of the Imperial Clan

At its outset, the Sung appeared to be nothing more than the sixth in a line of short-lived northern dynasties, and there was little to indicate that it would be any more successful than its predecessors. In retrospect, we can point to several factors that allowed it to become one of the great dynasties: the successes of its predecessors in reasserting central power, on which T'ai-tsu was able to build;[6] the forceful moves that T'ai-tsu quickly made to assert control over the military, particularly the commanders of the Palace Army; the combination of military force and diplomatic wooing to subdue the southern kingdoms; and, not least, the fact that for 37 years the Sung was ruled by emperors who were already adults at its outset, so that the dynasty was never threatened with the fate of the Later Chou. But even though the Sung claim to Heaven's mandate may have appeared less than secure, T'ai-tsu was a dynastic architect, conscious of historical precedents and mindful of posterity, and many of his actions can be seen as leading toward a lasting Sung order.

The issue of how to treat the imperial family is a case in point. The apparent simplicity of that formulation belies a number of social and political complexities. First and foremost, who constituted the family? From Chao T'iao on, T'ai-tsu's forebears had produced numerous offspring,[7] and T'ai-tsu had numerous Chao kin within his sphere of mourning relationships. Moreover, although in other dynasties the imperial clan came to consist of the offspring of the founding emperor, at the time of his accession T'ai-tsu was not the head of his family. That honor had been held by his mother, the Empress Dowager Tu, since his father's death in 956, which meant that his brothers were members of the core imperial family.

There is a document dated the twelfth day of the eighth month of 964 entitled "The Emperor T'ai-tsu's Great Instructions for the Jade Register" (i.e., the imperial genealogy).[8] Although T'ai-tsu's former tutor, the grand councilor Chao P'u (922–92), may have had a hand in its drafting,[9] the instructions are couched in the imperial first person and provide an invaluable view of T'ai-tsu's thinking about his family.

T'ai-tsu begins by invoking the metaphor of water: "We consider that people are rooted in their ancestors just as water comes from its source. When water flows far, streams diverge, and when people grow distant, they separate into branches. This is a fixed and natural principle." He then describes how the numerous descendents of his great-great-grandfather (Chao T'iao) have become dispersed, and without an accepted genealogical ordering, the ordering of their spirit tablets has become confused. The best way for them to satisfy their ancestors' intentions, he suggests, is for the intelligent among them to study, sit for examinations, and become officials. But what of a royal family? The instructions turn to the Chou dynasty and describe how, through the sagacity and enlightenment of the dynastic founders, the later royal clansmen came to be sent out to feudatories, as princes and lords.

This did not violate the original intention of the ancestors. Unfortunately, there were no branch characters [i.e., in their names] to distinguish the tablet-order for later generations. By the time of the Spring and Autumn and Warring States periods, kinsmen contested with each other, even to the point of enmity. What a misfortune!

This, he continues, is his concern for his offspring, so he offers the following prescription:

We, together with the Prince of Chin, Kuang-i, and the Prince of Ch'in, Kuang-mei, will constitute three branches. Each will establish fourteen characters [for generation names] in the Jade Register so as to distinguish the streams and give order to the [spirit] tablets. Although our posterity may be distant in time and in relationship, they will not lose their order.

Finally, after reiterating the importance of this practice for maintaining the clansmen as one, however distant their relationship may grow to be, he ends with a remarkable vision of a socially heterogeneous clan and a charge to future clansmen:

In our world when the streams have grown distant, you should hold the Jade Register in esteem. Whether you are an official en route or a traveling merchant, when you meet [other clansmen] in some place, you should recognize each other and identify yourselves according to the tablet-order, without favoring wealthy or spurning poor [clansmen], without favoring the noble or spurning the humble. Even in cases of rudeness and discourtesy, if it involves someone who is poor and whose family lacks the means to support itself, the wealthy and fortunate [clansmen] should exert themselves in offering help, and not allow him to go homeless, which would disgrace their ancestors. This should be remembered by everyone. Do not fail my instructions!

To the emperor's instructions was attached a companion piece by Chao P'u, dated the same day and called "A Preface to the Imperially Created Branches of the Jade Register."[10] In it are set out three sets of fourteen characters each, one for each branch of the clan, to be used sequentially so that all males of the same branch and generation would share a character in their personal names. The characters were drawn from the following 42-character poem:

Now original virtue should be completed,	若夫元德允克
Excellent virtue should be esteemed.	令德宜崇
Follow the ancients and emulate Mencius;	師古希孟
Timely learning glorifies the ancestors.	時學光宗
Good friends and accomplished scholars:	良友彥士
You will be recorded fairly [in the Jade Register].	登汝必公
Not only the eldest sons of princes	不惟世子
Should share in the pursuit of goodness;	與善之從
Whatever your fraternal order,	伯仲叔季
Your inheritance comes from a common source.[11]	承嗣由同

Together, these two documents defined the composition of the future imperial clan (the offspring of T'ai-tsu and his brothers) and detailed the generation names that were to serve as one of the most visible features of clan membership.[12] They also made the radical claim that all descendents of the three brothers were to be members of the clan and were to use the same series of generation names, a practice that ran contrary to earlier customs of denying clan status to those outside the emperor's mourning circle. As we will see in the following chapter, this became a contested issue in the late eleventh century, and its outcome had great significance for the future of the imperial clan. Finally, we should note the poem's stress on Mencius, scholars, and learning, for this prefigured another later development: the civilizing of the imperial clan, which occurred most markedly under the emperor Jen-tsung.

Notably absent from these documents, however, is any reference to the political role of the imperial clan or individual clansmen. Over the course of the next thirty years, especially during the reign of T'ai-tsung, the most important development involved a ban on clansmen holding any posts of political importance. This was closely linked to the issue of imperial succession.

Power and Succession

How to use—or not use—royal kin and especially princes is a problem innate to monarchies, and as we saw in the preceding chapter, it is one with which earlier Chinese dynasties struggled. Several competing needs—to reward one's kinsmen, to produce seasoned and capable emperors, to manage peaceful successions, and to avoid rivalry and internecine struggles—were difficult if not impossible to reconcile.

Although T'ai-tsu did not follow the Han—or later the Ming—practice of enfeoffing imperial princes in their own territories, he used his closest kin in positions of significant power. Chao Kuang-i (the future T'ai-tsung) served for many years as the metropolitan prefect of K'ai-feng, with responsibility for the capital's affairs during the emperor's frequent military campaigns. In 973 he was also named the Prince of Chin and given a protocol rank above that of the grand councilors.[13] His younger brother, Kuang-mei, in a similar fashion served as metropolitan prefect of Hsing-yuan fu (capital of Li-chou circuit) and then Ching-chao fu (the former T'ang capital of Ch'ang-an in Yung-hsing-chün circuit).[14] T'ai-tsu's sole grown son, Te-chao (AA; d. 979), in 973 succeeded Kuang-mei as prefect of Hsing-yuan fu.[15]

In the tenth month of 976, T'ai-tsu died suddenly in the middle of the night. According to Ssu-ma Kuang's (1019–86) dramatic though problematic account, the Empress Sung ordered the attending eunuch, one Wang Chi-lung, to fetch her son Chao Te-fang (AB; 959–81), apparently to be installed as emperor. But Wang, "knowing that T'ai-tsu's intention to pass the throne on to the Prince of Chin [i.e., Kuang-i] was commonly known," went instead to his residence. When Kuang-i then went to the palace to claim the throne, the empress was visibly shaken and said to him: "The lives of myself and my son now rest with you." To which Kuang-i replied, tearfully, "Together we will ensure prosperity and honor without distress."[16] And so the succession went to T'ai-tsu's brother, and not to one of his sons.

This lateral succession was a highly unusual occurrence, especially since T'ai-tsu left four sons, and it occasioned great discussion, by historians and others, as to why it occurred and whether it had, in fact, been T'ai-tsu's intention. The primary justification for it came from a conversation between T'ai-tsu and his mother, the Dowager Empress Tu. According to her biography, as she lay dying in 961, she asked him, "Do you know why you were able to gain the empire?" At first he refused to answer, but when she pressed, he said, "I gained the empire thanks to the accumulated merit of my ancestors and you." She replied, "No! It was really because Chou Shih-tsung left a child to rule the empire. Had he left an adult ruler, would the empire have been yours? For the sake of your posterity, you should be succeeded by your younger brother." T'ai-tsu tearfully indicated his accord ("Dare I not follow the empress's teaching?"), and the empress ordered Chao P'u, who was present, to record it and keep the document in a golden cupboard.[17]

Many historians have viewed this account as a later fabrication by T'ai-tsung to justify his succession. Indeed, some give credence to the popular speculation that T'ai-tsung murdered his brother—"the sound of the axe in the shadow of the flickering candle" (chu-ying fu-sheng)[18] as it was commonly described—if not personally, then at least through intermediaries.[19] Although the scene at Empress Tu's deathbed may well have been the fabrication of a usurping emperor, there are at least three reasons for accepting it. First, T'ai-tsu's acceptance of a plan for fraternal inheritance is consonant with his inclusion of the Kuang-i and Kuang-mei branches of the family in the imperial clan in the "Great Instructions." Second, Kuang-i's elevation to Prince of Chin in 973 seems to have made him the crown prince, for neither Te-chao nor any of his brothers had a princely title.[20] Third, according to the biography of Chao T'ing-mei (i.e., Kuang-mei) in the Sung History, some held that the intent of both Empress Tu and T'ai-tsu was for Kuang-mei in turn to succeed Kuang-i, with the line at that point passing back to Te-chao, T'ai-tsu's son.[21] Although such a rotation would have had little bearing on T'ai-tsung's emperorship itself, it would have effectively eliminated his own sons from the succession. Thus it makes little sense for him to have fabricated it.

Shortly after he became emperor, T'ai-tsung elevated T'ing-mei and Te-chao (see Table 2.1). T'ing-mei was named prefect of K'ai-feng (T'ai-tsung's former position) and elevated first to Prince of Ch'i and, soon thereafter, to Prince of Ch'in.[22] Te-chao, for his part, took T'ing-mei's post as prefect of Ching-chao fu and was ennobled as Commandary Prince of Wu-kung. Moreover, T'ai-tsung gave the two of them a protocol ranking above that of the grand councilors.[23] Both, however, subsequently fell from favor and came to tragic ends.

In 979, during the Sung campaign against the Khitans in Yu-chou (Hopei), T'ai-tsung, fearing that his retreat to the capital might be cut off by the enemy, secretly left camp with a small entourage. When the emperor was discovered missing that night, there was talk among the disgruntled troops about making Te-chao emperor, much to T'ai-tsung's later

Table 2.1

The Sons of T'ai-tsu, T'ai-tsung, and Wei-wang

Father	Sons
T'ai-tsu (K'uang-yin; 927–76; r. 960–76)	Te-chao (AA; d. 979)
	Te-fang (AB; 959–81)
	Te-hsiu (AC; 979–1008)
	Te-lin (AD; n.d.)
T'ai-tsung (K'uang-i; 939–97; r. 976–97)	Yuan-tso (BA; 962–1023)
	Yuan-hsi (BB; d. 992)
	Yuan-ch'ang, later Heng (968–1022; as Chen-tsung, r. 997–1022)
	Yuan-fen (BC; 968–1004)
	Yuan-chieh (BD; 972–1003)
	Yuan-wo (BE; 977–1018)
	Yuan-ch'eng (BF; 981–1014)
	Yuan-yen (BG; 987–1044)
	Yuan-i (died young; not in SS genealogy)
Wei-wang (K'uang-mei, then T'ing-mei; 947–84)	Te-kung (CA; 956–84)
	Te-lung (CB; 964–86)
	Te-jun (not in SS genealogy; 965–1003)
	Te-i (CC; 967–1015)
	Te-yung (CD; n.d.)
	Te-chün (CE; d. 1007)
	Te-ch'in (CF; 974–1004)
	Te-wen (CG; 975–1046)
	Te-yuan (not in SS genealogy; 976–99)
	Te-ts'un (CH; 982–1011)

displeasure. After the army's return to the capital, T'ai-tsung delayed giving out rewards because the expedition had been disastrous. When Te-chao raised the issue, the emperor was furious and taunted Te-chao: "If we wait for you to make them, the rewards will not take long." Te-chao went to his quarters and slit his throat. T'ai-tsung's response was one of sorrow if not remorse. He went to the corpse and said, in tears, "Silly boy, how did you come to this depravity?"[24]

T'ing-mei's misfortunes were more complicated. In the third month of 982, T'ai-tsung received reports that his brother was plotting with a number of military officers against him. Unwilling to deal with him ruthlessly, T'ai-tsung removed him from his K'ai-feng position and sent him to be prefect of Ching-chao; he also demoted or, in one case, exiled the co-conspirators. Shortly thereafter, Chao P'u, who had returned to court for another stint as grand councilor, reported allegations that T'ing-mei was plotting T'ai-tsung's death, this time with the minister of war, Lu Tuo-hsun (934–85), and others. At court a group of 74 ministers proposed death for all of them, but T'ai-tsung exiled Lu, confined T'ing-mei, and executed six of the conspirators. In addition, T'ing-mei's sons, daughters, and sons-in-law were all demoted. When T'ing-mei complained of his fate, he was sent instead into exile in Hupei, where he soon fell ill and died. T'ai-tsung grieved his death and gave T'ing-mei posthumous honors, but reportedly remained convinced of his guilt and lack of remorse.[25]

It is difficult to know how serious a threat to T'ai-tsung these plots were. The historians of the *Sung History* point to the manipulative hand of Chao P'u in determining T'ing-mei's fate, for Chao's opposition to the plan of fraternal succession was well known.[26] Others have condemned T'ai-tsung for his heartless treatment of his brother. In a structural sense, however, both Te-chao and T'ing-mei owed their fates to the fact that, by combining their successor status with active involvement in government, they constituted threats to the emperor; indeed, the conspiratorial elements of T'ing-mei's plots suggest the existence of a center of power that threatened to rival the emperor's. This was a common structure in virtually every other major dynasty in Chinese history and a frequent source of bloody intrigues.[27] T'ing-mei's case, however, was almost unique in history, and behind it seems to have been a decision to remove the imperial kin from politics.

The details of this change are unclear, for to my knowledge there are no contemporary records of discussions of it. As early as 983, with T'ing-mei already in disgrace, T'ai-tsung ordered that grand councilors take protocol precedence over imperial princes. When the grand councilors Sung Ch'i (917–96) and Li Fang (925–96) objected, the emperor replied: "The post of grand councilor is truly one of managing the hundred affairs. . . . Yuan-tso [his oldest son; BA; 962–1023] and his brothers are still young. I want them to know the way of modesty; ministers should not necessarily yield to them." And when in 992 the grand councilor Lü Meng-cheng (946–1011) asked

T'ai-tsung to reconsider this decision, he again refused.[28] Only two of T'ai-tsung's eight adult sons served in office, both as prefect of K'ai-feng—Chao Yuan-hsi (BB; d. 992) in 985 and Chao Heng (968–1022, the future emperor Chen-tsung) in 994—and neither had a noteworthy tenure.[29] Four of T'ing-mei's sons also served as prefects of lesser prefectures during the mid-980s, but their cases are instructive. When Chao Te-kung (CA; 962–1006) and his brother Te-lung (CB; 964–86) were appointed prefects at the end of 984, T'ai-tsung assigned them assistant prefects with these instructions: "Now that Te-kung and his brother are serving in prefectures, their good works should be praised, but if there are shortcomings, they should be vigorously rectified, and you will be held guilty."[30] However, the final example that I have found of an imperial kinsman holding a substantive post is that of T'ai-tsung's fifth son, Chao Yuan-wo (BE; 977–1018), who in 997 served as the commissioner for bridges, roads, hostels, and post stations for two prefectures in the northwest and helped to host a visit from the new emperor, Chen-tsung (r. 997–1022).[31] Thereafter for the next seventy years, it was accepted that imperial clansmen would be given high official ranks and often titles of nobility but would be kept away from power and barred from any substantive posts.

Imperial Kin in the Early Sung

Although T'ai-tsu in his Great Instructions clearly envisioned a large and far-flung imperial clan, during his reign and that of T'ai-tsung, the imperial kin were a rambling and often rambunctious extended family rather than a clan.

They were a remarkably fecund group. The three founding brothers had 23 sons, 59 grandsons, and 226 great-grandsons (see Table 2.2). At the time of T'ai-tsung's death the sons were in their adulthood and the grandsons (and their sisters) were children. The third generation of great-grandchildren had yet to begin appearing (see Table 2.3), but even so, the hundred-plus grandchildren in multiple households as well as the innumerable servants and guards already had made the imperial family a large group.

Wives, concubines, and daughters were an essential, though often ignored, part of the imperial family. There is little evidence concerning them for this period, but we know a little more about imperial marriage policies

Table 2.2

The Sung Imperial Clan: Generational Names and Numbers

Gene-ration	T'ai-tsu Name	T'ai-tsu No.	T'ai-tsung Name	T'ai-tsung No.	Wei-wang Name	Wei-wang No.	Totals
1st	Te	4	Yuan	9	Te	10	23
2d	Wei	8	Yun	19	Ch'eng	32	59
3d	Ts'ung/Shou	24	Tsung	75	K'o	127	226
4th	Shih	129	Chung	388	Shu	561	1,078
5th	Ling	564	Shih	1,499	Chih	1,425	3,488
6th	Tzu	1,251[a]	Pu	2,130	Kung	1,774	5,155
7th	Po	1,645	Shan	2,431	Yen	1,824	5,900
8th	Shih	1,490	Ju	1,022	Fu	1,666	4,178
9th	Hsi	1,140	Ch'ung	413	Shih	253	1,806
10th	Yü	110	Pi	19	Jo	24	153
TOTAL		6,365		8,005		7,696[b]	22,066

NOTES: The table does not include those in the eleventh and twelfth generations who had received names, nor does it include the direct descendents of Ying-tsung or Hui-tsung or the Nan-pan-kuan clansmen.

CSTP also gives data on the numbers of clansmen by branch for the first four generations. The numbers for the first generation are the same as those shown here; for the second through fourth generations, they are:

	T'ai-tsu	T'ai-tsung	Wei-wang	Total
2d	8	21	34	63
3d	25	64	124	213
4th	120	390	552	1,062

[a] WHTK gives 1,221, but this is an error, for it does not tally with the total given for all ten generations of T'ai-tsu's descendents.

[b] CYTC gives 7,296 and a grand total of 21,666, but the Wei-wang total is in fact 7,696 and the grand total 22,066.

SOURCE: CYTC, pt. 1, 1:24. The CYTC does not include the total shown in the last column. The same information with the error noted above can also be found in WHTK 259: 2056–57, but the CYTC was probably the source for the WHTK data. The CYTC's source was the *Hsien-yuan lei-p'u*, the official imperial genealogy.

Table 2.3

Birth and Death Years by Generation for the Sung Imperial Clan
(ranges and means)

Generation	Birth-year range (N)	Death-year range (N)	Mean years for births and deaths
1st	959–987 (15)	979–1046 (18)	971–1007
2d	966–1022 (12)	1010–70 (18)	994–1035
3d	998–1043 (34)	1034–1109 (45)	1022–1068
4th	1010–95 (51)	1041–1137 (62)	1049–84
5th	1049–1134 (28)	1056–1202 (45)	1078–1126
6th	1059–1144 (18)	1059–1224 (28)	1115–76
7th	1103–55 (21)	1161–1242 (23)	1132–94
8th	1109–1193 (19)	1167–1256 (22)	1159–1221
9th	1160–1230 (14)	1212–76 (16)	1183–1238
10th	1179–1267 (8)	1169–1330 (10)	1218–70
11th	1192–1286 (3)	1220–1332 (4)	1244–70

NOTE: These figures are drawn from the biographical list of all the clansmen on whom I found information (see Appendix A). Because in many cases only a birth or a death date is available for an individual, the numbers of reports (indicated here by the numbers in parentheses) are quite variable. This explains the apparent anomaly in the tenth generation: the first known death date is earlier than the first known birth date.

and wives. In the early years of the dynasty, the marriage of imperial off-spring clearly concerned the emperors personally. Priscilla Ching Chung has called attention to the founder T'ai-tsu's pledge in his famous drinking speech to unite his family with those of his generals in marriage.[32] His brother and successor, T'ai-tsung, was also clear about his intentions; at the time of the marriage of his second son, Chao Yuan-hsi, to the daughter of the border general Li Chien-p'u (915–76), he stated: "I have on occasion discussed my sons; now I will match them all in marriage to the families of generals, grand councilors, and great ministers."[33] And indeed, the early Sung marriages not only of princes but of clansmen and clanswomen generally seem to have been with the children of the mighty, although they were primarily from military rather than civil backgrounds.[34]

The women who gained the attention of the compilers of the *Sung History*—I have found no epitaphs for clan wives from this period—did so because of notoriety and clearly were not representative of clan women in general. Nevertheless, their stories are noteworthy. Lady Li, the daughter of the army officer Li Han-pin (fl. 976–83), was the wife of T'ai-tsung's fourth son, Chao Yuan-fen (BC), and apparently a strong-tempered woman who was constantly upsetting people. She is described as a jealous and cruel woman, who would beat—and even kill—palace maids on the slightest provocation, necessitating more than one imperial pardon. She was also involved in numerous breeches of decorum: not being in attendance on her sick husband when T'ai-tsung paid a visit; not participating in the mourning for T'ai-tsung after his death; giving her husband birthday presents that employed the forbidden imperial symbols of phoenixes and dragons; and not adopting a properly grieving demeanor after his death in 1004. These shortcomings seem to have bothered others more than Yuan-fen, for Chentsung, in responding to complaints about her behavior, chose not to disgrace her publicly, but simply reduced her noble titles and had her move to another residence, his reason being Yuan-fen's warm regard for his wife.[35]

In 992 another case incited greater imperial wrath. After the death of Chao Yuan-hsi—whose marriage was discussed above—allegations surfaced concerning his favorite concubine, Lady Chang. She was charged with being inclined to licentiousness and, unbeknown to Yuan-hsi, with having beaten a female slave to death. More seriously, she had summoned the souls of her parents at a Buddhist temple in the western part of the capital, a gross violation of sumptuary regulations. The emperor was furious. He sent a eunuch commissioner, Wang Chi-en (d. 999), to investigate, but she had already hung herself. The responsible officials were beaten, the coffins of her parents were destroyed, and all people connected to the affair were banished. In addition, four officials in the prince's establishment (wang-fu) were demoted, and Yuan-hsi was posthumously stripped of his ritual titles, although later emperors restored them.[36] As we shall see below, concubines were a ubiquitous feature of the huge imperial clan families of the eleventh century, but any attempt at social climbing by these women, whose unions stemmed from their sexual attractiveness rather than from family considerations (and imperial control), was considered threatening.

We know little about where the imperial family lived at this time. The emperor's children initially lived in the palace with him, although during adolescence they were usually sent to live in the Eastern Palace (Tung-kung).[37] Beyond that, the first formalization of the residences of the rest of the family occurred at the beginning of Chen-tsung's reign, when in the first month of 998 he decreed that each of the princes—in effect, the sons of the founders—inaugurate a house (*shih*), and a new complex of Southern and Northern residences (Nan-chai, Pei-chai) were established with teachers attached to them.[38]

At least some of the accounts that we have of life in the palaces are idyllic. T'ai-tsu's grandson Chao Wei-chi (AAB; 966–1010) was a favorite of his and spent his first eighteen *sui* in the imperial palace. On one occasion he reportedly jumped up and down in delight when the emperor, shooting at kites, hit one on his first shot. That so pleased his grandfather that he had a gold statue of unusual beasts and rare birds given to him. He also rode a small chariot and a small saddled horse, and T'ai-tsu ordered that he be allowed to come and go freely through the Yellow Gate to the palace.[39]

Other anecdotes, however, reveal a darker side to palace life. One victim of the recriminations and accusations involving Chao Te-chao and Chao T'ing-mei in the early years of T'ai-tsung's reign was his oldest son, Chao Yuan-tso. Yuan-tso was close to T'ing-mei, and when his uncle was sent into exile, he was the only one to defend him publicly. T'ing-mei's death in 984 reportedly drove him to madness, and he stabbed an attendant over a trifle. A year later his illness seemed to have been cured, and T'ai-tsung proclaimed a general amnesty in thanks. But it recurred at the time of the Double Ninth Daylight Feast. Enraged that he was not invited to the feast, Yuan-tso became drunk and burned down the palace. He was seized and, after an inquiry by censors, demoted to commoner status and exiled to Yun-chou (Chiang-nan-hsi). The emperor relented after 100 officials petitioned to have him remain in the capital, and he lived quietly for years in the Southern Palace (Nan-kung). In response to three officials who had had responsibility for Yuan-tso and asked to be punished, T'ai-tsung said, "This son, even I have been unable to reform through my teaching. How could you guide him?"[40]

The practice of appointing officials to oversee and instruct young princes had its origins—at least for the Sung—in 983, when T'ai-tsung appointed moral mentors (*yü-shan*) and advisors (*tzu-i*) to each of the princely establishments.[41] One of the mentors, Yao T'an (935–1009), had a series of disagreements with his charge, Chao Yuan-chieh (BD; 972–1003). From the outset, T'an frequently berated the young prince for being idle and lazy, and Yuan-chieh came to despise him. When T'an complained to the emperor, T'ai-tsung said: "Yuan-chieh is literate and enjoys learning; that should be sufficient to make him a worthy prince. If when young he is immoderate, then it is necessary to have entreaties to rein in his ridicule. But if you slander him without good reason, how is that going to help him?" On one occasion the prince—reportedly at the instigation of his friends—feigned illness and began skipping court. T'ai-tsung ordered daily checks on his progress, but when after a month he still ailed, the emperor was concerned. He summoned his wet nurse (ju-mu) and asked after Yuan-chieh. She said, "The prince basically is not sick; it's just that with Yao T'an checking up on him, he can seldom follow his inclinations, and thus has become sick." The emperor angrily said, "I have chosen upright scholars to help the prince be good. If the prince cannot use rules and practice, feigns illness, and wants to have me dismiss a proper man so that he can follow his inclinations, how can I comply? Moreover, the prince is young; this is a plot by all of you." He ordered her to be taken to a rear courtyard and caned several times. He then summoned Yao T'an and soothed him, saying, "When you are staying in the prince's palace, righting the wrongs wrought by a mob of bad men is no small matter. In cases like this, you should not be anxious over slander, for I will certainly not listen to it."[42]

Yuan-chieh's most famous confrontation with his mentor occurred after the prince had shown some talent at poetry and calligraphy and established himself as a bibliophile. He built a library to house his 20,000-chüan collection of books, and in the surrounding garden he had a pavilion and an artificial mountain (chia shan) built at great cost. When it was complete, he threw a drinking party for people to come and see it, but at the party Yao T'an, alone, refused to look at the mountain. The prince was startled and asked why. T'an replied, "When I was living in the country, I witnessed the prefectures and counties pressing [people] for their taxes, seizing fathers, sons, and brothers, and sending them to the counties to be flogged, so that blood flowed and bodies were broken. This artificial mountain was made by all of the peoples' taxes. If it is not a bloody mountain, then what is it?" When T'ai-tsung heard this, he ordered the mountain destroyed.[43]

However strained the relationship between Chao Yuan-chieh and Yao T'an may have been, their story contains several themes that were to be important for succeeding generations of clansmen—the imperial concern with their proper education, a focus on the arts of the literati, and the problem of profligacy by people raised amid almost unimaginable luxury.

THREE

Culture and Confinement

Chen-tsung, Jen-tsung, and Their Imperial Kin

With the reign of Chen-tsung (968–1022; r. 997–1022), the third Sung emperor, the period of dynastic founding came to an end. In contrast to the enormous changes wrought by T'ai-tsu and especially T'ai-tsung, Chen-tsung's reign was noted more for consolidation than innovation. Historically, his most important action was to conclude the Treaty of Shan-yuan in 1005, ending the long war with the Khitan and establishing a peace that was to last for over a century, albeit at the price of agreeing to a ritually inferior status vis-à-vis the Liao.[1] A desire to recover from the humiliation of the treaty agreement was undoubtedly behind the most flamboyant acts of his reign: the "discovery" of Heavenly Texts glorifying the Chao family and its ancient lineage, the performance of highly unusual—and controversial—imperial sacrifices at Mount T'ai and elsewhere, and the elevation of Taoism within the court.[2] For the imperial clan, these were important years. As we will see below, the functions of the Court of the Imperial Clan were expanded and formalized. But even more significant was the emergence of the imperial clan as a social entity under the benevolent attention of Chen-tsung, who was the first of the Sung emperors to have been raised in the palaces among his imperial kinsmen.

The biography of Chao Yuan-wo (BE; 977–1018), a younger brother of Chen-tsung, describes some of Chen-tsung's interactions with the clansmen in detail. "When Chen-tsung became emperor, he often stimulated scholarly activities among the youth of the clan. Yuan-wo, as head of the clansmen, also encouraged them. Whenever the emperor engaged in composition, all was peaceful. The emperor remarked on this to his ministers." Once he went with his entourage to Yuan-wo's palace, where they feasted and composed poetry. Yuan-wo toasted the emperor's health and was given clothing, a gold belt, money, and precious things. They also gathered with the clansmen for archery at the southwestern pavilion. After the attending officials had left, the emperor remained with his eunuchs.[3]

This impression of the emperor interacting freely and easily with his relatives is reinforced by numerous references in the biographies of the early eleventh-century clansmen. We are told that "whenever Chen-tsung entered the precincts of the [clan] palaces, he had sons and nephews in attendance."[4] He was known to have instructed clan youths personally and by no means limited his attention to close kin. Chao Ch'eng-i (CEF; 997–1053)—a cousin once removed from the Wei-wang branch—received the emperor's personal instruction at the imperial palace in the art of poetry.[5]

The most vivid example of Chen-tsung's close relationship with clansmen is his behavior toward Chao Ch'eng-ch'ing (CAA; d. 1039), of the same branch and generation as Ch'eng-i, although quite a bit older. Once on a fishing expedition, Chen-tsung asked his attendants (this was not a solitary undertaking), "Does this fishing please you?" The response was a unanimous affirmative except for Ch'eng-ch'ing, who volunteered, "I have one worry and one pleasure." All the attendants, we are told, blanched with fear at such impertinence. "What is it," the emperor asked, "that worries the great prince?" Ch'eng-ch'ing replied: "I noticed yesterday that the attendants at the imperial pavilion numbered several hundred and were standing on the railing. I could not but be worried. Now, when the imperial carriage arrived in the park for the feast, everyone pranced around and sang. In a time of great peace, with such plentiful happiness filling the place, I could not but be happy." The emperor said to his companions, "If the great prince loves me like this, you could learn [from him]," and gave him a gift of calligraphy.[6] On another occasion, during an archery outing at which Chen-tsung had lauded Ch'eng-ch'ing as a "spirit archer," the latter managed (had the good fortune?) to land his arrow directly beneath the emperor's, thus illustrating the proper relationship between sovereign and subject. His reward from the delighted Chen-tsung consisted of two gold belts, horses, and a poem.[7]

The last recorded conversation between the two men occurred in 1022, shortly before Chen-tsung's death, at a banquet for imperial clansmen and concerned the clan itself. "In this past reign, did you not report exhaustively on what you observed?" asked the emperor. "The affairs of this past reign were concerned with essentials of governance," replied Ch'eng-ch'ing, who mentioned the sacrifices on Mount T'ai and other events in which he had participated and thereafter recorded. "Record, in addition, family affairs without avoiding anything, for I want to hear [about them]," he was instructed, to which he answered, "If you allow me to take my leave, I will make a record of daily and weekly affairs," and proceeded to do so.[8]

The emperor Jen-tsung's (1010–63; r. 1022–63) earliest years were lived amid friendly interactions between emperor and clansmen, and as emperor he worked to maintain that tradition. He certainly encouraged individual clan youth with whom he had contact, such as Chao Shih-yen (AABAB; 1022–65), who as a young boy met Jen-tsung on a visit to the Chang-hsien empress. The emperor commented on his fondness for reading, tested him, and commanded that he learn poetry.[9]

The more typical form of interaction, however, was the imperial banquet for clansmen. This involved activities besides eating, sometimes archery,[10] but more often recitation and poetry composition. Chao Tsung-yen (BA-CA; 1008–50) was known for displaying his knowledge of poetry and the *Book of Changes* at feasts and once was rewarded by the emperor with a hundred bolts of silk in a poetry-writing contest.[11] The biography of Chao K'o-kou (CCBA; 1015–56) provides a commentary on the emperor's role in such affairs:

When the imperial clansmen were summoned to court, and all wrote poems based on one that the emperor had composed, that of the marquis [i.e., K'o-kou] came out first, and he received an edict of encouragement. The emperor commended the excellent [poems] to the clansmen and took pity on those without ability. That which he taught was uplifting and embracing; I only fear it was incomplete. When there was one case of excellence, he would immediately present gold and silk to give force to his educational ideas, and because the marquis was naturally outstanding, he was the recipient of many gifts.[12]

Competitions, like that described in this passage, also took the form of actual tests or examinations, usually of general learning.[13] These were *not* examinations for office and brought only imperial recognition and material rewards, but they were clearly an important step in bringing the clansmen into the culture of examinations that was coming to dominate Sung elite society.

The most striking difference between Jen-tsung's interaction with the imperial clan and those of his father lay in their increased formality: banquets and examinations in contrast to outings. This may in part reflect their personalities, but undoubtedly a determining factor behind the differences was demographic. Where Chen-tsung was dealing primarily with the 59 second-generation and 226 third-generation clansmen, under Jen-tsung—and especially in the latter half of his reign—the 1,078 fourth-generation clansmen had fully come into their own. According to one contemporary estimate, at Jen-tsung's death, clansmen and clanswomen numbered over four thousand.[14] It was impossible for Jen-tsung to know all the clansmen personally, and the occasions designed for their interaction must have been huge, very formal affairs.

As we will see in the following section, formality was hardly limited to interactions. Circumstances during the reigns of Chen-tsung and especially of Jen-tsung forced the creation of new institutions and greater procedural formality. Compared with the later Northern Sung and its panoply of rules and regulations, this formality was relatively limited, but most of the institutions that marked the fully developed imperial clan were in place by the end of Jen-tsung's reign.

Clan Institutions

The one imperial clan institution that the Sung inherited—in form, at least—from the T'ang was the Court of the Imperial Clan. At least as early as 973, the Sung had established a court with responsibility for maintaining the imperial genealogy and managing the major sacrificial sites: the Imperial Ancestral Temple (*T'ai-miao*), the temples of the empress(es) (*hou-miao*), and the imperial tombs.[15] For the first half-century of the dynasty, the court confined its activities to these duties and seems to have had little to do with the imperial clansmen themselves.

One remarkable and curious feature of the court in these early years is that it was headed by Chao kinsmen (*tsung-hsing*—imperially surnamed) who were not imperial clansmen (*tsung-shih*—imperial house). In fact, in 973 the first person we know to have held the post of vice-minister of the Court of the Imperial Clan (*Tsung-cheng shao-ch'ing*) was Chao Ch'ung-chi, a guard general who was appointed despite his military status, for there were no Chao kin with high civil rank.[16] What was behind this appointment, especially since T'ai-tsu had already explicitly limited the imperial clan to descendents of himself and his brothers? Two reasons suggest themselves. First, the imperial family sacrifices extended four generations back from T'ai-tsu, and there were a great many Chaos with legitimate claims to participate in them and therefore in the management of the court. Second, when the court began to function, "clansmen" were few in number, young, and mainly princes—thus not good candidates to serve as administrators.

The practice of using Chao kinsmen lasted for quite some time; a total of five are named through the reign of Chen-tsung.[17] Thereafter, the records seldom give the names of the court officials, although the rule restricting the top two offices to Chaos was rescinded only in the Yuan-feng period (1078–85).[18] However, this practice is an indication that distant non-clan relatives were not entirely forgotten by the Sung emperors.[19]

The Court of the Imperial Clan itself underwent two moves, the first in 999 out of cramped quarters near the palace, the second in 1015 when, following a fire at the court, a new complex was built in the Fu-shan quarter of K'ai-feng with two central halls: one for the Jade Register (the imperial genealogy), the other for the records of the imperial clan.[20] To this was added an imperial storehouse (*shen-yü-k'u*) in 1040 to store the rare and valuable objects used during sacrifices.[21]

Although the primary responsibilities of the court continued to be the imperial genealogy and sacrifices throughout Jen-tsung's reign, it came to assume another function—the oversight of the marriages of clansmen and women.[22] This was a natural extension from the court's genealogical concerns with births, marriages, and deaths, and as we will see below, it involved elaborate and restrictive procedures that bore directly on the lives of all members of the clan.

The Court of the Imperial Clan consisted of two supervisors (the minister [*Tsung-cheng ch'ing*] and vice-minister), at or above the rank of those serving in the Two Drafting Groups (*liang-chih-kuan*) of the government's

Administration Chamber (*cheng-shih t'ang*),[23] a recorder (*chu-pu*) of capital rank or above, and about thirty other officials to staff the various offices, temples, and tomb sites, as editors, clerks, and the like. Many of these were eunuch-officials, which is not surprising since the court in many ways was serving the inner, private interests of the monarchy.[24]

In the seventh month of 1036, Jen-tsung created a new clan institution to supplement the Court, one that had no historical precedents: the Great Office of Clan Affairs. The edict establishing it stated that it was necessitated by the huge growth in clan numbers and the crowding of clansmen in the great clan residences, and named two senior clansmen—Chao Yun-jang (BCB; 995–1059) from the T'ai-tsung branch and Chao Shou-chieh (AABA; n.d.) from the T'ai-tsu branch—to serve as its first administrator and vice-administrator (*chih* and *t'ung-chih Ta-tsung-cheng shih*), respectively. They were ordered to correct the shortcomings and transgressions of the clansmen.[25]

It took several decades before the functions of the Great Office were fully formalized (see Chapter 4), but the disciplinary authority given to it, and reaffirmed in a separate ruling in 1044,[26] made it the primary governing body of the clan. Unfortunately, extant sources for its activities under Jen-tsung are rare. However, a memorial from 1061 asking that two princely palace teachers be delegated to organize and edit the many imperial directives to the Great Office and regulations issued by it makes clear that it was very active (the emperor agreed to the request).[27]

The selections of Yun-jang and Shou-chieh, who together with a third clansman, Chao Yun-pi (BEA; 1008–70), led the imperial clan for most of Jen-tsung's reign,[28] were hardly arbitrary. Shou-chieh's father, Chao Wei-chi (AAB; 966–1010), had been a special favorite of T'ai-tsu's, and both Yun-jang and Yun-pi had been childhood companions of the future Jen-tsung.[29] As we will see in Chapter 4, clansmen from just a few elite lines within the clan dominated clan institutions for the rest of the dynasty.

Much closer to home—literally and figuratively—were the clan residences, which had their own regulations and bureaucracies. As noted in Chapter 2, the first move to house the clansmen—separate from the palaces of princes—occurred in 998, when the Northern and Southern Residences were built.[30] In 1011 the descendents of Chao Wei-cheng (AAA; n.d.) were moved to a Western Residence (Hsi-chai) under the supervision of a eunuch official.[31]

As the imperial clan grew rapidly during the early eleventh century, additional residences may well have been built in different parts of the capital, for in 1035, on the grounds that the scattering of princely establishments throughout the capital had made it difficult to enforce rules that barred clansmen from venturing abroad except for court attendance and other ceremonial occasions, the building of a new complex called the Mu-ch'in-chai (Residence of Profound Affection) was undertaken on the grounds of an old palace as housing for the collected offspring of T'ai-tsu and T'ai-tsung.[32] A year later the complex was completed and inaugurated, amid much fanfare, by an imperial visit.[33]

In 1047 the needs of the Wei-wang (Chao T'ing-mei) branch of the clan were addressed. The Northern Residence was renamed the Kuang-ch'in-chai (Residence of Wide Affection), and because they had outgrown it, the renovated and expanded estate of the late grand councilor Wang Ch'in-jo (962–1025) was incorporated into the complex.[34] Then in 1064 an annex for all clan branches called the Mu-ch'in Kuang-ch'in North Residence was built because both of the residences had become overcrowded. Prior to this, the emperor had allowed several high-ranking clansmen and their families from both the Mu-ch'in and the Kuang-ch'in complexes to move into the Shang-ch'ing Palace, but after complaints from a minister that the Palace was too small for this purpose, the beautiful Fang-lin Park in the northwest corner of the city was chosen for the intriguing reasons that "there were already many clansmen living there, and because the grounds were ample, it could be used without upsetting the people." The families that had moved into the palace were moved to the park.[35]

In later years additional residences were established for the offspring of individual emperors,[36] but until the beginning of the twelfth century, the Mu-ch'in and Kuang-ch'in Residences and the North Palace annex functioned as the primary residential complexes and housed the great majority of the imperial clan. Despite the government's attempts to confine the imperial clan to a few discrete locations, the fact that some clan families had already been living in the Fang-lin Park suggests that there were limitations on its ability to do so. Positive benefits were ascribed to the consolidation of clan housing described above. Wang Kuei (1019–85) noted that prior to the building of the Mu-ch'in Residence, with the princely palaces scattered throughout the capital, clan members seldom saw each other except at New Year's time, but that the Mu-ch'in Residence had brought people together.[37]

We know relatively little about the administration of the clan residences. The establishments of imperial princes (*ch'in-wang-fu*) were elaborately organized, as the following list of officials attached to them from the *Sung History* demonstrates: mentor (*fu*), administrator (*chang-shih*), assistant administrator (*ssu-ma*), administrative advisor (*tzu-i ts'an-chün*), companion (*yu*—literally "friend"),[38] secretarial aide (*chi-shih ts'an-chün*), princely establishment preceptors (*wang-fu chiao-shou*), and elementary preceptors (*hsiao-hsüeh chiao-shou*). Although the *Sung History* acknowledges that in practice many of these went unfilled, it notes various specific examples of officials attached to establishments, among them the appointment of mentors (*yü-shan*) and advisors (*tzu-i*) by T'ai-tsung in 983.[39] What little is known of the administration of the Mu-ch'in and Kuang-ch'in residences relates to education (see below). However, although the residences obviously did not have the panoply of officials assigned to the establishments of the imperial princes, they must have had large numbers of people attached to them as supervisors, bursars, recordkeepers, guards, maids, and other servants, for, as we shall see, the government provided for both the sustenance and the control of imperial clansmen and clanswomen.

Clansmen and Officeholding

One characteristic feature of the biographies of Northern Sung imperial clansmen is that in most instances the sequence of offices held—all military and most very august in title—forms the greater body of the text. Since these typically began in early childhood, when a boy received both a name and an office from the emperor (*tz'u-ming shou-kuan*), these posts did not involve actual military functions. In fact, as noted in the last chapter, by the end of T'ai-tsung's reign the decision had been made to deny the clansmen substantive political positions even while giving them high titular offices with lavish salaries and often noble titles.

Prior to 1017, the receipt of initial office by clansmen was somewhat ad hoc; most princes began as guard generals (*wei chiang-chün*); others received office according to the *yin* (protection) privileges of their fathers. That year, however, Chen-tsung accepted a proposal by the minister of the Imperial Clan Court, Chao An-jen (958–1018), to regularize appointments. Accordingly, it was ordered that the grandsons of T'ai-tsu, T'ai-tsung, and Hsuan-tsu (T'ai-tsu's father)[40] begin as guard generals, their great-grandsons as right palace attendants (*yu-shih-chin*), and their great-great-grandsons as right palace duty officers (*yu-pan-tien-chih*), although those who qualified were allowed to use their father's *yin* privilege to attain a higher office.[41] Even with this act, there was no standardization in the offices held by clansmen. Not only did the use of *yin* result in varied initial offices, but also generous promotions granted on the occasions of the Great Sacrifices (*ta-li*) in the southern suburbs had inflated the numbers, as well as the financial burden, of those in the higher offices. Then, in 1035, a standard initial office of vice-commandant of the Guard Command (*shuai-fu fu-shuai*) was established, as was the sequence of offices for promotion, all of them nominally connected to the imperial guard. The system of evaluations necessary for promotion was also regularized in an attempt to slow the rate of promotions.[42] Those who already held other offices—a group of 180—were given corresponding posts in this system of guard officials (*huan-wei kuan*).[43]

The imperial clansmen holding these guard offices were collectively called the "Southern Rank officials" (*nan-pan kuan*), in reference to their placement in the southern section of the courtyard during court ceremonies. This was not an empty appellation, for it described the primary public function of the rank-and-file clansmen—that of courtiers, attending court ceremonies en masse, to be seen and not heard—and undoubtedly helped to shape their sense of corporate identity, especially since they could be fined for non-attendance.[44]

In contrast to the southern rank officials, senior clansmen such as imperial uncles and the leaders of the Great Office could participate more substantively in audiences.[45] For example, Jen-tsung's uncle Chao Yuan-yen (BG; 987–1044)—the only clansman for whom we have a portrait (see Fig. 1)— regularly attended court and offered opinions on various matters of state until growing senility led him to cut back on appearances at court.[46]

Apart from providing clansmen with an official ceremonial role and prescribing their rank-order within that, the guard offices system was also used

Fig. 1 Portrait of Chao Yuan-yen (BG; 987–1044); woodblock print. A portrait of T'ai-tsung's eighth son from a later lineage genealogy, *Chao-shih chia-sheng* (1919). Yuan-yen, a friend of both Chen-tsung and Jen-tsung, was demoted after a fire in his palace quarters, but was an active participant at court audiences until senility restricted his activities.

to determine stipends, allowances (for food, clothing, and official expenses), and gifts for births, weddings, and the Great Sacrifices. A lowly vice-commander of the crown prince's right inner guard command (*t'ai-tzu yu-nei shuai-fu fu-shuai*)—the initial office in the guard system—received a monthly stipend of 20 strings of cash, winter and spring clothing allowances of 2 rolls (*p'i*) of fine silk (*ling*) and 5 rolls of raw silk (*hsiao*), and in the winter 40 ounces (*liang*) of cotton (*mien*) and a roll of light silk (*lo*). This was comparable to the salaries received by mid-level officials, but of course *all* the clansmen received these benefits as boys and had every expectation of advancing through the ranks. Those who advanced to military commissioner (*chieh-tu shih*), the highest rank open to clansmen, received 400 strings of cash per month, biannual gifts of 100 rolls of raw silk, 20 rolls of large fine silk (*ta-ling*), 30 rolls of small fine silk (*hsiao-ling*), and 10 rolls of light silk in the spring and 500 ounces of cotton in the winter.[47] Moreover, those clansmen who either received or inherited noble titles were the recipients of an additional array of benefits.

The court's support for the imperial clan, it is fair to conclude, was lavish, and in fact under Jen-tsung, at least, attempts to curb it met with little success. Although one of the stated goals of imposing guard offices on all clansmen in 1035 was to slow the rate of promotions—and therefore the income flowing to the clan—in the opinion of Wang Huai, the "reform" resulted in great increases in the numbers of clan officials.[48]

Fifteen years later—in 1050—Jen-tsung presided over an extravagant ritual celebration in which imperial largesse in the form of promotions was again in evidence. This was the ceremony for the Hall of Enlightenment (Ming-t'ang, literally "bright hall"), a hall serving "as a symbol of dynastic legitimacy and sovereignty,"[49] which claimed antecedents all the way back to the Yellow Emperor and which had played a significant role at the Han and T'ang courts.[50] The Sung did not build a new hall—the Ta-ch'ing Hall was used—but a new ceremonial guide (*Ming-t'ang li*) was compiled and used as a basis for the lavish sacrifice to honor T'ai-tsu, T'ai-tsung, and Chen-tsung. Over twelve thousand men—court ministers, academicians, and imperial clan members—participated in the imperial procession to the Hall and the ceremonies at the Hall. The role of the clansmen was significant, for in the debates that preceded the ceremony, several ministers argued that the focus should be on the emperor's filial duty to Heaven and his father, in contrast to ceremonies to the founding emperors, which took place at the Temple of Imperial Ancestors. It was Jen-tsung himself who insisted that the imperial ancestors be included, which accordingly entailed a role for the imperial clansmen.[51] According to Li T'ao, 87 clansmen received promotions as a result of their participation in the event,[52] although various clansmen's epitaphs make the rewards sound even more widespread. Chao Ch'eng-ts'ao's (CDD; 1022–58) says that "all the clansmen participated in the [Hall of Enlightened Rule] ceremonies and were promoted,"[53] and that of Chao K'o-chuang (CDCI; 1043–59), who was a young boy at the time, comments: "When the emperor sacrificed in the Hall of Enlightened Rule, all the imperial clansmen who assisted, regardless of age order or extreme youth, even including those not yet able to dress themselves, were ennobled and promoted."[54]

Imperial clansmen were also prominent in Buddhist-led ritual activities celebrating the emperor personally. These included imperial death-day observances at monasteries in the capital in which, on at least one occasion, the wailing of clansmen contributed to a general din that some observers found objectionable.[55] Clansmen also participated in the ceremonies honoring the portraits of imperial ancestors, such as celebrations inaugurating the renovation of the Temple of Spectacular Numina (Ching-ling kung), which housed the portraits.[56] Although the Buddhist (and Taoist) role in these affairs was objectionable to some Confucian ministers, this was mitigated by their public nature and, in the case of the latter, the emperor's personal participation. Such was not the case with the maintenance by some clansmen of private Buddhist temples that housed portraits of imperial ancestors, and indeed objections to this practice resulted in the confiscation of privately held portraits in 1071.[57]

Education and Civil Culture

As this last example indicates, the primary public function of the imperial clansmen was participation in ceremonies, whether sessions of court, ancestral sacrifices, or other religious rituals. In light of the Confucian state's preoccupation with ritual (*li*) as essential to the maintenance of the imperium and cosmos, this function was far from negligible. But the fact remains that they *did* very little, and that could lead to feelings of anxiety and depression, as was the case with Chao Ts'ung-chih (ABCC; 1007–50):

On occasions before it was light and he was waiting for dawn, he would go to the family's ancestral hall and prostrate himself. He would become troubled by the thought that, according to the organization of the dynasty, [clansmen] were not involved in official business and lacked responsibility for anything even minutely important in reality. And yet, in serving the lord their kinsman, they dared not be idle even for a day.[58]

This is hardly surprising, nor would it have surprised the Sung emperors who enforced the policy of keeping the clansmen politically impotent. But it raises the question of how the emperors addressed this issue of uselessness, of what they did to give the clansmen a sense of meaning and purpose. The answer, I believe, lies in their constant espousal of civil culture: education, learning and scholarship, and even examinations.

The espousal of education for imperial kin can be found early in the dynasty. In 983, just after T'ai-tsung had appointed advisors and moral mentors for the princes—they had to be court officials aged fifty and above who were men of classical learning and civil attainments—he gathered the ten who had been chosen and said to them: "Since all my sons have been born and reared deep in the palace and do not yet know worldly matters, I must provide excellent scholars as praiseworthy guides who will make [the princes] daily hear the way of loyalty and filial piety. You are the ones I have carefully chosen; each of you should encourage them."[59] In 995 he further appointed preceptors—termed *chiao-shou* to distinguish them from those teaching the princes—for the imperial nephews and cousins, and when in 998 the Northern and Southern residences were established, Chen-tsung ordered that three preceptors be assigned to teach in each residence.[60] We are told that from the year 1010 an order for all clan boys aged ten *sui* and older to attend school and study under a preceptor had been carried out, and in fact a few days later teachers in the Northern and Southern residences sent forward the names of five clan youths, proposing that they go to the Hall of Writing (*shu-yuan*) for lectures and readings of the Classics and history, and Chen-tsung commented, "I have often thought that among T'ai-tsung's instructions, [his injunction] to study and read books was the best."[61]

This system of education within the clan residences received little attention for the next half-century, but occasional references to it indicate that it
continued to function, albeit in a somewhat anemic fashion.[62] In Ying-
tsung's reform of clan education in 1064—which is discussed in the next
chapter—it was noted that the clan residences had only six preceptors, the
same figure mandated in 1010.[63] That said, both Chao Yun-liang (BGB;
1013–67) and Chao Yun-jang, two of the initial leaders of the Great Office
of Clan Affairs, are credited with promoting clan schools. The former asked
that Confucian scholars be selected to provide moral training and breadth
to clan youth,[64] and the latter's epitaph states that "clan boys who liked
learning were encouraged to advance; those who did not excel in studies
were warned of punishments if they did not change."[65]

There are also references in the epitaphs of clan youths to serious study
with renowned teachers, such as Lü Tsao (1024 *chin-shih*),[66] Wang Lieh,[67]
Yang Chung-ho,[68] and most notably, Sun Fu (992–1057). Despite his failure
in the examinations, Sun became the most eminent authority on the *Spring
and Autumn Annals* (*Ch'un-ch'iu*) of his day, a famous teacher, and an imperial
lecturer, and is identified as the teacher of two clansmen. One of them,
Chao Shih-ch'ung (AADDA; 1021–52), asked such a penetrating question
on Chou history that Sun reportedly marveled.[69] With only six preceptors
employed at the clan residences in 1064, it is not surprising that families
engaged tutors for their children, as Shih-ch'ung's family did in providing
for the education of his orphaned son, Chao Ling-pin (AADDAA; 1049–
82).[70] And in a case that I am sure was not unique, Chao Shih-heng (AA-
DAF; 1029–59) was educated by his mother and became known for his
understanding of Mencius, the *Odes*, and the *Classic of Changes*.[71]

In many ways Jen-tsung's encouragement of civil culture within the imperial clan was accomplished not through formal institutions, but rather
through highly visible cultural patronage and competition; in this it was not
unlike his encouragement of education and civil culture in the society at
large, which, at least in contrast to Shen-tsung and Hui-tsung's policies,
tended to be symbolic and informal. The epitaph for Chao Tsung-wang
(BDAA; 1020–63) contains a passage revealing of Jen-tsung's aims:

Once when Jen-tsung encouraged young clansmen to study the writings of Yü Yung-
hsing, Tsung-wang examined their calligraphy (*tzu-fa*) and submitted a thousand-word
memorial on them. The emperor liked the skill and agreeableness of his brush, and gave

him a special promotion to prefect (*tz'u-shih*). Later when the Court of the Imperial Clan held an examination on the writings of clan youths at the Yen-ho Hall, he placed first. When the emperor asked him what he wanted, he replied: a complete collection of the books [printed] by the Directorate of Education, so that he could encourage the studies of clan youths.[72]

A delighted emperor was happy to grant his request—and to ply him with various other gifts—for what could be more appropriate than rewarding literary accomplishments with literary works? As noted above, Jen-tsung liked to hold feasts for the assembled clansmen, glittering occasions at which poetry composition was often a featured activity. Another approach used by Jen-tsung was to reward clansmen for major scholarly accomplishments, such as the writing of books.

This last can be traced to an important edict of 1044, in which Jen-tsung ordered the preceptors in the clan residence schools to report cases of outstanding accomplishment in the Classics or literature. It begins with a broad claim for the symbolic importance of the imperial clan in the wider polity: "I think that among the rulers of antiquity, there were none who were not generous to their kin so as to support the royal house. Beginning from the family and city, they could then civilize the world." After citing some outstanding princely households from the Han, Jen-tsung turned to the Sung imperial clan with its flourishing numbers and history of generous imperial treatment. "We have also sent Confucian scholars to go [to the clan residences] and teach the lessons of the Classics. But while loyalty, filial piety, and diligence have become the custom of all the [clans]men, completed works of poetry and writing have been rare." He therefore directed that education in the "six arts" (*liu-i*) be encouraged, that abandoning one's studies be considered shameful, and that self-control be esteemed.[73] This edict was issued in the first month of 1044, when Fan Chung-yen and his reformist supporters were in power, and indeed it bears many of the hallmarks of the reformist educational program.[74] And like the Ch'ing-li Reforms, it took some time before effects of the proposed changes were evident. In 1046 a clansman was rewarded for producing an edition of Chen-tsung's poetry. Through the 1050s, a total of eight rewards were given for the production of books of one kind or another.[75] However, none of these seems to have brought its author renown in the wider literati world of letters.

As part of this policy of rewarding literary accomplishment, Jen-tsung frequently employed examinations. In some cases, recommended individuals were tested and rewarded with gifts;[76] in others, open examinations for clansmen led to generous rewards for those who placed at the top.[77] Although the rewards involved were almost always goods rather than promotions, these examinations had obvious parallels with the civil-service examinations, and in fact in the case of Chao Shu-shao (CABAA; fl. 1046–55), the parallels crossed. In 1046 Shu-shao placed first in an examination for clansmen personally administered by Jen-tsung. When in 1049, Shu-shao submitted his writings, the emperor ordered him examined by the Institute of Academicians, and he was then given a formal *chin-shih* degree, and with it an extraordinary promotion. At an imperial audience, Jen-tsung had him sit and take tea, and said to him: "There are quite a few clansmen who love learning, but only you have received a *chin-shih* by virtue of your writings. This has not happened before. I wish for the world to know the wise men from the clan. Do not forget your studies!"[78] This action, and an edict four years later directing any clansman who had mastered a Classic to be tested in it,[79] represented a logical step in the development of the clan's civil culture and made them increasingly resemble the civil elite.

In many ways, that process was extremely successful. Although there undoubtedly were many clansmen who engaged purely in hedonistic pleasures—and we must be mindful that we have biographies for only a small fraction of the clansmen—accounts of a wide variety of scholarly and intellectual pursuits fill the biographies and epitaphs. We find bibliophiles who accumulated huge libraries, and students of the Classics (the *Odes*, the *Changes*, the *Spring and Autumn Annals*, and Mencius), poetry, painting, calligraphy, music, archery, history, Buddhism, Taoism, medicine, astronomy, topography, and games, although not of Sun Tzu and, with the exception of archery, not of the military arts. It is difficult to distinguish scholars from dilettantes in biographies, but there are frequent references to collections of writings on individuals' specialties.

On occasion, however, a desire to do more than simply attend court and engage in scholarship and other leisured activities led some to challenge the imperial restrictions on their roles, although always with great diffidence. We saw in the Introduction how Chao Ts'ung-shih, Chao Shih-yung, Chao Shih-jung, and four others proposed—to no avail—in 1038 that they lead an expedition to put down Chao Yuan-hao's rebellion. During the Ch'ing-li period (1041–48), Shih-yung (AABAA; 1010–68) again tried to contribute to policy discussions with a ten-point plan for reforming the country, and again was rewarded but received no response to his proposal. As for Ts'ung-shih (ABBB; 1007–71), by the end of his life he was renowned for fifty years of unbroken court attendance under four emperors. But a comment that he made to a fellow clansman is revealing: "One has no responsibility and only goes to court for the rituals of serving the emperor. Yet still can one be idle?"[80]

What is remarkable about the clansmen under Jen-tsung is not that a few sought more active roles, but rather that the cocoon of inactivity crafted by imperial policy functioned so successfully, for it was in constant conflict with the Confucian ethical imperative to act, an idea that the clan youths confronted constantly in their studies. Late in Jen-tsung's reign, Liu Ch'ang offered this perceptive description of the clan in his epitaph for Chao Shu-she (CCFBA; 1056–59), who died as a young boy:

There are no people in the world who are noble at birth. Thus although there are sons of princes, they must first manage their own dress before being ennobled. They still have the responsibility for their duties, and sometimes their timing [i.e., premature death] makes it impossible for them to benefit fully from imperial grace. The dynasty has changed this system. Although public clansmen (*kung-tsu*, the imperial clan) may be distant [from the emperor], all become wealthy and honored through their offices and emoluments, and although to the end they have no responsibilities for duties, the treatment of them is still definitely complete. When they grow up and marry, it is even more so. Thus although Shu-she had not yet learned to talk, he was still an official.[81] But he still met an early death. What a fate![82]

Just how complete the government's treatment of the imperial clan was is the subject of the following section, which surveys the lives of clansmen and women from birth through death.

Life in the Imperial Clan

Although the births of children in imperial clan families—as in all Chinese families—were undoubtedly occasions for celebration, as far as the government was concerned their individual identities were set only some years later after the boys had received names and the girls were titled (*feng*). Many did not reach that point. In an earlier study of a thirty-*chüan* fragment of the thirteenth-century official imperial clan genealogy *Hsien-yuan lei-p'u* (Classified genealogy of immortal origins), which contains records of some 629 clansmen and 465 clanswomen, I found that 72 percent of the clansmen had not been named (*pu chi ming*) and 69 percent of the clanswomen had not been titled (*pu chi feng*).[83] These figures are sobering evidence of the high infant and early-childhood mortality rates in premodern societies within even the most affluent of groups, but they may also help explain the long delay on the part of the government, which ensured that only the survivors received names and titles.

Sung sources are silent on the titling of girls, but have a good deal to say about naming, especially since boys in the imperial clan simultaneously received names and appointment to titular office (*tz'u-ming shou-kuan*). The reason for the government's control of naming was genealogical; every effort was made to give each clansman a unique written name, and since one of the two characters in the name was always the same for all male members of the same generation, the result was often the use of exceedingly rare characters for the other element in the name.

In 1039, a memorial from the Great Office proposed that the past practice, which had been to provide names and offices to boys at the age of seven *sui*, be liberalized so that oldest sons could receive them at the first triennial Great Sacrifice after they were born, and younger sons could request them at the age of five *sui*.[84] These provisions were accepted, and reaffirmed in 1053,[85] but in 1061 they were drastically revised, and fifteen *sui* was set as the minimum age.[86] Although no reason was given, the likely cause was the great expense of conferring office upon large and increasing numbers of clansmen. As we will see in the next chapter, for just this reason, the conferral of names and offices became a critical issue during the reign of Shen-tsung, particularly since most of the clansmen no longer had a mourning relationship to the emperor.

Neither the institutional sources nor the biographies of these eleventh-century clansmen say much about their childhoods and early educations, except for the fairly stock language about literary precociousness common in literati biographies. Some of the biographies of clan wives make the point that they kept well-regulated women's quarters,[87] but they are silent concerning the raising of daughters. Much of the family's attention during childrearing went to the schooling of their sons—discussed above—which occurred both at home and in palace schools and which was probably much like that in literati families.

Clan marriage practices, however, differed dramatically from those in the wider society. The earliest record of imperial clan marriage regulations dates from 1029, when the proliferation of clansmen was already rendering the less formal matchmaking described in Chapter 2 obsolete. Each clan palace was ordered to submit a list of clansmen aged eighteen *sui* and clanswomen aged fifteen to be considered for marriages. While specifying administrative procedures including the appointment of eunuch investigators and the emperor's personal approval, the edict dictated that marriage partners "whose talent and age are suitable" should be sought from among "elite families of examination graduates" (*i-kuan shih-tsu*) untainted by members in the artisan or merchant classes, with no "miscellaneous elements," and no history of treasonous activities.[88]

These regulations, which remained in effect throughout the rest of Jen-tsung's reign, are remarkable on two counts. First, clan marriages were clearly considered state—or dynastic—business, and their importance is indicated by the stipulation that the emperor personally approve them. In contrast to non-clan families (elite and non-elite), for whom matchmaking was often a preoccupation, individual clan families had no formal say in the marriages of their children. Second, there was a great concern that marriage partners come from proper families. The proscribed categories of artisan, merchant, and "miscellaneous elements" were the same as those for examination candidates, but the requirement that they come from elite families—which meant families with a history of government service—was not.[89] The dynasty wanted to ensure that its marriage ties were with families from the ruling elite.

One attribute of clan marriages through at least the reign of Jen-tsung, which was not stipulated by any regulation, is that the matches, for both the emperors and members of the imperial clan, were made overwhelmingly with families of military officials.[90] By military officials I mean those whose titular offices came from the military rather than the civil service, a group that included active officers and many others with no particularly martial functions, as Winston Lo has shown.[91] Historians are agreed that although theoretically equal in rank to the companion civil service, the military service was widely viewed as inferior, was used to staff not only the military and military-support bureaucracy but also many bureaus and specialized offices, and relied much more heavily on the hereditary *yin* privilege and irregular methods of recruitment.[92] Since by the eleventh century the civil elite had become culturally and politically dominant, the imperial clan's marriages served to accentuate their distance from the former group. Liu Ch'ang's epitaph for Lady Li (1035–52), the wife of Chao K'o-ch'un (CEJA), contains a revealing comment. After describing her concern for others, her skill at women's work, her ability to write, and her knowledge of literature, he says, "Customs as good as these are not practiced in the families of hereditary officials or the military."[93] Since such families comprised the bulk of those supplying clan wives, one might read between the lines a not very high opinion of most of them.

Although the 1029 provisions for the marriages of clansmen and clanswomen were virtually the same, the differences between the two kinds of marriage were profound. Clanswomen were marrying out of the imperial clan, and the dynasty's immediate concerns were that their matches be honorable and the manner of their leaving appropriate to their high status, although the use of these marriages to cement political relationships was obviously a factor as well. Clanswomen, who before their marriages received allowances from the state, were provided generous dowries and their husbands received titular office in the military service if they were not already officials or promotions if they already were.[94] Their fate was frequently a difficult one, for they and their new families had constantly to struggle with the conflict between their subordinate status as women—deeply embedded in Confucian ideology and Sung social practice—and their superior status as natal members of the emperor's clan.[95]

For clanswomen, the only alternative to marriage was to become a Buddhist or Taoist nun, and I have found over a half-dozen cases in which they so chose—or had that fate chosen for them. The question of volition is generally unanswerable, for in most cases a daughter is simply identified as being a nun,[96] but a few cases provide more information. After Chao K'o-wen (CEDA; 1018–53) died at the early age of 36 *sui*, the emperor, as a mark of honor and sorrow, had one of K'o-wen's four daughters made a Taoist nun and the other three raised in the imperial palace.[97] All three daughters of Chao Ch'eng-hsun (CBA; n.d.) and Lady Chang (994–1059) were Taoist nuns at the T'ai-ho Palace;[98] and three out of the six daughters of Chao K'o-kou studied Taoism and lived as nuns at the Yen-ning Palace, where they had received their religious names from the emperor.[99] In these last two cases, however, it appears that their nunneries were part of the imperial palace complex, and taking orders hardly meant going into the outside world.

In contrast to clanswomen, clan wives came from the outside into the luxurious confines of the imperial clan. For the most part, their epitaphs praise them for the same virtues esteemed among literati women: filial service to their in-laws, successful childrearing, and good household management. We find praise for women who persevered through difficult circumstances, such as having to raise their children alone after the premature death of the husband,[100] and sorrow in one case for a woman, admired by all, who died at 22 *sui* without children.[101] And in the case of Lady Chang, mentioned above, the writer Liu Ch'ang demonstrates a remarkable perceptiveness of the double confinement faced by clan wives:

> However great their abilities, since none of the imperial clansmen has official duties outside the palaces, their words and actions are never renowned. But since the imperial clan wives have no activities outside the family, their lack of renown is even greater. However, when one considers her [Lady Chang's] service in the sacrifices and, within the imperial clan, her instruction of sons and grandsons, and her longevity and peacefulness, one can appreciate her virtue.[102]

Despite the hagiographic tendency of biographies—especially epitaphs—the discord that undoubtedly was a common feature of clan life occasionally appears, especially on those rare occasions when more than one source is available. A prime example is that of Chao Yun-ti (BGC; 1014–48), whose epitaph records that after his father's death in 1044, "in his observance of mourning there were things that did not accord with propriety," and he was demoted (though his offices were later restored after he had made amends). It also says of his second wife (his first having died), Lady Ch'ien of the Southern T'ang royal family: "Her ambitions still very strong, she was not happy with [Yun-ti's] family. She earnestly sought to enter a Taoist nunnery, and she was given a nun's hat and the name Great Teacher of Harmony and Correctness."[103] It is only from other sources that we learn that these two incidents were connected. Yun-ti had violated mourning by daily playing games with maids in the palace, and his wife reported him. Following his demotion—he was also barred from participation at court—she became a nun.[104]

The reference to maids (*nu-nü*) is suggestive, for most of the cases of scandal or discord seem to have involved other women in the clan residences—maids and especially concubines. That such women were a major element of clan life should come as no surprise, for the clan's immense financial resources allowed it to employ legions of servants, and the huge clan families could not have been produced by the wives alone.

Although few clansmen could match the fertility of Chao Ts'ung-hsin (AADF; 1010–60), who had 37 sons (24 of them named) and 19 daughters (13 of them titled), or Chao Tsung-yueh (BABA; 1003–post-1075), with 23 sons and 25 daughters,[105] the average size of the clan families was very large indeed. The 27 fathers from the fourth generation whose children are listed in the extant *Hsien-yuan lei-p'u* chapters—all of them from the T'ai-tsu and T'ai-tsung branches—had 257 sons and 157 daughters, which comes to 15 children per father (9.5 sons and 5.5 daughters).[106] This is a higher figure than one would get from Li Hsin-ch'uan's statistics in Table 2.2, in which 517 T'ai-tsu and T'ai-tsung branch clansmen of the fourth generation had 2,063 sons, or about 4 sons each. The differences are explained by two factors: many of these 517 clansmen did not actually become fathers of sons, and the 2,063 sons do not include boys who died before receiving names. One finding for which I have no simple explanation is the fact that the *Hsien-yuan lei-p'u* fathers had almost two sons for each daughter. Whether because of infanticide or childrearing practices that caused marked gender differences in mortality, girls were produced in far fewer numbers.[107]

Although T'ai-tsung's furious reaction to the presumptuous behavior of Chao Yuan-hsi's concubine—described in Chapter 2—probably endured as a warning to clan concubines, there is some evidence of lasting bonds between concubines and their sons, and of attempts by the latter to achieve some recognition for their birth mothers. Most notably, Chao Tsung-min (BCAB; n.d.) asked during a Great Sacrifice that his birth mother be ennobled, which was accepted and used as a precedent.[108] Nevertheless, the court continued to insist upon strict differentiation between wives and concubines, as Chao Tsung-ching (BEAD; 1032–77) discovered. After his wife had died and his mourning for her was complete, he sent his concubine out of the house, only to bring her back in marriage after a go-between had identified her as a "woman of a good family" (*liang-chia nü*). But when the emperor learned of it, he ordered Tsung-ching demoted a rank and the woman returned to her home.[109]

Although concubines appear only occasionally in historical records, references to maids are rarities. They are usually mentioned as the victims of violence, such as the maid killed by Chao Yuan-hsi's concubine.[110] The most dramatic example of this is that of Chao Tsung-yueh—noted above for having fathered almost fifty children—who during the Huang-yu period (1049–53) lost his name (*ch'u ming*) because of lewdness, or "not keeping the door curtains [separating the men's and women's quarters] repaired" (*wei-po pu hsiu*). Then, he was found guilty of killing a maid and was put under house arrest in the outer rooms of a vacant residence. After years of imprisonment, Tsung-yueh's son, Chung-min (BABAH; n.d.), made a tearful appeal in court to be allowed to take the place of his frail and elderly father. Shen-tsung—the emperor at this time—was moved but did not act on the request immediately. Chung-min left court unable to speak and then died on his return home. Tsung-yueh, it is reported, died alone.[111] In another case without sexual overtones, Chao Ts'ung-tang (AAAA; n.d.) was demoted and confined to a solitary separate residence for killing a bodyguard official. Although as a young man he had liked learning, in maturity he reportedly became mean and wasted, and in the end he slit his throat.[112]

The point to be made in recounting these anecdotes is not to suggest that such behavior characterized the imperial clan, but rather to indicate the kinds of problems that arose, at least on occasion, and which were striking enough to overcome the reticence of the biographers to speak ill of their subjects. And to those mentioned above, we might add references to family fights and alcoholism.[113] That said, it should be stressed that these examples are far outnumbered by positive accounts, such as the scholarly pursuits discussed above and tales of great filiality in the service of parents.

Filiality, of course, is so central to Chinese culture that praise for filial behavior is ubiquitous in biographies. What distinguishes the clan biographies from this period are the extremes to which the clansmen frequently went in serving sick parents. We find cases of clansmen pricking themselves and using the blood in prayers to the gods[114] and of others writing out passages of Buddhist *sutras* in their own blood.[115] Most controversial was the practice of cutting off pieces of one's flesh and feeding them to sick parents—or in one case, a brother—to heal them.[116] The case of brothers, which occurred in 1027, sparked a debate at court. Jen-tsung was so impressed by the action of Chao Ts'ung-chih (AADE; 1010–52) that he wanted to give him a large reward, but the grand councilor Wang Tseng (978–1038) and others objected, invoking the Confucian idea that harming one's body is an unfilial act and arguing that such self-mutilation was a vulgar practice not sanctioned by the sages of the past. Jen-tsung went ahead with the reward, but reduced it from what he had planned.[117] However, after Chao Shih-yung (AABAA; 1010–68) had written out a Buddhist *sutra* in his blood and his father then improved, Jen-tsung worried that this would lead his fellow clansmen to similarly demonstrate their utmost sincerity via mutilation.[118] Of course filial self-mutilation was hardly a preserve of the imperial clan (it was enshrined in the *Twenty-four Tales of Filial Piety*), but the hothouse conditions of clan life in K'ai-feng seem to have been particularly suited to its manifestation.

In dealing with death and the treatment of the dead, the imperial clan again followed strikingly different practices from those of the population at large. Imperial clan members were buried not in family plots but rather in vast mortuary complexes near the old capital of Lo-yang. A large plot of land was set aside for the descendents of T'ai-tsu and T'ai-tsung directly to the west of their tumuli at Yung-an ("eternal peace") county in Ho-nan fu, which had been carved out of Kung county by Chen-tsung during a visit to the imperial tombs in 1007.[119] The descendents of Wei-wang were buried at a secondary complex in Liang county, Ju-chou. Moreover, rather than individual burials for clan members, their coffins were kept temporarily in K'ai-feng (typically in Buddhist temples) and taken in batches on the fifty- to seventy-five-mile trip to the burial sites. This typically seems to have occurred every year or two, but the gap was occasionally much longer; the great interment of 1060 included coffins that had been stored for as long as nine years.[120]

Thus the three primary concerns of the premodern Chinese family— ownership of real estate (a house and lands), matchmaking and marriage, and funerals and tomb maintenance—were beyond the control of individual clan families. This made it even more difficult for clan families to create family traditions that would reinforce Confucian norms of behavior. People tried, most notably Chao Ch'eng-ch'ing (CAA; d. 1039), who wrote a three-chapter book called *Family Instructions* (*Chia hsun*), which reportedly forty years after his death continued to be taken to heart by his sons and grandsons.[121] But such attempts to create family traditions had to contend with the institutional weakness of the imperial clan family and the stultifying effects of the prohibitions on the movements of clan members.

Although the sources do not indicate when these prohibitions began, they were clearly in place by the middle of Jen-tsung's reign. As noted earlier, the reason given for the establishment of the Mu-ch'in Residence in 1035 was to enforce the prohibitions on clansmen coming and going except to attend court or other ceremonies.[122] Liu Ch'ang, writing around 1060, described the imperial clan as follows: "The emperor considered the imperial clan all to be relatives—near and far—within the degrees of mourning, and he gave them titular offices. Although they lacked responsibilities, they were given honored positions and outstanding ranks as a way of [demonstrating imperial] favor. But they were not supposed to mix with ordinary families."[123] Slightly later, in 1069, two clansmen who had been living outside the clan residences were ordered back, on the grounds that clansmen were not supposed to go out on their own authority and have private intercourse with commoner households.[124]

As this last example suggests, the prohibitions were not always followed or enforced. Indeed, certain activities seem to have been accepted, such as studying with teachers from the outside and socializing with affinal kin.[125] Still, this policy of seclusion goes a long way toward explaining the virtual invisibility of clansmen in the political, social, intellectual, and cultural worlds of K'ai-feng. As almost any book on the Northern Sung attests, imperial clansmen had little if any impact on their elite contemporaries.

Of course as this book bears witness, the imperial clan and its members were written about at length, and in the case of the epitaphs—at least those that are extant—the authors were elite men of letters. Yet these are precisely the documents that highlight most dramatically the social and cultural differences between the authors and their subjects. Unlike most Sung epitaphs, including those for Southern Sung imperial clansmen, which were typically solicited from well-known writers by the children of the deceased and in which the authors frequently describe their personal ties to the deceased, the eleventh-century clan epitaphs tend to be formulaic and rarely exhibit a personal knowledge of their subjects. In fact, most seem to have been written as a part of the authors' official duties. Chang Fang-p'ing (1007–91) wrote in 1048 that an edict had delegated responsibility for epitaphs to history officials.[126] When one examines the output of the most prolific producers of clan epitaphs, it is clear that most of their subjects died close to each other in time and were buried at the same time. Thus Chang Fang-p'ing's epitaphs were mainly for burials in 1048, Liu Ch'ang's (1019–68) and Ou-yang Hsiu's (1007–72) for 1060, Wang Kuei's for 1060 and 1064 (when Jen-tsung was buried), and Mu-jung Yen-feng's (1067–1117) for 1107.

Even in the less formulaic epitaphs that provide a more personal portrait of the subject—at times in considerable detail—there remains a sense of otherness, of the clan as apart from the rest of society. Liu Ch'ang, in his epitaph for Chao Shu-chan (CEAAB; 1034–58), a very ordinary clansman, laments that he died young and without an heir, but notes that the funeral ceremonies were complete with imperially delegated observers and that a literary minister (*tz'u-ch'en*, i.e., Liu) had written a memorial.[127]

More often, this sense exhibits itself in commentary on the human costs of the dynasty's great trade-off for imperial clan members—great wealth in return for seclusion and a lack of power—that has been the focus of much of this chapter as well. A number of examples are quoted above, most notably by Liu Ch'ang: for example, his comments on the added burdens borne by clan wives and his observation that clan members were not to mix with ordinary families. In another epitaph—to Chao K'o-wen—Liu remarked: "The emperor is certainly generous toward the imperial clan. The wealth of the marquis [i.e., K'o-wen] was sufficient to support wealth and honor and bring prosperity to the end of his days. But having long looked at the abundance of our great peace, I can see few famous [clansmen]."[128] For Chang Fang-p'ing, the pity of the situation is that talented clansmen were not allowed to realize their potential: "Now the court has appointed officials and established schools in order to lead the clan youths through virtue and righteousness, yet it is grievous when they do not realize a humble determination to advance by cultivating the character of their talent."[129] Sung Ch'i in one epitaph appeared to take a different position, arguing that the exclusion of imperial clansmen from positions of power had allowed the emperors to demonstrate great friendliness and provide lavish stipends without endangering the dynasty.[130] However, the fact that he was writing an epitaph for a clansman may have constrained him to emphasize the bright side of the equation, for elsewhere he delivered this blistering critique: "All those in the imperial clan generally have drowned in wealth and honor, are recklessly proud and boastful, and do not know propriety and righteousness. Even when reduced to poverty, they idle about seeking food, without work and without activity. They are called the 'branches of Heaven'; in reality they are discarded objects."[131]

Such criticism from an eminent observer like Sung, who among other things served as minister of works and was chief compiler of the *New T'ang History*, suggests that the elite's perception of the imperial clan was considerably more negative than the picture that we have drawn. However, tone aside, there is little difference between Sung and the other writers cited above concerning the causes for the clan's malaise. To cite one final example, Chang Fang-p'ing had this to say in his epitaph of Chao Shih-pao (ABBAB; 1019–41), a studious clansman who died in early adulthood:

Recently, very few of the royal clansmen have taken provincial offices. They have all stayed in the capital and do not even prepare for the Confucian examinations. The teaching officials make careful corrections and lecture. Externally, the clansmen simply serve in court and that is all. This [reflects] the court's principle (*i*) of friendliness to kin, of gathering the cordial and friendly, and is what distinguishes [the imperial clan] from the kin groups of commoners. It is not to be faulted. Yet within [the clan] there is a collection of talent, and I am concerned that there are able and knowledgeable people whose unfulfilled ambitions are not put to use—and so they die. Thus, using the records of one who was unable to attain [his ambition], I have written [this essay].[132]

Remarkably, this was written in the 1040s, two decades before the death of Jen-tsung. For by that point, there was a growing sense of crisis with regard to the imperial clan, and although much of it was spurred by the huge numbers and expenses of the clansmen, it was also driven by the sense of waste articulated so eloquently by Chang Fang-p'ing.

FOUR

The Clan Reoriented

The Succession of Ying-tsung

The late eleventh century proved to be a difficult period for the imperial clan. It confronted a variety of problems with a common cause: its own enormous growth. In the process of dealing with these problems, it became a very different institution from what it had been under Chen-tsung and Jen-tsung.

The succession to Jen-tsung, however, involved a clansman turned emperor, and thereby demonstrated the usefulness of the clan to the dynasty. Unlike many of his highly fecund kinsmen, Jen-tsung produced no male heirs—or at least none who lived to become heirs—and although precautions were taken by bringing two young clansmen into the imperial palace as potential heirs apparent, as his reign progressed, the lack of a designated successor came to be seen as increasingly problematic.

In 1055 Jen-tsung fell ill and became bed-ridden, which occasioned a request from his ministers for the early naming of a crown prince, but nothing was done. Over the next six years and long after he had recovered, however, the proposals continued. The most noteworthy came from the grand councilor Han Ch'i (1008–75), who suggested that a school be established in the palace for promising clan youths who loved learning, so that those who proved worthy and capable of great affairs could be identified. Jen-tsung responded that he was going to take one clansman or perhaps two into the palace to be prepared as a possible successor.[1]

By fall 1061, the matter had assumed added urgency, and Jen-tsung's leading ministers submitted a series of memorials emphasizing the importance of settling the issue of succession. This was, in their view, a matter of the utmost importance, bearing on the very existence of the dynasty. Their favored historical analogy was the Western Han emperor Ch'eng-ti (r. 33–7 B.C.E), whose inability to produce a surviving male heir had led to Wang Mang's usurpation of the throne. As Ssu-ma Kuang noted, Ch'eng-ti had not settled his succession by the time he turned 45, an age that Jen-tsung had already surpassed.[2] The palace censor Lü Hui (1014-71), who also invoked the analogy of Ch'eng-ti, hinted at schemes within the imperial clan: "I have also heard that recently in the imperial clan, false rumors have been hatched and have spread to the four quarters. People are alarmed and suspicious." Lü warned that continued inaction would lead to attempts by families to promote their offspring.[3] Jen-tsung proved amenable to their suggestions, but when he asked for their recommendations as to whom to select, Han replied that this was a matter about which ministers dared not speak; the choice had to be his.[4] Jen-tsung then noted that, of the two clansmen in the palace, one was very pure or sincere (*ch'un*) but not quick-witted (*hui*), but that the other one would do.[5] The "other one" was Chao Shu (originally Tsung-shih; BCBX), the future Ying-tsung (1032-67; r. 1063-67), and he was first elevated to be minister of the Clan Court, and then in 1062 formally made the crown prince.

Thus the Sung was spared the fate of the Former Han, and Lü Hui's suspicions of the imperial clan proved groundless. Ying-tsung's reign was noteworthy mainly for its brevity (less than four years in length) and his personal shortcomings; he was a serious but somewhat timorous individual who was extremely reluctant to accept the designation of crown prince,[6] and his first two years as emperor were marked by madness and a de facto regency by the empress dowager.[7] However, the succession crisis was successfully resolved, and Ying-tsung began a line of emperors whose rule was to last for a century.

Even before he attracted Jen-tsung's attention, Chao Tsung-shih was hardly a typical clansman. He was the fourteenth son of Chao Yun-jang (BCB; 995–1059), who as the first director of the Great Office of Clan Affairs was arguably the most powerful clansman for much of Jen-tsung's

reign. Moreover, as a boy Yun-jang had been brought into the palace by
Chen-tsung and served as a potential crown prince until the birth of Jen-
tsung in 1010, at which point he returned to his family.[8]

Ironically, Chao Yun-jang was also the cause of the major controversy of
Ying-tsung's reign, which concerned his proper nominal and ritual relationship to Ying-tsung. There was no question that the ritual father of Ying-
tsung, as Jen-tsung's adopted son and successor, was Jen-tsung, but the
court became badly split over the issue of whether Yun-jang (or the Prince
of P'u, his noble title) could also be recognized as a father—the alternative
being "imperial uncle" (*huang-po*). When Ying-tsung finally decided the issue
in 1066, he sided with the grand councilors Han Ch'i and Ou-yang Hsiu,
rejecting the designation "imperial uncle" in favor of "parent" (*ch'in*); shortly
thereafter the opponents of this position, all of them censors, were dismissed from their posts.[9] This dispute has been seen as a precursor of the
reform/conservative conflicts that were shortly to follow.[10] From the standpoint of the imperial clan, however, its main legacies were to provide a trou-
bling precedent that was revisited when Hsiao-tsung—the next imperial
clansman selected to become emperor—succeeded Kao-tsung in 1162, and
to establish the Yun-jang branch even more firmly as the pre-eminent lineage of the imperial clan.

During his brief reign, Ying-tsung displayed an interest in improving the
educational conditions of the clan. As an ex-clansman and past minister of
the Court of the Imperial Clan, he had firsthand knowledge of how the
growth of the clan had overwhelmed the residential teaching structure of the
Jen-tsung years. In 1064 he ordered the appointment of 21 teaching officials
to supplement the six already in place.[11] This still did not begin to address
the needs of the burgeoning clan population, but it nevertheless represented
a significant increase in the court's commitment to the education of clansmen.

The Crisis of Clan Growth

In the first month of 1067, Ying-tsung died following a two-month-long
illness and was succeeded by his oldest son, known to history as the emperor
Shen-tsung (1048–85; r. 1067–85).[12] Although a mere twenty *sui* in age at the
time of his accession, Shen-tsung was by all accounts a capable and bold

young man, determined to address the critical problems facing the empire, particularly the fiscal straits resulting from the four-year-long war against the Tangut Hsi-Hsia state in the 1040s, the heavy military expenditures that followed in its wake, and renewed threats from the Tanguts in the mid-1060s.[13] In 1069 he elevated to the position of vice–grand councilor the outsider Wang An-shih (1021–86), who the year before had proposed a wide-ranging program for reforming education, the civil service, agriculture, the military, and finances. The ensuing New Policies (*Hsin-fa*) program of reform under Wang, who was elevated to sole grand councilor in 1071, was unparalleled in Chinese imperial history for its breadth, scope, and commitment to state activism, and has given rise to an enormous literature.[14] By contrast, there has been little notice of the comparably radical changes that occurred within the imperial clan, changes generated by a sense of crisis.

The problems that faced the imperial clan by the late 1060s were threefold, involving genealogical distance from the throne, numbers, and expenses. By the beginning of Shen-tsung's reign, the clan was producing members of the fourth and fifth generations (see Table 2.3, p. 32), and most of them were beyond the five degrees of mourning (*wu-fu*) that traditionally defined mourning obligation. According to T'ang precedent, they should have been sent out of the capital, given land, severed from imperial support, and discontinued from the imperial genealogy. It is true that T'ai-tsu's Great Instructions, described in Chapter 2, foresaw an imperial clan that went far beyond the degrees of mourning, but T'ai-tsu had not had to contend with the pressures of growing numbers of clan members or the enormous costs that they entailed.

In 1064, at the time of Ying-tsung's appointment of 21 additional teaching officials to clan residences, it was reported that clan members with titular office—that is, clansmen of at least five *sui* and older—numbered over 1,200. Of these, 113 were 30 years old or above and an additional 309 were age fifteen and above, which left some 800 below the age of fifteen.[15] Although 1,200 clansmen represented a huge increase over earlier years, the real problem with these figures lay in the inevitably much larger growth that would occur once those clan youths became fathers themselves. And in fact, in the late 1070s Tseng Kung (1019–83), director of the Bureau of Three Ranks (San-pan yuan), reported that new entries in the imperial clan's genealogy numbered 487 in 1075, 544 in 1076, and 690 in 1077, whereas deaths num-

bered only around 200 per year.[16] What these figures reflect, I would suggest, is the arrival of the bulk of the 3,488-member fifth generation (see
Table 2.2, p. 31), with the larger sixth and seventh generations yet to follow.

The costs of supporting this assemblage of clansmen (and women) had
expanded to a significant portion of the imperial budget. In 1067, the
monthly support (in money and grain) for the clan exceeded 70,000 strings
of cash. By comparison, the entire capital bureaucracy cost some 40,000-
odd strings and the capital army 110,000. Moreover, this did not include
expenses for birthdays, marriages, and funerals, the seasonal clothing allowances, or other special disbursements, which could be quite high.[17] As an
example of the latter, in 1070 the Prince of P'u's palace—housing Ying-
tsung's siblings and their offspring—received 5,000 strings annually for
expenses.[18]

In sum, Shen-tsung faced a situation in which the burgeoning clan was
beginning to exceed the dynasty's capacity to maintain its lavish lifestyle, and
this was occurring precisely when the clan was reaching a point, genealogically, where there were historical precedents for cutting off that support.
Even under an emperor uninterested in reform, the situation would have to
have been addressed; under Shen-tsung and Wang An-shih, both intent on
bold reforms, major changes were in the offing for the imperial clan.

The Clan Reformed

From early in his reign, Shen-tsung was clearly mindful of the need for
change in the imperial clan. The figure of 70,000 strings for the clan's
monthly expenditure comes from an edict ordering a reduction in monthly
stipends and special gifts for weddings, birthdays, and the suburban sacrifices. Shen-tsung recognized, however, that budget cuts alone were inadequate, and that a structural reordering (*ting-chih*) of the clan was needed,
although out of respect for Ying-tsung, he agreed to his chief ministers'
advice to postpone that until his mourning was completed.[19]

In the second month of 1069—just after the second anniversary of Ying-
tsung's death—discussions began in earnest and lasted throughout that
year. On no less than four occasions, Shen-tsung consulted with the leaders
of the Secretariat and Bureau of Military Affairs (BMA), both singly and in
groups.[20] The emperor sought advice not only from Wang An-shih and his

allies such as Han Chiang (1012–88) and Ch'en Sheng-chih (1011–79) but also from representatives of the older order such as Tseng Kung-liang (999–1078) and three leading opponents of Wang's: Fu Pi (1004–83), Wen Yen-po (1006–97), and Ssu-ma Kuang (1019–86). Despite the diversity of the participants, their disagreements were minor. There was a broad consensus that the imperial clan had become too expensive,[21] that it needed restructuring, and that action required the personal leadership of the emperor himself. The only real issue of disagreement was that of the pace of change, with Ch'en Sheng-chih and Wang An-shih, in particular, arguing that the emperor should act resolutely, employing righteousness, whereas Fu Pi and Ssu-ma Kuang urged gradual change. Indeed, in the case of Ssu-ma—who in just a few months would be dismissed and retire to Lo-yang—Shen-tsung took him aside after an imperial seminar in the eleventh month of 1069 and asked him about reforming the regulations of the imperial clan. Ssu-ma replied, "I sincerely believe that they should be reformed, but that is best done gradually, without haste."[22]

It is no coincidence that these discussions occurred at the same time as the great reforms of Wang's New Policies, the first series of which were also being enacted in 1069, a time when the emperor was "strengthening the spirit of government," to quote Wang's brother, Wang An-li.[23] For both the imperial clan reforms and the New Policies, the general agreement over the nature of the problems broke down, at least in part, because of the hastiness of the solutions. In the case of the clan, Shen-tsung heeded not Ssu-ma's warning but Wang's advice. On the eleventh day of the eleventh month of 1069, the Secretariat and BMA submitted a detailed proposal for reorganizing the clan and, in particular, for dealing with the issue of distant, non-mourning kin. This was accompanied by an edict justifying the impending action that cited various Han and T'ang precedents in its support.[24]

Finally, on the twenty-third day of the twelfth month of 1069, Shen-tsung promulgated what is arguably the most important edict in the history of the Sung imperial clan. Brief and to the point, it stated:

According to the recent organization of the royal clan, those beyond the *t'an-wen* degree of mourning will no longer receive names and titular offices, but they may participate in the examinations. From now on, [the names of] those who have been born and died should be reported in [genealogical] order to the ennobled leader of the branch, each of whom will establish a register, and at the year's end they are to send these to the

Office of the Jade Register. Those who have yet to serve as officials may, according to past practice, enter the upper and lower schools.[25]

Since *t'an-wen* referred to the mourning relationship one step beyond the prescribed "five degrees" (*wu-fu*) and pertained to those clansmen whose imperial ancestor was five generations removed (that is, the last common ancestor was a great-great-great-grandfather),[26] the effect of this edict was to divest the T'ai-tsu and T'ai-tsung fifth-generation and Wei-wang fourth-generation clansmen and their offspring of the right to receive name and office, an act that had until this point been the foremost indicator of clan membership.

The edict contains several other noteworthy features. First, as compensation for their loss of automatic titular office, these non-mourning clansmen were given the right to take the examinations and, by extension, to serve as regular officials. Second, they were *not* dropped from the imperial genealogy, the primary written indicator of clan status. Third, we see the beginnings of an attempt to create a branch organization in the reference to the "ennobled leader," an innovation that was part of the reform plans. Finally, they continued to have access to the clan schools.

If we accept a story told by the Southern Sung writer Lu Yu (1125–1209), clansmen saw the 1069 action as a clear attack on the imperial clan. According to Lu, once when he was out riding, Wang An-shih was confronted by a group of angry clan youths, who reviled him, saying, "We are sons and grandsons of the imperial temple, and we say that the Grand Councilor–Duke [Wang] should look upon our ancestors' faces!" To which Wang heatedly replied: "All the ancestors' kin should be removed from the ancestral hall, especially all of you!" At this they scattered.[27]

Although the cutbacks that were the target of the clansmen's complaints were real enough, their long-term significance was not at all clear. In fact, the edict was replete with ambiguities concerning its implementation and implications. As the sections that follow make clear, that implementation resulted in great changes in genealogical practices, the examination system, officeholding regulations, residency patterns, marriage practices, and the organization of both the Court of the Imperial Clan and the Great Office. Moreover, it was only as these changes worked themselves out over the next quarter-century that the relationship between the emperor and kin—or state and clan—became clear, and what emerged was a considerably greater commitment to the clan than what Wang An-shih and Shen-tsung had originally had in mind.

The Clan Redefined

Even as the decision was being made to cut back on imperial support for the clan, many of the leading thinkers of the land were writing about the importance of patrilineal descent lines (*tsung*) and arguing for a return to their use. Responding to a diminution in the ability of kin groups to maintain themselves in positions of high status over time given contemporary conditions of commercialization and competition, Ou-yang Hsiu, Su Hsun (1009–66), Ssu-ma Kuang, and Ch'eng I (1033–1107), among others, proposed the revival of the *tsung*—a kinship institution described in Chou dynasty texts—which they argued could provide all individuals who could claim patrilineal descent from a common ancestor with a ritual center, genealogical identity, and the ability to counter the fragmentation of landholdings common in the practice of family division.[28]

The irony is that the imperial clan constituted the closest thing to a functioning *tsung* in eleventh-century China. Its very name, *tsung-shih*, meant "house of the [imperial] *tsung*." All clan members descended from Hsuan-tsung, and this was rigorously documented by the Office of the Jade Register. As we have seen, they lived together and were perceived as a mutual descent group. Moreover, in another important way, the clan appeared to be adopting an element central to much of the theoretical *tsung* discussion: the designation of clan heads (*tsung-ling*) as ritual leaders for each branch of the clan. These heads were distinguished both from the leaders of the Court of the Imperial Clan and the Great Office, who were appointed by the emperor, and from the clan leaders within the residences, the "respected elders" (*tsun-chang*). According to the detailed Secretariat/BMA memorial of 11/1069, which provided many of the specifics for the subsequent edict, these individuals were to be ennobled, hold guard rank, and participate in imperial sacrifices irrespective of their mourning relationship (or lack of it) to the emperor.[29]

In two key respects, however, the imperial clan heads departed from the classical model. First, there was no question of making the branches functioning economic entities under the control of the branch heads, as the classical model suggested. Second, there was no privileging of a particular patriline of eldest sons as branch heads. Instead, the eldest living member of the eldest surviving generation was selected as clan head, although there was considerable dispute over whether the post should be restricted to the sons of wives (thereby excluding the sons of concubines).[30] It was decided that all clansmen, regardless of the matrimonial status of their mother, would be eligible, and this principle was used in the inheritance of princely titles as well. Indeed, it is only because of the latter that we have documentation of this inheritance pattern, for the branch heads seem never to have been established successfully.[31]

In practical terms, the greatest significance of the *tsung* model lay in its open-ended character, for it supported the genealogical inclusion of non-mourning kin. Although the listing of ever more distant kin was true to T'ai-tsu's original vision of a vast and dispersed clan united by genealogical relationships, listing all members when the government no longer controlled the process of naming made genealogical clarity far more problematic.

Indeed, in 1070 the Court of the Imperial Clan even questioned whether clansmen beyond the *t'an-wen* relationship should be included in the genealogy, since they no longer received names and offices but came instead under the regulations for regular provincial officials. The Ministry of Rites, ordered by the emperor to consider the issue and report, argued that although by the sixth generation the relationship to the emperor was finished—the way of kinship (*ch'in-tao*) exhausted—the need to record names to the hundredth generation so as not to disorder generational records applied to mourning and non-mourning kin alike. Therefore, it recommended continuing to enter their names.[32] The practice was thus continued, and predictably problems increased. In 1092, the Court of the Imperial Clan complained that since the Hsi-ning (1068–77) reforms, clan families had been allowed to decide their children's names, and as a result there had been cases of duplication, of the use of taboo characters, of brothers not using the same generational character, and even of one-character names being given. The Court had already received permission to make changes in cases of duplicated names,[33] but they also asked that the palace officials be delegated to work on correcting the problems, and that the Court be given the authority to enforce the use of generational names. Both requests were granted.[34]

The Ministry of Rites limited its consideration of genealogical policy to the issue of mourning relationship versus the genealogical need for completeness, but in fact far more than names was involved. The genealogy defined the imperial clan, and so long as individuals were listed in it, they could claim clan membership and with it a status that set them off from the rest of society. Almost all clan members had a vital stake in the outcome of this issue. With the exception of the direct descendents of Chen-tsung and Jen-tsung—a tiny group—and those of Chao Yun-jang, the Prince of P'u, all fifth-generation members of the clan (fourth generation for the Wei-wang branch) were non-mourning kin. What was in question was the very existence of the imperial clan itself. It is understandable, therefore, that the dynasty found itself under great pressure to maintain a system of supports and privileges for all clan members, however distant their relationship. It was this more than anything else that set the Sung clan off from its predecessors and shaped its nature for the succeeding two centuries.

Policies for Non-mourning Kin

In the lengthy memorial detailing proposed reductions in support for the imperial clan, the Secretariat and BMA appear to have been moving toward cutting off distant clansmen entirely. After proposing the institution of clan branch heads, described above, they suggested a number of measures designed to effect this transition. The ending of the conferral of names and offices was the heart of the changes. In addition, the memorialists proposed the intermediate step for t'an-wen clansmen of allowing them to receive the less prestigious "three ranks" (san-pan) titular offices rather than Southern Rank guard offices. Succeeding generations had to make their way via the examinations, in which the t'an-wen clansmen could also participate, and considerable attention was devoted to how the examinations for them would function.[35] They proposed in addition that non-mourning kin (those of t'an-wen status and beyond) currently serving as officials as well as those who were not but whose parents and grandparents had died be permitted to establish their own residences in the capital as well as to invest in land. Those serving as officials, moreover, were allowed to purchase land and housing according to the laws for normal officials (wai-kuan fa). As for marriage practices, marriage allowances for both fifth- (t'an-wen) and sixth-

generation clanswomen were to be halved, and in addition the husbands of
the sixth-generation clanswomen were no longer to be given Southern Rank
titular office, although such women were still not allowed to marry men
from non-elite families (*fei shih-tsu chih chia*). They further suggested that
clansmen of the fifth and sixth generations who were poor and without
office be given land and, in the case of their orphaned young who had no
one on whom to depend and who were especially poor, that regardless of
their generational status their names should be written out and submitted,
to be discussed and considered for special assistance.[36]

These proposals are noteworthy in at least three ways. First, they
involved radical changes in the lives of the fifth- and especially the sixth-
generation clan members, essentially setting them on their own. Second,
they nevertheless qualified those changes in important ways, acknowledging
at least some responsibility toward distant clansmen and providing privileges for them. Third, if the continued restrictions on marriage partners
represented an attempt to assure clan members an elite status, the mention
of impoverished and needy clansmen—to my knowledge the first such reference—suggests that the cutbacks had begun producing non-elite clansmen, regardless of marriage partners.

There is no record that the 1069 proposals were implemented at that
time. However, the issues of examinations, officeholding, residency and
support allowances, and marriage and divorce were the subjects of frequent
discussion and legislation over the next few decades, and it is to those records that we now turn.

Examinations, Transfers from Guard Posts, and Officeholding

Shen-tsung's edict of 1069 set the stage for two centuries of participation by
the imperial clan in the examination system,[37] but it was some time before
clansmen began to be examined in the usual fashion. In the mid-1070s we
find notices of examinations for clansmen, but they involved tiny numbers,
and rather than representing new examination practices, they seem to have
had more in common with the occasional examinations given under Jen-
tsung.[38]

Of much greater import is an edict of 1072 found in the HCP permitting
clansmen beyond the *t'an-wen* generation to sit for an examination consisting

of three policy questions, one discussion essay, and ten questions on a major classic. An initial test was to weed out those who could not write grammatical Chinese (*pu ch'eng wen-li che*). The rest were to be retested. Half of the surviving candidates could be passed, but the total number of degrees given was not to exceed 50. Elderly examinees who had repeatedly failed could be nominated for special awards.[39] The *Sung History* and the thirteenth-century encyclopedia *Wen-hsien t'ung-k'ao* provide additional details about this legislation, which they call the "examination regulations for clansmen" (*tsung-tzu shih fa*). They specify that the *t'an-wen* clansmen were to be tested at the locked hall examination (*suo-t'ing-shih*—an examination for officials and the children of certain categories of officials). More distant clansmen were to be tested at the Directorate of Education and subsequently the Ministry of Rites (for the departmental examination), but their answers would be graded separately from those of other candidates, and half of them could pass, up to a maximum of 50. At the palace examination (the final stage in the examination process, but one used for ranking rather than selection), the clansmen were examined together with the other candidates on the important policy questions. Repeat candidates had to be over 40 *sui* to qualify for special nomination, and clansmen serving as provincial officials who did not wish to sit the locked hall examination in the circuit of their posting could instead take the Directorate examination.[40] The distinction between the *t'an-wen* clansmen, who took the locked hall examination since they already held official rank, and the distant kin without office, who took the Directorate (or Ministry of Rites) examination, had been suggested in the draft proposal of 1069[41] and was to remain a feature of the imperial clan examinations henceforth, joined, as we shall see, by two other categories of examination.[42]

Although the clansmen candidates were involved in the same sequence of examinations as regular candidates and, like them, received a *chin-shih* (advanced scholar) degree when successful, the regulations essentially created a separate and easier examination for them. The curriculum was somewhat easier, for although both had discussion and policy questions, the regular candidates had to prepare to be examined on a major classic as well as on the *Analects* and the works of Mencius, whereas the clansmen were tested only on a classic. The clan examination was also far less competitive: in the late eleventh century the ratio of successful candidates to examinees for the locked hall, Directorate, and departmental examinations was in each case around one in ten,[43] and whereas the chances of a regular candidate proceeding through the examinations to a *chin-shih* degree were about one in a hundred, for the imperial clansmen they were one in four.

When Shen-tsung died in 1085 and Empress Dowager Kao began a regency on behalf of her grandson, Che-tsung (born Chao Hsu, 1077–1100; r. 1085–1100), one of the most dramatic changes in Sung political history occurred, as the anti-reformers swept into power under the leadership of Ssu-ma Kuang. The impact of this change on the imperial clan was relatively minor, however. The major elements of Shen-tsung's reorganization were left in place, although the new government was less generous toward the clan, more inclined to erase the differences between the clan and the rest of society. In the examinations this took the form of an edict in 1088 abolishing the separate examination of clansmen.[44] For the next fourteen years, clansmen competed with non-clan literati in the examinations, although records are too sketchy to indicate whether they were truly competing on an equal footing or continued to receive privileges that made their task easier.

Whether this change made an appreciable difference in clansmen's examination success is hard to say. Clansmen accounted for only two *chin-shih* out of 500 in 1088, and eight out of 602 in 1092, but lest we conclude that discontinuing the separate examinations had a devastating impact, we should note that, according to the grand councilor Ts'ai Ching (1046–1126), by 1102 the clan had produced only twenty *chin-shih* in the 34 years since the start of the Hsi-ning period.[45] By way of comparison, Wang Sheng-to's tabulations of the numbers of mourning kin who received name and office in the late eleventh century show that they totaled 431 for the years 1070–77 and 396 for 1086–98. Even with missing years—in addition to 1078–85, there are no figures for 1093 and 1096—827 clansmen received office, 41 for each clansman *chin-shih*.[46] Considering, furthermore, the vast size of the fifth- and sixth-generation clan cohorts—totaling between them over 8,500—we can safely conclude that the importance of the examinations for the imperial clan during this period was minimal.[47]

Much more important than formal examinations was the transfer of clansmen with Southern Rank status into the regular military service. As described in the Secretariat/BMA memorial of 1069, this was to be limited to relatively low ranking clansmen, who could transfer to low military titular offices. Thus those with the guard rank of general (*chiang-chün*) could receive the titular rank of vice-commissioner in one of the various offices (*chu-ssu fu-shih*) or executive assistants of the Court of Imperial Sacrifices (T'ai-ch'ang ch'eng); commanders (*cheng-shuai*) could become imperial warders of the inner palace (*nei-tien ch'ung-pan*) or undersecretaries of the crown prince in the left Secretariat (*t'ai-tzu chung-yun*); and vice-commanders (*fu-shuai*) could become palace servitors in the clerical office (*hsi-t'ou kung-feng kuan*). In addition, *t'an-wen* clansmen over the age of twenty who had not received a Southern Rank office could be given the titular office of right palace duty group (*yu-pan tien-chih*).[48] All such appointees had to be recommended by the Great Office, to be guaranteed by the clan head of their residence and a clan teacher, and to pass an examination, albeit one far simpler than the regular examinations.[49]

This combination of transfer from Southern Rank offices and appointment of *t'an-wen* clansmen seems to have accounted for most of the movement by clansmen into the regular bureaucracy in the late eleventh century.[50] This entry, however, did not mean that clansmen had access to the full spectrum of posts. Through Shen-tsung's and much of Che-tsung's reigns, clansmen who had received *wai-kuan* status were limited to serving in the humble posts of state monopoly officials (*chien-tang kuan*), but over time that restriction eroded. Multiple postings became possible, and in 1092, clansmen were permitted under certain conditions to serve as county magistrates.[51]

The transformation of clansmen into regular officials was therefore a gradual and cautious process, and all the postings were initially, at least, humble. Yet neither this nor the clansmen's anger against Wang An-shih should obscure the significance of this change. Although Shen-tsung's reforms reduced the support they were receiving and caused insecurity for many clansmen, others welcomed the chance to assume a political role. Wang An-li, the brother of An-shih, describes the awakened, albeit unfulfilled aspirations of one clansman, Chao Chung-mou (BAADB; 1039–81): "In Hsi-ning when the emperor strengthened the spirit of government, he first decreed that clansmen of the *t'an-wen* relation and below who wished to serve as regular officials could exert their efforts [to that end]. Chung-mou wished to use the constant gratitude [he felt] as a close imperial kinsman to arouse himself and establish his name in the world. Unfortunately, before realizing his ambition he suddenly died. What a pity!"[52]

Residency and Living Allowances

The crisis in clan growth described above involved more than just money and numbers. The clan residences overflowed when fourth- and fifth-generation children began arriving in ever increasing numbers. As an edict from 1070 put it, "In the residences the boys and girls are many, and the buildings few."[53] Although the 1069 Secretariat/BMA memorial alluded to the issue of residency by proposing that non-mourning clansmen be allowed to own land and live on their own, the first formal act by the emperor was an edict in 1070 ordering non-mourning kin to leave their quarters, which were to be reallocated equitably by the Court of the Imperial Clan.[54]

The next thirty years witnessed a good deal of legislation concerning clan residential issues, most of it having to do with mourning kin who continued to live in the residences. Even before this, in 1068, clansmen were permitted to contract on their own with artisans to renovate their residences and to use official stores of building materials.[55] On several occasions clansmen were granted land on which to build residences in or adjacent to the residential complexes, and in two other instances mourning and *t'an-wen* clansmen were allowed to live in rented residences.[56] More frequently we find the court trying to control the physical movements of clan members. In 1070 the rules on entering and leaving the clan residences were relaxed; because moving many clan members out of the residences would necessitate more coming and going than before, clan members were excused from having to apply to the Great Office for permission to go out.[57] Seven years later, however, the emphasis was on restrictiveness. Citing a need to restrain the movements of clansmen who had not become normal officials (*wai-kuan*), an edict ordered them not to dismount from their horses en route to their destinations—that is, to make no stops. Moreover, if they left the "new city" (*hsin-ch'eng*) (most likely meaning K'ai-feng), they were required to submit a report to the Great Office, even if they had not spent the night away.[58] In 1081 a special dispensation was given to the director of the Great Office, Chao Tsung-tan (BAAC), allowing him to visit private households freely thereafter, although it was stipulated that he was to travel in a sedan chair with the curtains drawn.[59] In 1083 elderly and sick clan members were permitted to venture out in sedan chairs, although they were enjoined from using more than two lanterns when traveling at night.[60]

We can see in these varied actions an attempt to come to terms with the new reality of a dispersed clan, which made the control measures of the Jen-tsung era untenable. These were liberating times, and the desire for freedom from palatial confinements reached to the very top. Shen-tsung's two brothers, Hao (Ying-A; 1060-86) and Chün (Ying-B; 1056-88), asked repeatedly to be allowed to move out of the Eastern Palace, which neighbored the imperial palace, but were turned down by the emperor. They had to wait until 1086, when the empress dowager built them separate palaces in the Hsien-i quarter, where they lived out the brief remainder of their lives.[61]

The sources say little about how the non-mourning clansmen went about acquiring housing outside the clan residences or the problems they encountered, for the obvious reason that those were no longer concerns of the court. However, in 1092 the division of family property was permitted for clansmen of the *t'an-wen* degree and below who were living outside the clan residences. The provisions of this decree did not apply to mourning clansmen and also excluded "permanently held land" (*yung-yeh t'ien*) and sacrificial objects.[62] Nevertheless, the act was—as the supporting memorial noted—without precedent in the history of the imperial clan and constituted a critical step in the creation of the clan family as a socioeconomic unit.

The sources also say nothing about living allowances for non-mourning kin for most of Shen-tsung's reign. An edict of 1083 did decree that *t'an-wen* clansmen eligible for appointment as regular officials via *yin* but still too young to receive it and whose parents and grandparents had died could follow the precedent for non-mourning clansmen and receive a stipend. This was in response to a Great Office plea on behalf of a *t'an-wen* clansman from the Wei-wang branch who had no family member receiving a stipend for food.[63] The 1083 edict was, however, a narrow action, limited to clansmen who qualified for office via *yin*. In 1087, however, the court ordered that orphaned, non-mourning clansmen whose parents and grandparents were dead, who had no official stipend, and who were poor were to be reported to the Great Office and local officials (*suo-tsai kuan-ssu*), who were to investigate and verify their situation. The Ministry of Revenue was then to provide cash and grain allowances based on the number of family members (excluding married daughters).[64] The following year this was extended to include a housing allowance, and the Ministry of Rites was told to establish appropriate regulations.[65] In 1094 these provisions were spelled out in detail in a memorial—accepted by the throne—submitted by the Ministry of Rites. It specified that members of the *t'an-wen* and the next two generations of clansmen whose parents were dead and who either lacked official rank or were awaiting official postings were eligible for allowances, subject to verification and guarantees from the Great Office and local officials. A household of ten people and above was to receive a monthly allowance of twenty strings of cash, ten piculs (*shih*) of rice, and five rooms (*chien*) of housing. For a household of four to seven members, the corresponding figures were seven strings, five piculs, and three rooms; and for households of three or fewer members, two strings, one picul, and two rooms.[66] In 1095 these proportions were made more "equitable" by designating a per capita allowance of two strings and one picul per person, and a very restrictive two rooms for households of twelve members and below. Shortly thereafter a cap of twenty strings and six piculs per household was set.[67]

By the standards of Sung scholar-officials, and even more particularly of the imperial clan in which the entry-level office of vice-commander had a monthly stipend of twenty strings, these were modest amounts. For the government, however, the cumulative burden of these allowances was substantial, when one considers the thousands of fifth- and sixth-generation clans*men*, not to mention their wives, sisters, daughters, and daughters-in-law. Since the Ministry of Revenue rather than the Privy Purse was providing the allowances, they presumably involved a new expense for the regular treasury. But the true significance of these actions lay not in its finances but rather in the court's decision to undertake the support of *all* clansmen, at least through the seventh generation, albeit at greatly reduced levels. This marked the limits of the changes wrought by the 1069 edict abolishing the conferral of names and offices and in large part determined the subsequent nature of the imperial clan.

Marriage and Divorce

As we saw in Chapter 3, the court under Jen-tsung developed elaborate provisions for imperial clan marriages and particularly for controlling marriage partners. With the end of the conferral of names and offices for distant kin in 1069, all these were called into question. Should the court try to restrict the marriage of non-mourning clan members in any way? What should be done about the clanswomen's official dowries and the recruitment privileges given to their spouses? How should oversight be maintained for the mourning clan members in the changed circumstances of the clan? These issues and others resulted in much activity as the court wrestled with the restructuring of the clan.

The first proposal for a marriage policy for *t'an-wen* and non-mourning kin is found in the omnibus memorial from the Secretariat and BMA in 1069, which devoted a section to marriage. For *t'an-wen* clanswomen, the cash gift (the state's official dowry) was to be halved and their husbands were to be attendants of the three ranks (*san-pan feng-chih*), the lowest executory class of titular office. Non-mourning clanswomen were to receive a cash gift, but their husbands were not to receive office; if the husband had already received office, the procedures for advancement that applied to *t'an-wen* husbands were to be used. Finally, women marrying *t'an-wen* clansmen were to receive gifts. The memorial stated that non-mourning kin were to follow the marriage law for commoners (*shu-hsing fa*) but were nevertheless enjoined from marrying into non-elite families (*fei shih-tsu chih chia*).[68]

Since we do not know if this proposal was accepted, it is to an edict of 1077 that we must turn for the first definitive legislation concerning the marriages of distant kin (see also Table 4.1). *T'an-wen* clan members were prohibited from marriages with families of "miscellaneous elements" (*tsa-lei*)—defined as those with males who had been slaves or females who had been prostitutes—or those whose parents or grandparents had lived in border regions and served two regimes. Mourning clan members (*ssu-ma* and above) were further barred from marrying the sons or grandsons of clerks, officials who had gained rank via purchase or special skills,[69] artisans, merchants, "miscellaneous elements," or those found to be "evil and traitorous" (*o-ni*).[70] Non-mourning members were to marry according to the family law of commoners, and no additional restrictions were added.[71]

An edict of 1088 echoed the earlier edict in its prohibition of marriages to the offspring of clerks, officials via purchase, "miscellaneous elements," or the evil and traitorous but applied these restrictions to *t'an-wen* as well as mourning kin. The provisions for non-mourning kin remained unchanged.[72] Thus the court was growing at least marginally more inclusive in

Table 4.1

Imperial Clan Marriage Partners: Proscribed Groups

Year	Imperial kin affected (if specified)	Proscribed marriage partners
1029		Offspring of artisans, merchants, or "miscellaneous elements" or from families with a history of treasonous activities
1077	t'an-wen	From families of "miscellaneous elements": where males had been slaves or females prostitutes or where parents or grandparents had lived in border regions and served two regimes
1077	ssu-ma and above	Offspring of clerks, official via purchase or special skills, artisans, merchants, "miscellaneous elements," and those with a history of treasonous activities
1088	t'an-wen and above	same as ssu-ma of 1077
1088		relatives of eunuchs
1213	outside t'an-wen	families of clerks

SOURCES: SHY:CK, 20/4b; SS, 115: 2739; HCP, 409/4b; SHY:TH, 5/7b, 7/30a–b.

its demands for respectable marriage partners for clan members. Later the same year, a prohibition against marriages with families of eunuchs (*nei-ch'en chih chia*) was added, although this seems to have applied only to mourning kin.[73]

The edict of 1077 also contains a prescription for marriage matchmaking procedures, the first since that of 1029. Clan families planning marriages were to appoint a "clansman marriage master" (*chu-hun tsung-shih*), who was to identify suitable matches involving families with a three-generation history of local officials or officials of at least palace attendant (*tien-chih*) rank and send the family documents to the Great Office for inspection and guarantees. The Great Office would then forward them to the Palace Domestic Service (Nei-shih sheng). Provisions were further spelled out for treating cases of fraud.[74] In comparison to the earlier procedures, the court was yielding the active role in matchmaking to the immediate families while trying to ensure some control over the results. In 1086, there was an attempt to return to the old procedures, at least for mourning kin,[75] although the feasibility of this, given the growing size and increasing dispersion of the clan, seems questionable.

The 1077 edict also set policies for divorce. If there were legal grounds for separation or incompatibility, divorce petitions were to be allowed, with all wedding gifts being returned. If not, the couple was to be reunited and charges were to be brought, when appropriate. Divorced clanswomen who wanted to remarry could, but only after an investigation by the Court of the Imperial Clan; their husbands received reduced privileges.[76] The *Sung History* notes a subsequent edict to the effect that only clanswomen who were divorcees themselves were allowed to marry divorced men.[77]

In addition to legislation on marriage and divorce, Shen-tsung's reign also saw minor changes in privileges for the husbands of clanswomen and in the official dowries given to the women. In 1070 an edict prescribing privileges for the husbands of *t'an-wen* clanswomen stated that those without official rank could receive the office of attendant of the three ranks—as proposed in 1069—and that those who were already officials were to be granted a one-rank promotion. In the words of Wang An-shih, speaking in support of the measure, "This is a way of encouraging those who are officials to marry clanswomen and also [provides] a shortcut for entering officialdom."[78] We also possess a schedule of trousseaux (*lien*) to be given to clanswomen at marriage, according to their mourning rank. After the Hsi-ning period (1068–77), great-great-granddaughters of the founding emperors (i.e., fourth-generation descendents) were to receive 500 strings of cash; this sum decreased to 350 strings for fifth-generation descendents (i.e., *t'an-wen* clanswomen), 300 strings for the sixth, 250 strings for the seventh, and 150 strings for the eighth.[79] Although these are substantial figures—well in excess of the annual stipends for lower officials—they were modest by the standards of elite marriages, where dowries in the thousands of strings seem to have been common.[80] We must treat the dating of this list with caution, for its comes from two highly respected but non-annalistic Southern Sung works, and the inclusion of the eighth generation, which began appearing only in the early twelfth century, may make its likely date the late Northern

Sung. Nevertheless, it points to a process already visible in the Shen-tsung/Che-tsung era: the continuing support of the court for non-mourning generations of clansmen and women.

Clan Institutions in a Time of Change

Like the rules and practices governing the lives of clan members, clan institutions underwent significant changes in the late eleventh century. In the case of the Court of the Imperial Clan, these were relatively minor, perhaps because its functions at this time were quite narrowly defined. According to a document from the *Sung hui-yao* dated only as coming from Shen-tsung's reign (1067–85), the court had at its head four official personnel: a minister (*Tsung-cheng ch'ing*) of the upper fourth rank, a vice-minister (*shao-chi'ng*) of lower fifth rank, a recorder (*chu-pu*) of lower eighth rank, and an assistant minister (*ch'eng*) of lower seventh rank.[81] The primary task of the court was the compilation of the imperial clan's genealogy and census records, and the varied archival documents into which these are entered are described. Finally, it is noted that the charts are updated every three years, and the full compilations with biographical details are published every ten years.[82]

As for the Great Office of Clan Affairs, the *Sung History's* first description of its organization dates from Shen-tsung's reign, perhaps reflecting a formalization necessitated by its increasing functions. In addition to the administrator (*chih*) and vice-administrator (*t'ung-chih*), who were to be selected from among clansmen with a titular office of military training commissioner (*t'uan-lien-shih*) or above and a reputation for virtue, there were a supervisor (*p'an*), two assistant ministers (*ch'eng*) responsible for the affairs of the Mu-ch'in and Kuang-ch'in residences, a recordkeeper (*chi-shih*) in charge of documents and memorials, and twelve lecturer/preceptors (*chiang-shu chiao-shou*).[83]

Of these, the assistant ministers are noteworthy, first, because their assumption of oversight over the two major residential complexes represented a centralization of power under the Great Office. Second, they were to be selected from "civil or military officials of court rank or higher."[84] This use of non-clansmen for major posts within the Great Office was quite unprecedented, and in fact Shen-tsung questioned it when it was proposed. Wang An-shih, defending the proposal, cited precedents from the Spring and Autumn period, but added, with characteristic assurance, that "when sages establish laws, they do not always have to follow the precedents of former dynasties."[85]

The responsibilities of the Great Office included the education of clansmen, promoting social harmony, and dealing with litigation and discord. In cases of discord, the Great Office was to investigate, bring charges, and make judgments. If cases could not be decided, they were to be forwarded to the palace for judgment. The Great Office was also to keep seasonally submitted records from the residences concerning the daily comings and goings and annual reports on the births and deaths of clan members.[86] The *Sung History* also notes, somewhat cryptically, that the Great Office was divided into five sections (*an*) with eleven clerks (*li*).[87] These were quite likely the predecessors to the six sections (*an-hsi*) the Great Office maintained in 1122 (see Chapter 5), but we have no details concerning how they were organized at this time.

As noted above, the Great Office was responsible for verifying the need of poor non-mourning clan members for allowances. Finally, an edict of 1082 declared that the Great Office was *not* subordinate to the Six Ministries—presumably answering directly to the emperor instead—and stipulated that the civil assistant ministers were to be appointed by the Secretariat.[88] If the introduction of civil officials as vice-ministers involved an increasing role for the civil bureaucracy in the affairs of the imperial clan, that role remained circumscribed.

One continuity with the Jen-tsung period was the tendency for the Great Office to be dominated by a handful of clansmen with long tenures in office. Chao Tsung-tan (BAAC), praised by the *Sung History* for his easygoing but effective leadership of the clan, served as vice-administrator beginning in 1064–67 and as administrator from 1068 until 1082.[89] His brother, Tsung-hui (BAAK), served as vice-administrator before him, in 1061, but was dismissed in 1064 because of indiscretions with maids.[90] But he returned to the post in 1068 and served until 1082, when he became the administrator.[91] Slightly later we find Chao Tsung-sheng (BCBI; 1031–95) serving as vice-administrator in 1082 and administrator from 1084 to 1095,[92] and Chao Tsung-ching (BEAD; 1032–97), who was vice-administrator from 1085 to 1096. Like Tsung-hui, Tsung-ching had also earlier been disciplined for an indiscretion; determined to make his concubine his wife, he sent her out of his house, and then used a go-between to bring her back as a wife. But also as with them, this did not permanently damage his career.[93]

Two things are noteworthy about this group. First, all four were from the T'ai-tsung [B] branch of the clan; even though the T'ai-tsu branch [A] clansmen were theoretically eligible to hold Great Office posts, they were effectively excluded and would remain so until the Southern Sung. Second, each of these men came from exalted lines of the clan: the two brothers came from the senior T'ai-tsung branch, and Tsung-sheng and Tsung-ching were sons of two of the initial officials of the Great Office—Yun-pi (BEA) and Yun-jang (BCB). Indeed, we can see in Tsung-sheng's tenure the continuation of a long period of dominance for the descendents of Yun-jang.

The Li Feng Affair

Although the Great Office undoubtedly confronted numerous problems and crises during this period, most were too minor to merit the attention of the court and its historians. In 1075, however, a charge of sedition leveled against Chao Shih-chü (ABCCX), a prominent clansman, brought the imperial clan and the Great Office under intense scrutiny. The case is complicated but revealing not only of the imperial clan but also of the political culture of Shen-tsung's court.[94]

The case had its beginnings in the Shantung prefecture of I-chou in the first month of 1075. A commoner by the name of Chu T'ang accused Li Feng, the former registrar of Yü-yao county in Che-chiang and a native of neighboring Hsu-chou, of plotting rebellion. Wang T'ing-yun, a judicial commissioner sent to investigate, reported that although Li Feng was perverse, there was no evidence of a formal plot.[95] Dissatisfied with this finding, the emperor commissioned Chien Chou-fu, an acting judge from the Censorate, to go to Hsu-chou to investigate the plot. Chien's findings, reported by the beginning of the third month, were very different. Not only did he obtain a confession from Li, who was subsequently executed, but Li implicated Chao Shih-chü, a fourth-generation descendent of T'ai-tsu.

With Chien's report, the focus of the investigation shifted to Shih-chü. The directors of the Remonstrance Bureau and Proclamation Drafting Section—the latter the great erudite Shen Kua (1029–93)—were instructed to take up the investigation. However, when they found no discrepancies

(*i-tz'u*), the case was turned over to a K'ai-feng judge,[96] who together with a
clan official went to Chao Shih-chü's house on the eighth day of the third
month, inventoried his holdings, and took him into custody.[97]

At this point, the investigation took two directions. One concerned Chao
Shih-chü's relations with Li Feng. Chao was found guilty of having received
Li Feng at his house, perusing astrological charts (*t'u-ch'en*) with him, and
engaging in seditious talk. Involved with them were Chang Ching, registrar
for the Directorate of Palace Buildings; Liu Yü, a Han-lin usher and medical
official; and Ch'in Piao, a student at the Bureau of Astronomy, who had
provided a "Chart of Astronomical Calculations" ("Hsing-chen hsing-tu
t'u").[98] The most extravagant claims for Shih-chü's guilt came from Teng
Wan (1028–86), the acting palace aide to the censor-in-chief, who had been
ordered to examine Shih-chü's correspondence. Wrote Teng: "The original
intention of Li Feng, Chao Shih-chü, and others was to agitate as a result of
their embrace of astrological charts and the wild writings of Zoroastrians
(*hsien wang shu*)." In another document he charged: "When Shih-chü received the scoundrels, they discussed military [affairs] and embraced omens,
examined what was propitious and unpropitious for the dynasty, and came
and went at will, doing so year after year." Finally, Teng reported that a copy
of *An Illustrated Book of Offense and Defense* (*Kung-shou t'u-shu*) had been found
among the books in Shih-chü's library.[99]

The investigators also looked to Shih-chü's acquaintances, especially
those with whom he had engaged in correspondence. According to Ssu-ma
Kuang, Shih-chü was fond of literature, corresponded with *shih-ta-fu*, and
had acquired some renown,[100] and hence he had many acquaintances. Even
though the Censorate investigation of that correspondence had initially
found nothing amiss, and even Teng Wan conceded that all of it seemed to
be routine, two prefects found themselves accused simply because they had
corresponded with Shih-chü. In one case the emperor contended that his
correspondence contained "things that should not have been in them," although he could give no specifics when Wang An-shih pressed the issue; in
the other he said that the prefect in question had been acting fearful since
the correspondence had been discovered.[101] Even Shen-tsung's brother
Chün, the Prince of Chia, feared being tarred with guilt by association, since
he had made use of the medical services of Liu Yü, one of the alleged conspirators.[102]

The most intriguing individual charged was not an official but a commoner by the name of Li Shih-ning, a charlatan-like figure who had for
some time cut a wide swathe in K'ai-feng society. Again, to cite Ssu-ma
Kuang, who devotes an essay to Li in his *Su-shui chi-wen*, Li was a man of
unorthodox intellectual interests.[103] He was skilled at fortune-telling and,
although illiterate, could compose poems [orally] on the spot. He spoke of
portents and specifically misled people through what was to Ssu-ma reckless, even treasonous talk. He traveled around the country and, when he
came to the capital, gathered a wide following within elite society. He became especially friendly with Wang An-shih, and when Wang was grand
councilor, Li lived in his eastern residence for half a year, socializing daily
with Wang's brothers and sons. Moreover, when Wang was in mourning
for his father in Chin-ling (near modern Nanking), Li also lived there, and
it was alleged that their ambitions (*i-yü*) became similar.[104]

Li Shih-ning's friends included many in the imperial clan. Even during
Jen-tsung's reign, he had been able to gain access to the Mu-ch'in Residence,
where he informed the clansmen that because they were the original creations of T'ai-tsu, they deserved Li's blessings. More to the point, when,
ollowing the death of Ying-tsung's mother, Jen-tsung provided a funeral
dirge for her, Shih-ning changed the middle four lines so as to give the beginning and end a secret reference to Shih-chü as emperor. Shih-chü was
reportedly delighted and rewarded Shih-ning lavishly.

Li Shih-ning had no connection with Li Feng, but he was accused of
receiving an engraved dragon sword (*lung-tao*) from Shih-chü and, like Li
Feng, of dining with him. The accusation against Li Shih-ning, however,
gave Shih-chü's case an added dimension, for it was widely believed that
Wang's enemies at court, particularly Lü Hui-ch'ing (1031–1111), were using
it as a way to attack Wang. In the fourth month of 1074, Wang, stung by
various criticisms of the New Policies, resigned and left effective power in
the hands of his protégé Lü, then assistant grand councilor. During the eight
months that Wang was absent, however, Lü moved ruthlessly to consolidate
his own position, attacking both reformers and anti-reformers alike. An
alarmed Shen-tsung recalled Wang in the second month of 1075, and there
ensued a period of contention between the two, which culminated with the
demotion of Lü to the prefectship of Ch'en-chou (Ching-hsi-pei) in the
tenth month of 1075.[105]

When Wang returned from retirement, the K'ai-feng investigation of the Li Feng case was just about to begin. Li T'ao discounts the idea that Lü Hui-ch'ing actively used Li Shih-ning's association against Wang, mainly on the grounds that Ssu-ma Kuang does not make the charge in his essay, but whether Lü did or not, Wang's connection to Li Shih-ning clearly made him vulnerable. Perhaps for this reason, Wang urged restraint regarding those charged with associating with Chao Shih-chü and in particular argued with the emperor, who was far readier to proclaim widespread guilt. To give one example, when Shen-tsung cited a remark by Wang Kung, a case reviewer in the Court of Judicial Review, to the effect that "[Chao] Shih-chü was like T'ai-tsu," Wang quoted a Tu Fu poem with the line "whiskers like T'ai-tsung's" and asked how they differed. Wang's advice was to treat Shih-chü with the full force of the law, but to show mercy to his family and move cautiously with the others who had been accused. Reflecting on the potential impact of the case, he advised:

In this affair we have punished the responsible officials and we have offered generous rewards for informers. I fear that this will open us up to false accusations [submitted for] rewards, and officials, in order to avoid punishment, will implicate others. I hope that Your Majesty will carefully scrutinize this matter. In the climate of today, those who do not shirk from destroying human life or falsely accusing other people's families in order to advance themselves are many.[106]

In this plea, he was only partially successful. Li Shih-ning, flogged and exiled to Hunan, probably owed his life to Wang's intervention. Others were less fortunate. Chao Shih-chü was allowed to commit suicide. His sons and grandsons were spared execution but lost their clan names, were dropped from the imperial genealogy, and were imprisoned for a period of time. All his brothers, uncles, and nephews received demotions, and his wife, daughters, and daughters-in-law were forced to become nuns in a palace nunnery.[107]

Among the other primary conspirators, Liu Yü was put to a slow death and his wife exiled to Kuang-nan to serve as an army slave; Chang Ching was cut in half and his wife and parents were flogged and exiled to Kuang-nan; Ch'in Piao was banished to Hunan. All those accused of associating with Shih-chü were demoted and removed from office.[108] And Wang T'ing-yun, the judicial commissioner who had initially found the charges against Li Feng to be groundless, strangled himself while under impeachment.[109]

Punishments were also meted out to Great Office officials. Administrator Chao Tsung-tan was demoted for not having investigated the visits of Li Feng, as was Vice-Administrator Chao Tsung-hui for having lent a military book to Shih-chü. In addition, demotions were given to several minor officials in the Great Office.[110]

From our historical remove, it is impossible to determine how much credence to give the charges leveled against Li Feng and Chao Shih-chü. Concerning Chao, at least, despite Teng Wan's talk about the "framework of a rebellion," no evidence was offered to suggest that an insurrection was being planned. But there is ample evidence to indicate that a witch-hunting atmosphere prevailed in spring 1075, as all acquaintances of Chao Shih-chü and his "co-conspirators" became fair game.

The very disruptiveness of the affair, however, provides us with rare views of K'ai-feng and the imperial clan in the mid–Northern Sung. First, we see revealed the iron fist of the Sung state, in contrast to the velvet glove to which the imperial clan had undoubtedly grown accustomed. In matters that threatened the throne, if only symbolically, the emperor was prepared to act drastically. Although we have no reports of clan responses to Chao Shih-chü's fate, the members must have been traumatized. Second, the success of an individual like Li Shih-ning is revealing. Of course, charlatans are to be found in every society and age, demonstrating the gullibility of the respectable. But the fact that Shih-ning (and Li Feng) could have penetrated the residences of the imperial clan with such great ease suggests that the attempts of the court to segregate the clan from the rest of society were inadequate at best. Third, one of the themes running through the accounts of this affair is the power of the written word, especially when tied to portents and astrology or the military. In fact, one of Teng Wan's reports on the misdeeds of Shih-chü was coupled with a proposal for the banning, collection, and burning of all astrological charts and books (*t'u-ch'en wen-shu*). His idea was accepted, and an edict enacted announcing a two-month period of grace in which people could turn in books without punishment; this was to be followed by rewards of 100 strings of cash for informers and death sentences for those subsequently found with such materials.[111] And yet the prevailing impression is one of the inability of the government to exert wide-ranging controls over human behavior. In the cosmopolitan, commercial, and literate atmosphere of K'ai-feng, neither books nor the movements of people could effectively be limited. The best that the court could do was to move harshly against individuals when the opportunity arose and hope that the example would have some effect.

The Clan Adrift

One of the problems in treating the history of the imperial clan in the late Northern Sung is that the epitaph record, so useful in presenting the human faces of the clan throughout most of the Sung, is relatively silent. As noted in the preceding chapter, Northern Sung epitaphs tended to be written by commissioned officials and produced en masse, whereas Southern Sung epitaphs were usually written at the request of family members, often by friends or acquaintances of the deceased. Unfortunately, the only late Northern Sung examples of the former type are the epitaphs of Mu-jung Yen-feng, written mainly of clan members who died at the turn of the twelfth century, and they tend not to be very informative. But the latter type of epitaphs had yet to appear, an indication, I believe, of the continuing social gulf between most clansmen and *shih-ta-fu* society.

Another lacuna—if a lacuna it is—is the absence of evidence attesting to personal interactions between the emperor and the clan. Although Shen-tsung certainly discussed problems of the clan at length with his ministers— witness the case of Chao Shih-chü—neither he nor Che-tsung continued Jen-tsung's practices of holding banquets for the clan or sponsoring special competitions for them. Considering that the main thrust of Shen-tsung's policies was to reduce the court's support of the clan and cut off non-mourning kin, this is understandable, but it meant that the clan was losing one of its most valued resources: proximity to the emperor.

The massive institutional documentation of the clan in this period points to what has been a central theme of this chapter, that the clan was under-going a fundamental reorientation resulting from a crisis in numbers, money, and attenuated genealogical relationships. Yet those same docu-ments also reveal an uncertainty about the most pressing question of all: whether non-mourning kin should lose all support from the state. By the end of Che-tsung's reign, even though the court had made some critical moves to ensure a continued connection, the future character of the imperial clan was still unclear.

There was, in short, a lack of direction, a sense of the clan adrift. Although sources shedding light on the internal dynamics of clan families are rare, one that has survived depicts a bitter family quarrel in which one clansman accuses his brother's family of stealing[112] whereas another describes brothers creating a fraternal association, the Flower and Calyx Society (Ti-o hui).[113] In an age when clan families were having to operate increasingly like other elite families, family concord and discord became important issues.

Nowhere was the new and ambiguous status of the clan more at issue than in its marriage relationships. We noted above the greater role given to individual clan families in arranging their own marriages and the removal of most—though not all—restrictions on the marriages of non-mourning clan members. With these changes, however, came a realization that not all clan marriages would be with the most desirable families, particularly since the recruitment privileges offered to the spouses of clanswomen proved to be a magnet that attracted all sorts of families. Wang An-shih may have felt that this was a useful way of ensuring that clanswomen married officials, but others were doubtful.

Chao Shih-k'ai (AAEAC), for one, protested during an audience with Shen-tsung that in the marriages of clanswomen, wealthy families considered the women commodities whose chief value was that the family no longer had to compete for office. This impressed the emperor, who offered him a position as a clan official (which he declined),[114] but in fact the complaint was not a new one. In 1068 the censor Liu Shu (1034 chin-shih), in arguing unsuccessfully that clanswomen's marriages be restricted to currently serving civil and military officials, had asserted that wealthy villagers falsely used the official genealogies of others to marry clanswomen. "For entangling the rules of the country," he wrote, "and dirtying that which is under Heaven, there is nothing worse than this."[115]

In his rich collection of Northern Sung anecdotes, Chu Yü (1075–after 1119) provides a vivid example of this problem from the Yuan-yu period (1084–93):

A man named Liu from the foreign quarter of Kuang-chou (Kuang-tung) married an imperial clanswoman, and received the office of tso-pan tien-chih. When Liu died, the clanswoman had no sons, and his family fought over the division of property, causing someone to use the memorial drum to complain. The court was alarmed that a clanswoman had married [a family in] the foreign quarter, and forbid it. It required that [the groom's family] have at least a generation of officeholding in order to marry a clanswoman.[116]

That a commoner probably of foreign origins from the southernmost part of the empire could marry a clanswoman and that his family could subsequently wrangle over the division of property after his death (undoubtedly the issue was the large dowry she had brought with her) provide eloquent testimony to the lack of control exercised by the court by the beginning of Che-tsung's reign. Even more remarkable, metaphorically and substantively, is a 1088 memorial by the drafting official P'eng Ju-li (1041–94) asking for a clarification of the marriage regulations for *t'an-wen* clansmen and women. Noting that they were barred from marrying with "non-elite families" (*fei shih-tsu chih chia*), he said he did not know what was meant by that phrase because the specific occupational prohibitions applied only to mourning kin, thus opening the way to marriages with officials via purchase and even those with treasonous backgrounds. He then continued:

In my opinion, that which accumulates greatly will flow lengthily and, when far from the source, will form a great lake. That is the nature of things. Now among the Son of Heaven's kin, if the ancestors reaching to the seventh generation are not forgotten, then their descendents stretching into the distance also cannot but be acclaimed. Even though the *t'an-wen* kin have all issued from the imperial ancestors and are identically connected to the body of the state (*kuo-t'i*), they are made dirty, rustic, and remote, and all can be taken [in marriage] as commodities. This does not honor the imperial ancestors.[117]

The consequences of this he then painted in vivid if melodramatic colors:

Powerful merchants and great traders, using wealth to dominate their communities, now pay from three to five thousand strings of cash to enter [officialdom] as instructors and registrars, and so steal the name of "elite family" (*shih-tsu*). By further payment of several thousand strings, they can seek to become palace kin [i.e., marry with the imperial clan] and thus gain the status of "official household" (*kuan-hu*). Stealing favor, robbing the state, relying on force, and humiliating the weak, how can this not be a disgrace to the state?[118]

With this last assertion, P'eng adds a dimension to our notions of clan marriage exchanges, for here we see a different, sub rosa, exchange of money for marriage and its attendant office, or at least allegations of it. Even more striking are the images he uses and the attitudes they reveal. Although the common Sung metaphor for the imperial clan was "Heavenly branches,"

P'eng talks of the "body of the state," which can be sullied (thus echoing Liu Shu), but even more about a stream that flows to make a lake. His concern is with the purity of the imperial kin, and that was most threatened by the marriage of women.

In his choice of metaphors, P'eng aptly illustrated the dilemma that the imperial clan posed to the state in the late eleventh century. If non-mourning kin were part of the Heavenly lake, how could its purity be maintained even as those kin were being severed from the court's support? The allowance provisions for non-mourning kin enacted under Che-tsung indicate a recognition that total severance was not desirable, but as we will see in the following chapter, this, too, was not deemed a satisfactory solution.

FIVE

The Creation of Secondary Centers

Between the year 1100, when the young Chao Chi (1082–1135) succeeded his prematurely deceased brother Che-tsung to become Hui-tsung (r. 1100–1126), the eighth Sung emperor, and 1126, when the Jurchen Chin invaded from the north to capture the retired Hui-tsung, his son Ch'in-tsung (1100–61; r. 1126–27), and thousands of imperial clansmen, the imperial clan underwent dramatic change. Clan families, which were in the process of dispersing among the general population, found themselves uprooted again, this time by the costly and ambitious reform program of Hui-tsung and his primary grand councilor, Ts'ai Ching (1046–1126). Even more than the decision a generation earlier to continue allowances and privileges for non-mourning kin, this program distinguished the Sung clan from its historical predecessors, marking it as unique even before the dramatic traumas of 1126 and beyond.

Ts'ai Ching's Reform

The start of the new direction for the imperial clan can be dated with some precision, for on the twelfth day of the eleventh month of 1102, Ts'ai Ching submitted a long memorial dealing with a broad spectrum of clan affairs, and it was accepted on all counts by the emperor. At this point Hui-tsung had been on the throne for just under two years, but only in the latter half of 1102 had the general direction of the court's policies become apparent.

Hui-tsung himself had been an unexpected choice as emperor after the heirless Che-tsung died at age 24 *sui* following a short illness. Only nineteen *sui* at the time and the eleventh son of Shen-tsung (although he was the second oldest surviving son), Chao Chi, who was then the Prince of Tuan, was not in line to become emperor and became so only at the insistence of the Empress Dowager Ch'en, who overruled the protests of the grand councilor Chang Tun (1035–1105).[1] One reason for the empress's support may have been his youth and presumed malleability, and for the first three months of his reign, Hui-tsung ruled jointly with the empress dowager acting as co-regent.[2] Once he began ruling on his own—particularly after her death at the beginning of 1101—he began to move decisively (or disastrously, in the view of many historians). As had Che-tsung when he gained his majority in 1094, he favored the reformers who traced themselves to Wang An-shih against the "anti-reformers" who had flourished during the Yuan-yu regency; one of his first actions was to declare a new reign period beginning in 1102 called "exalting [Hsi-]ning" (Ch'ung-ning), in honor of his father's Hsi-ning period. Unlike Che-tsung, he employed ministers whose zealous partisanship and vindictiveness were extreme, even when measured by the standards of the earlier reform and anti-reform periods.

Among Hui-tsung's ministers, the most important by far was Ts'ai Ching, who, with a few breaks, served as grand councilor from 1102 until 1125; indeed, such were his power and influence that it is difficult to discern which initiatives were his and which Hui-tsung's, much like Shen-tsung and Wang An-shih in the first decade of Shen-tsung's reign. Ts'ai, a native of the Fu-chien commandary of Hsing-hua, received his *chin-shih* in 1070 and was an ardent supporter of the New Policies, although that did not deter him from aligning himself with Ssu-ma Kuang in 1085 when the latter proposed restoring the "drafted service system" (*ch'ai-i fa*) for village administration, thereby undoing one of the major reforms of the New Policies.[3] Although Ts'ai became minister of revenue in 1094, and was associated with Chang Tun, his dramatic rise to the grand councilorship is generally credited to the patronage of the eunuch commander T'ung Kuan (d. 1126), who met Ts'ai in Hang-chou in early 1102 when T'ung was collecting rare rocks and other objects for the emperor and Ts'ai was serving in administrative exile.[4]

In the months that followed Ts'ai's appointment as grand councilor in the fourth month of 1102, the court, at Ts'ai's request, moved in two directions. First, it took steps to cripple the political opposition, labeling 120 members of the Yuan-yu faction a treasonous clique and inscribing their names in stone, and demoting over 500 opponents in all.[5] Second, it undertook a number of major legislative initiatives. These included the revival of an empire-wide tea monopoly;[6] the consolidation of the entire salt administration under the control of the central government;[7] the establishment of a system of charity clinics throughout the empire;[8] the creation of an educational system (the San-she fa or Three Hall System), which mandated an integrated hierarchy of government schools extending from the counties through the prefectures to the Imperial University in K'ai-feng;[9] and the program for the imperial clan. These measures shared a statist approach: institutional boldness, control by the central government, and a willingness to commit significant resources—often those of the local governments.

Ts'ai Ching's memorial on the imperial clan consists of nine sections, each with its own recommendations. One deals with education, four with the examinations and other methods of official recruitment, one with the support of poor clan members stranded in the provinces, and three—the centerpiece—with a proposal to create two regional residential complexes.[10] For Ts'ai, the clan's problems stemmed from the huge increase in the numbers of non-mourning kin who were both deprived of social and economic security and largely beyond the control of the government. The picture that he paints of these clansmen is bleak: "Today, the distant kin live all over the capital. . . . Coming and going [at the residences] is not prohibited, and social intercourse is not regulated. Laws and prohibitions are constantly violated. The poor [clansmen] who cannot provide [for themselves] are virtually like the common people (*ch'i-min*), without the means to support their parents and children, and without houses for shelter from the wind and rain."[11] The distant clansmen had been given land, noted Ts'ai, but that merely exacerbated matters, for "with residences spread out in the nearby prefectures, there is nothing that we can do when they break the law."[12] Moreover, the position of the clansmen had not been significantly improved by giving them access to examinations and official service, as Shen-tsung had hoped. The appointment of clan teachers had lapsed, thus depriving clan youths of a meaningful education. Few had availed themselves of the opportunity to take even the undemanding *liang-shih* (measurement examination), an examination for clansmen that had been in existence since 1069 and was comparable in status—though not in other particulars—to the facilitated examinations.[13] Moreover, the few who had succeeded were narrowly trained and poorly prepared to serve as officials.[14]

The solutions that Ts'ai proposed addressed all these elements: land and residence, education and examinations, and official service. The first of these was the primary one, however, for using the notion of land grants, he proposed reconsolidating the imperial clan, bringing all the distant kin into two vast residential complexes, which he called *Tun-tsung yuan*, or Halls of Extended Clanship.

The Tun-tsung Halls

Ts'ai Ching took as his starting point the idea that distant kin be given land. Although land grants had been mentioned in the restructuring of the imperial clan under Shen-tsung, and Ts'ai cited that fact, there is no evidence that clansmen were in fact given such grants on a broad scale. However, the idea of land grants had many pre-Sung precedents, and it is hardly surprising as a foundation for Ts'ai's reforms.

Specifically, Ts'ai proposed that in the Western Capital (Ho-nan fu, or Lo-yang, some 175 kilometers west of K'ai-feng) and Southern Capital (Ying-t'ien fu, some 125 kilometers east-south-east), the local governments collect unsold "government land" (*kuan-t'ien*) from the metropolitan and surrounding prefectures. Within each prefecture, an "imperial clan official estate"(*tsung-shih kuan-chuang*) was to be established and managed by a local official, who would oversee it jointly with the vice-prefect. Two clerks were to handle the day-to-day affairs of the estate, and one-third of the income of each was to be kept in reserve against floods or droughts, with the remainder used for the support of clan members. The program was to begin in the Western Capital, and Ts'ai proposed an initial appropriation of 10,000 *ch'ing* of fields, the equivalent of over 160,000 acres.[15]

With the income from these endowments, Tun-tsung Halls were to be established in both capitals. Ts'ai does not appear to have envisioned these as unitary residences, for he suggests that government buildings be used. If government buildings were insufficient, residences could be built on open lands far from the marketplaces, although it was also possible for clansmen to live in residences in neighboring prefectures of the two capitals. In each capital, an Outer Office of Clan Affairs (Wai tsung-cheng ssu) was to be established, headed by sagely clansmen, with two officials from the prefectural staffs appointed to serve as aide and registrar. These offices were to be responsible for clan affairs outside K'ai-feng.[16]

Although the Tun-tsung Halls were generally intended for all clansmen beyond the *t'an-wen* generation, Ts'ai specified that the first group to take up residence in the halls should be those who had neither parents nor brothers and who lacked a titular office at the level of general (*chiang-chün*), vice-commissioner (*fu-shih*), or above. Those with parents and brothers could move into the halls if they wished. Finally, boats outfitted like those for regular officials were to be obtained to transport them to their new homes.[17]

The biographical records are silent on the subject of the Tun-tsung Halls, and we do not know how clan members reacted to the order to move to the secondary capitals; some may have viewed it as a welcome opportunity, but others undoubtedly saw it as a form of exile that took them away from their friends and relatives and from the pleasures and excitement of the great metropolis of K'ai-feng. The actual transfers of the clan members seem to have been somewhat gradual, for in the ninth month of 1104 it was reported that 325 clan members had arrived at the Southern Capital, which must have represented only a portion of those who were supposed to move. The context of this figure is interesting, for the memorial in which it was cited concerned the right of clan members to receive a monthly allowance of grain from the public granary for the production of wine. The ensuing edict determined that adult members should receive two piculs (*shih*) per month of distillery grain, and children from five to fifteen *sui* half that, and that children younger than five should not make wine.[18] Apparently the privilege of wine making was one of the economic prerogatives given the clan in their move to the provinces.

The next general report on the Tun-tsung Halls is in an edict from the third month of 1109, which painted a dismal picture. In it Hui-tsung noted that the original intention of the Tun-tsung Halls had been to provide housing outside the capital, to support those without stipends, and to educate the youth. "Yet, year after year some of the clansmen in the other capitals ignore [this] and break the law. The officials cannot stop them, and the people consider them to be a disturbance. The Confucian teachers are numerous, yet the students few. The officials are excessive and affairs troublesome." He therefore ordered the closing of both Tun-tsung Halls and the termination of the related official posts. Clan housing would return to local government control, and the clan estates be placed under the ever normal granaries. The clan families were to have two months to vacate, they were to be given boat and postal station passes, and they were permitted to reside in or near the Mu-ch'in and Kuan-ch'in residences.[19]

It is hard to know what to make of this edict, for we lack corroborating documents that would help explain it. That the clansmen were difficult to control is quite understandable; given the newness of their presence in the Western and Southern capitals and their august imperial connection, local officials must have been perplexed as to how they should best be handled. But it is also possible that the Tun-tsung Halls' fate was linked to that of Ts'ai Ching, for just over two months after this edict Ts'ai was removed from the grand councilorship, accused by critics of treasonous activities. It would be almost three years before Ts'ai returned to office, and in that time severe cutbacks were made in his educational program.[20] More to the point, in the seventh month of 1112, just three months after Ts'ai's reinstatement, the Tun-tsung Halls were revived.

The edict of 1112 was reminiscent of Ts'ai Ching's 1102 memorial in stating as its central concern the ever growing numbers of clansmen, including many among the distant kin who were too poor to sustain themselves, and it noted that their predicament was a result of Hui-tsung's having disbanded the halls. The emperor therefore ordered the total restoration of the two halls as they were prior to 1109, generous allowances for clansmen and clanswomen, and more liberal provisions for officeholding, a point discussed below.[21]

In the years that followed the re-establishment of the Tun-tsung Halls, they flourished and grew. A report from 1114 on both the capitals describes the building of sixteen clan residences (*kung-yuan*) with 1,427 rooms (*chien*). The halls were functioning in accordance with the pre-1109 rules, there were ample funds for the wedding expenses of clanswomen, the Outer Offices of Clan Affairs had recently prepared housing for another 48 clansmen who were expected to arrive shortly, and 215 clan youths had been persuaded to enter the clan schools.[22] Impressive as these figures might be, they are over-shadowed by statistics from an edict of 1120, which, while objecting to the overly generous treatment accorded certain clansmen and the general costli-ness of the halls, notes that the two complexes had an endowment of 44,000 *ch'ing* of fields (ca. 660,000 acres) and over 23,600 rooms.[23]

These figures, which almost certainly represent the maximum size of the Tun-tsung Halls, must give us pause. Although there are no figures for the number of clan members in residence at the halls, we can make some esti-mates. The specially targeted population consisted of the two generations beyond *t'an-wen*, that is, the sixth and seventh for the T'ai-tsu and T'ai-tsung branches, and the fifth and sixth for the Wei-wang branch. The clansmen in this group, we know from Table 2.2 (p. 31), numbered just over 10,600, although we must keep in mind that many clansmen in the seventh genera-tion, especially, were not born until the Southern Sung (see Table 2.3, p. 32), and many clansmen in the T'ai-tsung branch were mourning relatives and remained in K'ai-feng.[24] With that in mind, a conservative guess would be that the Tun-tsung Halls housed some 5,000 clansmen in all. Adding an equal number of women would give 10,000 clan members in the halls,[25] which would mean that each member was supported by over four *ch'ing*—or over 60 acres—of land, a generous level of support by any measure.

By way of comparison, in 1109 it was reported that empire-wide the Three Halls System of schools, which Ts'ai Ching had also established in 1102, had a total of 105,990 *ch'ing* of fields, 155,454 *ying* (another term for room) of buildings, of which 95,298 were in school buildings, and 167,622 students.[26] Thus the school system had roughly twice the landholdings and almost seven times the buildings as the two clan complexes, but its students outnumbered clan members at least sixteenfold (or if only clansmen are considered, at least 32-fold). But whereas the schools and their landholdings were spread throughout the empire, the Tun-tsung Halls were limited to two regions. Unfortunately there is to my knowledge no evidence pertaining to the impact of the halls upon the Southern and Western Capitals, but we will see below that Ch'üan-chou, which housed one of the two major clan centers in the Southern Sung and which was a far larger metropolis than either of these capitals, found maintaining a much smaller clan population costly and troublesome.

The government's support for the non-mourning imperial kin, we can only conclude, was generous. Although we lack allowance schedules for clan members like that described in Chapter 4 from 1094, all clan members were entitled to monthly food and cash allowances, allowances of grain to make wine, and special allowances for marriages and funerals. In addition, special arrangements were made at the Tun-tsung Halls for orphans, widows, and divorced clanswomen who had returned to the halls. In fact, there were even allowances for the remarriage of clanswomen.[27]

One important issue, for which there is mixed evidence, is the extent of choice that distant kin had in deciding to live at the Tun-tsung Halls. Although Ts'ai Ching's memorial of 1102 stressed that relocation was voluntary for those with parents or brothers in K'ai-feng, it appears that others had no choice. In 1106 an edict forbade officials to force clansmen to move against their wishes, and it seems that there was a desire to avoid sundering families, especially in cases in which there were grandparents to be cared for.[28] At the same time, barriers were erected to stop clansmen in the Tun-tsung Halls from returning to K'ai-feng. In 1116, elaborate procedures were enacted for clansmen traveling to K'ai-feng to visit relatives or to take examinations.[29] And a year later, an edict ordered all clansmen from the Tun-tsung Halls who had moved to K'ai-feng to be sent back to the two capitals.[30]

Although the initial rationale for the halls was to view them as a form of land grant that had historically been given to distant imperial kin, the result was to return the non-mourning kin to the paternal embrace of the government. Their lives were less affluent and certainly more provincial than those of their kin who remained in the Mu-ch'in and Kuang-ch'in residences, but one wonders if they were essentially different.

There was one change, however: to a large extent the Tun-tsung Halls were a concern of both the Great Office of Clan Affairs—to which we next turn—and the regular government, and not simply of the emperor and court. The management of both the halls and the imperial clan estates involved local officials in the Western and Southern capitals. And as noted above, the moving force behind them seems to have been Ts'ai Ching rather than Hui-tsung. Not only was the general approach much like that of Ts'ai's other major reforms, but the halls' fortunes were closely linked to Ts'ai's personal ups and downs.[31] Moreover, Ts'ai penchant for acting through elaborate bureaucracies, as in the Tun-tsung Halls, was also evident in the Great Office, which reached the height of its complexity in this period.

The Great Office and Its Sections

Our primary source for the Great Office under Hui-tsung comes from a remarkable memorial submitted by the Secretariat in 1122.[32] This followed Ts'ai Ching's penultimate fall from grace (he was to return as grand councilor briefly in 1125), and like many other documents from this period, it is concerned with retrenchment rather than new initiatives—in this case, reductions from the inflated levels that had been achieved back to what they had been under Shen-tsung—but what stands out are not the reductions but rather the organizational complexity that the memorial describes.

At this time, the Great Office was divided into six sections (*an-hsi*), and the memorial describes the functional responsibilities of each:

1. The Scholar Section (*shih an-hsi*) oversaw the affairs of Southern Rank clansmen as well as the mourning and *t'an-wen* kin: specifically, marriage, housing, the receipt of name and office, requests for office by the husbands of clanswomen, recommendations for imperial grace, and requests for both temple guardianships and transfers from guard official to regular official status.

2. The Household Section (*hu an-hsi*) handled petitions from the Southern Rank and other clansmen, but dealt primarily with the non-mourning kin. Its responsibilities included the reporting of genealogical information (births, marriages, deaths), family segmentation, marriages, housing, and the care of those who had become orphaned, indigent, or otherwise "worn out," and particularly the allowances allotted for these needs.

3. The Rites Section (*i an-hsi*) oversaw court attendance, sacrifices, affairs of the Imperial Ancestral Temple, and requests to enter monastic orders, and supervised clan education and the measurement examination (*liang-shih*).[33]

4. The Military Section (*ping an-hsi*) was responsible for clansmen serving as personal guards (presumably the honorific guard officials) and the supply of horses for the clan.

5. The Legal Section (*hsing an-hsi*) was concerned with legal and punitive

matters, especially those involving the clan/non-clan interactions. The punishments that it oversaw included demotions and incarcerations.

6. The Works Section (*kung an-hsi*) was responsible for the building and repair of residences outside K'ai-feng and other miscellaneous business.

Because this document stands alone, we can say little about unmentioned functions or how the sections worked. The *Sung History's* description of the Great Office derives from the Shen-tsung era (see Chapter 4) and mentions the existence of five sections; so it seems likely that the office grew piecemeal under Hui-tsung rather than developing dramatically, as the Tun-tsung Halls had. At the same time, with the creation of satellite residences and clan institutions in the Western and Southern capitals, the organizational problems of the Great Office were undoubtedly multiplied, for it continued to have authority over most aspects of life for the entire clan. Concerning two of those aspects—education and recruitment, and officeholding—the records say a great deal.

Education and Recruitment

As we saw in Chapter 4, although examination competition was accorded a central role in Shen-tsung's reforms, few clansmen passed the examinations either in his reign or in Che-tsung's. A major reason is that little was done to improve the education of clan youths. In particular, no special educational provisions were made for non-mourning clansmen. Although a proposal to create a clan school (*tsung-hsueh*) had been approved in 1091, nothing had come of it, and although Hui-tsung ordered the project revived in 1101, there is no evidence for the existence of a single clan academy at any time in his reign.[34]

Instead the emphasis continued to be on schools and teachers in the clan residences, as it had long been, but Ts'ai moved vigorously in his 1102 memorial to give substance to both. Each residence (*kung*) was to establish upper and lower schools (*ta-hsueh, hsiao-hsueh*) and employ teachers (*chiao-shou*) in each. The schools were to employ a testing and selection system (*k'ao-hsuan fa*), with monthly essays and seasonal examinations used to select those most accomplished in the literary arts. Clan youths of 10 *sui* and above were to study at the lower schools, and those 20 and above at the upper schools, although boys below 10 and 20 could enter the lower and upper schools, respectively, if they wished. Attendance was mandatory, and a schedule of punishments for absences was described, not only for the boys but also for the responsible officials.[35]

Ts'ai's attempt to improve clan education met with some success, at least in part because the government continued to stress it. In 1106 and 1107, teachers were rewarded for having successful students, and although in the first case the teacher was from a K'ai-feng residence school, in the second the school was at a residence in the Southern Capital.[36] In 1108, two officials (one a clansman) were demoted for proposing that clansmen who had failed a school examination nevertheless be advanced to the next level.[37]

Even more informative are a memorial and ensuing edict from 1108 that attempted to work out the linkage between the clan schools and the Imperial University. This was an important matter, for the Three Hall System consolidated the schools of the empire into a single system. Every school had graded classes or halls—outer, inner, and upper, in ascending order—and students progressed through them on the basis of tests and evaluations. From the county schools, students progressed to the prefectural schools, and then to the outer hall of the university, which had its own campus called the Pi-yung, and finally to its inner and upper halls. Moreover, graduation from the upper hall of the university replaced the examinations, with the graduates receiving *chin-shih* degrees.[38] The memorial noted that clansmen from the upper halls of the clan schools were permitted to take the departmental examination along with the prefectural school graduates and that six in ten were passed—a remarkably generous figure, since the ratio for other candidates was one in ten.[39] The problem was what to do with the unsuccessful clansmen. The prefectural graduates had the right to stay and study in the Pi-yung, but the clansmen were sent back to their schools. In response, the emperor gave the clansmen the right to enroll at the Directorate School (Kuo-tzu hsueh—literally "School for national sons"), an adjunct to the university reserved for the children of officials. This demonstrates the increasing integration of clansmen into the recruitment structure of the empire at large. The clansmen maintained significant privileges, to be sure, and they would continue to do so, but this was nevertheless an important step in their general movement into the ranks of the literati.

A rare description of contemporary clan education from the epitaph of Chao Tzu-chou (AAEBFAE; 1089–1142) provides a brief glimpse of the clan examinations in practice. Tzu-chou, a precocious and brilliant youth, enrolled in school at the Southern Capital shortly before 1107. His biographer states that at that time the attitude in the clan examination halls was that "one could pass without studying," and that when examinations were held, "even before the essays were submitted, people came and went, laughing and jeering." Despite this, Tzu-chou placed first in the clan examinations of 1107, receiving a *chin-shih* degree, and went on to a distinguished and precedent-setting official career.[40]

In the period following Ts'ai Ching's return to the grand councilorship in 1112—there are no records of educational activities in the 1109–12 period—educational conditions in the clan apparently improved; at least references to them are generally positive. In 1114, the emperor hosted a feast for clansmen—the first recorded by the *Sung hui-yao* since Jen-tsung's reign—and spoke of his delight at the improvements that had been accomplished within the clan. He rewarded those in attendance lavishly, and after noting that he had counted over a hundred clansmen in the genealogical register without office, he granted those without office official rank and promoted those with office.[41] In the same year a clansman serving in a minor office was given permission to enter the local prefectural school and participate in its examinations, thus setting a precedent for clan access to the government schools.[42] Finally, in 1117 the emperor promoted the clan head of a princely residence in the Western Capital because of the success of students in his residence's schools.[43]

Although sketchy, the historical evidence suggests that it was during Hui-tsung's reign that the imperial clansmen first became significantly engaged in education and the examinations. This certainly was the goal of Ts'ai Ching, whose role as the creator of the Three Hall System made him one of the outstanding educational reformers in Chinese history. In an attempt to provide some impetus to the clansmen's examination efforts, Ts'ai proposed in his 1102 memorial that a one-time special examination consisting of two questions on either the Classics or law be held for clansmen age 25 *sui* or older, with those passing to be considered "supplemental *chin-shih*" (*fu chin-shih*).[44] It is noteworthy that in the clansmen's biographies it is among those who came of age under Hui-tsung that we first find frequent note of examination success. In addition to Chao Tzu-chou, noted above,

Chao Tzu-sung (AADBDFA; d. 1132) received his *chin-shih* in 1106,[45] Chao Ling-chin (AADBHF; d. 1158) in 1108,[46] Chao Hsun-chih (CABBFH; d. 1129) in 1112,[47] Chao Tzu-ch'eng (ABBACEA; d. 1144) and Chao Shih-tsan (BCAAHA; 1095–1160) in 1119,[48] Chao Ling-ken (AADCBK) in 1120,[49] and Chao Tzu-hsiao (AADEHAF; 1102–67) in 1124.[50] Most remarkably, examination success could even be found in the imperial palace, for Chao K'ai (Hui-B, Fl. 1118-26), the third son of Hui-tsung, placed first in the palace examination of 1118, received a *chin-shih* degree, and went on to take charge of the capital security office (Huang-ch'eng ssu) during the 1120s.[51]

Examination success, of course, was not an end in itself but rather a means to an official career. But before we consider the record of clansmen as officials under Hui-tsung, we should acknowledge a little noted but important provision in Ts'ai Ching's 1102 memorial, namely, that non-mourning kin be permitted to use the *yin* privilege to receive official rank, in accordance with the provisions for regular officials.[52] The thrust of this was to make office vastly more accessible to the non-mourning clansmen, since virtually all had fathers and grandfathers with relatively high rank (almost all guard offices were quite high in rank).

Clansmen as Officials

Thanks to their increasing success in the examinations and their expanded access to officialdom through the *yin* privilege, clansmen began appearing in growing numbers as regular officials during the Hui-tsung years. Of course, there had been some clansmen-officials as early as the 1070s, but they were few in number. One such example was Chao Tzu-ch'ih (AADBDAD; n.d.), who as a child had been called a "steed" (i.e., a genius) by a visiting Su Shih (1036–1101). After receiving office through exercise of the *yin* privilege, he began a distinguished career by serving as registrar (*pu*) of the Directorate for Imperial Manufactories and then in a provincial post in Ho-nan under Che-tsung.[53] Chao Shu-tan (CDADA; 1051-1103) was also able to break out of the confines of monopoly office postings when he served as military administrator for infantry and cavalry in Huai-tung and then in Ching-hsi-nan.[54] But these were exceptions, and most clansmen-officials held posts that were minor and unremarkable.

Under Hui-tsung, two noteworthy changes accompanied the growing numbers of clansmen-officials. One was the development of a body of legislation concerning the distribution of clansmen in provincial posts, and the other involved the increasing spread of clansmen into the prestigious posts involving personal governance of the people (*ch'in-min*), such as magistracies and prefectships.

In the appointment of clansmen to provincial positions, the court exhibited understandable concern about where they were sent and in what numbers. In 1101, extra-quota positions for clansmen (*t'ien-ch'ai*—positions beyond the normal quotas) were terminated for the northeastern circuits of Ho-tung and Shensi, although these were offset by increases in such positions in more central and southern circuits.[55] In the same vein, in 1116 and again in 1119, the emperor prohibited clansmen from serving in border posts, where security concerns were greater.[56]

In 1111 a more general kind of limitation was initiated, when it was decreed that no more than one clansman could hold a senior military or civil position in any prefecture, and that no more than three clansmen could serve concurrently in a prefecture and no more than two in a county.[57] Although this was most likely a precautionary step rather than a response to a problem, this edict was important in serving as a model for similar quota legislation in the early Southern Sung.

One way of handling ranked officials who were clansmen (and nonclansmen for that matter) was to appoint them to extra-quota positions without duties (*pu-li-wu*), which provided them with a titular post and income. I have found no record of clansmen being given such positions, but it must have occurred, for in 1120 and again in 1124, objections were raised to such practices, and they were ordered stopped, although the very fact that the order was repeated suggests that the practice was entrenched.[58]

Evidence for the increase in the numbers of clansmen holding positions of local governance—the second change in officeholding under Huitsung—is primarily biographical. Whereas the biographies contain only a handful of instances of clansmen serving as regular officials from the late eleventh and early twelfth centuries, and then almost always for state monopoly positions, for the 1120s I have found seventeen clansmen-officials: seven prefects, three magistrates, three vice-prefects, two vice-magistrates, one minor civil official, and just one state monopoly official. Of course, this distribution undoubtedly reflects the bias of literati authors, among other things. But just as clearly, the figures reflect the maturation of a cohort of clansmen into more prestigious and senior civil positions in local government.

The official service of one clansman stood out from all others: Chao Tzu-ch'ih (AADBDAD), whose "steed"-like promise and service under Che-tsung is mentioned above. From his start with the Directorate for Imperial Manufactories, Tzu-ch'ih rose through positions within the fiscal bureaucracy, such as a river official on the Ts'ai River near K'ai-feng and then as fiscal vice-commissioner for Shan-hsi. Thanks perhaps to his river post experience, during the Ch'ung-ning (1102–6) and Ta-kuan (1107–10) periods he supervised numerous construction projects, even though his acquaintances apparently looked down on him for such mundane undertakings. Then in the Hsuan-ho period (1119–25), Tzu-ch'ih became the center of attention when he proposed to Hui-tsung that iron coins be minted to relieve the hardship caused by Ts'ai Ching's minting of tin coins (copper coins had long been the standard). Not only did Hui-tsung approve, but he also gave Tzu-ch'ih the responsibility for overseeing the distribution of over one million strings of the new coins in the five central circuits, where they were to be exchanged for the old copper coins held by people and used to stabilize grain prices. However, when Tzu-ch'ih subsequently became convinced that the government was moving too quickly and coercively in the coin exchange—he reportedly received hundreds of complaints a day—he petitioned for relief for the people. Ts'ai was then able to attack him for having destroyed the fiscal system, and he was removed from office.[59]

What is remarkable about this case is not that Tzu-ch'ih lost out in a dispute with Ts'ai Ching, but rather that he was involved—indeed was a central player—in a weighty dispute over fiscal policy at all, for this clearly marked a departure from limitations hitherto placed on the political activities of clansmen. It would be interesting to know if his accusers called attention to his imperial clan status; the sources do not say, but it seems quite possible that it was an issue. At the same time, we must not overstate the case, for even when commissioned by Hui-tsung to oversee the distribution of the new coins, there is no indication that he was given high permanent office. Moreover, his very uniqueness makes it difficult to generalize from his example.

At the Northern Sung's End

Given the catastrophic changes that soon were to engulf the imperial clan, it might be useful to consider the character of the clan in the last years of the Northern Sung and trends within it. Although there is much that we do not know about the clan in this period, at least two points can be made with some assurance.

First, with the continuation of allowances and privileges for non-mourning clan members under Shen-tsung and Che-tsung, and even more with the creation of the Tun-tsung Halls, the government had committed itself to the indefinite support of the broader clan. The only reasonable place to truncate the clan was at the divide between mourning and non-mourning kin, and although Shen-tsung certainly moved toward cutting off the latter in 1069, subsequent actions rejoined them. This involved a price for the non-mourning kin; living in what must have been regarded as the backwaters of the Southern and Western capitals exemplified their second-class status. Nevertheless, given the resources that the state committed to the Tun-tsung Halls, theirs was hardly an impoverished existence. Moreover, as the mourning generations died out in K'ai-feng, the succeeding generations could look forward to increasing numerical dominance within the clan as a whole, and quite possibly provisions made for the return of at least some of them to the K'ai-feng residences.

Second, the transformation of clansmen from honorary guard officials to active regular officials was clearly under way. Clansmen still had far to go in terms of producing well-educated examination graduates who could compete with the *shih-ta-fu* for the more prestigious positions in local government, and with the exception of Chao Tzu-ch'ih, postings within the central government remained a terra incognita fraught with potential problems. Nevertheless, there is no reason to doubt that both these developments would have occurred, albeit slowly. Indeed, movement of clansmen into the *ch'in-min* positions was already well under way, as we have seen.

In two quite unintended ways, the imperial clan's unique configuration at the end of the Northern Sung was to prove vitally important. First, when the Jurchen conquered K'ai-feng and took into captivity the vast majority of clan members there, the existence of the two satellite centers enabled large numbers of clan members to escape to the south, and thus saved the clan as a significant institution. Second, those members who made it to the south, although overwhelmingly non-mourning kin, nevertheless constituted a reservoir of potential emperors. This surely was not a factor in Hui-tsung's thinking when he created the Tun-tsung Halls, for he had 31 sons and the idea that any of his successors might be heirless would have seemed far-fetched. Yet as we shall see below, on two occasions succession was to involve the adoption of clansmen who were non-mourning kin.[60] Thus the commitment to support the non-mourning kin and to define the clan broadly saved the dynasty.

SIX

Captivity, Resistance, and Opportunity

In 1126 disaster struck the Sung. Rampaging Tungusic Jurchen forces swept down from Manchuria, overrunning the north China plain, besieging and capturing K'ai-feng and with it both the sitting and the retired emperors, and then moving south. Reconstituted by an imperial prince in the south, the dynasty's existence hung for a time on the slenderest of threads, at least until a treaty in 1142 offered some respite.

Like the dynasty, the imperial clan came to the verge of extinction in 1126, at least as a privileged clan. When the Jurchen took as many as 3,000 K'ai-feng clan members, imperial relatives, and Sung officials into captivity, it must have seemed as if the end had come. In fact, for them it had. Yet for those clansmen who eluded the Jurchen, and there were many who fled south and contributed to the resistance to the invaders, the tragedy offered opportunities. For some it was the chance to die as martyrs opposing the Jurchen armies; others who made their way to the south discovered new social and political roles. Less and less was it possible to define the imperial clan simply as an appendage of monarchy. The unprecedented political and military activities of clansmen forced a redefinition of their relationship to the emperor and bureaucracy in ways that set the limits of their roles for the Southern Sung. In this chapter, we will consider both the political and the military events surrounding the fall of the Northern Sung, the flight to the south, the capture of most of the clan, resistance among clansmen-officials, and the establishment of a revived dynasty in southern China.

An Overview of the War

Narrowly considered, the Sung loss of northern China was the result of a disastrously ill-conceived alliance. In the eyes of Sung leaders, the rise of the Jurchen people in northern Manchuria (their sinicized Chin dynasty was founded there in 1115) presented an opportunity to defeat their old enemy, the Liao. In an agreement reached in 1120, both countries undertook to attack the Liao and to share thereafter in the spoils, and in 1123, with the Liao in full retreat (thanks to Chin rather than Sung fighting), a Sung-Chin treaty agreed on the return of Yen-ching and sixteen prefectures to the Sung. However, following the Chin capture of the Liao king in 1125 and Sung complaints that its share of Liao territory was insufficient, the Chin moved swiftly against the Sung. A two-pronged Jurchen campaign in the last months of 1125 resulted in the Sung loss of two prefectures and the besieging of the northern capital of T'ai-yuan in the west, and the Chin occupation of the north China plain above the Yellow River in the east. Although temporarily thwarted in their attempt to cross the river, the Chin returned the following year. In the fourth month of 1126 they besieged K'ai-feng, left following payment of a huge indemnity, but returned again in the eighth month and began a second siege, which lasted for four months and led to the surrender of the Sung court.[1]

Certainly there was more to this debacle than a poor alliance. The corruption and ineffectiveness of the Sung army, the court's vacillation over the proper response to the Chin invasion, eunuch interference in politics (particularly the infamous T'ung Kuan, who deserted his post as commander of Sung forces in the T'ai-yuan region in the face of Jurchen attack), as well as the general wastefulness of Hui-tsung's court, which weakened the empire, have all been named as contributing factors.[2] Even the most intelligent Sung statesmanship, however, would have had trouble containing the military might and aggressiveness of the Chin.

However we might view the causes of the Jurchen invasion today, for many at court in late 1125, responsibility for the disaster lay with the Son of Heaven. The historical analogy cited by loyalist ministers like Li Kang (1083–1140) was that of T'ang Hsuan-tsung, whose failure to abdicate when he fled Lo-yang and the rebel An Lu-shan in 755 complicated the situation for his successor, Su-tsung. In the last month of 1125, Hui-tsung assumed full responsibility for what had happened and designated his eldest son, Chao Huan (1100–61), crown prince. A month later he abdicated in favor of Huan, who became the ninth Sung emperor, Ch'in-tsung. This action was unprecedented in Sung history, and as John Haeger has argued, created a crisis for the Sung monarchy. Hui-tsung cooperated fully in turning over the reins of power to his son, and even left K'ai-feng for the Southern Capital so as to give him a free hand. But in contrast to the contemporary monarchy of Heian Japan, where the institution of retired emperors was venerable, the Sung had no such tradition, and Hui-tsung, by his very existence, inspired doubts about the authority of Ch'in-tsung.[3]

By all accounts, Ch'in-tsung was popular with most of the court and the populace of K'ai-feng, in no small part because he purged some of the most unpopular of Hui-tsung's ministers and curbed the power of the eunuchs.[4] However, he was no more successful than his father in the war against the Chin, in considerable part because the court continued to vacillate between resisting Chin demands and capitulating to them. In early 1126 the Jurchen besieged K'ai-feng for 33 days, withdrawing only after receiving a large indemnity from the Sung. But when in the eighth month Ch'in-tsung refused the Chin terms for peace, a new offensive began. The Jurchen armies returned to K'ai-feng, where a four-month siege ensued. After a failed Sung counteroffensive and increasingly desperate conditions, with people driven to starvation and cannibalism, the city fell. In early 1127, Ch'in-tsung and Hui-tsung (who had returned to K'ai-feng before the siege), together with over 1,300 people from the inner palace and somewhere between 900 and 3,000 members of the imperial clan, as well as numerous officials, attendants, and servants, were transported to the northern city of Yen-ching, where the great majority lived out the rest of their lives in captivity.[5]

That the Sung survived was due to the escape of Hui-tsung's ninth son, Chao Kou (1107–87), the Prince of K'ang, who was able to reconstitute the dynasty in the south. Early in 1126, the prince accompanied a Sung diplomatic mission to the Jurchen, who had demanded a Sung prince as a hostage. By one account he was released from Chin control and sent back to K'ai-feng after shooting so well in an archery contest that the Chin commander was convinced that he must be an imperial clansmen with military training rather than a prince.[6] But instead of returning to K'ai-feng, he was active in Hopei, attempting to rally loyalist forces on behalf of the court, and in late 1126 Ch'in-tsung bestowed him with the title of grand marshal (*ta yuan-shuai*) of all the armed forces. But following word of the fall of K'ai-feng and capture of the two emperors, he came under increasing pressure from his attending officials and others who had flocked to his banner to claim the emperorship. This he finally did on the first day of the fifth month of 1127 at the Southern Capital, becoming the tenth Sung emperor, posthumously known as Kao-tsung (r. 1127–62).[7]

To reign was not necessarily to rule, and the achievement of a legitimate and viable Southern Sung empire was a lengthy process with numerous crises in which dynastic extinction was narrowly averted. Although the war with the Chin lasted for another fifteen years, until 1142, the first four years were the most critical. In early 1128 a Chin sortie almost resulted in the capture of Kao-tsung at his temporary capital in Yang-chou, where he had moved a few months earlier. Escaping with a few followers by a nocturnal boat ride across the Yangtze, Kao-tsung moved first to Chien-k'ang (modern Nanking) and then further south to Hang-chou. In early 1129 a military coup in Hang-chou resulted in the forced and, it turned out, temporary abdication of Kao-tsung in favor of his three-year-old son. With the help of loyal ministers and generals, the coup was bloodlessly suppressed, but the fragility of Kao-tsung's regime had been revealed. Late that same year, a major Chin offensive south of the Yangtze again almost ended the dynasty. As the Jurchen army, having defeated the Sung army around Chien-k'ang, swept through the Yangtze delta, Kao-tsung fled to the coast and then to sea, making his way down to Wen-chou and even then only narrowly escaping the Chin pursuit, which had also taken to the sea. He was thus able to evade the Jurchen army—which was an expeditionary force rather than occupying army—until it withdrew to the north in the spring of 1130.[8]

The following twelve years witnessed a great deal of fighting, not all of it as one-sided as the encounters described above, but over time a standoff emerged, with the Huai River serving as a general border between the two empires in the east. In 1140 the Sung general Yueh Fei (1104–42) countered a Chin offensive so successfully that his troops drew to within a dozen miles of K'ai-feng, only to be recalled by Kao-tsung and the grand councilor Ch'in Kuei (1090–1155).[9] In Hang-chou, which had become the Southern Sung capital, Yueh was subsequently arrested and executed on trumped-up charges. This betrayal of Yueh, and with it the ending of the one serious threat by the Sung to retake the north, has been condemned by generations of Chinese, for whom Yueh has become a potent symbol of Chinese nationalism. For Kao-tsung, however, peace with the Chin and control over the military were more important than the reconquest of the north. Moreover, peace had the added benefit of keeping Ch'in-tsung in captivity, for until his death in 1156 he remained a potential threat to the legitimacy of Kao-tsung.[10]

Even while recognizing patterns in the Sung-Chin conflict such as those just described, we must be cognizant of the profoundly unsettled state of all of China in this period, especially in the late 1120s. The Chin capture of K'ai-feng and the imperial court did not ensure their control of northern China generally. For a few years at least, Sung loyalists continued to hold prefectures in the north and command significant forces. Similarly, the Jurchen did not constitute the only threat to Sung rule in the south. The country was awash with bandits and rebels, who often posed a more immediate challenge to the Sung than did the Chin.

Against this backdrop of extended warfare and disorder, the doings of the imperial clan were colorful, eventful, and often tragic. Most of the clan was taken into captivity, but many were actively involved in the resistance to the Jurchen, and not a few died as martyrs. The southward flight of clan families—at least those who had evaded the Jurchen—and institutions was complex, involving virtually every part of the southern empire. Finally, as clan members settled into unfamiliar locales, they found that more than the scenery had changed, and they began to explore the possibilities offered by the radically altered political and social realities as well as the dangers posed by them.

Captivity and Flight

Such is the nature of our sources that we can only imagine the humiliation and horror visited upon the K'ai-feng members of the imperial clan—and those captured elsewhere—when, first, their residences were looted by the Sung in order to meet Chin demands for indemnity, and then they were taken into custody and transported as prisoners to the north. But from the accounts of imperial princes, some sense of that horror remains.

In 1127, shortly after K'ai-feng's fall, the Jurchen demanded that the Sung court give up the crown prince, Chao Ch'en (Ch'in-A; b. 1117), then age eleven *sui*. Sun Fu (1078–1128), the co-administrator of the Bureau of Military Affairs and the prince's former tutor, wanted to find a look-alike who could be killed so that a body could be sent. But nothing came of this, and after five days, the prince's fate had become a matter of concern to the city populace. Fearing a popular uprising over the issue, several officials decided to settle the matter through compliance. The prince and his mother were seized by imperial guards and placed in a cart. According to the *Sung History*, officials and soldiers followed the cart protesting, and university students knelt in front of it. The prince called out, "Save my life, my people," and the sound of crying shook the heavens. But the cart went north.[11]

He did not go alone. According to a contemporary enumeration, the inner-palace entourage alone consisted of the two emperors, 23 imperial princes, seven other princes, sixteen imperial grandsons (including Chao Ch'en),[12] eight imperial sons-in-law, 181 empresses and imperial consorts (143 from Hui-tsung's harem, 38 from Ch'in-tsung's), 21 imperial princesses, 30 imperial granddaughters, 52 wives of princes, and 23 of their daughters. Moreover, they were accompanied by 146 eunuch attendants and 832 maids and serving women.[13]

From other princes we get scattered impressions of the trip north. The Prince of Ching, Chao I (Hui-D), who had briefly served as an envoy, was noteworthy for the devotion of his service to Ch'in-tsung while on the road. He served him daily, slept without undressing, and refused to eat meat; by the time they reached the north his hair had turned white.[14] While on the road, Ch'in-tsung encountered two of his uncles, Shen-tsung's tenth and twelfth sons, Chao Wu (Shen-B) and Chao Ssu (Shen-C), and said to them, "I wish we could die together." In fact, Wu died of starvation during a stop in Ch'ing-yuan fu, and Ssu died shortly after arriving in the north.[15]

Some princes and clansmen managed to escape en route. The most prominent was Ch'in-tsung's brother Chao Chen (Hui-O), the Prince of Hsin, who escaped in Chen-ting fu in Hopei and rallied forces in the area to the Sung cause, as we shall see below.[16] Chao Shih-ch'ien (BCBLHE) also escaped while in the two emperors' party, entered a Buddhist monastery, and disguised himself as a monk. Some time later he was able to make his way south, in monk's garb, and joined Kao-tsung's court in Shao-hsing, where he was received with honor.[17] Less fortunate was Chao Shih-ch'i (BCBGCB), who also escaped and with the help of local magnates in Hsing-chou (Hopei) began to resist the Chin, for he was soon captured and executed.[18]

The treatment meted out to the imperial captives varied. The two emperors were given noble titles,[19] and they and their immediate entourages were able to maintain at least a surface respectability, but the veneer was paper-thin. Stories circulated in the south that Kao-tsung's mother, the Lady Wei, had been taken by a Chin general as a concubine. James T. C. Liu dismisses these stories but notes that many palace women were mistreated, which added credence to the tales at the time.[20] In one case, which must have been the cause of great dissension, one of Ch'in-tsung's brothers, Chao O (Hui-L), the Prince of I, and his brother-in-law Liu Yen-wen, reported that the emperor's associates were plotting rebellion. The Chin authorities ordered Ch'in-tsung to investigate, and after three days the two Sung officials delegated—one of them Ts'ai T'iao, son of Ts'ai Ching and an imperial son-in-law himself—elicited confessions from Chao and Liu themselves, who were then executed by the Chin.[21] Thus the handling of the matter was left to Ch'in-tsung, even though the outcome—the death of the "guilty" party—was undoubtedly predetermined.

All the rest of the captives—princes, clan members, eunuchs, and officials—were made slaves, receiving meager allowances and utterly at the mercy of the Jurchen. According to Chao Tzu-ti (AADBDEB; d. 1128), a clansman who managed to get permission to go south, where he joined Kao-tsung's court and wrote an account of his time in the north, 1,800 clanswomen and imperial in-laws in a group under the Prince of P'u, Chao Chung-li (BCBGN), were quartered at the Hsien-lu Temple in Yen-shan (Liao Yen-ching and, later, Chin Chung-tu) and provided with a daily allowance of one *sheng* (just under a quart) of rice and a monthly ration of a *sheng* of salt. The men, however, did not fare as well. "Enduring hardship on the road and the bitterness of solitude," the prince, his Sung guards (and presumably accompanying clansmen, although they are not mentioned), were seized, bound, and constantly observed. After a year, 80 percent had died, leaving only 398 men.[22]

Clan members who evaded capture by the Jurchen headed south individually and in groups and began appearing in virtually every part of southern China. Initially their obvious destination was Kao-tsung's court, and
indeed a memorial from the administrator of the Southern Clan Office,
Chao Shih-niao (BCBIAG; 1084–1153), offers an informative overview of
affairs in the eighth month of 1127, three months after Kao-tsung's accession.
Clan members had entered Huai-nan in search of provisions, but in that
circuit only Yang-chou had sufficient space and resources for accommodating them. Shih-niao, however, expressed concern at their vulnerability, concentrated as they were north of the Yangtze, and suggested that if the clan
members crossed the river to Chen-chiang fu (he used the pre-1113 name of
Jun-chou), they would not be dependent for their support solely on the
Huai-nan administration. In response, Kao-tsung ordered clan members
from the Southern Capital to go to Chen-chiang, those from the Western
Capital to Yang-chou, and those from K'ai-feng to Chiang-ning fu.[23]

Two points should be noted here. First, imperial clan members were not
typical refugees. They were branches of the imperial tree, and every effort
had to be made to provide them with adequate housing, food, and clothing.
We have no descriptions of the clan en route, but it seems likely that they
took as many of their possessions as they could, and further, that they were
a demanding group, since they were accustomed to being fully supported.
Since that support necessarily had to come from local governments, there
were good economic reasons for splitting them up. Second, congregations
of clansmen were highly visible and potentially vulnerable as targets of the
Jurchen, since each represented a potential Chao claimant to the throne.
This was the first of a series of measures taken to move them south, as far
from the Jurchen as possible.

Over the next few years, this policy of moving the clan south combined
with various specific exigencies to create a remarkable fragmentation. In
early 1128, supervision over the Western Capital clan members was divided,
with Chao Shih-ts'ung (BCBGFA) heading one group in Kao-yu chün, and
Chao Ling-k'uang (AADFCH; 1069–1143) heading another in T'ai-chou,
both in Huai-nan-tung.[24] In the fourth month of 1129, a memorial from the
administrator of the Great Office, Chao Chung-ts'ung, described problems
that had arisen in accommodating clan members in Chiang-ning fu. Despite

a scarcity of housing owing to the demands of the military, they had put clan members up in temples and public buildings, but such were their numbers that Chung-ts'ung asked that they be sent further south, suggesting either Hsin-chou in Chiang-nan-tung or Ch'ien-chou in southern Chiang-nan-hsi. The latter was designated, although guard official clansmen were exempted so that they could serve at court.[25]

Three months later, the clansmen from Chiang-ning together with the Great Office personnel had traveled beyond Ch'ien-chou to Kuang-chou (Canton) in the far south, where for the next three years the Great Office was to maintain its headquarters. The exemption that allowed some clansmen to remain with the court was already coming under fire, both because of the difficulty of finding housing and coping with inflation at the temporary capital (at this point, Hang-chou), and because of Great Office objections to having the Southern Rank clansmen—who at this point were their primary charges within the clan—in two such widely separated locales. It therefore proposed that the Southern Rank clansmen in Hang-chou be sent to Kuang-chou, and Kao-tsung approved, although whether this was carried out we do not know.[26]

In the last month of 1129, the Southern Capital clan offices and clan members, who had earlier been in Yang-chou, voyaged by sea to the southern Fu-chien metropolis of Ch'üan-chou.[27] Although there was some planning, with clan officials being given funds to hire ships and an advance contingent going ahead to make preparations, the fact that this occurred at just the time that Kao-tsung himself was fleeing the Jurchen by sea suggests that the Southern Capital clansmen were also engaged in flight. But whatever their reasons for going, the Southern Capital clansmen stayed in Ch'üan-chou, which was to become the pre-eminent center for the imperial clan in the Southern Sung.

Elsewhere, the situation was chaotic, with temporary clan offices springing up in numerous locations to deal with the scattered clan. These included Hung-chou (Chiang-hsi), where a temporary office (*chih ssu-suo*) had been established, which was given permission to obtain housing and financial support from local officials according to the Chiang-ning precedent;[28] Ch'ien-chou, where in late 1130 clan officials asked that their office be moved to Chi-chou further north because of Ch'ien-chou's miasmic atmosphere and the threat of bandits;[29] and Nan-hsiung chou, just south of Ch'ien-chou in Kuang-tung, where Great Office officials asked for financial relief to support clansmen originating in the Western Capital.[30] A report from 1131 provides an added twist concerning the Western Capital clansmen, saying that their office had been moved to Hu-chou in Liang-che.[31]

In a very different vein, an edict from 1129 addressed the plight of clanswomen and wives who had become separated from the men in their families and made their way south. It directed prefectural and county officials to give them cash and food allowances. Those with active officials in their families were to join them; the others were to go to the Western and Southern Clan Offices, as appropriate.[32] The story of Chao Po-shen provides an example of such sundering of families. His father, Tzu-hui, was serving in the military in Ti-chou (Ho-pei-tung) when the war broke out and was captured by the Jurchen. Po-shen, then very young, and his mother, Lady Chang, traveled to Ti-chou and stayed there to await his father's release. But his father was killed, and when the Jurchen made their push across the Yellow River, he and his mother were separated. Making his way south, for over twenty years Po-shen traveled the empire in search of her. In 1151, he finally found her in Ssu-ch'uan, and they were tearfully reunited.[33]

In the ninth month of 1131, a drafting official in the Secretariat, Hu Wen-hsiu, submitted a report in support of a proposal by the Prince of P'u, Chao Chung-shih (BCBGF; d. 1137), to combine the Western and Southern Clan Offices so as to reduce the administrative personnel, and in it provided an invaluable census of the clan members under the two offices (see Table 6.1).[34] Since we know that clan members were scattered throughout the empire, the 217 men and 298 women cannot be taken as a measure of clan members in the south. Nevertheless, these were far and away the two largest groupings of the clan, and the fact that, combined, they came to just over five hundred, provides at least an indication of the enormous losses that the clan had suffered.

Writing about seventy years later, the historian Li Hsin-ch'uan cites virtually the same numbers of clan members and provides in addition figures for the government's annual expenditures on the Western and Southern clansmen circa 1131: 60,000 strings of cash for the larger Southern branch; 30,000 strings for the Western branch.[35] These were enormous amounts for

Table 6.1

Clan Members with the Southern and Western Offices, 1131

Category	Southern Capital Clan Office	Western Capital Clan Office	Totals
Clansmen	122	95	217
Clanswomen	126	49	175
Clan wives	78	30	108
Birth mothers (i.e., concubines)	13	2	15
total	339	176	515

SOURCE: SHY:CK, 20/37b–38a.

the fledgling Southern Sung government, representing some 180 strings annually per clan member. For a comparative perspective, however, we should recall that the K'ai-feng clan in 1067 was supported by expenditures of 70,000 strings *per month*. By that measure, the lifestyles of the Southern Sung clan members were necessarily more modest.

Chao Chung-shih's proposal to merge the two branches was not accepted—quite possibly out of concern about overburdening a single locality with responsibility for the support of both branches. Instead, the Western branch established its offices and residences in the northern Fukienese prefecture of Fu-chou, paralleling the Southern center in Ch'üan-chou.[36]

By 1133, the institutional outline of the Southern Sung imperial clan had become clear. In addition to the major centers in Ch'üan-chou and Fu-chou, the Court of the Imperial Clan was located in Shao-hsing fu (formerly Yueh-chou) in Liang-che, and the capital Lin-an (formerly Hang-chou) housed the Great Office and also the newly constructed Mu-ch'in Residence, the residence for the Southern Rank clansmen who served the emperor at court and who constituted the last remnant of the mourning kin.[37] Throughout the rest of the Sung, in every prefecture where clan members resided, a clan elder was to be delegated to lead the clan members and oversee distribution of the cash and grain allowances to which clan members were entitled.[38]

Clansmen in the War

These patterns of migration and resettlement were of great importance for the future of the imperial clan in the Southern Sung, and we will return to them in later chapters. However, they do not compare in drama or political significance to the record of the clansmen involved in resisting the Chin and serving the Sung in a wide variety of roles during these tumultuous times.

Because of the personnel policies for the imperial clan, discussed in the preceding chapter, when the war broke out, clansmen were serving in local government posts throughout the empire, and not a few had become magistrates and prefects. During the wars and rebellions of the ensuing years, when most jurisdictions were left to their own devices and much of the conflict involved siege warfare, numerous clansmen distinguished themselves.

Chao Pu-ch'ün (BCBAAKA; n.d.) is a noteworthy example. A graduate of the *liang-shih* examination for clansmen, he was magistrate of Chang-ch'iu county (Chi-nan fu, Ching-tung-tung) in 1126, where he recruited 5,000 soldiers, strengthened the city's defenses, and was thereby able to withstand a two-month siege. Then as prefect of Ch'en-chou (Hunan) and Ting-chou (Ching-hu-pei) in central China, he resisted rebel attacks successfully. At his next post, as prefect of Lu-chou (Huai-hsi in 1128), the Sung general Li Ch'iung rebelled and took Pu-ch'ün north as a prisoner. He was later released and went on to serve as the vice–fiscal intendant for Liang-che.[39] The story of Chao Tzu-li (AAXXXXX d. 1137)—a *chin-shih* from 1091—is simpler; he was credited with the successful defense of Ju-chou (Ching-hsi-pei), which was the only prefecture in the region to remain under Sung control during the Jurchen army drive into the Ching-hu region (Hunan and Ho-pei) in 1129.[40]

Chao Shih-wu (BCBPAM; 1108–53) was not an official in 1126, but through pluck and audacity he was able to make his mark in the defense against the Chin. Imprisoned and taken north with the other K'ai-feng clansmen in 1126, he discussed escaping with other clansmen when they passed near Ming-chou (Ho-pei-hsi), which was still held by the Sung. He managed to escape on a donkey, but it was stolen by thieves, and he arrived on foot at an inn and announced, "I am an imperial uncle." However incongruous this claim may have appeared in the mouth of a bedraggled teenager, local officials provided him with a hundred-man guard. Proceeding to Tzu-chou to the west, Shih-wu raised a militia to lift the Chin siege of Ming-chou, and within ten days had attracted 5,000 "superior troops" and "tens of thousands of followers." This force successfully raised the siege of Ming-chou and captured the Chin general. For his efforts, Shih-wu was appointed prefect and defense commissioner of Ming-chou, where he served until a Chin siege in 1128 forced him to flee, at which point he made his way south.[41]

The besieged city was the archetypal locale for the Sung defense against both Jurchen and rebels, and many clansmen spurned either flight or surrender, choosing instead martyrdom. Chao Shu-chiao, the military director-in-chief of Te-chou (Ho-pei-tung) in 1128, commanded the defense of the besieged prefecture through six battles. When he discovered that his subordinate Chiang Che had plotted with the prefect to surrender, he had him beheaded—even while weeping for him. The city soon fell, and Shu-chiao was captured while fighting in the street; refusing to submit, he was executed.[42]

Frequently, an explicit connection was made between the imperial status of the clansman and the need for resistance unto death. Chao Pu-shih (BAAKLCC) was serving as prefect of Hsiang-chou (Ho-pei-tung) in 1127 when the town came under siege. After a time the situation appeared hopeless, with no relief from Sung forces in sight and the soldiers and people demoralized. Pu-shih said, "The town's food is now exhausted, and we will not be rescued from outside. *Pu-shih is an imperial clansman and in righteousness cannot surrender.* So what are we to do?" His solution was to climb the town wall, in full view of all. He then threw his family into a well, jumped in himself, and on his orders the well was filled with earth. In this way, he spared the populace from slaughter.[43]

In the case of Chao Shih-lung (BAANBE; 1080–1131), the price demanded of the clansman's family for his loyalty was also fearsome, although the enemy in this case consisted of the rebel Li Ch'eng and his followers, who had mounted a serious rebellion in the Chiang-Huai region. Shih-lung, who had made a career with the military ever since abandoning preparations for the civil examinations during his youth, was the military supervisor of infantry and cavalry for Huai-nan-hsi and had been instrumental in resisting rebel attacks on three occasions, including once against Li's subordinate, Ma Chin. In 1131 Shih-lung found himself besieged in the city of Chiu-chiang leading the fight against Li's troops. After a hundred-odd days had passed, the food ran out and Shih-lung's fellow officials fled, leaving him with only a contingent of government slaves. The rebels entered the city, killing many, and seized Shih-lung. Li Ch'eng offered to make him rebel defense commissioner, but Shih-lung mocked him: "Does the rebel wish to capitulate to me?" Shih-lung managed to smuggle out instructions for his sons written on silk he had torn from his robes: "The rebels have not killed me, [but] in righteousness I cannot live. You must all escape and avenge me." He then killed himself with poison, which so infuriated Li Ch'eng that he had over ten members of Shih-lung's family killed.[44]

The anger that Li vented on Shih-lung's family may well have been compounded by the fact that two imperial clansmen had successfully resisted him already. Like the clansmen, Li was a northerner (from Shantung) brought south by the tides of war; unlike them he was a wandering brigand who in 1126 had gathered a following of uprooted men. The main thing to distinguish him from the countless other bandit leaders was his belief, stemming from the prophecy of a Taoist monk, that he was destined to become the hegemon of Ssu-ch'uan.[45] This may also have been the reason for his refusal to accept Sung authority for any more than brief periods of time. In 1126 he was still in the Shantung region, and his troops besieged the city of Tzu-chou (Ching-tung-tung), where Chao Shih-tsan (BCAAHA; 1095–1160), was acting prefect, the prefect having fled on the pretext of illness. Shih-tsan personally organized the defense of the city, which lasted for 49 days, when the rebels' food ran out and they left.[46]

The next clansman Li Ch'eng encountered was Chao Ling-ch'eng (AADBHD; d. 1129)—later to meet his death in Huang-chou at Chin hands—who successfully resisted an attack by Li and Ting Chin on that prefecture.[47] Although undated in Ling-ch'eng's biography, this event probably occurred in 1128 or early 1129, by which time Li had established himself as a power in the Huai-nan area. In response, the Sung court attempted to buy him off with the title of military commissioner (*chen-fu shih*) for Shu and Ch'i prefectures (both in Huai-nan-hsi). However, by the second month of 1129 he was again on the warpath, attacking towns throughout the central Yangtze region.[48] For several years Li posed a significant threat to the Sung. Chao Shih-lung was one of many killed by Li, yet all Sung attempts to either defeat or control him were stymied, and in fact as a quintessential survivor Li managed, first, to join the ranks of the pretender Liu Yü (1073–1146) and his Ch'i dynasty and, then, after its collapse to become a ranking Chin commander.[49]

Like Chao Shih-lung in Chiu-chiang, Chao Ling-ch'eng (AADBHD) mocked his captors, when as the prefect of Huang-chou (Huai-nan-hsi) he fell into Chin hands. In fact he had saved the city from rebels earlier, but in early 1129 left to mourn his mother. When the Jurchen began their southern campaign later that year, he was urgently recalled and, despite illness, rushed back to Huang-chou, arriving in the middle of the night. However, the city fell the next day. Dressed in his armor, he confronted the Chin, who wanted him to surrender. He refused to submit or to drink the wine the commander offered him. "Why should I submit," he asked. "I owe obeisance only to my ancestral emperors; how could I give obeisance to dogs and pigs?" Although whipped to a bloody pulp for this speech, he continued cursing the Chin until he died.[50]

Imperial clansmen had no monopoly on martyrdom for the Sung cause; the chapters on "loyal and righteous" individuals in the *Sung History* from which most of these examples are drawn are full of examples of non-clan loyalists. I would suggest, however, that the imperial status of the clansmen set them apart from others, since for them dynastic and family identities merged. Chao Yü-chih (CEDBBA) was a very junior military official in T'an-chou (Hunan) when the Chin army attacked in 1129. While inspecting the city's defenses, the prefect Hsiang Tzu-yin (1086–1153) said to Yü-chih, who was in charge of defending the east wall: "As an imperial clansman, you cannot be insignificant like the others." Yü-chih was moved to tears, and when the city fell and most of the other officials (Hsiang included) had fled, he died fighting in the streets.[51] Finally, Chao Shu-p'ing, the military administrator of Shan-chou (Yung-hsing lu) in the northwest, managed to smuggle a letter out to his son—also an official in Yung-hsing circuit—in which he wrote: "Since ministers should die [during their] country's difficulties, how much greater is our obligation, who are closely related? Can we disgrace our mandate? We must die!" In fact no one surrendered, and Shu-p'ing led all the city's officials and officers, some 51 men in all, to their deaths.[52]

The clansmen described above were of secondary importance historically and are remembered primarily for their loyalty and heroism, but there were some who did not fit this mold. For example, the Prince of Hsin—Chao Chen—after escaping from the Jurchen during the trip north became a significant rallying point for the dynasty in the far north (Hopei and Shansi). Joining forces with local military leaders, he sent one of them to Kao-tsung's court to solicit aid, authorization to stockade troops west of the mountains, and a military appointment. Despite suspicion at the court over the bona fides of the messenger and his letter, Kao-tsung recognized his brother's handwriting and appointed him marshal for forces beyond the Yellow River.[53] When a rumor that the Prince of Hsin had crossed the Yellow River and was moving on K'ai-feng subsequently reached Kao-tsung's court, there was great excitement and plans were begun for an expedition north. In fact, the prince had done no such thing. Shortly thereafter his forces were defeated by the Chin, and he disappeared. As a final note, in 1131 a rebel named Yang claiming to be the Prince of Hsin began a rebellion in the border regions between the Sung and Chin, but it was quickly put down.[54]

Chao Tzu-sung (AADBDFA; d. 1132) played an even more important role in the war, albeit one that was ultimately ill-fated. In 1126 he was serving as prefect of Huai-ning fu in Ching-hsi-pei and thus had troops at his call even as K'ai-feng fell. Upon learning that the Prince of K'ang had escaped to the south, he got into contact with him and recommended an aggressive strategy against the Chin. That advice was not taken, but the prince appointed Tzu-sung grand marshal for militias in the southeast (i.e., the Huai-nan area). While not an independent command, this was an important position, and Tzu-sung was particularly engaged in making sure that Chang Pang-ch'ang (1081–1172), the Chin-installed pretender in K'ai-feng, received no support from his native region of Huai-nan.[55] A vigorous participant in policy discussions at Kao-tsung's court, Tzu-sung was named prefect of Chen-chiang fu—a strategic prefecture in northern Liang-che on the Yangtze—and chief military administrator of infantry and cavalry for Liang-che. Here his luck deserted him, however. When Chao Wan began a rebellion in Chen-chiang, Tzu-sung dispatched troops to attack the rebels and raised a militia to defend the prefectural city. However, the government troops lost, the militia deserted, and Tzu-sung retreated to a nearby temple while the rebels took the city. Capping this disgrace was a report that reached Kao-tsung that Tzu-sung had quoted a saying by Miao Ch'ang-i, the director of astronomy, that "the offspring of the T'ai-tsu line would again possess the empire." In a fury, Kao-tsung demoted Tzu-sung and sent him into exile in Nan-hsiung (Kuang-nan-hsi). Although pardoned in an amnesty in 1132, Tzu-sung died there that same year.[56]

Chao Tzu-sung was not the only clansman accused of disloyalty or harboring imperial ambitions. Chao Shu-hsiang, from the Wei-wang branch of the clan, fled Lo-yang before it was conquered by the Chin and attempted unsuccessfully to launch an expedition to rescue the emperor. Later, however, his subordinate Yü Huan rebelled, and Shu-hsiang was implicated. In response, the court ordered him seized and executed.[57]

The most interesting clansman-"rebel," however, was another Wei-wang descendent, Chao Shu-chin (CDCKG; d. 1128), although his story is complicated.[58] In 1127, one of the many rebellions faced by Kao-tsung's court was led by a Hang-chou soldier named Ch'en T'ung. General Hsin Tao-tsung was ordered to suppress it, but his troops, too, got out of hand and attacked the prefectural capital of Hsiu-chou, north of Hang-chou. Chao Shu-chin, the prefect of Hsiu-chou, was able to talk the troops into dispersing. Subsequently named judicial inspector of Liang-che, Shu-chin met with Ch'en and was able to convince him to return to the Sung side along with several score of soldiers. Shu-chin explained in a memorial that Ch'en T'ung was not a traitor at heart and had rebelled only because he had been insufficiently rewarded in the past.[59] But even though Kao-tsung found Shu-chin's proposal to pardon Ch'en acceptable, it was vetoed by the Censorate.

After Shu-chin returned to Hsiu-chou, Ch'en was murdered by General Wang Yuan, who gained entrée to Ch'en's house by announcing himself as "Chao of Hsiu-chou." Wang, who hated Shu-chin for having taken his mistress—Lady Chou, a prostitute—from him while in K'ai-feng, proceeded to slander Shu-chin, accusing him of colluding with rebels. This was enough to get Shu-chin replaced as prefect of Hsiu-chou. However, so unpopular was Chu Fei, the replacement, that he was imprisoned by a common soldier, who then asked Shu-chin—who was still in Hsiu-chou—to return as prefect and pacify the situation. Shu-chin agreed, but only as a temporary measure, and wrote the court asking that a new prefect be appointed.

But before the arrival of Shu-chin's memorial, the court ordered General Chang Chün (1097–1164)—a subordinate of Wang Yuan and later a military hero and grand councilor—to lead a punitive expedition against him. Upon Chang's arrival in Hsiu-chou, Shu-chin came out to welcome Chang, only to find himself cursed and his right arm cut off. "I am an imperial clansman!" Shu-chin shouted, to which Chang replied: "You have followed the rebels; how can you say 'imperial clan'?" Even before Chang had finished speaking, his men had beheaded Shu-chin. The popular response was outrage and outbreaks of incendiarism, but Chang seized and executed the man responsible for imprisoning the prefect and also found Lady Chou and returned her to Wang Yuan. The story has an epilogue: in 1139—two years after Chang had been dismissed as grand councilor—the Censorate claimed that Shu-chin had been wronged, and he was posthumously promoted.

So far as one can tell from the records, none of these cases involved a serious threat to the throne or an intent to commit treason. That said, Shu-chin in twice taking the side of those whom others regarded as rebels was certainly stretching—and breaking, it turned out—the limits of official tolerance. As for Tzu-sung, his assertive behavior together with the fact that, had no princes been able to escape the Jurchen in 1126, he would have been well placed to claim the throne himself, made him an easy target to his enemies. I would suggest, too, that both men were emboldened by their clan status to act forcefully, as when Shu-chin protested, "I am an imperial clansman." This was also true of the martyred clansmen described above, but with one difference—the dead did not pose a threat. After generations in which clansmen were denied anything but the most circumscribed power, these clansmen found themselves with much power in a situation with few rules. As we will see below, the early years of the Southern Sung saw the crafting of new regulations and expectations—explicit and implicit—that redefined the acceptable political roles for clansmen.

Service by Clansmen and the Issue of Fraud

The clansmen described above held a wide variety of military and civil posts. Just how widespread they were in the government at this time is impossible to say, but that they had become a common presence is suggested by the legislation related to clansmen-officials. In the late 1120s, with a military situation that was often desperate and a dearth of officials available for postings, the imperial clansmen were a valuable resource. On the first day of the fifth month of 1127—the very day of his accession—Kao-tsung, as part of a general amnesty, gave official rank to *chü-jen* of the Southern Capital and elsewhere and to clansmen who had participated in the examinations; he also made it easier for clansmen-officials to receive postings without out delay.[60] In 1129, declaring that "imperial clansmen are the branches and leaves of the state," he noted in an edict that many clansmen had been kept from pursuing a military career and cleared the way for them to apply to become officers, subject to the scrutiny of the Executive Office of the Council of State.[61] Later that same year, the court issued new quotas for the maximum number of clansmen-officials who could serve in a given prefecture or county. As can be seen from Table 6.2, these new quotas came close to doubling those set in 1111, and they were increased again in 1133 before being cut back in 1142. The existence of these quotas does not imply that the typical prefecture and county had that many clansmen-officials; rather, the quotas should be seen as a way of avoiding undue concentrations of them in individual jurisdictions. Nevertheless, the very fact that the quotas were raised in 1129 and again in 1133 would suggest that in some localities, at least, there were enough clansmen-officials to necessitate the larger quotas. Moreover, the fact that the quotas were reduced in 1142—as the court was making its peace with the Chin—points to the early years of the Southern Sung as a particularly hospitable period for clansmen-officials.

Perhaps the most vexing problem facing the government—and clan officials—regarding the imperial clansmen and their service as officials concerned the evaluation of claims to clan membership. When Kao-tsung's court was constituted in the Southern Capital in 1127, it had no governmental records. The problem went far beyond the imperial clan; indeed the lack of officials' personnel files and examination records posed a particular challenge.[62] The loss of the clan's genealogical records, however, meant that claims to clan membership—with it the right to allowances and often official status—were difficult, sometimes impossible, to evaluate. Additionally, some non-mourning clansmen reportedly claimed to be mourning kin and therefore eligible for guard rank status.[63]

Engaged with more pressing matters—among them, survival—during

Table 6.2

Maximum Numbers of Clansmen Allowed to Serve
in a Given Prefecture or County

Year	Prefecture	County
IIII	All prefectures: 3[a]	All counties: 2
1129	All prefectures: 7	All counties: 3
1130	All prefectures: 7	All counties: 3
1133	Prefectures with:	Counties with:
	10+ counties: 10	over 10,000 households: 3
	5–9 counties: 5–9	under 10,000 households: 2
	3–4 counties: 5	
	1–2 counties: 3	
1142	Prefectures with:	All counties: 1
	10+ counties: 5	
	7–9 counties: 4	
	5–6 counties: 3	
	1–4 counties: 2	

[a] Only one of the clansmen was allowed to serve in a senior civil or military position.

SOURCES: SHY: IH, 5/23b (1111), 32b–33a (1129); 6/2a–3a (1133), 16a–b (1142).

the first years of the Southern Sung, the court turned to the issue of fraudulent claims only in the early 1130s. Its approach to the problem was two-pronged. First, in the absence of records, formal guarantees were employed to verify claims to clan membership. At their most elaborate, these consisted of guarantees by two clansmen with a mourning relationship to the claimant. In their absence, guarantees from two clansmen of military administrative status (*ta-shih-ch'en*) or three clansmen with military executory status (*hsiao-shih-ch'en*) sufficed. The claims and guarantees, moreover, were to be examined by local officials, and fraudulent claims would entail the "loss of name" (i.e., the loss of clan status) for the guarantors.[64] In addition, rewards of 50 strings were announced for anyone uncovering false claims to clan membership.[65]

Second, the government undertook the arduous task of reconstructing the imperial genealogy. In the fourth month of 1132, officials of the Great

Office, the Western and Southern Offices, and the East Palace Gate Office (a eunuch bureau) were instructed to gather records from all prefectures and counties relating to the clan's genealogy. Early in 1133 their authority to demand cooperation from local officials was strengthened.[66] As a memorial from later in 1133 indicates, however, the task was extremely difficult, especially given the many fraudulent claims. The writer of the memorial took particular exception to making genealogical outlines widely available, since that would simply make fraud easier.[67] Although these efforts led to the production of a reconstructed genealogy in 1137, it was the acquisition of fifteen volumes (*ts'e*) and over 2,000 woodblocks of the Northern Sung genealogy during a brief Sung reconquest of K'ai-feng in 1139 that made it possible to produce a reliable clan genealogy in the 1140s and thereby end much of the fraud.[68]

The Crises of 1129

The newfound prominence of clansmen-officials was not limited to the provinces and battlefield; they were equally visible at the court and in the central government as well. Two early examples of clan prominence in the workings of the court can be found in two crises from 1129: a coup against Kao-tsung in Hang-chou and the dramatic flight by the Lung-yu Empress Dowager through Chiang-hsi to evade capture by the Jurchen.

If Kao-tsung's escape by sea in late 1129 represented the high point of Chin attempts to destroy the fledgling Southern Sung court, the coup by elements of the imperial army in Hang-chou earlier the same year posed the most serious internal threat to Kao-tsung. On the fifth day of the third month of 1129, Miao Fu (d. 1129) and Liu Cheng-yen (d. 1129), the commander and vice-commander, respectively, of the imperial bodyguard, seized control of Hang-chou, which had just been designated the temporary capital, and forced the abdication of Kao-tsung in favor of his three-year-old son, with Empress Meng (1077–1135) —the Lung-yu Empress Dowager—to serve as regent during his minority.[69] The reasons for this undertaking appear to have been, first, frustration among the northern generals and their men at the bleak military situation and the timid leadership of the emperor and, second, anger at the high-handed ways and influence of eunuchs at the court. Indeed, one of the first actions taken by the plotters was to kill over a hundred eunuchs.[70] Knowing that their position was precarious, Miao and Liu solicited the support of generals and officials outside Hang-chou, but to no avail, for the loyalists were able to command broad support against them. An Imperial Relief Army (Ch'in-wang chün) was raised in the Yangtze Delta region, and with the help of effective diplomacy by the grand councilor Chu Sheng-fei (d. 1138), Miao and Liu were forced to back down.[71] Kao-tsung was peacefully restored, and Miao and Liu were given promotions. Fearing—with reason—that their lives were in danger, however, both fled and were subsequently captured and executed.

During the 25 days that elapsed between the overthrow of Kao-tsung and his restoration, three imperial clansmen are recorded as playing roles in the loyalist cause. One was very minor: Chao Tzu-hsiao (AADEHAF; 1102–67) was serving as judge and concurrent pacification officer in Ch'ü-chou, to the south of Hang-chou, and held off mutinous units in the area sympathetic to the coup.[72] By contrast, Chao Shih-niao (BCBIAG; 1084–1153) and his son Pu-fan (BCBIAGA; n.d.) were close to the center of the action. Shih-niao entered Hang-chou in disguise and secretly sent letters to Chang Chün, an important general supposedly under Miao Fu's command, and Lü I-hao (1071–1139), pacification commissioner for Chiang-nan-tung and prefect of Chiang-ning, urging them to rescue the emperor and save the dynasty. A little later, when Chang had gotten into trouble with Miao, Shih-niao wrote him again, stressing the absolute necessity of getting rid of the rebels.[73] Pu-fan, for his part, acted as the messenger to Chang Chün, concealing his father's letter in an opening cut into his thigh.[74]

Since neither the primary histories of this period nor the biographies of Chang and Lü make mention of these letters,[75] we may question their importance, especially since both men played important roles throughout the brief interregnum and both are portrayed as committed loyalists throughout. Nevertheless, the fact remains that clansmen were involved close to the center of the intrigues and were rewarded for their actions; Shih-niao was promoted to junior guardian and vice-director of the Great Office of Clan Affairs, and Pu-fan received a two-rank promotion and civil official status.[76] The limits of acceptable political activity for clansmen had been broadened a little.

Later in 1129, even as Kao-tsung was fleeing the Jurchen on the coast of China, another drama was under way in Chiang-hsi, as the Chin chased

Empress Meng through the province. The emergence of Empress Meng as an important figure in the early Southern Sung is remarkable.[77] A secondary empress of the emperor Che-tsung, she had been the victim of political attack under Hui-tsung and lived through most of his reign in obscurity. At the time of the Jurchen capture of K'ai-feng, Empress Meng was living in a temple, for her palace had burned, and was overlooked when the imperial harem was taken to the north. As the sole empress outside captivity, she suddenly acquired great symbolic authority. From 1126 to 1129, she was used to validate, in turn, the puppet government of Chang Pang-ch'ang in K'ai-feng,[78] the accession of the Prince of K'ang as Kao-tsung,[79] and finally the brief reign of Kao-tsung's infant son during the abortive coup by Miao Fu and Liu Cheng-yen. In fact, since she opposed the coup and made it clear (to Chang Chün in particular) that her loyalty remained with Kao-tsung, she was honored more than ever when his rule was restored.[80]

In late 1129, as Kao-tsung prepared to leave Lin-an fu (as Hang-chou had been renamed), he sent Empress Meng with an imperial guard west into Chiang-hsi, apparently so that were he to be captured or killed, a source of dynastic legitimacy would remain.[81] This was well understood by the Jurchen, who split their forces and sent an army across Huai-nan into Chiang-hsi to capture her. They almost succeeded when, to the astonishment of Sung commanders, they crossed the Yangtze a mere two hundred *li* (approximately seventy miles) from Hung-chou, where the empress was staying.[82] With the Chin in hot pursuit, she was taken south to Chi-chou and then on to Ch'ien-chou. So unsettled was Chiang-hsi at this time and so desperate the dynasty's situation that every stage of the trip proved perilous: the empress's party was nearly captured by the Chin, the guard-escort mutinied in Chi-chou, and there was a popular uprising amid near famine conditions in Ch'ien-chou. After the crisis in the east abated, Kao-tsung recalled her to Lin-an, and she returned in honor.

Three imperial clansmen played noteworthy roles in Empress Meng's adventures in Chiang-hsi. Chao Shou-chih (CEFCBC) was postal relay station supervisor for four prefectures in central Chiang-hsi. When the empress's party fled Chi-chou for Ch'ien-chou, the prefect of Chi-chou took the bulk of the prefectural garrison to her and left Shou-chih as acting prefect of Chi-chou in an extremely perilous situation, although in fact he managed without incident.[83]

Chao Hsun-chih (CABBFH; 1112 *chin-shih*, d. 1129) was serving as magistrate of Yung-feng county (in northeastern Chi-chou) when the empress's guard mutinied and one of their allies led an attack on Yung-feng. Resourceful in their battlefield tactics, Hsun-chih and the sheriff—one Ch'en Tzu-jen—managed to thwart the attack but at the cost of their own lives.[84]

Finally, Chao Shih-ch'iung (BCBIBH; d. 1151) was a Southern Rank clansman traveling in the empress's party whose persuasiveness proved critical on two occasions. En route to Chi-chou, the party encountered a group of several hundred displaced soldiers headed for the mountains and intent on brigandage. Shih-ch'iung showed them paintings of Hui-tsung and Ch'in-tsung that were being transported on one of the party's boats[85] and observed that material rewards for loyalists greatly outweighed those for brigands, who from morning to night were concerned with their next meal.[86] In response the soldiers declared their loyalty. Later in Ch'ien-chou, when fighting broke out between the empress's guard and a local militia, Shih-ch'iung counseled the granting of a pardon to the militia.[87] If people could be assured that they would not be executed, they would congregate peacefully, and if the town was pacified, then troubles outside would subside. According to Shih-ch'iung's biography, at least, the pardon was granted and the situation resolved.[88]

As in the Hang-chou coup affair, none of the clansmen involved in the flight of Empress Meng was among the principal actors, yet their actions were significant. Moreover, with Chao Shih-niao in Hang-chou and Shih-ch'iung in Chiang-hsi, we see clansmen acting *within* the court. This was clearly the result of exigency rather than any considered policy change on the part of Kao-tsung. Nevertheless, emboldened by their experiences in the provinces, on the battlefield, and at court, clansmen during the 1130s played a prominent role in politics, until that role itself became an issue.

The Clan in Politics

Examples of imperial clansmen who came to occupy important bureaucratic and political roles in the early years of the Southern Sung are numerous. Chao Shih-tsan (BCAAHA; 1095–1160), who had successfully repelled Li Ch'eng in 1126, at various times held the crucial prefectships of Lin-an and Shao-hsing fu and served as vice–fiscal intendant of Chiang-nan-tung.[89]

Chao Pu-ch'ün (BCBAAKA; n.d.), whose successful defense of Ju-chou was described above, ended his career as vice–fiscal intendant of Liang-che.[90] Chao Tzu-ch'ih (AADBDAD; n.d.), whose prominent role under Hui-tsung in the reform of coinage is discussed in Chapter 5, served under Kao-tsung first as the director of the Western Clan Office and then as the fiscal intendant of Chiang-hsi.[91]

Chao Tzu-chou (AAEBFAE; 1089–1142) is especially noteworthy because of the precedents that his career set for his fellow clansmen. He began as a local official under Hui-tsung with a variety of postings, including the prefectship of Mi-chou in Ching-tung-tung. When the Jurchen invaded the north, he escaped south with his mother, hiding for a period in the mountains of Hsin-an. In the 1130s he held a variety of important positions in the central government. He served as personal escort to Chin envoys in 1133, vice-minister to the Chamberlain of Ceremonials, vice-minister of rites, and chief recipient of edicts for the Military Commission. He was the first imperial clansman to hold this last position, which was important because of its control over the flow of documents, and also the first to hold the position of attendant (*shih-ts'ung*), which gave him personal access to the emperor.[92]

Inevitably, imperial clansmen who entered the upper realms of government in the early Southern Sung found themselves vulnerable to political intrigues at court, and many were caught up in the controversies surrounding Yueh Fei, the general on whom hopes for the reconquest of the north rested, and Ch'in Kuei, who in the 1130s was consolidating his tyrannical hold on power, which was not to be shaken until his death in 1155. Imperial clansmen could be found on opposing sides in these controversies. Chao Pu-ch'i (BAADADA; n.d.), for example, is described by his biographer as a crony of Ch'in's who helped him bring down one of his enemies.[93] Chao Shih-tsan was also considered to be a Ch'in ally, although his father-in-law was a political victim of Ch'in's.[94]

However, most of the politically active clansmen, like the greater body of scholar-officials, were opponents of Ch'in. Chao Tzu-chou, for example, clashed with him and as a result was forced into retirement for the last seven years of his life.[95] The stakes proved even higher for Chao Pu-yu (BCA-BACA), whom we noted in the last chapter for having turned his back on literary studies and undertaken a military career. In 1126 he had gathered a force in the Hopei/Honan region and became a subordinate ally of Yueh Fei. Although he apparently spent a period of time serving Kao-tsung in court, he kept his army and participated in Yueh's expedition to the north in 1140. When Yueh was recalled by Ch'in Kuei—returning to his arrest and eventual execution—Pu-yu followed him. After Yueh's death, he was stripped of his army and sent into administrative exile in Heng-chou (Hunan), where he died.[96]

Probably the most vociferous critic of Ch'in Kuei among the clansmen was Chao Ling-chin (AADBHF; 1108 *chin-shih*, d. 1158), a clansman whose outspokenness got him in trouble a number of times in his life. Although he never advanced beyond prefect in his career, his reported criticisms of Ch'in Kuei and his family infuriated Ch'in, and in fact, at the time of Ch'in's death, Ling-chin was being held at the Southern Clan Office in Ch'üan-chou and being investigated on a charge of plotting rebellion along with Chao Fen, the son of the late grand councilor Chao Ting (1085–1147) and not a clansman. With Ch'in's death, the charges were dropped, and Ling-chin was rehabilitated.[97]

In terms of the fortunes of the imperial clan, however, the most important controversy involving a clansman during these years concerned Chao Shih-niao, whose role during the Hang-chou coup is discussed above. Following that affair, Shih-niao had been named vice-administrator of the Great Office of Clan Affairs, and shortly thereafter administrator.[98] Although a vigorous administrator through the 1130s, he seems not to have become controversial until late 1141, when he joined the debate over Yueh Fei, whose life hung in the balance. He spoke out on several occasions in defense of Yueh and on one occasion reportedly said to Ch'in Kuei: "The central plain has yet to be pacified, and misfortune has reached to the loyal and righteous. You have forgotten the two sages [i.e., Hui-tsung and Ch'in-tsung] and do not wish to return to the central plain."[99] A furious Ch'in Kuei accused him of conspiring with Yueh and having secret dealings about "matters threatening the imperial person." To Kao-tsung, Ch'in said: "Shih-niao is a close relative; outside [the court] he has friendly relations with generals and inside with executive officials. The matter concerns the emperor's person."[100] As a result, Shih-niao was dismissed from his post and exiled to Chien-chou (Fu-chien), where he died. Moreover, the edict ordering his dismissal also ordered an examination of the imperial clan by the Ministry of Justice and banned imperial clansmen from social intercourse with officials.[101]

The New Political Limits

There is no evidence that the ban on social intercourse with officials issued upon Chao Shih-niao's dismissal was ever carried out in the Southern Sung—although it had been a fact of life in Northern Sung K'ai-feng—even if one interprets it as applying only to the Southern Rank clansmen within Lin-an.[102] However, Kao-tsung's restrictions seem to have had a chilling effect on the access of clansmen to high office within the central government. In fact, during a discussion in 1144 with Ch'in Kuei concerning the imperial clan, the emperor said that "ever since the founding emperors, we have not used imperial clansmen as grand councilors. With concerns of such long standing, we should use them to the level of attendant (*shih-ts'ung*) but stop with that."[103] To my knowledge, this is the earliest statement of a prohibition on clansmen as grand councilors, although a half-century later when a clansman became a grand councilor, the prohibition was frequently cited as a policy of the founding emperors. As a product of the early Southern Sung, the prohibition is perhaps best seen as the capstone of a decision by Kao-tsung to curb the political power of the imperial clan.

But even though curbed, the imperial clan remained a significant presence in the polity of the Southern Sung empire, and not simply because clansmen-officials were numerous. For although there were numerous examples of clan status becoming a source of suspicion, the imperial clan remained an extension of emperorship and that connection proved too useful to be ignored by either clansmen or the emperor. Chao Tzu-hsiao, whose distinguished career spanned four decades and whose role in the coup of 1129 is discussed above, had a special audience with Kao-tsung before leaving to take a post in Chiang-hsi, at which the emperor said: "You may send secret memorials. Clansmen are the body of the state, and it is appropriate for them to know my feelings."[104] And in fact, if one were to point to the most commonly shared trait of Southern Sung clansmen-officials, it would probably be a boldness rooted in their imperial status and in a perception that they had the emperor's ear.

That said, what most distinguished the clansmen-officials from their Northern Sung ancestors was the extent to which they had come to resemble the non-imperial scholar-officials. Yet as members of the elite with imperial status, they occupied a political, social, and cultural space between the emperor and the non-imperial elite that was fraught with tension toward both groups, and it is in the variety of resolutions to that tension over the next century and a half that we find the distinctiveness of the Southern Sung imperial clan.

SEVEN

Settlement and Privilege

The Southern Sung imperial clan, dispersed throughout the empire and, for the most part, genealogically distant from the emperor, differed in many respects from its Northern Sung predecessor. Governmental support was more modest, and access to office was largely by way of the conventional routes of success in the examination and the exercise of *yin*, although clansmen's use of both was highly privileged. Moreover, whereas the dramatic policy shifts of the late Northern Sung had created for the clan—as for the government at large—an almost rhythmic pattern of change, in the Southern Sung imperial policies evolved but seldom underwent dramatic and systemic change. As a result, this chapter and the next two to an extent abandon a straightforward historical narrative so as to explore more fully the social and political realities of the clan vis-à-vis both throne and other elites.

In approaching the Southern Sung clan, we must also acknowledge the peculiarities of the historical sources and the ways in which they shape our knowledge. Although the kinds of sources available are much the same for the two periods, their mix and informativeness are not. Those sources associated with the dynastic recordkeeping and the Bureau of History—the *Sung History*, the *Sung hui-yao*, and Li Hsin-ch'uan's *Hsi-nien yao-lu*—are excellent for the early Southern Sung, good through the early thirteenth century, and sorely deficient thereafter. This periodization does not hold for the sources produced by the elite; epitaphs, local histories, and the jottings and essays of individual authors are plentiful throughout the Southern Sung and provide a richness of information unseen in Northern Sung writings.

This is particularly true for the epitaphs of clan members; whereas those in the Northern Sung were usually commissioned by the government and tended to be formulaic, Southern Sung epitaphs were typically the result of personal ties and solicitations and are therefore far more detailed and revealing. But because they were not produced en masse and because the early generations of clansmen, virtually all of whom were mourning kin of the emperor, were more likely to receive at least passing attention from the writers of the *Sung History*, we are faced with a paradox. We have far fewer biographies of clansmen in the Southern Sung—especially when considered as a percentage of their generations—but we know far more about them (see Table 7.1).

This finding should be taken not as a problem to be solved but as a given of which we must be mindful. This is especially true with regard to two dichotomies that did much to shape the Southern Sung imperial clan. One was a division between the successful few and the far larger number whose circumstances were modest to marginal. The other was the geographical and social distinction between clan members residing at the clan centers in Lin-an, Fu-chou, and Ch'üan-chou and those living independently elsewhere. That the biographical record should come overwhelmingly from the successful few is only to be expected, but it makes all the more important the search for evidence concerning the unseen majority. Less expected is the fact that the epitaphs are almost all of clansmen living *outside* the clan centers, a finding to which we will return below.

Finally, I would caution that the attenuation of narrative in these Southern Sung chapters should not be taken as a denial of its importance. In the realm of politics, especially, the role of imperial clansmen can be understood only in the context of Southern Sung political history and of the actions of the two emperors who spent their youths as clansmen, not princes: Hsiao-tsung (r. 1162–89) and Li-tsung (r. 1224–64). As we shall see, the personal interest of Hsiao-tsung, and to a lesser extent of Li-tsung, in the imperial clan was a key to the public role played by clansmen in the Southern Sung. But before surveying the historical record of clansmen in Southern Sung politics, we need first to consider their position in Southern Sung society, particularly settlement patterns, support structures, schooling and examination participation, and interactions with other members of the elite.

Table 7.1

Biographies of Clansmen as a Percentage of All Clansmen

Generation	Total clansmen[a]	Number of biographies	Percentage with biography
1st	23	15	65.2%
2d	59	18	30.5
3d	226	55	24.3
4th	1,078	62	5.8
5th	3,488	54	1.5
6th	5,155	46	0.9
7th	5,900	37	0.6
8th	4,178	33	0.8
9th[b]	1,806	22	
10th[b]	153	20	
11th–12th[b]	n.a.	26	
total	22,066	388	1.8%

[a] These figures are the same as the totals shown in Table 2.1 above.

[b] Because the data on the number of clansmen derive from around 1200, the totals shown from the ninth generation on are incomplete, and any percentages computed from them would be meaningless.

Settlement Patterns

In contrast to the precise figures of 339 and 176 clan members who settled in Ch'üan-chou and Fu-chou, respectively, in the early 1130s,[1] we have little information about the numbers settling elsewhere. That they were believed to be widely dispersed throughout the empire is clear from early Southern Sung edicts dealing with the treatment of the imperial clan, but I have found no record of an empire-wide census of the clan.[2] However, by analyzing the evidence that is available, we can at least venture a guess as to where they were concentrated. Table 7.2 presents the distributions of two sets of clansmen: those with epitaphs that specified where they were buried, since burial was one of the most important indicators of where a family considered its residence to be; and members of the imperial clan who received the *chin-shih* degree in 1256 for whom residency was specified.[3]

Table 7.2

*Geographical Distributions of Clansmen with Known Burial Sites
and of 1256* Chin-shih

Province	Burial sites of clansmen	Percentage of total	1256 clan *chin-shih*[a]	Percentage of total
Liang-che	29	47%	19	40%
Fu-chien	11	18	11	23
Chiang-hsi	10	16	3	6
Chiang-tung	9	15	7	15
Ssu-ch'uan	0		6	13
Kuang-tung	1	2	1	2
Hu-pei	1	2	0	
Hu-nan	1	2	0	
TOTAL	62	100%	47	100%

[a] The residences of 28 clansmen are not known; they are excluded from the total and the percentages shown here.

Each measure has its limitations, most notably a clear bias toward the successful—the clan elite, if it is possible to use such a term. That said (and the point accepted), these two distributions are in striking agreement on the dominance of Liang-che and the secondary importance of Fu-chien, followed by the interior circuits. The only striking point of disagreement concerns Ssu-ch'uan, for which there are no recorded burial sites but six *chin-shih*. The obvious historiographic explanation is the great losses of Sung—and other—records during the turmoils that later embroiled that region on more than one occasion. As noted below, there was a significant clan presence in Ssu-ch'uan and discussion about how to treat it.

The dominance of Liang-che and Fu-chien, on which these sources are agreed, is only to be expected, for these were the most developed regions of the empire economically and the most successful in the examinations. Furthermore, Liang-che was the site of the capital (although none of the 1256 *chin-shih* was from Lin-an),[4] and it was quite natural that imperial clan families settled there disproportionately. It is to these two southeastern regions that most of our attention will be devoted.[5]

Maintaining the Clan as a Whole

The kinds of support available to all clan members reveal much about members who otherwise would be invisible. Records in the *Sung hui-yao* for the early decades of Kao-tsung's reign betray anxiety about the chaotic conditions under which many imperial clan members were living, which had led to both real poverty and improper, even scandalous activities. In 1133, two *chin-shih* from Chiang-yin commandary (Liang-che) complained of extortion, theft, and meddlesome behavior on the part of clansmen there.[6] In late 1139, a minister related scenes of orphaned clansmen and clanswomen and wives "scattering among the people, coming and going to the marketplace, and mixing with commoners."[7] A month later, a memorial described with even greater alarm how clan members were scattered, refugees without resources and unable to return home. Some had even become involved in commerce, were consorting with merchants and runners, and were beyond the control of clan authorities. It proposed that all the prefectures and counties gather clan members together and give them support money, temporary housing, and travel allowances (to be supplied from privy purse funds) so that they could return to the jurisdiction of the clan authorities. In this way, "people would esteem and love [the clansmen], understand their difference from the common stream [of people], and thereby praise Your Majesty's ideal of measured generosity."[8]

Three points are worth noting here. First, in all these documents we see evidence of how ordinary clan members attempted to cope with dislocation: rubbing elbows with the mainstays of Sung urban society—peddlers and merchants, runners and other government functionaries—and throwing their weight around on occasion. Second, in the last memorial we have a revealing statement about the significance of the imperial clan from the standpoint of the court. That the clan is different from the "common stream" calls to mind the metaphor of the clan as a heavenly lake, and by tying treatment of the clan to the emperor's "ideal of measured generosity," the memorialist affirms the clan as an extension of emperorship. But therein also lay the problem, for how could the ideal of the clan as different from the "common stream" square with the reality that many clansmen were behaving like that stream? Third, court policy toward the imperial clan focused on residency—removing members from the midst of commoner society, preferably to the clan centers—and the provision of sufficient allowances and privileges to allow them to be maintained as a "heavenly lake." This policy was contested, most vigorously by those successful clansmen who were busy at this same time establishing ties and integrating their families into local elite society. I would even venture that this separatist/integrationist tension was fundamental to the identity of the imperial clan throughout the Southern Sung.

On the issue of clan housing, the court alternated between two positions, one of which was the proposal that clan members be returned to the clan authorities (i.e., go to clan centers). The other can be seen in a document by Chao Tzu-ch'eng (ABBACEA; d. 1144), later to gain fame as the father of the emperor Hsiao-tsung. While serving as vice-prefect of Hu-chou (Liang-che) in 1135, Tzu-ch'eng submitted a memorial, which met with Kao-tsung's agreement. In it, he proposed that since clansmen without homes were to be found throughout the empire, each prefecture should establish a residence on official land. He suggested that one clansman among each prefectural group serve as a "respected elder" (*tsun-chang*) and verify the identity of all the other clan members, and that a gatekeeper be appointed to control casual coming and going. He further proposed that all clan boys age fifteen *sui* and above be permitted to attend the prefectural school, be supported according to the school's support provisions for regular students (but presumably with funds from the prefectural rather than school coffers), and be allowed to take the prefectural examinations.[9]

Four years later—and a month before the 1139 memorial proposing to send homeless clan members to the clan centers—a ministerial report addressed the specific issue of needy clansmen in Lin-an, the temporary capital. Over the preceding decade, nineteen buildings (*suo*) of clan palaces (*kung-yuan*) had been established to house clan members when they were in the capital. This included not only the Southern Rank (*Nan-pan*) clan members, who lived in the Mu-ch'in Residence and were a part of the Sung court, but also many orphans and wives, who though receiving support were not formally registered in the palaces and thus could not be kept from "scattering among the people, coming and going to the marketplace, and mixing with commoners." The report proposed the building of additional residences in the Western and Southern centers and in Shao-hsing fu, so that these clan members could be housed there. Most particularly, clan members were to be discouraged from living among the people or in Buddhist temples, and support was to be made dependent on residing in an official residence. In response, the emperor ordered the Ministry of Rites to work out the details in accordance with clan regulations, and it seems quite likely that the 1139 proposal to send homeless clan members to the clan centers was the result.[10]

The contradictory nature of these different measures suggests that none of them was very effective, and in 1143 the Ministry of Rites proposed yet another approach, albeit one closer to Chao Tzu-ch'eng's. The fiscal intendant's office in each circuit was to establish a Tun-tsung Hall for the clansmen in the circuit. Each prefecture and county was to investigate the particulars of all clan members in its jurisdiction and find out if they preferred to move to the Southern or the Western clan centers and provide travel allowances if they did. As a temporary measure, prefectures and counties could house clan members in temples, but for no longer than a month.[11] This proposal, too, was accepted, but the sources are silent as to whether it was enacted; I have come across no other references to circuit Tun-tsung halls.

None of these proposals mention the clan families, found in many localities, that had acquired land and residences and established themselves (see below). What seems likely is that once the acute problems of the refugee families had subsided, most clan families were either independently established or in residence at the clan centers. The residual individuals—and they undoubtedly existed—would have constituted a chronic source of annoyance to local officials, but not numerous enough to justify a whole set of institutions.

As for the general support allowances, perhaps the most striking fact is that the level of aid provided in 1132 was virtually unchanged from the late eleventh century: one picul (*shih*) of rice and two strings (*kuan*) per month for orphaned clansmen or those without official rank.[12] In 1095, when these figures had initially been set, there was an additional "allowance" for housing, but, as we have seen, the Southern Sung government made every effort to provide clan members with housing.[13]

There is one puzzle in the early Southern Sung legislation on allowances, namely, that much of it focuses exclusively on mourning kin. For example, in 1130 special provisions were made for clan wives who had neither sons nor the stipends of office on which to depend. All wives of mourning kin (*ssu-ma*) were to receive 96,000 cash, 36 piculs of rice, and 28 rolls (*p'i*) of silk (*po*) annually, whereas wives of the *t'an-wen* generation were to be given the same amounts of cash and grain but only half that amount of silk.[14] Similarly, in 1141 a funeral allowance of 300,000 cash was designated for mourning kin, 100,000 for *t'an-wen* kin.[15]

The curious feature of these provisions is that, strictly interpreted, they would have benefited very few people, for the vast majority of clan members were in the sixth to ninth generations and thus had no mourning relationship, not even that of *t'an-wen*, to Kao-tsung. (The main exceptions were those in the Prince of P'u [BCB] subbranch of the T'ai-tsung branch.) I would suggest that it makes much more sense if we take the references to "*t'an-wen*" to mean "*t'an-wen* and beyond," a shortened form of the phrase used in 1095: "*t'an-wen* and the two following generations."[16] It is suggestive, in this regard, that the one-third *t'an-wen* allowance levels legislated in 1130 were 32 strings and 12 piculs per year or 2.7 strings and one picul per month, which is very close to the 1132 figures cited above, and in fact more liberal than the 1095 provisions for non-mourning kin cited in Chapter 4.[17] Moreover, later, when special increases in allowances were granted on such occasions as the suburban sacrifices, the nomenclature of mourning relationship was abandoned altogether.[18] Finally, we might note a reflective memorial from the registrar of the Great Office written in 1212 in an attempt to elicit greater cooperation from local officials in providing the clan allowances. It describes how, in the early Southern Sung, the emperor acceded to the request that members of the "Heavenly clan" receive equal benefits and says that support was approved for all clan members lacking other means of support (such as stipends) "without limitation on the number of generations" (*pu hsien shih-shu*) of those supported.[19] This, in fact, is the essential point. Clan membership, whether for allowances, other privileges, or status, ceased in the Southern Sung to become a matter of mourning relationship or generation. All patrilineal descendents of the three founding Chao brothers were equally leaves on the imperial branches, a metaphor invoked by the 1212 memorialist.

In addition to the annual allowances and the special allowances for such occasions as funerals, the court also continued and, indeed, extended the privileges accorded husbands of clanswomen. Here again, the evidence is somewhat indirect. Writing in the late twelfth century, Hung Mai (1123–1204) described the basic privilege for husbands of *t'an-wen* clanswomen as the receipt of low civil rank (*chiang-shih lang*) if they were *chü-jen* (graduates of the preliminary examinations) or low military rank (*ch'eng-hsin lang*) otherwise.[20] The *chü-jen* stipulation was new in the Southern Sung, and in fact Li Hsin-ch'uan dates it to 1171, but states that "when men who had passed the preliminary examinations married clanswomen, they would enter service as civil officials," and makes no reference to *t'an-wen* status, which provides further support for the notion that *t'an-wen* had become a shorthand term to designate clan members with no formal mourning relationship to the emperor.[21]

This privilege was not the only marriage benefit the court conferred on clanswomen, although it probably was the most important. The schedule of official dowries, established in the Hsi-ning period (1068–77), which designated the payments to be made beginning with imperial princesses and extending through clanswomen of the eighth generation (see Chapter 4) was revived in 1137, albeit at greatly reduced levels. Seventh-generation women were to receive approximately 70 strings of cash, and those of the eighth generation 50 strings.[22] And how did these distant kin fare in reality? The same sources go on to say that some officials refused to disburse these funds, making it impossible for some poor clanswomen to marry. In 1162, at the request of the administrator of the Southern Clan Office in Ch'üan-chou, the emperor sent court funds there to cover these expenses. Since the eighth generation was flourishing in the mid-twelfth century (see Table 2.3, p. 32), they may have accounted for the bulk of these payments. But at some point these dowries were extended to later generations, for Fang Ta-ts'ung (1183–1247), writing much later, noted that "according to precedent, when clanswomen get married, they are to have a cash dowry," and in fact he was critical of pressures put upon young clan girls to marry so that the dowry could be obtained.[23]

Finally, the court in 1166 created one further privilege for clanswomen, and that was the right to nominate one son for official rank, regardless of how many sons her husband or his family were entitled to name through the *yin* privilege. Since we learn of this measure in a description of a cutback enacted around 1201 to restrict the number of sons named by clanswomen to one, the implication is that at times more than one was named.[24]

In summary, although the policy of the court toward the support of the imperial clan in general was constantly evolving during the early decades of the Southern Sung and had few clear turning points, it was on the whole generous and inclusive toward the increasingly distant membership of the clan. In many ways, however, the factors most important in the lives of individual clan members were related to their local circumstances, particularly in Lin-an, Shao-hsing, Fu-chou, and Ch'üan-chou, the major centers of the clan.

The Clan Centers

There could hardly be a more striking comparison than the one between Northern Sung K'ai-feng and Southern Sung Lin-an as centers of imperial clan activity. Even at the end of the Northern Sung, when the Tun-tsung Halls at the Western and Southern capitals had drawn many clan members, K'ai-feng was unchallenged as the clan center, with thousands of members living in opulence in their palatial residential complexes. The clan's presence in Lin-an, by contrast, was always small and usually unremarkable. For example, among the clansmen represented in Table 7.2, none of the 1256 *chin-shih* and just two of those with identified burial sites were from Lin-an, and both of them in fact lived outside the city itself.

Two factors explain the low profile of Lin-an in clan life. First, the official Mu-ch'in Residence was reserved for Southern Rank clan members, and there were not many of them. Second, the government actively discouraged other clan members from living in the capital—with the exception of those who were there as officials—as spelled out in the 1139 memorial concerning the clan's presence in Lin-an discussed above.

The Southern Rank clansmen played a visible if limited role in the court life of the capital. Like their much more numerous Northern Sung predecessors, they were courtiers who, as their name indicates, occupied the southernmost rank or section at court and in other ceremonies.[25] Their numbers were small; we know that in 1129 some 30 of them went to Kuang-chou under the supervision of Great Office officials, although that number probably included women as well as men.[26] In 1142 the Great Office administrator expressed alarm at the fact that, due to deaths, the number of Southern Rank clansmen resident in the capital had declined from seventeen to thirteen and asked that some be transferred from Shao-hsing fu, where Southern Rank clansmen also resided.[27] This seems to have improved their numbers somewhat, for in 1156, twenty clansmen benefited from a general promotion for Southern Rank clansmen.[28]

Small as their number were, the Southern Rank clan members must have seemed a demanding group to the authorities in the capital. In the sixth month of 1132, the prefect of Lin-an complained that the Southern Rank clansmen were objecting to the new residency complex being built for them and demanding the quarters of the Korean Relations Institute (T'ung-wen kuan) and the side corridor of the Ming-ch'ing Temple for their residence. Kao-tsung concurred with the prefect's suggestion that the clan members be required to accept the designated buildings. The Mu-ch'in Residence was completed four months later.[29] Ironically, the clan complaints appear to have had some merit, for in 1136 it was acknowledged that the residence was too crowded, and the Secretariat was ordered to come up with a plan to address the problem.[30] The Southern Rank clan members were also reported in 1135 to be suffering from the galloping inflation that plagued Lin-an at that time; in response they were made eligible to pay the discounted prices for foodstuffs used by the imperial kitchens.[31] Later the same year, Kao-tsung was worried about their ability to survive the winter and gave them presents from the privy purse totaling 3,600 rolls of raw silk and 10,000 ounces of cotton. This action won the emperor both the praise of the grand councilor Chao Ting (1085–1147) for its generosity and criticism for doing it without informing him.[32]

As virtually the only mourning kinsmen of the emperor, the Southern Rank clansmen were the only clansmen who continued to receive names and guard rank offices as children, as had all clansmen a century earlier. This, together with their much higher salaries and allowances, put them in an enviable position relative to other clansmen. It also had its drawbacks, the chief of which were the mandatory court attendance and the lack of political responsibility, in contrast to those clansmen pursuing active official careers. Some Southern Rank men chose to give up their guard status and transfer to the regular military or civil service,[33] but since these cases were individually—and only occasionally—reported, the practice seems to have been the exception rather then the norm.

Lin-an also housed the Office of the Jade Register, the Court of the Imperial Clan, and the Great Office of Imperial Clan Affairs, the last of which had jurisdiction, in theory at least, over clan affairs throughout the empire. The first two were housed together, at least after their permanent quarters were built in 1150, and seem to have concerned themselves primarily with genealogical issues.[34] But even the Great Office seems to have maintained a low profile in the Southern Sung. It was centrally located next to the grand councilors' offices, to the north of the central gate of the imperial palace,[35] but according to a complaint by the administrator Chao Shih-k'ua (BCBMCB; n.d.) in 1147, the quarters were quite inadequate. Despite responsibility for clan affairs in all prefectures, the need to record the births and deaths of clansmen and clanswomen, marriages, entry to office, allowances, and the like, they had so little space that some of the clan officials had no offices. Shih-k'ua asked that either the quarters be enlarged or that buildings be acquired from people living nearby. The emperor directed the Lin-an officials to take care of the matter, which is the last we hear of it.[36]

More to the point, it is almost the last that we hear of the Great Office as an institution in the Southern Sung. In part this may have been because of the lackluster quality of its administrators. Li Hsin-ch'uan, the preeminent historian of Kao-tsung's reign, argues that in the early years of the Southern Sung, its administrators were drawn from the Southern Rank clansmen and were mediocre individuals who did not serve as exemplars for their fellow clansmen and who ruthlessly exploited their positions for their own ends. His only good words are for Chao Pu-hsi (BCBFAFA; 1121–87), a highly admired clansman whose appointment broke precedent—he came to the post from a successful career in the civil service.[37] In confirmation of this point, of the four individuals with biographies who served either as administrator or as co-administrator of the Great Office in the twelfth century, only one is credited with innovative activities during his tenure. That was Chao Pu-hsi, who while serving as administrator late in his career energetically promoted educational reform for clansmen (see below).[38]

Information concerning the activities of the clan centers outside Lin-an is not plentiful, but what we have is interesting. Not all these activities took place at the three major centers. In 1209, a Buddhist temple complex was created at the prefectural offices of Chia-hsing fu (Liang-che), the birthplace of the clansman Chao Po-ts'ung (ABBACEAB), who was selected by Kao-tsung as his heir and reigned as Hsiao-tsung. The monastery, known as the Hsing-sheng ssu, served as a site for memorializing and performing devotions to Hsiao-tsung until virtually the end of the dynasty, and drew upon both the local government and the community for support. However, as Mark Halperin has shown, imperial clansmen played a central role both in the establishment of the monastery and in its maintenance.[39] Some of the half-dozen whom Halperin identifies were closely related to Hsiao-tsung. For example, Chao Hsi-tao, who as prefect of Chia-hsing oversaw its initial construction, was the grandson of Hsiao-tsung's brother Po-kuei (ABBA-CEAA; 1125–1202).[40] However, others like the painter and poet Chao Meng-chien (AABCDBADBEAA, 1199–ca. 1267) were only distantly related, although all were members of the T'ai-tzu branch of the clan. Thus the ritual veneration of imperial ancestors, which in the Northern Sung had been confined to K'ai-feng and kept out of the hands of the imperial clan, took a local and popular turn, with imperial clansmen playing a prominent role.

Scenic Shao-hsing, another clan center, was home to many of the Southern Rank clan families that did not live in Lin-an, but its greater claim to fame was as the mortuary center for the dynasty in the south. Here were buried emperors, empresses, and the princes of P'u—but not as a rule clan members (the decision to bury the emperors rather than holding their coffins for a later burial in the north came only after much debate following the death of Kao-tsung in 1187).[41] With far fewer clan members under its jurisdiction than the offices in Fu-chien, the clan office at Shao-hsing—called the "temporary office" (*hsing-ssu*) in some documents—was quite marginal. In 1171, a proposal to move the Shao-hsing office to Ssu-ch'uan, which had large numbers of clan members, was seriously discussed at court,[42] and although nothing ever came of it, that same year the Shao-hsing office was formally subordinated to the Great Office in Lin-an.[43]

With its 300-plus clan members, the Southern Office in Ch'üan-chou was the largest of the clan offices. Almost from the outset, the burden of supporting these huge numbers was sorely resented by the local officials. In the fifth month of 1133, Hsieh K'o-chia (1097 *chin-shih*), the prefect of Ch'üan-chou, submitted a plea for financial relief. Hsieh noted that the prefecture's regular sources of revenue were barely adequate for its normal expenditures and totally inadequate to support the clan members. They had been aided by a grant of some 20,000 strings of cash from the fiscal commissioner's office, but even so during the preceding ten months they had run a shortfall of over 62,400 strings. In response, the emperor authorized the sale of 250 ordination certificates for monks, with the proceeds to go to the prefecture.[44] These are considerable figures; indeed, the sum of 82,400 strings averages to almost 275 strings per clan member (82,400/300 = 275), an order of magnitude greater than the basic allowance of 2.7 strings of cash and one picul of rice. Of course, there were also the stipends for those with official rank, the other allowances to which members were entitled, the administrative costs of the Western Office, and possibly even the cost of residential construction, since the move to Ch'üan-chou had occurred only three years earlier. Nevertheless, the burden was great, and as we will see in the next chapter, became greater yet as clan numbers swelled.

As time went by, various practices evolved concerning the roles of the Western and Southern Offices in clan affairs. One was ritual, for Fu-chou clan members were given the singular privilege of maintaining imperial portraits and conducting appropriate rituals for them.[45] Another was penal; when clansmen were found guilty of an offense requiring incarceration, they were sent to Ch'üan-chou in odd-numbered months and to Fu-chou in even-numbered ones.[46] Also, in 1156 an idea first proposed in 1133 came to fruition, and that was for annual meetings between the officials of the Western and Southern Offices to discuss common problems.[47]

The administrators of the Western and Southern Offices at this time were, respectively, Chao Shih-k'an (BCBGFF; n.d.) and Chao Shih-hsueh (BCBLFD; 1108–62), second cousins in the Prince of P'u sub-branch of the clan. It seems that they became too cooperative in their annual meetings, for in 1161 both were removed from office in a scandal. According to the *Hsi-nien yao-lu*, Shih-k'an's crime involved the forcible purchase of an oceangoing junk.[48] The fuller *Sung hui-yao* account explains. A Chang-chou merchant, Wang Ch'iung, who owned a ship that plied the overseas trade, was bankrupted by expenses following the death of his father, who died while traveling in another locality. Officials insisted that he even sell his empty ship to pay his debts, and it was sold to none other than Chao Shih-k'an, operating under an alias and certainly using crooked means to pressure Wang, in the view of his accuser. When the court learned of this, it ordered the Fu-chien

judicial officials to return the ship to Wang. However, given his debts and
the additional interest they had accumulated, he had had to sell it and it
again entered the possession of Shih-k'an, and in fact the memorialist reporting this saw no further recourses open to Wang.[49]

As to Chao Shih-hsueh, he, too, had illegally seized a large ship from a
merchant. For three years this matter went unrectified; in 1159 a new
Ch'üan-chou prefect, Fan Ju-kuei (1102–60), had heard the merchant's suit
and settled it according to the law. According to Chu Hsi, who chronicled
this affair, Fan's reward was removal from office after being slandered by
Shih-hsueh.[50] Curiously, Shih-hsueh's epitaph makes no mention of his
dismissal, saying only that in 1161 his request for a temple guardianship was
accepted and that he died the next year while en route. It also notes that he
was promoted to high ceremonial office in 1159 because of his excellent governance of the Southern Office and praises his service there: "In guiding the
clan members, he was able to lead them through his personal kindness, first
and foremost toward the orphaned and friendless. While severe, he was
not cruel. In the unity of the clan's culture, there was an air of nobility, like
that reported in antiquity."[51] Even Chao Shih-k'an, the primary culprit in
this affair, seems to have weathered it without too much disgrace, for two
years later he and his brother Shih-chien (BCBGFE) were praised by the
new emperor Hsiao-tsung for offering to give half of the imperial gifts that
had just been bestowed on them to support the war effort against the
Chin.[52]

Personalities aside, the Wang Ch'iung affair had two important out-
comes for the imperial clan. The first was an absolute prohibition on the
involvement of Western or Southern Office officials in the overseas trade,
thus depriving them of a potentially lucrative source of revenue (as we will
see in Chapter 9, however, the prohibition did not stop clan involvement of
various sorts in the trade).[53] Second, in appointing replacements for Shih-
k'an and Shih-hsueh as the administrators of the Fu-chien offices, the emperor approved going outside the pool of Southern Rank clansmen—from
which all past appointments had been made—and selecting "honest and
upright clansmen from the ranks of civil and military officials." According
to Li Hsin-ch'uan, from this time on civil official–clansmen were frequently
selected for leadership posts in the clan.[54]

We do not know whether the implications of this policy change were discussed, but they were significant. When it ended the monopoly of the Southern Rank clansmen on clan offices, the court turned not to clansmen-officials from either the Fu-chou or Ch'üan-chou centers but rather to men who lived with their families independently of the centers. These men emerged in the early Southern Sung as the new elite of the imperial clan.

The Independent Clan Families

One subject about which the sources on the Southern Sung clan centers are silent is the life of clan members—how they lived, with whom they socialized, whom they married. I would suggest that this silence is not accidental but the result of the insularity of the clan centers. As had been the case with the Northern Sung residences in K'ai-feng and the two minor capitals, clan members lived together in large numbers and were discouraged from socializing with those outside the centers. In marked contrast, the clan families that lived independently in southern China were by and large integrated into local society. Although the individual families could constitute sizable establishments,[55] clansmen outside the clan centers necessarily interacted with their neighbors—especially the local elites—a fact that undoubtedly benefited them in their official careers as well.

The decision by a clan family to settle in a particular locality was made for a variety of reasons, but the most common was related to official service. For example, Chao Shih-ts'u (BEAGFE; n.d.) served as an official in Shao-wu chün (Fu-chien) in the early Southern Sung, liked its scenery, and made his home there. Shih-ts'u's son, Pu-che, reportedly had few ambitions beyond raising his sons properly. When Pu-che's son Shan-kung (BEAG-FEAC; 1148–1217) excelled in his studies and went on to pass the qualifying examinations in 1166, which resulted in his being named a wine-tax official, his father said, "This son is the one who will make our family (*chia*) flourish." And he was right, for Shan-kung went on to receive a *chin-shih* degree in 1172 and had an extremely distinguished career.[56] Chao Po-lu (AAAA-CEBB; 1135–1202), who had been orphaned as a boy of six and had a brief career in minor posts, settled in Chi-shui county of Chi-chou (Chiang-hsi), where he had served as tax collector. He quickly put down roots, impressing his neighbors with his harmonious household, hiring teachers to instruct his sons and brothers, and even handling the burial of a clansman-official who had died while in office but was not a close relation—an instance of social solidarity among clansmen that I have encountered only rarely. Finally, his epitaph was written by none other than Chou Pi-ta (1126–1204), a former grand councilor who was among the most eminent Chi-chou natives of the day.[57]

Chou also wrote the epitaph of Chao Yen-wu (CCCCEBAA; 1137–1201), whose father had been an official in Lu-ling county of Chi-chou and settled there. Yen-wu had a moderately successful career as a local official, serving at the time of his death as a county magistrate in Hunan, and is credited with engaging with local worthies in literary pursuits. His family is also portrayed as being modest in resources—it had to borrow money to pay for his coffin—but since Yen-wu was also Chou's nephew by marriage (through his second wife), we must be cautious about reading poverty into that fact.[58]

At least some clansmen-officials did not purchase a residence and land but relied instead on residences attached to official posts. We are told that the father of Chao Shih-hsin (AADEAAEAC; 1148–90) led his family south and settled in Yin, the metropolitan county of Ming-chou. They lived frugally and modestly in official quarters, saving salary money to realize their plans.[59] Chao Pu-hsi's case was somewhat different. An official of great distinction who—as noted above—was the first clansman active in the regular bureaucracy to be appointed administrator of the Great Office, he could hardly have been financially needy. Yet such was his sense of propriety that he lived with his family unostentatiously in official quarters, and when traveling to Ssu-ch'uan to serve as the assistant fiscal intendant, he took his entire household—some fifty in all—with him on a single boat and refused expensive gifts from officials en route.[60]

If an official posting determined the residence of some clan families, others settled where the tides of war cast them as refugees. Chao Mu-chih (CHABEF; 1101–59) in 1127 led his mother, younger brothers, and orphaned nephews from Lo-yang south into central Hunan. They stopped and settled in Heng-shan county of T'an-chou, where they were joined by his widowed older sister. He supported his family by serving as a bridge toll official and led a successful defense of the town against a bandit attack after the other officials had deserted. Although he held only the one minor position (he had a low military service rank thanks to exercising his father's *yin* privilege), he became highly respected in his community (local people called him a Buddha, *fo-tzu*), and had his epitaph written by Hu Hung (1106–62), the outstanding Hunanese philosopher of the twelfth century.[61]

In their flight south, Chao Kung-mai (CABCAGC; 1115–79) and his brothers arrived in Hui-chou (Chiang-tung-tung) in 1131 and settled there. Despite his youth, Kung-mai did well in a poetry examination (not the regular examinations), which earned him military rank, and then received a *chin-shih* degree in 1154. Throughout a career that took him to posts in Chiang-hsi, Liang-che, and Fu-chien (where he was the registrar at the Western Office), his home remained Hui-chou, where he also supported his orphaned nephews on his salary. Their residence was not in the countryside but in the prefectural city near the market, and Kung-mai bemoaned the fact that, without farmland, the family could not eat its own produce.[62]

Just a year younger, Chao Po-shu (AADDGADA; 1116–68) began much like Kung-mai by settling in Wu-yuan county in Hui-chou, where it fell to him to manage the family's affairs since his father was away in official service. A first cousin of Po-shu's grandfather Chao Ling-ch'ih (AADDEA; 1061–1134), a prince and clan official, took an interest in him and wanted to nominate him for official rank. Po-shu declined, for he wanted to devote himself to his studies, but he did accompany Ling-ch'ih to Lin-chiang chün in Chiang-hsi. There he joined a circle of young scholars who were preparing for the examinations, and in 1145 managed to place eighth in the palace examination, an unprecedented feat for an imperial clansman. After that promising start, his career was disappointing, and he died while serving in a county post in Hunan. However, since he was buried not in Hui-chou but in Lin-chiang, it would seem that his move to Lin-chiang was a permanent one.[63]

There were clansmen who had the luxury of choosing a locality in which to settle. Chao Shih-tsan (BCAAHA; 1095–1160), whom we saw in the preceding chapter successfully resisting the rebel Li Ch'eng and later becoming identified as an ally of Ch'in Kuei, provides an interesting example. Sun Ti (1081–1169), a prominent local official and the author of Shih-tsan's epitaph, recounts their initial acquaintance, which occurred during the Chien-yen period (1127–30) in I-hsing county of Ch'ang-chou (northern Liang-che), where Shih-tsan, in between postings as a prefect, was living in a Buddhist hall on the estate of Hu Mao-lao, an academician. Shih-tsan, Sun, Hu, and Tung Ling-sheng, another official, spent ten days eating, drinking, and writing poetry, and became fast friends. Years later Sun returned to I-hsing to find that Hu had died, but Tung and Shih-tsan were still there, the latter having bought an estate south of the town to which he had retired, and they renewed their friendship. In the interim Shih-tsan had had a long and successful career, but never served in I-hsing or Ch'ang-chou.[64]

Also revealing is the case of Chao Pu-t'ien (BCBTGDA; 1144–81). He was a Southern Rank clansman who was born and raised in the Mu-ch'in Residence in Lin-an; his parents died while he was an adolescent, and he spent most of his youth overseeing the education and marriages of his four younger brothers. Then he said, "I am not happy staying in the capital and want to acquire mountains and forests in order to live in accord with my nature." Hearing that Su-chou had abundant fertile land, he bought land in K'ai-yuan, a hamlet in Ch'ang-shou county and built a residence there. Its description is idyllic; it had running water in front and green hills behind, a clear pond with a bridge, trees, flowers, and scattered bamboos. There he devoted himself to a gentry lifestyle, entertaining guests with drink and poetry, befriending Buddhist monks, aiding the poor and needy in the community (often by forgiving debts), and mediating local disputes. So rooted was he that for years he did not even travel into the city—presumably Su-chou—and when, late in life, he was offered a post in another part of the Yangtze Delta, he turned it down. Yet curiously, Pu-t'ien's epitaph was written not by a Su-chou scholar but rather by one Yang Hsing-tsung (1160 *chin-shih*), a Fukienese official who never served in Su-chou. Clearly, Pu-t'ien's social world went well beyond the confines of Ch'ang-shou county.[65]

Chao Pu-t'ien is not the only clansman whose estate is described in his epitaph. To cite just a few of the many other examples, the father of Chao Po-huai (AABDEFBA; 1120–77) took his family to Huang-yen county in T'ai-chou (Liang-che) and purchased land that turned out to be quite barren. As the oldest son, Po-huai took responsibility for family affairs, which included urging the estate employees to "energetic cultivation"; his efforts resulted in a productive enterprise.[66] The politically successful Chao Tzu-chou (AAEBFAE; 1089–1142), whose career was described in the preceding chapter, converted his success into a grand estate in the southern suburbs of Ch'ü-chou (Liang-che), with spacious lands and a garden with ponds and pavilions where he entertained his friends.[67]

What of those clan families that lacked the resources to establish themselves? Since they tended not to have epitaphs written for them—at least not epitaphs by writers prominent enough to have their collected writings survive to the present—they are for the most part invisible. Chao Kung-heng (CDCFIDB; 1138–96), however, comes close to being an archetypal "poor clansman." When his father and uncles came south, they settled in the Yangtze River prefecture of Chiu-chiang, where they reportedly lived in rustic poverty. When Kung-heng was fifteen *sui*, his father died of an illness, as did his uncles shortly thereafter, and the family was dependent on the orphan's allowance for clan members. At some point they moved to Lu-ling county in Chi-chou, where, like Chao Pu-t'ien, Kung-heng devoted himself to local pursuits. He became knowledgeable in Taoism, astronomy, medicine, and divination, helped those who were sick or in need, and was extremely filial in serving his mother, who lived to the age of 79. Never taking the examinations or holding office—although he received military rank late in life—he styled himself as a "tranquil retired scholar." Yet however modest his accomplishments, Kung-heng still had claims to prominence, such as his official rank, his community leadership, and the fact that all four of his sons received *chin-shih* degrees and became officials. Most notably, he was the only clansman for whom I found two epitaphs, and they were written by none other than Chou Pi-ta and Yang Wan-li (1127–1206), perhaps the greatest poet of the Southern Sung.[68] Thus even though Kung-heng is among the least prominent of the clansmen for whom we have records, in terms of Chi-chou society he seems not to have been marginal at all.

Also related to residency is the question of burial practice, for in general, where a family buried its dead was taken as one of the surest signs of residence.[69] As we saw above, the imperial clan was different, for in the Northern Sung all clan members—except for clanswomen who had married out of the clan—were buried at one of the two great mortuary centers in Honan. In the Southern Sung those centers were of course out of reach, and so far as we know, except for the imperial tombs in Shao-hsing, the government made no attempt to establish a new mortuary center for the imperial clan.[70] The epitaphs give precise burial information for 62 clansmen, and present a clear pattern. Grave sites were obtained and used by individual families in the localities in which they were residing, and they did not cooperate with other clan families in the same localities. We have records of two or more clansmen being buried in the same county—from Chi-chou (Chiang-hsi) and the Liang-che prefectures of Ming-chou, T'ai-chou and Su-chou—but with only one curious exception clansmen from different families were not buried at the same site.[71] Thus one of the sociocultural practices that most distinguished the clan disappeared, making the independent clan families even more like the local elites with whom they were interacting.

Marriages and Affines

If grave sites were the most enduring signs of residency in Sung society, marriage was the pre-eminent marker of social connection. For this reason, and also because historical records lend themselves to marriage analysis, much of the most exciting research in recent years on Sung social history has focused upon marriage. One of the most important hypotheses has been that of Robert Hymes, who, working from a superbly researched study of Fu-chou (Chiang-hsi), has argued that a social closure occurred in the early Southern Sung, a shift in social and political focus from the national (or empire-wide) to the local level. Central to his analysis is his finding that marriages by families in the Fu-chou elite were much more local (that is, occurring within the prefecture) in the Southern Sung than they had been before.[72] Beverly Bossler has taken issue with this model, suggesting that the changes Hymes describes are in fact historiographically generated—a result of the much greater quantity of historical records available in the Southern Sung. Using data drawn from the records on the families of grand councilors and Wu-chou (in southern Liang-che), she argues for a more fluid elite society, one in which both local and extra-local marriage ties played a role.[73] (I mention this debate not because I intend to resolve it here—although it seems likely that at least some of the difference between Hymes and Bossler can be explained by differences between Chiang-hsi and Liang-che—but rather to provide some perspective for my findings on clan marriages.)

The clansmen's epitaphs contain a number of revealing accounts of their marriage matches, and in the early Southern Sung some of these were quite unconventional. For example, Chao Yen-meng (CCAAAABA; n.d.) took refuge in Hui-chou (Chiang-nan-tung) during his flight south. There he married the daughter of the military commander, Meng Keng, who was himself a northerner from P'u-chou (Ching-tung-hsi). Yen-meng accompanied the Mengs to their new home in Ch'ien-shan (Hsin-chou), and lived with them until establishing his own residence there. When his son, Ch'ung-fu (CCAAAABAA; 1134–1218), proved bright and precocious in his studies, Meng Keng was impressed and arranged his marriage to a Meng granddaughter (i.e., Ch'ung-fu's cousin). We might further note that despite the family's humble beginnings, its estate in Hsin-chou came to have a tower and a building called the Eastern School, where the sons and grandsons of the family gathered for their studies.[74]

Chao Shan-hsi (BCABACAA; 1141–98) was the son of Pu-yu, the general who—we saw in the preceding chapter—was banished and died in disgrace following the death of his patron, Yueh Fei. Although Shan-hsi was only an infant at the time, the indignation he felt over his father's fate fueled his determination to succeed. A month after marrying a Lady Li from a vice-prefect's family in Lin-chiang chün (Chiang-hsi)—he himself was from Ming-chou—he left her with his maternal uncle's family in Wen-chou and rented a room in a Buddhist monastery, where he devoted himself to studying for the examinations. After three years he passed the examinations, was named a capital official, and finally set off to see his wife. En route he met an official named Hsiao and asked after his father-in-law. Hsiao replied: "Alas, he died. His daughter married into the imperial clan but is now drifting about. I hear that she has been cut off now for several years." Shan-hsi laughed and recounted his story—which he later told to Hsiao-tsung in court. Notwithstanding Shan-hsi's three-year desertion, his marriage apparently was a success, for he proceeded to have five sons and a daughter.[75]

To cite one more example, Chao Kung-yü (CEFCBCB; 1136–1203) was a resident of Chi-chou (Chiang-hsi), where his father had settled after serving there in the late 1120s. Kung-yü had two wives, the second of whom was the daughter of a judicial official. The first, however, came from a local Chi-chou family and the match followed from Kung-yü's friendship with her grandfather; they would gather with friends to drink and recite poetry in woods west of the prefectural city.[76]

Apart from offering unusual stories, these examples illustrate the three

major groups with which the imperial clan families intermarried: northerners, local elite families, and official families from other locales. But how
common were these kinds of marriage? This question is not easy to answer,
for Sung epitaphs typically provide the names and ranks (or offices) of male
in-laws, but not their residences; we can determine the kind of marriage only
in those cases where residency can be independently ascertained. However,
in the clansmen's epitaphs there are some 32 in-laws whose residences can
be identified (seventeen fathers-in-law, fifteen sons-in-law), and in those
marriages, eighteen of the spouses (56 percent) were from the same prefecture, ten (31 percent) were from outside the prefecture, and four (13 percent)
were northerners.[77] These figures differ considerably from those presented
by Hymes, who found overwhelming percentages of local marriages for Fu-
chou in the Southern Sung, and the number of cases is so small that we
must avoid reading too much into them. Still, they do indicate that the
independent clan families actively engaged in both local and interregional
marriages. Like the prominent families—especially those of grand councilors—dealt with by Bossler, they moved in both worlds at once.

The epitaphs are considerably more revealing about the official status of
imperial clan affines. Tables 7.3 and 7.4 summarize the available information
on fathers- and sons-in-law of clansmen over a 250-year period. Bear in
mind that Table 7.3, on fathers-in-law, reflects the marriages of clansmen;
assuming an average marriage age of around twenty, the dates for the marriages would lag around twenty years behind the birthdates. Similarly, the
sons-in-law table reflects the marriages of clanswomen, with an average lag
of approximately fifty years (thirty years for the clansmen to marry and
father a daughter, and twenty years for the daughter to reach the age of
marriage).

Both tables depict a dramatic change in the composition of imperial clan
affines: the virtual disappearance of affines in the military service counter-
balanced by the rise of those from the civil service and, on a smaller scale, by
examination graduates and those without official status.[78] These last two
groups are most evident among the sons-in-law and can be explained at least
in part by the fact that the fathers-in-law (necessarily deceased since the data
derive from their epitaphs) were being described in mid- to late career, when
their daughters were getting married to young men whose careers were just

Table 7.3

Status of Clansmen's Fathers-in-Law,
Grouped by Clansmen's Birthdates

Clansmen's birthdates	No. of clansmen	No. of fathers-in-law	Not an official	Military official	Civil official
960–1009	10	11	0	10 (91%)	1 (9%)
1010–59	17	20	1 (5%)	16 (80%)	3 (15%)
1060–1109	5	6	0	1 (17%)	5 (83%)
1110–59	15	19	2 (11%)	2 (11%)	15 (79%)
1160–1259	12	12	3 (25%)	1 (8%)	8 (66%)
TOTAL	59	68	6 (9%)	30 (44%)	32 (47%)

NOTE: In cases in which no father-in-law but a more distant relation was given, the most closely related relative was used instead. Specifically, eleven grandfathers-in-law, one great-grandfather-in-law, and one uncle-in-law were used.

Table 7.4

Status of Clansmen's Sons-in-Law,
Grouped by Clansmen's Birthdates

Clansmen's birthdates	No. of clansmen	No. of sons-in-law	Not an official	Examination graduate	Military official	Civil official
960–1009	11	40	0	0	40 (100%)	0
1010–59	25	54	12 (22%)	0	40 (74%)	2 (4%)
1060–1109	15	30	2 (7%)	0	11 (37%)	17 (57%)
1110–59	27	77	20 (26%)	2 (3%)	6 (8%)	49 (64%)
1160–1259	15	32	12 (38%)	3 (9%)	0	17 (53%)
TOTAL	93	233	46 (20%)	5 (2%)	97 (42%)	85 (36%)

NOTE: The figures for sons-in-law include fourteen husbands of granddaughters.

beginning. Also, in light of the recruitment privileges offered to husbands of imperial clanswomen, at least some of the 46 non-official sons-in-law were probably marrying in order to gain official status. We should also remember that their lack of an official position at the time of the father-in-law's death does not mean that they were not from official households or that they did not acquire a position some time after the epitaph was written. That said, the increase in the number of fathers-in-law who were not officials suggests that the social scope of clan family marriages broadened over the course of time, probably out of necessity.

Despite these minor differences, the two tables agree on the military to civilian transformation of clan marriage ties, one that had its beginnings in the late eleventh century at the time of the profound changes that accompanied the appearance of the first non-mourning generations. Certainly by the Southern Sung, it would appear that the imperial clan was marrying almost exclusively with the civil elite, which is very much the group studied by Hymes, Bossler, and in fact virtually all social historians of the Sung.

There is a problem with this picture, however; virtually all the authors of the Southern Sung epitaphs were members of that civil elite with which the clan families were marrying, and they wrote their epitaphs either because they were friends of the deceased or because they had been approached by the family. (By contrast, as we noted above, most Northern Sung epitaphs were written in batches by officials commissioned to write them.) Thus the question arises; how representative are these findings?

The *Hsien-yuan lei-p'u*, the twenty-*chüan* fragment of the imperial genealogy (see Chapter 3), offers another perspective on the issue of marriage ties, for despite its limitations in terms of generation and time, it has the great advantage of treating *all* clan members and not simply those who were successful or prominent. Moreover, whereas the epitaphs present the situation found at the time of the father's death and would not mention data on the husbands of as yet unmarried daughters, these records deal with the daughters across their own life-spans rather than that of their father; thus this work presents a truer cross-section of the clan than the sample drawn from epitaphs. Table 7.5 shows the status of 222 husbands of some 210 clanswomen from the late eleventh and early twelfth centuries.

There are some telling differences with the data derived from the epitaphs. For these clanswomen, at least, the dramatic increase in spouses with

Table 7.5
Status of Clanswomen's Husbands,
Grouped by Clanswomen's Birthdates

Clans-women's birthdates	No. of women	Un-married	Twice married	Hus-bands	No office	Military official	Civil official
1050–79	37	0	0	37	25 (68%)	10 (27%)	2 (5%)
1080–1109	140	30	8	118	47 (39%)	60 (51%)	11 (9%)
1110–39	103	55	2	50	5 (10%)	27 (54%)	18 (36%)
1140–69	22	7	2	17	3 (18%)	8 (47%)	6 (35%)
TOTAL	302	92	12	222	80 (36%)	105 (47%)	37 (17%)

SOURCE: *Hsien-yuan lei-p'u.*

careers in the civil service began with those born in 1110 and later, or basically with women who married in the Southern Sung. Also, the large number of unmarried women in the 1110–1139 cohort undoubtedly was the result of their captivity under the Chin. But the most surprising difference is the fact that, even in the twelfth century, military service spouses continued to account for half of the marriages and civil service spouses for just a third.

The explanation for these seemingly contradictory findings, I would suggest, lies in the select nature of the epitaph records, for they reflect only the independent clan families that were prominent enough to have epitaphs. That group, quite clearly, became integrated almost exclusively into the local elites—in particular, into the *shih-ta-fu* or scholar-official stratum of those societies. If this is the correct explanation, then the large number of military service marriages would have been concentrated among the clan families living in the clan centers and essentially continued the marriage patterns of the Northern Sung clan.

Schools and Education

But if there was a de facto hierarchy within the imperial clan that followed lines of residency and marriage, all clansmen were united by the fact that the primary path to advancement was through the schools and examinations—as it was for the wider society—and by the privileges that they shared within the educational world. As we saw in earlier chapters, the court's policy of relying upon education and examinations to serve as the primary vehicle for the entry of non-mourning imperial clansmen into officialdom was firmly established in the last half-century of the Northern Sung. In the early Southern Sung, however, it became even more critical, and much attention was paid to meeting the educational needs of the clansmen.

Clansmen came to make use of a wide variety of schools, the most important of which were the clan schools in Lin-an and the clan centers. Although we know much more about the former, the earliest reports of activity in the Southern Sung come from the latter. In 1132, it was decreed that both the Western and the Southern Office could appoint a teacher (*chiao-shou*) to "teach and guide clan youths" within each of their jurisdictions.[79] In the 1140s steps were taken to clarify the status of the teachers at the Western and Southern Office schools—the general principle was that their status was comparable to that of prefectural school teachers[80]—and in the late 1140s several students from the two schools were exempted from the *chin-shih* qualifying examinations because they had done well in two years of study there.[81] Unfortunately, there is little information on either school that would give a sense of what they were like as institutions. The best description I have found comes from the epitaph of Chao Hsiang-chih (CCFHIA; 1128–1202), who served as administrator of the Western Office late in his career. When he arrived, the imperial clan in Fu-chou had a school, teachers, and a temple to the sages (*fu-tzu-miao*), but no ceremonial activities or clan covenant. Students had no ceremonies, although in the spring and fall they could participate in the prefectural school ceremonies. Hsiang-chih lectured at the school, and after someone asked how they could venerate the former sages without ceremonial implements, Hsiang-chih drew up plans and got funds, and by the next year ceremonies had commenced.[82] In this anecdote we might note both the powerful influence exerted by the prefectural school as a model center of ritual as well as study,[83] and the fact that it took the Fu-chou clan school over half a century to adopt the model fully.

As mentioned earlier, teachers in the clan schools had one curious responsibility—oversight of the incarceration of clansmen. In 1174 the Western Office in Fu-chou reported on the case of Chao Pu-ch'en (possibly BCAAEAJ). Because his offspring (*tzu-hsing*) had been causing disturbances in the marketplace and extorting goods from the people, one was sent to the

Western Office and two to the Southern Office, where they were put under the supervision of teachers at the clan schools. However, according to a report by one of the teachers, Pu-ch'en was 66 and complaining of illness. Given the problems of supplying him with medicines and caring for him, it was not convenient to keep his children separated from him. And so the three were allowed to return home.[84] The palace schools in Lin-an also had this punitive function. Seven years later, in response to a request from the Great Office administrator, Chao Pu-hsi, the palace schools were instructed to create isolation rooms (*tzu-sung-chai*) for the confinement of clansmen guilty of crimes.[85] This curious use of schools may simply reflect that fact that, apart from the residences themselves, only the schools had the physical facilities and personnel to handle an incarceration. However, another purpose may be detected as well, for in his request Pu-hsi asked that the isolation rooms be provided with books, so that the miscreants could read while confined.[86] In good Confucian fashion, clan administrators looked to education for the reform of individuals, and even those clansmen guilty of criminal behavior were spared from being treated as criminals.

The schools in Lin-an had their beginnings in 1134 when the upper and lower princely palaces schools (*wang-kung ta hsiao hsueh*) were established,[87] and a year later permission was given to appoint two teachers (*chiao-shou*) each to the upper and lower schools.[88] Further developments followed in 1144, when Kao-tsung accepted a Great Office proposal to permit clansmen from outside Lin-an to enter the palace schools if they wished, and set student numbers at 50 for the upper school and 40 for the lower school.[89] At this time, a peace with the Chin had been secured and Kao-tsung was actively encouraging the development of schools throughout the empire. To a contemporary, the palace schools would have appeared to have a promising future.

In fact, over the next half-century, their lot was a troubled one. In a revealing memorial from 1157, the palace school teacher Ch'en T'ang asked that the palace school move beyond teaching just the *Analects* and the *Mencius*, which it had been doing for over twenty years on the grounds that more would be too demanding. Noting that the regular examinations placed classical studies first, Ch'en asked that both major and minor classics be taught.[90] Ch'en's proposal was accepted, although with questionable effect, for during the Lung-hsing period (1163–65) the two teaching lines were reduced to one,[91] and according to Li Hsin-ch'uan, teachers at this time would simply go into the school hall, bow once, and retire.[92]

Conditions improved considerably in the 1170s under the leadership of the Great Office administrator Chao Pu-hsi, an excellent scholar (he had received a *chin-shih* degree in 1157) who was highly regarded by the philosophers Chang Shih (1133–80) and Chu Hsi. Pu-hsi, the official responsible for the isolation rooms at the palace school, renovated the palace school and increased student numbers. He also wanted to provide for the boarding and support of clan youths, as was the custom at the Imperial University, and while this was not accepted, his efforts apparently had some results, for he personally encouraged clan youth to study and recommended several score of them, many of whom were outstanding.[93]

These successes did not long outlast Pu-hsi's tenure as Great Office administrator. Claiming that "although clan schools have been established, their affairs have been a formality, with name but not reality," in 1191 the palace school teacher Wang Shih proposed that a group of young and outstanding clansmen without official rank be sent to study at the Imperial University. There they would be housed in a separate dormitory but would in all other respects be treated like the other students. The proposal went nowhere, however, for both the Ministry of Rites and the Directorate of Education opposed it, and Kuang-tsung (r. 1190–94), concurring with their opposition, reasoned that "the purpose of my ancestors in establishing separate clan schools was to provide clansmen with the best treatment, and it would be difficult to command royal [kinsmen] to return to the [Imperial] University."[94]

The emptiness of this rhetoric can be seen in Kuang-tsung's rejection, that same year, of a proposal by the administrator of the Great Office, Chao Po-kuei (ABBACEAA; 1125–1202), to create a separate clan school (*tsung-hsueh*) for the "clan youths of the empire," which would hold monthly and seasonal examinations, as did the Imperial University. Lou Yueh, the author of Po-kuei's epitaph, notes that although nothing came of the proposal, "those who knew of it thought him correct."[95] As well they should have, for the problem with the palace schools is that they were designed for the Southern Rank clansmen, a group that, as we have noted, was small and relatively insignificant.

Finally, in 1214 under another emperor—Ning-tsung (r. 1195–1224)—a clan school was established in Lin-an. Its prescribed size was virtually identical to that of the palace schools in 1144: 100 students in six dormitories. But rather than teachers (*chiao-shou*), the school was to have a professor, or "erudite" (*po-shih*), thus making it more comparable to the university, as well as four educational officials to supervise the corridors and a leader for each dormitory. In justification for the new school, it was stated that in contrast to the late Northern Sung, when K'ai-feng had a clan school and the Western and Southern Capital complexes had palace schools, in the Southern Sung, there were schools for clan youths in Fu-chou and Ch'üan-chou but *not* Lin-an.[96] The palace schools, it would appear, were defunct at this point.

Among the several alternatives to the clan schools, the most important were the government schools. As noted earlier in this chapter, in 1135 clan youths throughout the empire were permitted to attend the local prefectural schools, and in fact a year's attendance was set as a prerequisite to sitting for the examinations.[97] For example, Chao Po-shu (AADFABFB; 1121–88) entered the prefectural school in Hung-chou (Chiang-hsi) as a teenager. There he is described as studying day and night, eating salted cabbage (i.e., ordinary food), and becoming accomplished in the civil arts. More than once he placed first among the many scholars sitting for examinations, and he received a *chin-shih* degree in 1148 (he was ranked 114 out of 122 in the fourth class).[98] Such hard work and brilliance clearly were not the norm. In 1157 a palace school teacher complained that clan youths around the country were simply enrolling in the prefectural schools to meet the examination requirement, but not attending classes, and he asked that—and the emperor instructed—both the Great Office and local officials crack down on the practice.[99] When he was prefect of Ming-chou in 1169–70, Chao Po-kuei, who in 1191 was to propose the creation of a clan school, went a step further. In conjunction with extensive renovations of the prefectural school, he required local imperial clan youths who were not already preparing for the examinations to enter the school and be subject to the same rules as other students. As a result, many of them passed the examinations.[100] We do not know how much use clansmen made of this access to the government schools, but the privilege of attendance was considerable. Although much criticized, the county and prefectural schools were the most widespread and best-supported educational institutions in the empire, and entry to them was often competitive. The clansmen's unrestricted access was unique.

The remaining educational alternatives were the same as those available to others: study at the academies, which in the late twelfth and thirteenth centuries were spreading throughout the empire,[101] or in the family with private tutors, or in family schools. Although examples of clansmen pursuing these routes to education are few, they can be revealing, as in the case of the ninth-generation descendent of T'ai-tsu, Chao Hsi-kuan (AADBBE-GADA; 1176–1233). Born in Ch'ang-shan county of Ch'ü-chou (Liang-che), Hsi-kuan was a bright child and at an early age demonstrated unusual discipline and ambition. Even before he was capped, he accompanied his father to a post in Hunan and studied with P'an Chih (1126–89) at the newly revived Stone Drum Academy (Shih-ku shu-yuan), which P'an had recently revived. Later he studied with two renowned Wen-chou (Liang-che) scholars—Ch'en Fu-liang (1137–1203) and Hsu I (1144–1208)—and in 1196 at the age of 21 *sui* passed the *chin-shih* examinations. Hsi-kuan's biographer, Wei Liao-weng (1178–1237)—himself one of the great Confucian scholars of his day—also noted that although the prefectural school had "a large and elegant dormitory for the noble youths of the dynasty" (i.e., the imperial clansmen), Hsi-kuan refused to enter them, saying, "I am simply cold and plain." This aversion to luxury, however, should not obscure the fact that his education was truly superlative.[102]

In at least one instance, an academy was created for the education of clansmen. In the early thirteenth century, Wang Yen, the prefect of Yun-chou (Chiang-hsi) and a sixth-generation descendent of the Northern Sung grand councilor Wang Tan (957–1017), became concerned about the poor education of the many clan youths in the prefecture. So he built the Delight in Goodness Academy (Lo-shan shu-yuan) next to the prefectural school. The academy's campus had a lecture hall flanked by two corridors and six dormitories. It had an endowment of a thousand *mou* of land to support twenty clan students. They were to be selected from among youths with no official rank and were to study the Classics and the histories. Chou Pi-ta, who wrote the commemorative essay for the academy and whose connections with the imperial clan were numerous, placed this project in the tradition of the sage ruler Shun educating his sons and the Chou dynasty's emphasis on the education of royal princes and foresaw a flourishing imperial clan with eminent scholars.[103]

Less grand but undoubtedly more important for the clan—as it was for the *shih-ta-fu* as well—was the education provided in family schools and with tutors. Earlier, we noted the school that Chao Ch'ung-fu built on his estate. Similarly, Chao Po-kuei had a family school (*chia-shu*) on his estate, where, for forty years, he regularly led the family in ceremonies to the former sages.[104] In two cases, we also know of clan youths who studied in the family schools or homes of neighbors. When the future grand councilor Shih Hao (1106–94) was serving as sheriff of Yü-yao county (Shao-hsing fu), Chao Shih-lung (AABBABDCA; 1143–93), then a child of seven *sui*, studied alongside two of Hao's sons and impressed Hao with his precociousness.[105] A generation later, Chao Ju-sui (BCBGNAGCC; 1172–1246) attended the family school of Lü Tsu-ch'ien (1137–81), which was renowned for the many scholars it produced; there he studied the works of Chu Hsi.[106] These can hardly be considered typical examples, but they nevertheless indicate the kinds of opportunities available to clan youths. Given the prestige and affluence of the imperial clan and its ready access to office, it was probably the rare clan family that could not afford a decent education for its children.

Examinations and Recruitment

Although Confucian culture had always stressed the moral and civilizing functions of education, by the Sung education had become thoroughly interwoven with the examinations. Moreover, the remarkable principle that people should be ranked on the basis of their performances on tests and that those rankings should be used not only to advance students through schools but also to determine eligibility for office and promotions in the bureaucracy had become a central postulate of the political order. The early generations of the imperial clan did participate in contests and examinations, but the members of the clan began to have a real stake in the examinations only after Shen-tsung's reforms. By the Southern Sung, examinations had become central to the lives of most if not all clansmen. Chao Kung-heng, whose individualistic pursuits in Chi-chou are described above, was probably not unique in "being unwilling to take even a single examination for official service,"[107] but there could not have been many like him.

"Examinations," we must remember, included far more than the prestigious *chin-shih* examination. For those looking to government service in some form, the alternatives included placement examinations for those utilizing the *yin* privilege, facilitated examinations for *chü-jen* who had tried and failed the departmental *chin-shih* examinations on numerous occasions, military examinations, examinations for prodigies, and decree examinations (used primarily for promotions within the bureaucracy rather than recruitment into it).[108] There were also examinations exclusively for imperial clansmen. Although in many cases we know only that individuals passed an "examination for clansmen,"[109] the two main institutionalized forms of examination for clansmen were the measurement examination (*liang-shih*) and the special examinations that they took for the *chin-shih* examination.

As noted in Chapter 5, the measurement examinations were more or less equivalent to the facilitated examinations in terms of prestige, in the kinds of rank awarded successful candidates, and in their status as examinations of last resort for those unable to pass the regular examinations. However, unlike the facilitated examinations, they had no formal ties to the regular examinations. According to a formulation from 1162, imperial clansmen sitting the measurement examination were examined on one Classic, poetry and poetic description (*shih fu*), and a discussion (*lun*) of political or philosophical principles.[110] This was more demanding than the Northern Sung test, which examined a candidate on either a Classic or the law, but it lacked the policy questions (*ts'e*) that were generally considered the most difficult part of the *chin-shih* examination. The reward for passing was the prestige title of "gentleman of trust" (*ch'eng-hsin lang*, military rank 9B) for all except the top candidate, who was given the slightly higher title of "gentleman for fostering temperance" (*ch'eng-chieh lang*).[111] That these were military titles—in fact the same titles given to graduates of the military examinations (*wu-chü chin-shih*)—clearly indicates the distinction made between the measurement examination and the regular *chin-shih* examinations.[112]

Although we know little about the number of measurement examination degrees awarded during most of the Southern Sung, a group of documents for the years 1162–72 provides invaluable information about them. In 1663, 1166, 1169, and 1172, the names of the successful measurement examination candidates were announced at virtually the same time as those of the *chin-*

shih, the facilitated *chin-shih*, and military examinations. Following a practice similar to that described above, the top three graduates in the measurement examination were given the higher rank of "gentleman for protecting righteousness" (*pao-i lang*) and the rest *ch'eng-chieh lang*.[113] The numbers of degrees granted in those years were 50, 39, 38, and 41, respectively, or an average of 42 degrees per examination. In comparison, the number of those passing the military examinations averaged 30, the *chin-shih* examinations 398, and the facilitated *chin-shih* examinations 336 for the same four years.[114]

In two of these years, however, an additional measurement examination was given and extra degrees conferred. One involved just a handful of individuals; in 1169, eight clansmen who had twice qualified for the regular examinations passed a measurement examination and were made *ch'eng-chieh lang*.[115] However, in 1163 something very different occurred. It was reported that 30 percent of the over 700 clansmen who had taken a measurement examination had demonstrated relative understanding (and competence), but that the others either did not answer the questions or wrote on some other question. Hsiao-tsung ordered that those who had passed (i.e., demonstrated understanding) be selected, although a few candidates with past disciplinary problems (*tsa-fan*) had to wait for two years before receiving official rank.[116] Although the sources are not explicit, it seems clear that this measurement examination was an extraordinary one, for the upshot was that 216 clansmen received the title of *ch'eng-hsin lang*, which was one notch lower than the *ch'eng-chieh lang* usually received by measurement examination graduates.[117]

Two features of this mass conferral of degrees are noteworthy. First, rather than selecting the most competent or talented, as Sung examinations usually did, this measurement examination rewarded all who could demonstrate a minimal competence, and almost five hundred of those examined could not. Second, the timing of this act, I would suggest, argues that it was related to Hsiao-tsung's recent enthronement. As we shall see below, Hsiao-tsung, who was truly a clansman-emperor, initiated a number of policies that served to enhance the identity and visibility of the imperial clan. It would therefore have been quite in keeping for him to have addressed the pent-up demand of clansmen desiring office through examination by holding an extraordinary examination and giving degrees to all who qualified.

Indeed, after the announcement of names of the 216 successful candidates, Hsiao-tsung granted the title of *ch'eng-hsin lang* to clansmen 40 *sui* or older who had failed the measurement examination.[118]

Although this brief period provides our only figures for the measurement examinations, Hung Mai (1123–1202) wrote at the end of the twelfth century that over a thousand imperial clansmen had passed the measurement examination, received the title of *ch'eng-hsin lang*, and as a result entered officialdom.[119] Hung does not indicate the span of time involved, but even viewed cumulatively, the figure represents a remarkable degree of imperial largesse.

Crucial as the measurement examinations were for many imperial clansmen, they were still viewed as a poor alternative to the regular examinations. Given the difficulty of the latter, it was the rare clansman who participated in them in the late Northern Sung, but this seems to have changed at the very end of the Northern Sung, at least in part because the court carved out separate tracks within the regular examinations for clansmen. These tracks are clearly alluded to in a memorial from 1139 by one Chao Shan-shih (BA-BAVAAB), who described the examinations for clansmen as they existed after 1121, when regular examinations were resumed following the period when the government school system had been used to select *chin-shih* recipients:

I have noticed that in the examination class of Shen Hui [i.e., 1124], when the Three Hall System was first discontinued and the regular examinations (*k'o-chü*) revived, imperial clansmen were divided into three classes and received three levels of grace. Those with official rank who had taken the locked hall examination were promoted two ranks and transferred to civil status. Of those without office deserving of selection (*ch'ü-ying*), the top three were to be made gentlemen for protecting righteousness and the others gentlemen for fostering temperance. Those without office who had been selected as suitable (*ying-chü* [i.e., who had taken the directorate examination]) were to be made gentlemen of good service (*hsiu-chih lang* [an unranked civil executory title]).[120]

The first and third of these classes were the same as they had been in the later Northern Sung: the locked hall examination for clansmen who already held official rank and the directorate examination for clansmen without office. In contrast to the Northern Sung practices, clansmen taking the former were not as a rule *t'an-wen* kin, since there were few if any of them, but rather clansmen who had received office through some other means such as the *yin* privilege.[121] The *ch'ü-ying* category, however, was new. This involved clansmen taking first the qualifying examination at the fiscal intendant's office or a re-examination at the Directorate of Education and then the departmental and palace examinations.[122] But in contrast to the other two categories, the *ch'ü-ying* examinations were simpler, and, in 1145 at least, there were no quotas, which allowed degrees to be conferred on all who wrote acceptable examinations.[123] Not surprisingly, with the exception of the top-ranked individual, the *ch'ü-ying* graduates were not counted as regular *chin-shih*.[124]

The extent to which clansmen-candidates in the *chin-shih* examinations should be tested alongside the other candidates was the subject of a confusing array of decisions, which probably reflects a certain irregularity of practice. For the preliminary examinations, a memorial and edict from 1145 allowed clansmen to compete at the circuit-level fiscal commissioner's office examinations or at the capital in the Directorate of Education examinations or the locked hall examinations. In 1162, Fu-chien, with the bulk of the clan population, was permitted to follow the precedent of Kuang-nan-tung and -hsi and send all clansmen who wished to go to the capital to take the preliminary examination at the directorate.[125] Although we have one report, dating from 1194, in which clan youths sat the prefectural examinations with other candidates—this occurred in Chien-k'ang fu (Chiang-nan-tung) under the clansman-prefect Chao Yen-yü (CCACCBAB; 1130–1225)[126]—this appears to have been an exception to the general practice of segregated qualifying examinations.

Integration within the higher examinations was more forthcoming. In 1145, Chao Po-shu, whose study at the Hung-chou prefectural school is described above, became so renowned for his academic brilliance that he was allowed to participate in the 1145 palace examination, and in fact finished in the first of the five classes of graduates.[127] Finally, in 1155, clansmen who so wished were permitted to sit for the departmental examination with other candidates.[128]

Taking the examinations with the other candidates did not mean directly competing with them, however. The 1155 action also gave clansmen the option of being examined separately. In fact, clansmen competed with each other and were selected according to quota-ratios that were far less competitive than those used for others. In 1145, seven clansmen who were already

officials took the preliminary examinations in Lin-an and three were selected, as were four of the seven clansmen who were not officials.[129] These
quotas were subsequently reduced to one successful candidate for every
seven taking the examination, a ratio that was also used for clansmen at the
departmental examination (in the Ch'un-hsi period [1174–89], the latter was
reduced to one out of ten).[130] By comparison, the quotas for the prefectural
examinations in 1156 were supposed to be based upon a ratio of one successful candidate for every 100 examinees, and the ratio for the departmental
examinations fluctuated between one out of fourteen and one out of seventeen during this period.[131]

Special favor was also shown in the ranking of the clansmen who passed
the *chin-shih* examination, for they were kept out of the fifth—and lowest—
class. According to Li Hsin-ch'uan, this practice began in 1124.[132] Southern
Sung records say little about this custom, but in the examination lists of 1148
and 1256, large numbers of clansmen are found at the end of the fourth class,
and none in the fifth.

Such munificence toward the imperial clan swelled the numbers of
clansmen-officials and made them an increasingly significant group within
the bureaucracy. In 1148, 16 out of the 330 *chin-shih* were imperial clansmen
(4.8 percent).[133] Writing in the thirteenth century, Chang Hao (ca. 1180–
1250) made the remarkable claim that in the 128 years between 1080 and
1208, 1,340 clansmen received *chin-shih* degrees.[134] It seems likely that this
figure includes graduates of the measurement examinations, for the 1,340
figure works out to an average of 33.5 clansmen per triennial examination,
and we know that in the late Northern Sung there were very few clansmen-
chin-shih. But perhaps the most reliable measure of the clansmen in the
bureaucracy comes from Li Hsin-ch'uan's 1213 breakdown of the civil and
military services by the form of entry into the bureaucracy (Table 7.6).

There are some questions about the figures for clan members in the table,
especially the relatively tiny number of those in the civil administrative
group, for the 24 listed are identified as "imperial clansmen recruited after
passing the Rites" (*tsung-tzu kuo li pu-kuan*), and although that could be taken
to mean "passing the [Ministry of] Rites [examination]" (i.e., the departmental examination), that seems unlikely in light of the fact that the terminology is not used elsewhere for examination graduates. Similarly, the 584

Table 7.6

Imperial Clansmen in the Civil and Military Services, 1213

Type of position	Civil Service			Military Service		
	No. of clansmen	No. of officials	Percent-age	No. of clansmen	No. of officials	Percent-age
Adminis-trative[a]	24	2,392	1.0%	425	3,866	11.0%
Executory	584	17,006	3.4	2,914	15,506	18.8
TOTAL	608	19,398	3.1%	3,339	19,372	17.2%

[a] Includes only administrative officials in ranks 6 through 9.

SOURCE: CYTC, pt. 2, 14: 528. For more detailed tabulations, see tables 2 and 3 in Chaffee, *Thorny Gates of Learning*.

clansmen in the executory category of civil officials are identified as "imperial clansmen deserving of grace" (*tsung-tzu kai en*). Again we do not know if the clansmen–*chin-shih* are listed here or among the 4,325 executory-level *chin-shih*.[135] Thus, these figures should be taken as minimums rather than maximums.

That said, three points about these statistics stand out. First, as in the case of the marriage relations of the clan, our focus on examinations and civil officials—and in this I am following the sources, which say little about recruitment into the military service apart from the measurement examinations—is at odds with the numerical dominance of military service–clansmen, a fact that is borne out by the *Hsien-yuan lei-p'u* records.[136] Second, the sheer magnitude of the clan's representation in the bureaucracy is impressive.[137] Their numbers are such as to defy comparison with even the most successful non–imperial kin groups, such as the Shih of Ming-chou studied in such brilliant detail by Richard Davis.[138] Third, the role of clansmen in the bureaucracy had grown dramatically since the beginning of the Southern Sung, both as a result of their increasing presence in the examinations, as described above, and because the clan itself was growing.

In remarks to his disciples while serving as prefect of Chang-chou (Fu-chien) in 1190, Chu Hsi (1130–1200) reflected on this new reality and expressed his concerns about it:

In one instance in Chang-chou, over sixty imperial clansmen became officials in a single day, thanks to the act of grace upon [Kuang-tsung's] succession and to the imperial clan's emphasis upon examinations for official recruitment. For the prefecture this sudden increase of so many salaries [to be paid] almost means that there will be nothing to pay [even] me. The court is not concerned with the distant future, when the constant increase in the imperial clan will become a crisis for [all] prefectures, as it has already become for one or two.[139]

Chu had good cause for concern, and as we will see in the next two chapters, his concern was shared by other officials who had to wrestle with the consequences of the generous recruitment provisions for the imperial clan.

But these findings raise other, more direct questions as well. What were the political consequences of this influx of clansmen into the bureaucracy? What roles did they play in governance? And did they have a shared identity that informed their actions, if only on occasion? It is to these questions that we turn in the next chapter.

EIGHT

Politics and the Limits of Power

The Selection of Hsiao-tsung

In 1129, Kao-tsung's only son, Chao Fu, died suddenly of convulsions at just four *sui*, leaving a distraught emperor, who complained that he had lost his delight in the pleasures of the bedchamber.[1] So despite the fact that he was still in his early twenties, in 1131 Kao-tsung ordered a search within the imperial clan for boys to be raised as possible successors. His initial charge was to select four or five boys age two to three *sui*, although that was later changed to ten boys of seven *sui* or below. Most remarkably, he specified that the search be limited to boys with the "*po*" character in their names, that is, the seventh generation of the T'ai-tsu line.[2] His reason was that T'ai-tsu had managed to pacify the world with a martial spirit, but that since then his offspring had been scattered and suffered greatly. It was necessary for him to establish a great plan that satisfied the spirits of Heaven.[3] More prosaically, it might be noted that Kao-tsung had no near relatives such as nephews living in the south to whom he could have turned, and that available T'ai-tsu offspring greatly outnumbered those of the T'ai-tsung branch, since the latter had been concentrated in K'ai-feng and most had been taken into captivity by the Jurchen.

Chao Ling-chih (AADDEC; 1061–1134), the administrator of the Great Office, and Chao Ling-k'uang (AADFCH; 1069–1143), the founding administrator of the Western Office in Fu-chou, were responsible for the search. Of the ten boys brought into the palace, we have the names of only three: Chao Po-hao (ABABAIAB; n.d.), Chao Po-chiu (AADFFCDA;

1130–80), and Chao Po-ts'ung (ABBACEAB; 1127–94), the son of Tzu-ch'eng (d. 1144), a local official of scholarly inclinations (on Tzu-ch'eng, see Chapters 5 and 7 above).[4] As descendents of T'ai-tsu, none of them was a mourning kinsman of the emperor, and had not the definition of imperial clansmen been liberalized in the late Northern Sung, they would not even have been clansmen in any formal sense.

The boys were raised in the imperial palace by palace women under the watchful and benevolent eye of the emperor. But if the stories that have survived concerning them are to be believed, they were constantly being evaluated and even trivial incidents could be decisive. According to one story, Kao-tsung at one point had decided that either Po-hao or Po-chiu would be selected as one of the final two boys and chose the fat Po-hao rather than the thin Po-chiu. But before the boys left, the emperor told the two to stand together so that he could have a final look at them. While they were standing, Po-hao kicked a cat that was passing by. Kao-tsung responded: "What did the cat do to deserve being kicked? This boy is not mentally stable. How can he bear the heavy responsibility later." So Po-hao was eliminated and sent on his way with 300 taels of silver.[5]

Po-ts'ung (renamed Shen) and Po-chiu (Chü) remained in contention for years. As adolescents they moved into the matching Eastern and Western Palaces, and only in 1153 was a choice publicly announced, with Shen being named Prince of Chien and the heir.[6] By one account, Shen's superior calligraphy was a factor.[7] By another, faced with a court divided between backers of the two adopted princes, Kao-tsung gave Shen and Chü ten maids each for their personal service. Shen's tutor, the future grand councilor Shih Hao, warned him that the gift was a test, and he should treat them carefully. This he did. When, a short time later, the maids were ordered back to the palace, all of those assigned to Chü had been violated whereas Shen's remained "pure as jade," and the emperor decided on Shen, the future Hsiao-tsung.[8]

Whatever the truth of these stories, the fact that they circulated indicates a public perception of the selection process as lengthy and openly contested. In this it differed dramatically from the selection of Ying-tsung as Jen-tsung's successor; Jen-tsung's ministers forced him to make a choice, but Jen-tsung made the choice with little input from others, so far as we know. As for the future Hsiao-tsung, I would suggest that the long period of uncertainty before the decision strengthened his sense of identity with the imperial clan, the group from which he had come and to which he could easily have been returned. That, in fact, is precisely what happened to Chü (Po-chiu) after Shen became crown prince. He was sent out of Lin-an and spent the rest of his life as a clan official, first as the supervisor (*p'an*) of the Great Office in Shao-hsing fu and then as administrator of the Western Office in Fu-chou.[9] The point is not just academic, for in 1162 Kao-tsung broke with precedent and abdicated in favor of Chao Shen, who became the emperor Hsiao-tsung (r. 1162–89). And it was during his reign that the imperial clan not only increased its representation in the bureaucracy but also developed politically, experimenting with new roles.

Hsiao-tsung and the Imperial Clan

Like Kao-tsung, Hsiao-tsung came to power in the midst of a war with the Chin. In 1161, the Chin emperor—the infamous Prince of Hai-ling—invaded the Sung, quickly reaching the Yangtze River, although the Sung army managed to thwart his attempts at crossing. Fortunately for the Sung, the prince's men mutinied and assassinated him. Subsequently the Sung attempted to carry the war north, and although unsuccessful, the war dragged on until 1165, when a peace at least somewhat more advantageous than that of 1142 was concluded.[10] Kao-tsung's decision to abdicate was in part a result of weariness with the war as well as a testimonial to his trust in his heir, a trust that the remarkably capable Hsiao-tsung was to repay amply.[11]

As a result of the war situation, a number of Hsiao-tsung's first actions vis-à-vis the imperial clan involved retrenchment. These included personnel reductions at the clan centers and decreases in the size of imperial gifts (such as birthday presents) to clan members, although this latter economy was made at the suggestion of clansmen themselves.[12]

These cutbacks did not reflect Hsiao-tsung's general policy toward the clan, however. The growing presence of clansmen in the examinations and bureaucracy discussed in the last chapter remains imperfectly understood, but it is significant that early in his reign—in 1163—Hsiao-tsung conferred 216 measurement-examination degrees on clansmen, thereby demonstrating his desire to provide recognition through the granting of official status to all clansmen who could demonstrate even a minimal competency. This is not to say that he always favored clansmen. As we saw in Chapter 7, the quota-ratios used in the *chin-shih* examinations were made stricter under Hsiao-tsung. He also—in late 1162—reiterated a long-standing prohibition on clansmen serving as educational or examinations officials,[13] and in 1165 when the young Chao Ju-yü (BAAKFBDAA; 1140–96) wrote the best examina-tion for the palace examination, Hsiao-tsung refused to allow him recogni-tion as the top graduate (*chuang-yuan*).[14] Historically, however, decreases in quota-ratios were used to respond to growths in candidate numbers rather than punitively against a locality or group. And as early as 1170, exceptions were allowed to the prohibition on clansmen serving as examination offi-cials,[15] and Ju-yü, although not the *chuang-yuan*, was nevertheless highly regarded by Hsiao-tsung, who used him in various capacities.

Hsiao-tsung's solicitude toward—and trust in—the imperial clan was also evident in three other acts. One was his willingness to make use of his second son, Chao K'ai (1146–80), the Prince of Wei, in a genuine provincial post after passing over him in his selection of an heir. In 1174 the prince was named prefect of Ning-kuo fu (formerly Hsuan-chou, Chiang-hsi). When he arrived, the senior official there proposed that he and his assistant take care of all matters for the prince, but he replied:

I have been commanded to be prefect of the prefecture. Now if I specifically delegate [power to] the administrator and his assistant, it will become an empty, useless posi-tion. Moreover, if three people serve as prefectural administrators, I fear that disputes between officials and the people will be numerous, and we will see only disturbances. The administrator and assistant should be in charge of money, grain, litigation, and so forth, presenting things to me for decision. Then the people below will be tranquil and affairs easily managed.

More remarkable than this quite understandable response is the fact that the emperor fully backed him up, and in Ning-kuo and in a subsequent posting as prefect of Ming-chou, the prince was able to use his position to benefit the prefectures, as when he succeeded in increasing the *chü-jen* ex-amination quota for Ning-kuo.[16] Although the prince was not an imperial clansman as such, his service was a noteworthy signal of yet a further loos-ening in the Northern Sung policy of keeping all imperial relatives out of power.

Second, in 1166 Hsiao-tsung decreed that one son of every clans*woman* be permitted to gain office through *yin*.[17] The addition of this potent inducement for elite families to marry with the clan suggests that some clan families, at least, were having difficulty marrying their daughters off. Then in 1179, every prefecture and commandary in the empire was ordered to reserve places on its staff for military service by imperial clansmen. In two detailed edicts—the second for Ssu-ch'uan, an area that had not been included in the first—specific quotas spelled out exactly how many personal governance (ch'in-min) posts, monopoly (chien-tang) posts, and temple guardianships (i.e., sinecures) each prefecture was to provide. In all, the reserved positions totaled 215, 431, and 690, for the respective categories, for a total of 1,336.[18] Presumably, the posts already being held by military service clansmen were included in these quotas, and thirteen hundred new positions were not being created for them. Nevertheless, Hsiao-tsung's willingness to commit significant government resources for the employment of clansmen-officials is a striking sign of his encouragement of the clan.

In another measure aimed primarily at civil clansmen-officials, Hsiao-tsung in 1163 ordered everyone serving as an attendant (shih-ts'ung) or as censor and remonstrator (t'ai chien)—categories that in effect were the entire top layer of civil ministers—to recommend two outstanding clansmen-officials.[19] We have no way of assessing the overall impact of these recommendations, but several epitaphs discuss them at some length.

Lou Yueh (1137–1213), in his epitaph for Chao Shih-hsin (AADEAA-EAC; 1148–99), describes his search for an official to recommend. His choice was Shih-hsin, who by 1163 had served with distinction in several posts and whom Lou knew well since Shih-hsin was married to his niece.[20] Lou had already used his two recommendations—one of them for Shih-hsin's older brother—and so could not help Shih-hsin. Neither could Hsieh Shen-fu (1166 chin-shih), the administrator of the Bureau of Military Affairs and an enthusiastic supporter of Shih-hsin's, for he too had used his recommendations. However, when the minister of rites, Liu Te-hsiu (d. 1208), asked Hsieh for suggestions of deserving clansmen, Hsieh praised Shih-hsin, and Liu happily recommended him, saying in his memorial that "in the luxurious thickets of the Heavenly clan, talented men are numerous."[21]

Although recommended in 1163, Shih-hsin remained a minor official with no recorded contact with the emperor. That was not true of two others. Chao Hsiang-chih (CCFHIA; 1128–1202), who in 1148 had gained distinction as the highest-ranking clansman in the palace examination, was recommended by the minister of personnel, Hsiao Sui (1117–93)—a fellow *chin-shih* from the 1148 class—who also suggested that he be appointed prefect of Ying-chou (Ching-hsi-nan). Hsiao-tsung, noting that he had been much impressed by Hsiang-chih's memorials, said that he ought not be stuck in Ying-chou but "should be one of my ministers," and so he was appointed vice-director of armaments. But soon thereafter Hsiang-chih offended a high minister by a funeral essay that he had written and as a result was named the ever-normal granary commissioner for Hunan. At his audience with the emperor upon departing for his new post, he greatly impressed Hsiao-tsung with his ideas about the functioning of the granaries, and perhaps as a result his posting was changed to granary commissioner for Chiang-nan-tung and then to Western Office administrator, where as we saw in the preceding chapter he was instrumental in renovating the clan school.[22]

Chao Yen-tuan (CBAECAAA; 1121–75), a brilliant official who had received a *chin-shih* degree at the age of seventeen *sui*, was also recommended and summoned for an imperial audience. Hsiao-tsung welcomed him, saying, "I have long heard of the minister's eminent talent." Unwilling to simply engage in pleasantries, Yen-tuan addressed the issue of political discourse at the court:

I am an imperial clansman and especially share the joys and sorrows of the dynasty; so I must speak. In the past those discussing [policies] have hated to have people disagree with them, and hence ministers near at hand have engaged in unceasing intrigue, and distant ministers have dared not advance their ideas. If we are to avoid regrets such as [those] we have for the war at hand, then in the future Your Majesty will have to be informed that the collected advice [presented to the emperor on an issue] can be useless [without full discussion]. I hope that this will be a profound warning for the future.

Although this might have seemed audacious advice coming from someone who at the time was a judicial official in Fu-chien, Yen-tuan was awarded a capital post as secretary of the Directorate of Education.[23]

Two things stand out in these examples of recommended clansmen. One is Yen-tuan's presumption of a common identity and shared interests with the emperor, which he then used to justify his frank criticism. The second was Hsiang-chih's demotion despite the support of the emperor. Both were typical rather than the exception; clan status gave many—if not all—clansmen-officials a special sense of identity with the emperor, and this sense was often viewed suspiciously and even with fear by others.

This emperor-clansman tie was not new with Hsiao-tsung. We saw in Chapter 6 how Kao-tsung said to Chao Tzu-hsiao (AADEHAF; 1102–67): "You may send secret memorials. Clansmen are the body of the state, and it is appropriate for them to know my feelings." In his next post, as military bursar for Chiang-nan and Huai-nan, Tzu-hsiao actively curbed graft, thereby enraging generals, who sent false accusations to court; Kao-tsung's response was to promote Tzu-hsiao.[24] Under Hsiao-tsung, however, the phenomenon seems to have been much more common.

To cite a few examples, Chao Pu-hsi (BCBFAFA; 1121–87), one of the outstanding clansmen-officials of the twelfth century whose long career included important civil, military, and clan positions (we saw him earlier as administrator of the Great Office), was known for his willingness to take on the powerful and wealthy when necessary, and for the outspokenness of his memorials. In summarizing Pu-hsi's career, Yeh Shih (1150–1223) noted that his memorials were often long, forthright, and fearless. Some the emperor followed, others he did not, but the emperor never doubted Pu-hsi's loyalty and commended him at a feast as "a worthy imperial clansman."[25]

Chao Shan-yü (BCABGHEB; 1143–89), as vice-fiscal intendant for the T'ung-ch'uan circuit, was confronted with the problem of a notoriously dishonest prefect. He first snubbed him, then impeached him, and when the prefect's patron, the grand councilor Wang Huai (1126–89), blocked the impeachment, Shan-yü dismissed the man directly.[26] Chao Yen-chen (CDADAFAB; 1143–96), in his very first posting, as an administrative supervisor (*lu-shih ts'an-chün*) to Fu-chou (Chiang-nan-hsi), became upset at the harsh conditions in the prison, for which he was responsible but which he found himself powerless to change. When a Ministry of Justice envoy visited from Lin-an, Yen-chen charged that the provisioning in the prison was unjust. The envoy proceeded to explode in anger, thoroughly intimidating Yen-chen's subordinates, who wanted to drop the matter. Yen-chen, however, shouted at them to leave the room and then drew up a list of his accusations. The impressed envoy not only agreed to submit them to the ministry, but also wanted to recommend Yen-chen, who declined. When told of his son's audacious behavior, Yen-chen's father is reported to have sighed and said, "That's my son."[27]

The defense of the poor and the willingness to combat injustice at personal cost were essential elements of the Confucian ideal of service and thus common currency in Sung elite culture. The examples given above certainly demonstrate that these clansmen, at least, had thoroughly assimilated that ideal, but not that they were different from other conscientious officials. Yet I would suggest that there was a difference, that their imperial connection made them more willing to speak out, and it made their opponents more cautious about challenging them—just as it undoubtedly provided unprincipled clansmen with the means to ill-gotten wealth and power.

The early career of Chao Hsi-kuan (AADBBEGADA; 1176–1233) offers a vivid example of the clansman-official as viewed by others. Just after receiving his *chin-shih* degree in 1196, Hsi-kuan was appointed expectant revenue administrator for T'ing-chou (Fu-chien), although he had to wait for eight years until the post became vacant. Just two months after arriving in T'ing-chou, the rebellion of Li Yuan-li (d. 1211) broke out in the mountains between Fu-chien and Chiang-hsi, and T'ing-chou was threatened by it. The local officials gathered to discuss the defense of the prefecture, and throughout the meeting Hsi-kuan was silent. At the end the prefect remarked on it and asked him if he had no views. He replied that guarding the city walls—the apparent plan of the group—was no solution and that the government troops should make their stand at an old wall that guarded a pass some thirty *li* away. The group accepted this proposal, and Hsi-kuan was placed in charge of the troops, led a successful defense against the rebels, and became the hero of the prefecture. But the most telling statement about Hsi-kuan occurs after his deputation by the prefect to lead the troops: "At the time he was an imperial clansman in his first office, and everyone regarded him as dangerous."[28]

This aura of royal power that apparently surrounded Hsi-kuan was a mixed blessing, of course, for although it may often have engendered respect and compliance, it could also give rise to resentment and suspicion, and damage or even finish careers. It is hard to say whether that was a factor for Chao Keng-fu (CCABHBACB; 1173–1219), whose career came crashing to a halt when, in his first post as a wine office official, he tried to take on wealthy merchant families only to find himself impeached and cashiered,[29] or Chao Shan-tai (BCBPAAAC; 1138–88), who after years of distinguished service was accused by a fiscal intendant of wrongful expenditures and, despite an investigation that cleared him and the support of the grand councilor Chou Pi-ta, was unable to advance any further.[30] In Shan-tai's case, however, another factor may have been at play, and that was opposition to giving imperial clansmen positions at court (excepting the ceremonial Southern Rank guard positions).

The fundamental difference between clansmen-officials and their non-clan colleagues is that the clansmen were potential emperors and therefore not to be trusted with too much power. Thus, Ch'in Kuei and Kao-tsung initiated the prohibition on clansmen serving as grand councilors and generally not allowing them to advance above the level of attendant (*shih-ts'ung*).[31] In contrast to the apparent innocence of Chao Shan-tai, his son Ju-shu (BCBPAAACA; n.d.), despite becoming an attendant and holding the important prefectship of P'ing-chiang fu (Su-chou, Liang-che), was viewed with suspicion because of his transparent ambition, according to the *Sung History*.[32] One even finds clansmen voicing concerns on this subject. Because of his literary abilities, Chao Yen-tuan, whose criticism of the prevailing tenor of policy discourse at court was quoted above, was proposed more than once for the post of editorial clerk (*wen-tzu*)—a position of great importance since it involved the actual drafting of edicts and other official documents. Each time he declined, on the grounds that imperial relatives in the editorial office might use their position to gain entry to the inner palace.[33]

One of the most intriguing examples of the perils that could accompany the political rise of a clansman-official is that of Chao Shan-hsi (BCABA-CAA; 1141–98), the clansman who as a youth left his bride for three years while he prepared for the examinations. In his early postings as a county aide, then magistrate, and then as vice-prefect of Lin-an, Shan-hsi gained a reputation as an outstanding official. More important, in the Lin-an post he came to the attention of the emperor, who had him attend court, gave him a gold-lettered plaque, and named him prefect of Hsiu-chou. But when Hsiao-tsung then tried to bring him to court, the move was blocked by the vice–grand councilor Huang Hsia (1122–1200), apparently because while in Hsiu-chou Shan-hsi had enraged Huang by citing Huang's recommendation of relatives. After another posting as a prefect—of Chiang-chou in Chiang-nan-hsi—Shan-hsi was brought to the capital as director of the Bureau of General Accounts and provided the emperor with much valued advice on military affairs. But when Hsiao-tsung then named him prefect of Lin-an, trouble again arose, for the chief ministers repeatedly (the epitaph says "ten times") refused to receive the nomination. Appointed instead the vice-chamberlain for palace affairs, he found himself accused by the Censorate of unnamed crimes. Hsiao-tsung was furious and had the accusation destroyed, but he also removed Shan-hsi from office. This was not the end of Shan-hsi's career. He went on to serve with distinction as prefect of Hui-chou (Chiang-nan-tung) and in other provincial posts, but never again at the capital. Indeed, when Kuang-tsung tried to make him a coinage commissioner, that, too, was blocked.[34]

We do not know what inspired such strong and long-lasting opposition to Chao Shan-hsi; the antagonism of Huang Hsia is hardly an adequate explanation. But whatever was at the heart of the opposition, it almost certainly fed on a general belief that clansmen-officials should not serve in substantive positions at court. Moroto Tatsuo, in an analysis of the nineteen clansmen listed by Li Hsin-ch'uan as having attained the title of attendant (*shih-ts'ung*) from the Hsuan-ho (1119–25) to Chia-t'ai (1201–4) reign periods, argues that although many held important provincial positions, they were systematically excluded from positions at court.[35] I would concur, for although I have found no explicit enunciation of such a policy, such an exclusion seems generally to have been in effect through Kao-tsung's and Hsiao-tsung's reigns.

In Shan-hsi's case, one factor that may, ironically, have increased opposition to his serving at court was his unusually close relationship with the emperor. Even the most loyal clansman had the potential of breaching the divide between inner and outer court and thereby subverting the authority of the grand councilors. Yeh Shih addressed this issue at some length, describing Hsiao-tsung as satisfied, intimate, and friendly in response to Shan-hsi's simple and unpretentious manner during audiences. Hsiao-tsung once said to him: "Each day all of the world's affairs must pass through my heart. I keep you here so we can face them together; you must not go far." Yet despite such sentiments, the emperor's wishes were thwarted. Yeh commented: "There were suspicions [of Shan-hsi], but they were groundless. Still, those of eminence who were known by the ruler of men [the emperor] were demanding and rude, strongly opposing this 'orphan from outside.' So although [the emperor] intended to support [Shan-hsi], he could not overcome the hundred schemes for rejecting him. Alas!" Elsewhere in the epitaph, Yeh wrote that "although the emperor long wished to employ him, Shan-hsi was crushed by the outer palace."[36]

The success of the ministers in this contest of wills with the emperor casts an interesting light on the common depiction of Sung monarchy as autocratic, especially since Hsiao-tsung was one of the most forceful and activist of the Southern Sung emperors.[37] Immense as the emperor's power was, I would suggest that the proper political role of imperial clansmen was seen as a fundamental issue within the political order—akin to the English "unwritten constitution"—and that the emperor could simply not change it on his own.

Nevertheless, change was in the offing. The large numbers of clansmen entering the bureaucracy through both *yin* and the examinations ensured that Chao Shan-hsi would not be unique, that there would be others of ministerial caliber who would challenge the policy of excluding clansmen from the highest offices. In fact, just after Hsiao-tsung stepped down from the emperorship in 1189, that challenge occurred in the person of Chao Ju-yü (BAAKFBDAA; 1140–96).

Chao Ju-yü, Clansman as Grand Councilor

Chao Ju-yü's political success was not based on the success of his immediate forebears, who, though successful, were not particularly distinguished.[38] Under his great-great-grandfather, Chung-ch'i (BAAKF; 1055 1088), his family had moved to the Western Capital.[39] Ju-yü's grandfather, Pu-ch'iu (BAAKFBD; n.d.), moved his family south during the Jurchen invasions—we are not told how—and settled in Yü-kan county in Jao-chou (Chiang-nan-tung), where he was serving at the time of his death.[40]

Ju-yü's father, Shan-ying (BAAKFBDA; 1118–77), was not especially successful as an official—his highest post was as military director in chief (*ping-ma tu-chien*) for Chiang-nan-tung—but he set a family style of frugality, bookishness, and philanthropy that was to characterize it for generations.[41] Although family members described it as poor, such perceptions are relative, for the family married well[42] and was very large. Shan-ying's biography speaks of a hundred living together, and Ju-yü's of three thousand (if accurate, the figure must include servants).[43]

Chao Ju-yü's political career spanned some thirty years. He first gained fame when, as noted above, it became known that he had written the best palace examination in his *chin-shih* class of 1165, though because of the tradition that the highest ranking be given to a commoner, the title of *chuang-yüan* went to another.[44] In subsequent years, through three periods of service in the capital—following his examination success, in the late 1170s, and from 1191 on—and a variety of civil and military posts in Fu-chien, Chiang-hsi, and Ssu-ch'uan in between, and despite one impeachment that was found to be baseless,[45] he achieved a reputation for honesty, rectitude, and capable administration.

Although Ju-yü generally seems to have avoided calling attention to his imperial clan status, his contemporaries remarked on it constantly. In addition to his examination success, he was the first clansman to serve as director of the departmental examinations, the first to be promoted to the position of councilor, and finally the first—and only—clansman in the Sung to be made grand councilor. Ju-yü in his actions and extant writings showed little concern with clan affairs, but he was almost certainly knowledgeable about them, for he was close to Chao Po-kuei (ABBACEAA; 1125–1202) in Lin-an in 1191 when Po-kuei, a confidant of Hsiao-tsung's, was administrator of the Great Office of Clan Affairs.[46] And although there were several clansmen, like Po-kuei, with whom he was friendly or identified politically,[47] others numbered among his bitterest critics.

Like many of the clansmen-officials described above, Ju-yü was known for his fearless outspokenness, whether in recommendations and impeachments or in advice to the throne. And when he took up local posts, others were clearly aware that they were dealing not merely with a well-known official but with a kinsman of the emperor. Chu Hsi wrote in a letter to him that, although you "are physically out [in the provinces], as an imperial relative you have the importance of an envoy and a heart that ever loves your ruler and is concerned for the country."[48] As for his relations with the emperor, his epitaph declares that in addressing the emperor, "those things that he [Ju-yü] said were things that all ministers find hard to say."[49]

In early 1189, Hsiao-tsung followed Kao-tsung's example by retiring and yielding the throne to his third son, Chao Tun (1147–1200), who became the twelfth emperor, Kuang-tsung (r. 1189–94). It is curious that Hsiao-tsung, still a vigorous man, chose to do so, but one factor seems to have been the unconcealed impatience of Chao Tun, who had been named crown prince in 1180.[50] Initially this arrangement worked well, but as time went by Kuang-tsung began to act erratically, most particularly by cutting back on audiences and on his visits to his father, to the dismay of the court.[51]

Chao Ju-yü's rapid rise at court began under Kuang-tsung. In 1191, he was brought from Fu-chien, where he had been pacification commissioner and prefect of Fu-chou, to serve as minister of personnel.[52] Although unprecedented for a clansman, this promotion seems not to have been controversial. However, in 1193, when he was named co-administrator of the Bureau of Military Affairs (his first appointment at the level of councilor, *chih-cheng*), the chief investigating censor Wang I-tuan cited a dynastic policy of not employing imperial clansmen as councilors and for good measure accused Ju-yü of faction building.[53] Wang's attack had little effect—he was demoted, and Ju-yü shortly thereafter was promoted to sole administrator of the Bureau of Military Affairs—but it was significant for the issues that it raised, issues that were to be resurrected in the future.

Indeed, the remarkable fact is that Ju-yü received these promotions, since, as we have seen, not only had the court followed Kao-tsung's prohibition against clansmen serving as grand councilors, but it had even kept them from lesser court positions. One reason cited for overruling the objections of Wang I-tuan in 1193 was that Kao-tsung had been acting to check the machinations of Ch'in Kuei,[54] but that was an obvious rationalization. The real reason seems to have been Ju-yü's force of character; he was respected by his fellow scholar-officials, and he was trusted by Hsiao-tsung, Kuang-tsung, and initially Ning-tsung (r. 1194–1224). Moreover, so far as we can tell, the trust was deserved, for in the critical days of 1194 he had ample opportunity to betray it but did not.

When Hsiao-tsung took ill in the spring of 1194, Kuang-tsung ceased visiting him. The occasional remonstrances of his ministers against his neglect of his father were supplanted by urgent memorials and massed gatherings of ministers and courtiers outside Kuang-tsung's palace, where they entreated him, to no avail, to pay respects to his ailing father. When Hsiao-tsung died on the eighth day of the sixth month of 1194, the emperor proved so incapacitated as to be unable to perform the mourning ceremonies. A full-fledged dynastic crisis was at hand. Into this breach stepped Chao Ju-yü, for as the histories tell it, in the month that followed he engineered a successful resolution to one of the most serious internal threats the empire had faced.

Never were the ritual and symbolic functions of the Chinese patrimonial state more in evidence than in the days following the death of Hsiao-tsung, for Kuang-tsung's refusal to conduct mourning, specifically to lead the ceremony initiating the donning of mourning garments (*t'an-chi*), brought the government to a virtual halt. Ju-yü and the grand councilor Liu Cheng (1129–1206) first approached the Senior Empress Dowager Wu (Kao-tsung's widow) through her nephew, the junior mentor Wu Chü, and proposed that she rule from "behind the screen" as regent, but she refused. The alternative was abdication, but for that to be accomplished, a crown prince had to be named and Kuang-tsung himself had to agree to the naming and then abdicate. After some delays, the first was accomplished on the twenty-fourth day of the sixth month of 1194 with the naming of Chao K'uo, the Prince of Chia and Kuang-tsung's third son,[55] and the following day the assembled ministers received a written message from the emperor expressing his desire to step down: "Having passed through many affairs and years, I remember my wish to retire." As conciliatory as this was, Liu Cheng was shaken by it—perhaps because of the gravity of their actions in forcing an abdication. He left first the court and the next day the capital, and Ju-yü found himself single-handedly heading the government.[56]

In the days following Liu's departure, tensions within the capital were at their peak, and there were rumors of military intervention and pending anarchy. To secure the military, Ju-yü enlisted the help of Chao Yen-yü (CCACCBAB, 1130–1225), the minister of works and a fellow imperial clansman, and together they secured a pledge of support from Kuo Kao, the palace commander.[57] To get the Dowager Empress Wu's consent to an abdication decree, Ju-yü enlisted Han T'o-chou (1151–1207), the administrator of the palace postern (that is, the critical keeper of the palace gate), who himself used the services of the eunuch Kuan Li. The result was that on the fourth day of the seventh month of 1194, the Prince of Chia conducted the mourning ceremonies and acceded to the throne as the emperor Ning-tsung (r. 1194–1224), but only after Ju-yü persuaded him to overcome his reluctance to do so. When the prince protested that taking the throne would be unfilial, Ju-yü countered: "The Son of Heaven should pacify the spirits of the soil and grain. To settle the state is filial. Currently people within and without worry about chaos. If such a state comes to pass, where will you provide for the Senior Emperor?"[58]

The accession of Ning-tsung marked the apex of Ju-yü's fortunes, in fact if not in name. Acting on his advice, the emperor quickly recalled Liu Cheng to office, appointed Chu Hsi as lecturer in waiting, and brought "outstanding scholars from the countryside" to the capital.[59] Ning-tsung also tried to appoint Ju-yü as right grand councilor, but he declined, saying: "If ministers have the same surname [as the ruler], it is unlucky and will cause difficulties between ruler and minister."[60] Instead he was confirmed in his current position as administrator of the Bureau of Military Affairs. But this did not last long, for in the eighth month Han T'o-chou engineered a sudden demotion for Liu Cheng (much to Ju-yü's dismay), and the emperor once again named Ju-yü right grand councilor. After three attempts to refuse, he reluctantly accepted, the first (and last) Sung imperial clansman to be so honored.

Unfortunately for Ju-yü, the dismissal of Liu Cheng proved more predictive of his future fortunes than did his promotion. For despite his evident loyalty, Ju-yü as right grand councilor was vulnerable to attack. Han T'o-chou proved adept at making Ning-tsung suspicious of Ju-yü's activities, and his suspicions seemed confirmed when Ju-yü's erstwhile ally Chao Yen-yü submitted a list of the "worthies of the day" labeled "Ju-yü's faction."[61] There were those, moreover, who would have been delighted had Ju-yü entertained higher aspirations. Yu Chung-hung (1138–1215), who had served as a subordinate to Ju-yü in Ssu-ch'uan, wrote him a letter during the succession crisis proposing that Ju-yü become regent himself. Ju-yü read the letter, was terrified, and burned it without answering; he later refused to respond to two similar proposals from Yu.[62] Thus although Ju-yü himself was not involved, it is quite possible that loose talk by followers like Yu may have fueled the emperor's suspicions.

Although Chu Hsi and others recognized that Han, the brother-in-law of the new empress and a relative by marriage of Senior Dowager Empress Wu, was a threat to Ju-yü and suggested that he recommend Han for a promotion that would at the same time curtail his power, he dismissed their advice and attempted to pre-empt Han and his supporters. Han quickly made his power felt. Over Ju-yü's strenuous protests, Chu Hsi was dismissed for criticizing the emperor's arbitrary personnel decisions, and this was followed by the demotions of P'eng Kuei-nien (1142–1206), Wu Lieh (n.d.), Liu Kuang-tsu (1142–1222), and Ch'en Fu-liang (1137–1203), all men whom Ju-yü had recommended. In the second month of 1195, Ju-yü himself became the target of attack, when one of Han's followers, the director for palace buildings, Li Mu, impeached him, saying, "Ju-yü as an imperial clansman has occupied the position of grand councilor. This is not good for the state. I ask that you end his governance."[63] The emperor agreed, and Ju-yü was given a prefectural position, although this was changed to a sinecure to allow him to remain in the capital. Still the attacks and the dismissals of his supporters continued. He was accused by the investigating censor Hu Hung[64] of being a student of spurious learning and of using false omens from his dreams to further his imperial designs. He was attacked by Wang I-tuan, who compared him to two infamous imperial clansmen of the past, Liu Ch'ü-li of the Han and Li Lin-fu of the T'ang. Chao Shih-chao (AACF-CGAIC; n.d.), another imperial clansman, proposed that he be beheaded.[65] Finally demoted to pacification commissioner of Yung-chou (in the distant reaches of Hu-nan), Ju-yü left the capital, only to die en route in Heng-chou (Hu-nan). According to his *Sung History* biographer, "All under Heaven grieved when they heard."[66]

But although Ju-yü had died, the vendetta begun by Han continued in full force. The charge of "spurious learning" (*wei-hsüeh*) that Hu Hung had leveled against Ju-yü became the label of a purge directed generally against some 59 ministers, officials, and scholars, who were attacked as a "rebellious clique of spurious learning" (*wei-hsüeh ni-tang*), particularly against Chu Hsi and his disciples, who advocated the Learning of the Way (*tao-hsüeh*). Teachers were forbidden to teach such dangerous ideas, and students of spurious learning were barred from the examinations, prohibitions that only began to be lifted several years after Chu Hsi's death in 1200. Once lifted, however, the Learning of the Way came increasingly to be honored by the state and regarded as the correct or orthodox way of interpreting China's classical tradition. Thus the succession crisis has been viewed primarily in terms of the "spurious learning" controversy, as a repressive action that elicited a reaction leading to the Neo-Confucian dominance of the late imperial period.[67]

Although the struggle between Chao Ju-yü and Han T'o-chou came to involve broad issues such as the Learning of the Way, Ju-yü's downfall can be attributed first and foremost to his imperial clan status. According to his biographer, Han T'o-chou was advised that given Ju-yü's imperial surname, "you can falsely accuse him of plotting to endanger the state, and as a result [Han] had Li Mu submit the accusation that led to his dismissal as grand councilor."[68] Through it and the later accusations by Hu Hung and Wang I-tuan ran the charge of treasonous intentions. The concerns of Kao-tsung appeared to have been realized. Yet the legacy of Ju-yü's brief tenure as administrator of the Bureau of Military Affairs and then grand councilor was complex. Throughout the succeeding 30 years of Ning-tsung's reign, clansmen were rarely to be found at even the ministerial level at court, although as we will see, they held important roles in the provinces. But over time, with the posthumous vindication of Chao Ju-yü and with the succession of another clansman-emperor, their stock rose once again.

Clansmen-Officials Under Ning-tsung

The 30-year reign of Ning-tsung can be divided by the tenures of the two grand councilors who dominated the court under him. Following his successful campaign to discredit and banish Chao Ju-yü and to accuse his opponents generally of "spurious learning," Han T'o-chou was able to pack the court with his supporters so effectively that he was virtually unassailable for the next decade. His downfall occurred as a result of an extremely ill-conceived war that he pursued against the Chin in 1207–8, which led directly to his assassination at the hands of his own ministers.[69] One of Shih Hao's younger sons, Shih Mi-yüan (1164–1233), orchestrated the coup against Han and emerged as the dominant minister at court, a position he was to hold until shortly before his death in 1233.[70]

As the preceding section made clear, clansmen-officials were to be found on both sides of Chao Ju-yü's struggle with Han T'o-chou. Among Ju-yü's clan supporters, the brothers Ju-t'an (BCBFAFAAA, d. 1237) and Ju-tang (BCBFAFAAB, d. 1223) were perhaps the most prominent. Minor officials at the time, they had submitted a memorial demanding that Ju-yü be retained and Han executed. Both were kept out of office until after Han's death.[71] Chao Hsi-i (1155–1212; AAXXXXXXXX), who early in his career had served under Ju-yü, displayed considerable courage when, after Ju-yü's death, he dared to recommend Ju-yü's oldest son, Ch'ung-hsien (BAAKFBDAAA; 1160–1219), calling him the "son of a worthy minister."[72]

Perhaps as a result of this, Hsi-i's many successes as an important provincial official, including pacification commissioner and fiscal intendant, never translated into a court appointment, much to the regret of his biographer, Chen Te-hsiu (1178–1235).[73] As for Ju-yü's sons themselves, although Ch'ung-hsien never advanced beyond the level of prefect,[74] his younger brother Ch'ung-tu (BAAKFBDAAE; 1175–1230) rose to become the director of the Right Section of the Ministry of Revenue and then the vice-minister of personnel, although these occurred at the outset of Li-tsung's reign (r. 1224–64). Long before that, after Han had died, it was Ch'ung-tu who approached the emperor asking that the "false and crooked histories" of the events surrounding his father and Han be revised, a request to which Ning-tsung agreed.[75]

Among the clansmen-officials who had opposed Ju-yü, little is known about the later career of Chao Shih-chao, who had demanded his execution. As for Ju-yü's one-time ally who later accused him of factionalism, Chao Yen-yü, in the following decade he held two important prefectships—in Ming-chou and Ch'eng-tu fu—and served as military commissioner for Ssu-ch'uan, governing with distinction in each case. Then in 1208 his career ended abruptly, ostensibly for not having done more to curb the power of the warlord Wu Hsi, who revolted in 1206, but undoubtedly also because of his close connection to Han.[76]

Although not known as an opponent of Ju-yü, the clansman most associated with Han—and politically the most important member of the imperial clan during Han's tenure—was Chao Shih-i (AADDFEBEA, 1149–1217). Perhaps unique among the T'ai-tsu branch clansmen of his generation, Shih-i had been born in the clan residences in Lin-an, for his father, Po-su, had been a friend of Kao-tsung's in K'ai-feng and had served in Kao-tsung's court. According to Yeh Shih, Shih-i, having received his *chin-shih* degree in 1175, came to the notice of Hsiao-tsung, who, remembering Shih-i's clan status, wisely gave him early advancement and extraordinary attention. Shih-i frequently submitted memorials concerning affairs of state, and in private talks with the emperor—as the clepsydra would pass through several *k'o* (half-hour units)—"there was nothing that he dared not say."[77] Over the next two decades Shih-i served successfully in a variety of important provincial posts as well as positions at court and demonstrated particular acumen in financial matters.[78]

According to Shih-i's biography in the *Sung History*—which provides a much more critical account of his life than does Yeh Shih's epitaph—he "attached himself" to Han T'o-chou after the latter was in power, thus suggesting that he did not play a role in the downfall of Ju-yü. In return, he received the coveted prefectship of Lin-an, a post that he had held briefly a few years earlier but had had to resign upon his mother's death and one he was to hold four times in all. Reactions to his governance were mixed. During his first tour, he gained some fame by arresting a monk engaged in sorcery and having him branded on the face, and during the last he was credited with stabilizing grain prices in the capital, which had been rising rapidly.[79] Yeh Shih also credits him with vigilance against treasonous underlings and a concern for maintaining the streets of the city, and quotes people as saying, "With a million households inside the Ch'ang-an Gate, all are like family members of Minister Chao. Our feelings are like the mountains and sea. Except for Prefect Chao, who knows them all?"[80]

But Shih-i received the contempt of others—especially in the scholarly world—for his extreme sycophancy toward Han T'o-chou. According to the *Sung History*, his appointment as prefect of Lin-an was the result of two incidents. On the occasion of a birthday party for Han, at which officials and ministers vied to give him rarities, Shih-i was the last to arrive. He took out a small box and said, "I would like to present you with a few nuts to eat." In the box were over one hundred large pearls, and it caused a sensation. Shih-i, it turned out, had discovered that Han was in a quandary over discord among his fourteen concubines, for he had been given a present of four pearl tiaras, which he then gave to four of them, only to have the others demand tiaras as well. So Shih-i spent 100,000 strings of cash to buy the pearls and had ten tiaras made. Reportedly at the insistence of the concubines, Han named Shih-i the minister of works.[81] It is hard to say whether the sums of money involved or Shih-i's obsequiousness were more remarkable, but the latter was spectacularly in evidence in the second incident. One day Han and Shih-i ate together on the grounds of the Southern Garden, a large park that Han had been given by the Empress Tz'u-fu in 1197 and in which a rustic village had been constructed, an instance of Sung urban pastoralism.[82] After eating, they walked through the park, passing by a mountain farm, wattled fences, and thatched huts, and Han said to Shih-i, "This truly has the character of rural life, but it's missing the barking of dogs and

crowing of roosters." A few moments later when the barking of a dog suddenly sounded from the undergrowth, Han discovered that it was Shih-i
and roared with laughter. Subsequently, he named Shih-i prefect of Lin-an,
in addition to his ministerial post.[83]

Han T'o-chou and Shih-i eventually had a falling out over the issue of
the war, for Shih-i strongly opposed it, and in fact was forced to resign because of his opposition.[84] Again, the sources differ in their treatment of his
opposition, with Yeh Shih emphasizing the sincerity of his misgivings about
the war, and the *Sung History* pointing to his ambitions.[85] Planned or not,
this rupture with Han allowed his career to continue at a time when Han's
supporters were being purged.

Shih-i's major appointment in the post-Han period was as prefect of Lin-
an (his fourth tour) and concurrent minister of war, and in two respects it
was his least successful. At this time (1209–10), Lin-an was experiencing
rampant inflation, driven generally by the tendency of the Southern Sung
government to issue excessive amounts of paper money (particularly mul-
berry paper money) and specifically by the inflationary impact of the war.[86]
As noted above, Shih-i is credited with having stabilized prices, but his
methods involved the use of price controls enforced by draconian punishments for those who did not honor them, and they were controversial.
Among those opposed was his vice-prefect, Chao Shih-t'ung (CBABBCA-
AAB; 1161–1221), who argued that, with prices unnaturally low, demand had
outstripped supply, merchants had been driven into smuggling, and many
people unnecessarily arrested. According to Chen Te-hsiu, Shih-t'ung's
biographer, Shih-i was talented but suspicious, and fearful that Shih-t'ung
would dominate the debate and thus prevail, he used slander and brought
false charges against Shih-t'ung and drove him from office.[87]

More serious for Shih-i was a dispute that he had with students at the
capital, which effectively terminated his career. In 1210 two students from
the military school were brought to the prefecture for some infraction, and
Shih-i had them flogged and banished. This roused the students at the
university as well as the military school, and together they demonstrated
against him with placards. Attempts by the grand councilor Shih Mi-yuan
to placate them failed, and the protestors raised the issue of Shih-i's relations with Han T'o-chou. Shih-i was forced to resign, and he lived the last
seven years of his life in retirement.[88]

It should be noted that Chao Shih-i's clan status apparently played only a minor role in his fortunes, after his crucial early friendship with Hsiao-tsung, that is. This is not to deny that it was never a factor; for example, the 100,000 strings that Shih-i spent on the gift of pearls may well have reflected his wealth as a clansman raised in the clan residences in the capital. Yet for all their differences, neither of the biographical accounts gives any indication that being a clansman either helped or hurt Shih-i, and in his conflict with Chao Shih-t'ung—which we know only from the latter's epitaph—no attention is called to the fact that both were clansmen.

Apart from Chao Shih-i, to the best of my knowledge no other clansman-official rose to the level of minister under Ning-tsung, although several served as vice-ministers.[89] The most prominent clansman in Ning-tsung's court was Chao Hsi-kuan—the hero of T'ing-chou whose imperial status so impressed the people there—and his case is instructive. After his tour in T'ing-chou, he served in the fiscal intendant's office for K'uei-chou circuit in western China, where he proved very successful at solving production problems at the government's salt wells in Ta-ning. For this he was promoted and appointed magistrate of Yü-shan county in Hsin-chou (Chiang-tung), but at his departure audience he so impressed the emperor with his ideas and knowledge—his talk included a history of the Ta-ning salt wells and the problems of the Ssu-ch'uan examinations—that he was appointed instead to three positions at the capital: assistant minister of the Court of Judicial Review, vice administrator of the Great Office for Clan Affairs, and vice-minister of the Ministry of Works. His subsequent work in the Great Office was noteworthy. He aided poor clansmen who had been unable to receive their official names thanks to the unceasing demand for bribes by the officials responsible for processing their cases, and he worked to increase the numbers of clansmen in ceremonial attendance at court. Hsi-kuan was then transferred from civil official to guard official status, beginning with an appointment as Chi-chou "prefect" (*tz'u-shih*), a nominal title only, for in effect he had become a clansman-courtier. There followed a series of promotions, to surveillance commissioner (*kuan-ch'a-shih*), which carried the rank of 3B, by the time of Li-tsung's accession in 1224, and to military commissioner (*chieh-tu-shih*, rank 2B) and Duke of the Hsin-an Commandary by the end of his life.[90]

According to precedent, the change to guard status should have made

Hsi-kuan a silent attendant in court, seen but not heard. However, shortly after his transfer a court minister ruled that clansmen who had been transferred into the guard but who had passed the *chin-shih* examinations should be permitted to participate in discussions if they wished.[91] Hsi-kuan subsequently played an active role in court debates, speaking out on the shortcomings of courtiers, the education of imperial clan youth, and inadequacies in court sacrifices. He even lectured a young Li-tsung on the proper duties of the sovereign.[92]

The absence of clansmen-officials from the highest level of government should not be taken as a sign that they had become unimportant, for outside the capital they were more important than ever, especially in the critical realm of military affairs. By the early years of the thirteenth century, the dynasty faced a host of threats to its security. The Chin threat was clearly demonstrated by the war of 1207–8, and the fact that the Chin were themselves threatened by a new East Asian power, the Mongols, translated not into relief for the Sung but rather into renewed attacks by the Chin against the Sung over the period 1212–24.[93] This chronic warfare provided the opportunity for independent warlords such as Li Ch'üan to establish themselves in the contested border region between the Sung and Chin that stretched from Ssu-ch'uan to the Pacific. Elsewhere, although conditions were not as unsettled as they had been in the years following the fall of the Northern Sung, banditry was endemic and not infrequently mushroomed into serious rebellion. This was especially true for the peripheral regions of central China, such as the mountainous belt stretching from western Fu-chien, through southern Chiang-hsi and Hu-nan, to eastern Ssu-ch'uan.[94]

Examples abound of clansmen who played significant roles in military affairs, both as civil and as military officials. Most of these involved clansmen-officials serving as military commissioners, coastal defense commissioners, and the like—for example, Chao Hsi-i's noteworthy role as Chiang-hsi pacification commissioner in helping to quell the Black Wind district rebellion of 1208–11—and not as commanders of armies.[95] But a number in fact raised and led armies in response to the threats of rebellion or war: the aforementioned Chao Hsi-kuan in T'ing-chou; Chao Ju-k'uan (BCADAC-BBB, 1172–1230), who raised a force to oppose another rebellion in Fu-chien in 1230;[96] Chao Ju-sui (BCBGNAGCC, 1172–1246), who led an army against bandits in southern Hu-nan;[97] and Chao Shih-i, who, as prefect of Lin-an, raised and equipped a corps of 3,000 men to defend the capital when the war of 1206–8 was going poorly.[98] Provocative as it might have seemed for a clansman to create an army at the capital, his action seems to have had little effect other than to anger Han T'o-chou, with whom he had already broken.

The most striking example of the involvement of a clansman in sensitive military matters is that of Chao Shen-fu (CABCBCCBE, 1162–1222), who spent most of the period from 1200 to 1220 in the contested border region of Huai-nan. While serving as magistrate of Chiang-tu county (Yang-chou), he successfully resisted a Chin army attack and quelled a peasant rebellion. He is credited with having improved the military readiness of the critical border prefecture of Ch'u-chou, which lay on the border with the Chin. Most notably, while serving as prefect of Lu-chou, he received a report of a Chin army approaching from the west at a time when he had a force of less than 10,000 men at his disposal and a vulnerable prefectural city, since construction of a new wall on the western side of the prefectural city was only partially completed. Suspecting a ruse—for the most likely spot to ford the Huai River was to the east—Shen-fu sent contingents in both directions to probe for the enemy, and was thereby able to discover them and force their retreat. Rather than receiving a reward for his actions, he was cashiered by the military commissioner, who on the basis of incomplete information accused him of timidity. However, in a subsequent investigation, the full facts emerged, "the emperor knew his loyalty," and shortly thereafter he was appointed director of the Imperial Treasury in Lin-an.[99]

The remarkable element in Shen-fu's story is not his success in acquitting himself so much as the fact that he was serving as an important official in Huai-nan-hsi at all. As noted in Chapter 5, in the late Northern Sung clansmen-officials had been banned from serving in border prefectures, presumably for fear of the mischief that they could cause were they to rebel or change sides. This ban was not renewed in the Southern Sung, but one might have thought that the appointment of clansmen to Huai-nan would still be restricted given the constant danger and intrigue, not only from the Chin but also from the contending warlords and bandit leaders. The uncontroversial nature of the service of men such as Shen-fu in Huai-nan is a measure of the court's trust in the clansmen-officials, and it was a trust that Southern Sung clansmen justified. With just one unusual exception, which we will consider in the next section, rebellion among the clansmen-officials was unheard of.

The Succession of Li-tsung

Among the many problems that Ning-tsung confronted during the three decades of his reign, one was familiar to the dynasty, especially in the Southern Sung: the lack of sons to inherit the throne. Just why the emperors from Kao-tsung on had trouble producing heirs is something of a mystery, but the facts are indisputable. Apart from Hsiao-tsung, who saw three sons grow to maturity, and Kuang-tsung, who had one surviving son (Ning-tsung), Kao-tsung's one son and Ning-tsung's nine all died in infancy, and Li-tsung had no sons.[100]

With dynastic precedents to guide him—particularly that of Kao-tsung—Ning-tsung acted expeditiously in the matter of an heir, but his luck was poor. Following the death of his eldest son, the Prince of Yen, in 1197, Ning-tsung adopted a clan youth age six *sui* named Chao Yü-yuan (1192–1220; Ning-H)—a descendent of Chao Te-chao (AA)—who was given the name Yen and brought into the palace. When he was eventually made crown prince, his name was changed to Hsün, the Prince of I, and he was carefully groomed to be emperor, receiving daily visits from the grand councilor for discussions of state policies.[101]

Unfortunately, Hsün died in 1220 at the age of 29, thus disrupting the carefully nurtured plans for succession. Ning-tsung commanded that selected tenth-generation offspring of T'ai-tsu (with the generation name of Yü-) of at least fifteen *sui* be brought to the palace for education.[102] With Ning-tsung then over sixty, that was deemed too slow a process, and in 1221 the emperor adopted and named as crown prince Chao Hung (d. 1225), the natural son of Chao Chün, himself a clansman originally named Hsi-ch'ü (ABAAACBAAC) who had been adopted as heir for Hsiao-tsung's second childless son, K'ai. More to the point, under the name Kuei-ho, Hung had been heir to Hsün, he had been reared in the palace, and he was an adult.[103]

Although the choice of Hung to succeed Ning-tsung was logical, it did not sit well with the grand councilor Shih Mi-yuan and his close ally in the palace, Empress Yang. Two incidents are reported to have convinced Mi-yuan that Hung should not become emperor. First, he told others of coming across the prince in his quarters one day lying drunk on the floor, and second, a musician-spy he had infiltrated into Hung's establishment reported that Hung was vowing to exile Mi-yuan to the far south, once he was emperor.[104] Secretly, Mi-yuan began to prepare an alternative in the person of Chao Kuei-ch'eng (1205–64; AABDEAEABBX), who had been born in Shan-yin county of Shao-hsing fu to Chao Hsi-lu (AABDEAEABB; n.d.), an obscure clansman about whom nothing is known. Mi-yuan chose Cheng Ch'ing-chih (1176–1251), a university instructor and future grand councilor, to oversee a crash education for Kuei-ch'eng, who is described in the *Sung History* as a serious, studious young man of few words,[105] and he periodically received reports on Kuei-ch'eng's progress.[106]

On the twenty-first day of the eighth month of 1224, Ning-tsung became ill and ceased holding daily court. Six days later Kuei-ch'eng was elevated to the status of imperial son and renamed Yun,[107] and five days after that Ning-tsung died, according to one version poisoned by Shih Mi-yuan.[108] At that point, Mi-yuan had Ch'ing-chih fetch Yun rather than Hung to the throne room. Only after he had arrived was Hung summoned. He hurried to the throne room, which he was allowed to enter only after being separated from his attendants and bodyguard. Once there, he was puzzled at being directed to stand in his customary spot, but was assured that this was just a formality for the reading of the edict declaring the new emperor. However, the edict named not him but Yun, and the lamps, we are told, cast the single shadow of Yun's figure on the throne. Hung's protest was fleeting and futile. When all others prostrated themselves before the new emperor, Li-tsung, Hung alone remained standing, but only until the palace commander pulled him down.[109]

As Richard Davis has noted, the historical sources are so biased against Shih Mi-yuan that it is impossible to know how much of this account is dependable. The allegation of poisoning, in particular, seems far-fetched, for it would have been in Shih's interest to have had more time before the death of Ning-tsung, so as to further prepare Yun and to engineer a more proper succession. But the indisputable fact in this story is that Mi-yuan and his supporters installed as emperor an individual who was not the crown prince and whose legitimacy rested upon an edict that may or may not have represented the will of Ning-tsung.[110] He was also young, and until Mi-yuan's death in 1233 Empress Yang ruled as regent. Moreover, in contrast to the furor that perceived violations of the norms of emperorship had touched off—the issue of the forms of address to be used by Ying-tsung in mourning Jen-tsung comes to mind—Mi-yuan's installation of Li-tsung met with virtual silence. One reason may have been that Mi-yuan moved immediately to appease his potential critics by having Li-tsung promote the "venerable Confucians" of the day.[111] There were a few voices of protest. The eminent Chen Te-hsiu, who had just been named an academician, is reported to have told Lou Yueh that they should immediately leave court so that the ancestral hall would know that there were those who were unwilling to serve, and in fact he repeatedly asked for a provincial assignment.[112] Chao Ju-t'an became ill in his grieving for Ning-tsung, and his congratulatory memorial to Li-tsung was so strong in its censure that it was likened to a censor's statement.[113] But these voices were mere ripples in the general calm.

Li-tsung's succession story has one further chapter. After Chao Hung was passed over for the emperorship, Li-tsung made him the Prince of Chi and sent him to nearby Hu-chou to live in palatial exile. In early 1225, a group of commoners in Hu-chou launched a rebellion in the name of the Prince of Chi. After initial resistance, Hung was persuaded to cooperate with the rebels and held court in the Hu-chou prefectural offices, even though "he knew that they would not succeed." The rebels claimed the backing of 200,000 troops and the support of the powerful Huai-nan warlord Li Ch'üan. In fact, they had no significant following, and the army dispatched by the court had no trouble in subduing them a mere two weeks after they had raised the banner of rebellion. Hung was quickly executed by strangulation.[114]

Chao Hung's rebellion clearly shocked his contemporaries, since it was the first Sung rebellion of an imperial kinsman and involved the man whom most had expected to become emperor only six months before. From a broader comparative perspective, it is the exception that demonstrates the remarkable stability of Sung imperial institutions. Whether in China in the Han, T'ang, Ming, and Ch'ing dynasties, or in other premodern empires like the Roman and Ottoman, fratricidal succession struggles were commonly used to decide succession. In this, the most irregular imperial succession of the dynasty, the fact that the just deposed and very vigorous ex–crown prince could not garner significant support when, however unwillingly, he raised the banner of rebellion, bears witness to the essential civility of Sung political culture, an aversion to the use of violence to achieve political ends.

The imperial clan played a distinct part in this culture of civility, especially in the Southern Sung. With thousands of clansmen-officials serving the dynasty, such problems as venality, sloth, and arrogance were undoubtedly much in evidence, as they were among all officials. Disloyalty and sedition, however, were not. Indeed, under Li-tsung, the third and last of the clansmen-emperors, clansmen-officials were more widespread at the upper levels of government than ever before.

Clansmen and Politics Under Li-tsung

The forty-year reign of the emperor Li-tsung (1224–64), though by no means free of crisis, encompassed the last significant periods of political stability in the Sung. Two issues dominated the court for much of his reign. Foremost was the question of how to deal with the threat posed by the Mongols, who during Li-tsung's reign were conquering most of the Eurasian continent. Initially the Mongols were viewed as offering an opportunity to wrest back northern China from a weakened Chin, but when the short-lived northern expedition of 1234 ended in disaster, only to be followed by Mongol armies attacking the south in 1235–36, thoughts of glory gave way to fears for survival. In fact, the dynasty survived for another forty years, thanks both to the strength of the Southern Sung navy and to political instability within the Mongol empire for most of the 1240s, but its foreign posture was purely defensive. A second issue concerned the Learning of the Way (*tao-hsueh*), which had been so bitterly attacked by Han T'o-chou and his followers; through the enshrinement of the Northern Sung masters and Chu Hsi in the Confucian temple, special recognition for academies associated with *tao-hsueh*, and the promotion of leading *tao-hsueh* thinkers, Li-tsung (the "ancestor of principle") effectively provided state recognition of the primacy of this particular school of Confucianism.[115]

Although there is no reason to doubt the sincerity of the young emperor's imperial blessing on what had become the prevailing philosophical stance among the literati at large, clearly his policies were also aimed at bridging the profound sense of alienation felt by many scholar-officials outside the capital toward the court and central government. But just as clearly their success in this regard was limited, for despite the promotions and court appointments of leading *tao-hsueh* thinkers—among them Wei Liao-weng and Chen Te-hsiu—there was little change at the top.[116] Indeed, for most of Li-tsung's reign, the government was effectively controlled by just three men, two of them close relatives and all from Ming-chou: Shih Mi-yuan, who was virtually unchallenged up until his death in 1233; Cheng Ch'ing-chih, Mi-yuan's protégé, who had earlier been tutor to the future emperor and who served as grand councilor from 1232 to 1236 and from 1246 to 1251 (he overlapped with Mi-yuan for two years); and Mi-yuan's nephew Shih Sung-chih (1189–1257), who dominated the government from the late 1230s until his fall in 1244.[117] Thus the sense of alienation persisted for many, who saw in the domination of these men and their followers a fundamental cause of dynastic weakness.

From the available biographies, it would appear that the clansmen-officials who played prominent roles in Li-tsung's court were not, as a rule, protégés or followers of these grand councilors.[118] If anything, they were outspoken critics of those in power, and in at least some cases paid for their criticism by being dismissed from court.

Chao Pi-yuan (BAAKFBDAAAA; 1214 *chin-shih*; d. 1249) provides a good example of this outspokenness. A grandson of the grand councilor Chao Ju-yü, Pi-yuan was raised in a family whose traditions included both service at court and close ties with Chu Hsi and other *tao-hsueh* leaders. His official career began in 1201, when he received official rank through exercise of his grandfather's *yin* privilege, although he went on to pass the *chin-shih* examination in 1214. After more than thirty years of outstanding service in a variety of local positions, including several important prefectships, Pi-yuan came to the capital in the mid-1230s, first as an aide in the Court of Judicial Review and then as vice-minister for general accounts. Over the next decade he served in a variety of posts at the capital, including vice-minister of the Court of the Imperial Clan, vice-minister of personnel, and minister of revenue.[119]

Shortly after coming to the capital, Pi-yuan submitted a memorial that dealt with personnel practices. After some introductory praise for the emperor's virtue and ability to make judgments, he turned to his concerns that appointments and dismissals were often made arbitrarily and without adequate information, that the grand councilors were often deferred to in personnel decisions, and that some appointments were so irregular that people did not know who had made them. As a result, he continued,

the people begin to distrust Your Majesty. Once appointment letters have been announced, once orders have been sent out, although they did not come from the eunuchs, people will suspect that they did; even though they were not the result of private visits, people will suspect that they were; *even though they did not come from the residences of imperial in-laws and clansmen, people will suspect that they did.* Now, the world is the world of the imperial ancestors; it is not the private domain of your majesty. Although Your Majesty has the desire (*hsin*) to get rid of unworthy [things], you are taking a suspect path. How can Your Majesty be happy with that?[120] (Emphasis added)

Pi-yuan's rhetorical choices are striking. His willingness to acknowledge the suspicions that people harbored toward the imperial clan is unique among the memorials of clansmen that I have read, but it also served to underscore his clan status and thereby give added weight to his warning to the emperor not to view the world as his private domain.

In subsequent memorials and imperial audiences, Pi-yuan spoke out on a number of issues, the war of 1234–37, border defenses, and monetary policy among them, but his strongest protests dealt with problems within the court: the overbearing power of grand councilors—he mentioned at one point the need "to rectify the guilt of the dictatorship of the former grand councilor"[121]—and the stifling of policy discussions among scholar-officials. At an audience upon being appointed director of the Left Office and concurrent vice-minister for the Court of the National Treasury, he used the imagery of the human body in arguing for the ailments of the body politic:

Proper spirit (*cheng ch'i*) has been daily and monthly dissipating, even down to the present. It is not simply that the officials and degree holders (*chin-shen*) dare not discuss affairs, but even rustic scholars are all tongue-tied. In early Tuan-p'ing [ca. 1234] era, when the sinking sickness [i.e., Shih Mi-yuan] had been expelled and new ills had not yet arisen, Your Majesty was still encouraging inquiries, and our fears were not realized. Now, the illness has attacked the heart and stomach, and they are sure to break and burst. If we do not seek a medicine that will disturb and so draw out this danger, then our delusion will be great.[122]

Although Pi-yuan's dire warnings apparently met with no action, neither did they damage his position at court, at least until the mid-1240s. Then, two of his memorials angered Shih Sung-chih, and in short order he was relieved of his positions in the capital and named prefect of Fu-chou (Fu-chien), where he died in office.[123]

Like Pi-yuan, Chao Yü-huan (AADFCHAGBXA; n.d.) received a *chin-shih* degree in 1214 and was a fearless minister in Li-tsung's court, but in other respects they were quite different. Whereas Pi-yuan served for decades as a local official, most of Yü-huan's career was spent at the capital, although that included three tours in the critical prefectship of Lin-an, where his brand of humane governance earned him the popular nickname of "Buddha Chao." Moreover, although Yü-huan had little firsthand experience with military affairs—apart from a brief stint as a border affairs envoy (in Huai-nan-hsi) early in his career—he was outspoken on military issues. As a result he was given the responsibility in 1237 for creating a "loyal and resolute" army of 3,000 to help bolster the defenses of Lin-an and also served as acting minister of war. With subsequent appointments as minister first of revenue and then of personnel, by the early 1240s he was one of the senior ministers in Li-tsung's court.[124]

Like Pi-yuan, Chao Yü-huan could be extremely critical in his memorials and audiences, on one occasion causing the emperor to lose his composure over allegations of heterodoxy and "small men" at court.[125] A believer in portents, Yü-huan used the occasions of solar eclipses, great storms, and "star changes" (*hsing-pien*—a nova?) to issue warnings about sedition, border affairs, and the need for imperial virtue. In the last instance, he argued that the "great fire" of a "star change" was a "calamitous burning." Confessing his own faults, he asked that he be permitted to resign, but also added that "I wish only to fear the wrath of Heaven and think that for virtue truly to reach the people, it must begin with the emperor himself." In response the minister Fang Ta-ts'ung praised his earnestness, knowledge, and righteousness and proposed that "ministers great and small all accept blame." Yü-huan was rewarded with appointment as minister of revenue.[126]

Chao Yü-huan's most direct involvement in political controversy came in the ninth month of 1244, when the emperor recalled Shih Sung-chih, who had only the day before resigned to mourn his father's death. Although there was ample precedent for such an action, on this occasion the frustrations of those who had chafed at years of Shih's highhandedness burst into the open. Protests were not restricted to officialdom but included hundreds of students at the various schools in the capital, including 34 at the imperial clan school.[127] When Yü-huan was asked by Li-tsung for his opinion, he did not prevaricate: "Master Sung-chih spends lavishly and is intimate with the avaricious and wealthy. He improperly established his reputation and should not be used again."[128]

After several months of crisis, Li-tsung found himself forced to accept Shih Sung-chih's resignation, but controversy continued when four of Shih's severest critics, including his nephew Shih Ching-ch'ing (d. 1245) and the junior grand councilor Tu Fan (1182–1245), died under mysterious circumstances. Even though an official investigation into the causes of their deaths was inconclusive, it was widely believed that Shih had had them murdered.[129] Again, Yü-huan played a small but notable role, for he asked that compensation be given to the families of two of the dead officials, and after the emperor concurred, he drafted the compensation edict.[130]

In contrast to Yü-huan, who in his later years became something of a ministerial fixture in Li-tsung's court, Chao Shan-hsiang (BCBGFCJA; d. 1242), despite service in 1231 as minister of war, spent his career largely in the provinces. Yet that career was itself exceptional, for a series of high-level military responsibilities made him one of the most important and powerful of the thirteenth-century clansmen-officials.

Chao Shan-hsiang came from the prefecture of Ming-chou, where his father, Pu-lou (n.d.), had settled in the early Southern Sung, because he had heard that it was home to many famous Confucians. Shan-hsiang passed the *chin-shih* in 1196 and wrote prolifically on the Classics throughout his life. His early career involved a conventional sequence of posts but rapid promotions through them, and by 1211 he was given the first of a number of appointments as a prefect. Even at this time, his successful suppression of tea bandits (*ch'a k'ou*) while serving as vice-prefect of Wu-chou (Liang-che) pointed to military talents that were to become increasingly important as time went by.[131] During the 1220s, Shan-hsiang's postings included that of administrator of the Great Office of Clan Affairs, but more to the point, pacification commissioner of Chiang-hsi, naval commissioner in Chien-k'ang fu (Chiang-tung), and pacification commissioner of Chiang-tung. In the course of this service he was rewarded for pacifying bandits in Ku-shih county (of Kuang-chou, Huai-nan-hsi), strengthening the Chiang-tung army, keeping the peace in the Huai army, and subduing the rebel Liu Ch'ing-fu. Then, in 1230, according to his biography, he was charged with suppressing Li Ch'üan, the Huai-nan warlord who had been a thorn in Sung sides for the better part of twenty years. And following his report the next year that Li had been killed, Shan-hsiang was named minister of war.[132]

It is impossible to tell from Shan-hsiang's biography just what his personal role was in these events. In Li Ch'üan's biography in the *Sung History*, Shan-hsiang rates only a brief mention, as the official reporting Li's death to the court, and a much more central role is accorded the brothers Chao Fan (n.d.) and Chao K'uei (1186–1266)—neither of them clansmen but both important figures in Li-tsung's court.[133] That Shan-hsiang's biography describes him as a protégé of the Chao brothers, ever solicitous, responsive to their concerns, and even sending his sons to study with them suggests that his promotions may have owed as much to political connections as to military prowess. Moreover, since we are also told that he was closely connected to Shih Mi-yuan—his youngest son had married a daughter of Shih's—he clearly does not fit the earlier generalization of clansmen-ministers as unbeholden to the dominant ministers at court.[134] However, Shan-hsiang's contemporary Chang Tuan-i (1179–1250) credited him with having broken into Chin-ling, where Li Ch'üan had been holed up with his army, and killing him.[135]

Whatever the reality of his military activities, Shan-hsiang was again credited with military successes in 1232, when as military commissioner for Chiang-nan and Huai-nan, he was rewarded for recapturing four cities in Huai-tung from the Chin and for defeating the Chin general Na-ho Mai-chu.[136] But then followed his impeachment by a censor. His biography does not state the charges, but Chang Tuan-i offers a clue that they may have involved concern about his clan status. Following Shan-hsiang's victory over Li Ch'üan, says Chang,

there were those who argued that imperial clansmen should not command troops, and in consequence there was slander at the palace. I recall that when the general was in command of the Ch'ih-chou army, a scholar had a copy of the *Southern Rank Book* (*Nan-pan shu*). This said that according to the statutes of the founding ancestors, the management of armies should not be entrusted to imperial clansmen, and it feared that statutes had been violated.[137]

The censor's charges, whether these or others, went nowhere, for the emperor himself defended Shan-hsiang, noting that his achievements included punishing rebels and retaking cities, and Chang concluded by saying that "recently generals have all been recommended and selected from the ranks of imperial clansmen." The impeachment, however, may have succeeded in curbing Shan-hsiang's career, for his only substantive post thereafter was prefect of Ch'ing-yuan fu and coastal commissioner for Che-tung, where, as recounted in the Introduction, he fled mutinous troops only to have his successor, Chao I-fu, redeem the situation, although this incident is not mentioned in his biography.[138] But despite this unhappy ending to his career, Shan-hsiang's repeated postings and military responsibilities in the critical war zone along the Yangtze River bear eloquent testimony to the degree to which clansmen had become trusted in the military as well as the civil sphere.

Although Li-tsung seems to have respected both Chao Yü-huan and Chao Shan-hsiang, neither was personally close to the emperor. By contrast, Shan-hsiang's rescuer in Ch'ing-yuan fu, Chao I-fu (CECBCCDAD; 1189–1256), had a career at court marked by both high office and a very personal bond with the emperor.

From a modest family line in the Wei-wang branch of the clan that had settled in Fu-chou in the early Southern Sung, Chao I-fu was not an obvious candidate for prominence. His father died when I-fu was just nine *sui*, and he took office through the *yin* privilege, but went on to receive a *chin-shih* degree in 1217 after placing first in the locked hall examinations in Kuang-nan-hsi, where he had been serving as a minor official. That earned him a magistracy, and over the next twenty years he served with distinction in a succession of provincial posts, in which he excelled at such diverse activities as fiscal governance, local institution building, and bandit pacification.

For about six or seven years beginning in the mid-1230s, I-fu's career alternated between court and countryside. In 1238, following a period of service at the vice-ministerial level in the capital, I-fu was appointed prefect of Ch'ing-yuan fu, where his quelling of the army mutiny described above led to his appointment as chief recipient of edicts for the Bureau of Military Affairs in Lin-an. However, thanks to a strongly worded memorial that he wrote even before leaving Ch'ing-yuan fu, he came under attack from some officials at the capital and retired to his home in Fu-chou. A shift in the political winds brought him back to the capital as an attendant gentleman in the Ministry of Justice, where the quality of his memorials and recommendations gained the emperor's attention. That paved the way for his appointment, in 1240, as pacification commissioner for Chiang-nan-tung and state farm commissioner for three prefectures in neighboring Huai-nan-hsi. This was a war zone, which had just witnessed several years of fighting between the Sung and the Mongols, and the posting provides more evidence of the perceived trustworthiness of clansmen-officials. As luck would have it, 1240 marked the beginning of a decade-long respite in serious fighting. Even so, I-fu distinguished himself through his improvement of troop conditions and training—paid for in part by his donation of gifts from the emperor—and through his role in capturing a Mongol general who had led a foray into Huai-nan-hsi. As a result he was brought to the capital to serve as acting minister of justice, and there he was to remain for the next decade.[139]

I-fu's first audience with Li-tsung after his return from Chiang-nan was memorable. The emperor began, "You have had two years of great toil, minister." I-fu modestly replied, "My memorials have all reflected Your Majesty's virtue. I have not had a hair of [individual] merit." The emperor: "You discussed urgent matters like preventing rebellions, [settling] imperial succession, and the drought that hit Chiang-nan and Hu-nan." I-fu: "King T'ang [of the Shang] reproached himself over the six affairs. Your Majesty should determine whether in the present circumstances there is a 'six affairs' [situation].[140] In name the treasonous are expelled, yet secret memorials are used and rare baubles are given [to the palace]. In name frugality is esteemed, yet the Lung-hsiang Hall is built and presents of food [i.e., bribes] are elicited; the palace is like this. As in the past, loyal and upright [ministers] are expelled and degraded, while favorites come and go spreading rumors and slander—abusing their position."[141]

This was bold—or reckless—talk for a minister fresh from the provinces and could well have ended I-fu's career. Instead, we are told that the emperor was "fear-stricken" (*sung jan*) and turned the conversation to I-fu's writings on the *I-ching* (*Book of Changes*), which was his scholarly specialty. The next day, I-fu was named imperial reader-in-waiting and imperial genealogy compiler, and the emperor ordered that a day be set aside for divining with the *I-ching*. The account is too brief to allow for psychoanalysis, but clearly something had clicked between the two men. We are told that Li-tsung next asked for I-fu's analysis of a visiting Mongol envoy and was so delighted with the result that he gave him a twelve-character placard.[142]

Promotions continued as well: acting minister of personnel, minister of justice, and supervising censor.

In the years that followed, I-fu's postings included director of the Imperial Clan Genealogical Office, minister of rites and of personnel, supervisor of the palace examinations in 1250, senior compiler in the History Bureau, and supervisor of the Palace Library. I-fu also submitted two books: *Tu I t'ung chung p'ien* (Reading the *I-ching* for complete understanding), which he had authored; and *Kuang Ning erh-ch'ao pao hsun* (Precious admonitions from the courts of Kuang-tsung and Ning-tsung), a compilation he edited that was undoubtedly a fruit of his work at the History Bureau. Li-tsung praised both and presented I-fu with a volume of his own poetry. He is said to have read the book on the *I-ching* frequently and continued his discussions of the *I-ching* with I-fu, on one occasion interpreting the "family hexagram" (*chia-jen kua*) as applying to female officials in the palace.[143]

As might be expected in the case of an outspoken official serving at the capital for a number of years, not all went smoothly for I-fu. In 1248 he was demoted for his criticism of the appointments of two officials, one of them being Shih Chai-chih (1205–49)—the son of Mi-yuan—as administrator of the Bureau of Military Affairs. Chai-chih, though unpopular with many in the central government, was an old and close friend of Li-tsung's, who had earlier attempted unsuccessfully to get him a post in the capital. I-fu expected to be sent out of the capital, but after he submitted a self-criticism, the emperor relented and restored him to his former positions.[144]

A more serious problem arose when I-fu aroused the enmity of the grand councilor Cheng Ch'ing-chih, a former supporter, because of his criticisms of ministerial corruption and Cheng's policies.[145] Faced with Cheng's complaint that "this attendant minister has repudiated his ministerial rectitude and capital rank," Li-tsung gave I-fu a temple guardianship, although he kept him in the History Bureau as a reader-in-waiting. But worse was to come when the History Bureau came under attack for alleged misrepresentations of affairs in the palace quarters. Although Liu K'o-chuang, I-fu's biographer and his predecessor at the History Bureau, absolves him of wrongdoing, I-fu's heated defense of his own actions only increased the emperor's anger. I-fu was impeached and left the capital in disgrace, never to return.

Despite this unhappy note, the emperor continued to display goodwill toward I-fu. After his departure, Li-tsung called I-fu his "assisting minister" (*fu ch'en*) and said: "When he had long been at the [hall for] expounding the Classics, in any consultation he was always able to come up with an answer applying the authority of the ancients to the present. From among the clansmen, [his kind] is not easily to be gotten." In 1255, after three years of distinguished service as administrator of the Western Clan Office in Fu-chou, I-fu was named minister of rites and reader-in-waiting, but he declined, citing illness. On hearing this, the emperor reportedly sighed in sorrow and gave him an unusually large promotion from "grand master for proper service" (*cheng-feng ta-fu*, rank 4A) to "grand master for splendid happiness" (*kuang-lu ta-fu*, 2B). Following I-fu's death in early 1256, Li-tsung posthumously gave him the highest of prestige titles: area commander unequaled in honor (*k'ai-fu i-t'ung san-ssu*).[146]

Imperial Clansmen and Southern Sung Politics

The clansmen-officials examined in this chapter were active in politics and government under five emperors, from the mid-twelfth to the mid-thirteenth centuries. What can be concluded about the roles that they played?

The most obvious point is that by the late Southern Sung imperial clansmen were to be found in virtually every part of the government. They were ubiquitous in county and prefectural government. We find them in circuit posts, including military ones. Although there were attempts in the early Southern Sung to keep them out of any but clan offices and ceremonial postings in the central government, by the thirteenth century clansmen frequently served in vice-ministerial and ministerial positions. Restrictions against clansmen serving as examination officials, foreign envoys, and most notably as military commanders, similarly gave way in the mid–Southern Sung.

There was an important exception in this record of widespread service: clansmen rarely served as grand or assisting councilors, posts that included the administrators of the Bureau of Military Affairs. This policy, which had been enunciated by Kao-tsung, was overridden by Kuang-tsung's use of Chao Ju-yü, first as administrator of the Bureau of Military Affairs and then as grand councilor, but it also served as one of the grounds for his enemies' successful attack on him. Thereafter, the sources are silent on the issue, which I would take to represent a consensus accepting the prohibition. The key fact is that, after Chao Ju-yü, no clansman either served or—to the best of my knowledge—was proposed for service in this top tier of posts.[147]

A second point is the role played by the Southern Sung emperors themselves in the development of political roles for clansmen-officials. As we saw in Chapter 6, it was Kao-tsung who, in the crisis years of the late 1120s, gave clansmen their first opportunity to hold significant civil and military office, although he was also responsible for many of the restrictions placed on that service. The role played by Hsiao-tsung, the clansman-emperor, was even more striking, for he both promoted outstanding clansmen and found himself frustrated by his ministers who upheld the earlier prohibitions, even though these were increasingly eroded during his reign. Nor should we forget that it was Kuang-tsung who broke precedent in his successive promotions of Chao Ju-yü. If Ning-tsung and Li-tsung seem to have been less involved, personally, with this issue, perhaps it was because of the consensus on the prohibition of clansmen in top offices that we suggested above.

There is, finally, the question of what effect, if any, clan status had upon the clansmen who served as ministers or even ordinary officials in the Southern Sung. One characteristic shared by virtually all the individuals we have discussed in this chapter was boldness, a willingness to speak out critically against ruling ministers or even the emperor. Fearless remonstrance—whether of a parent or a ruler—was a cardinal ideal of Confucian practice, however, and by no means a prerogative of imperial clansmen.[148] How often the clan status of a clansman-official made a difference, either to those around them (for example, the young Chao Hsi-kuan, who was regarded by his colleagues as "dangerous") or for them personally in terms of self-confidence, we cannot say. However, I have found no suggestion of the opposite, of clansmen fearing to speak out either because their unique status made them second-class officials or because their clan status rendered them especially vulnerable to attack.

Indeed, the most interesting instances of clansmen's outspokenness occurred when they invoked their clan status, as when Chao Yen-tuan said, "I am an imperial clansman and especially share the joys and sorrows of the dynasty, so I must speak." An even more intriguing example comes from late

1246 when Chao Shih-huan (CDADADBFBA; 1201–57), then a Palace
Library assistant, addressed the childless Li-tsung following a solar eclipse:
"Liu Hsiang [of the Han] argued that an eclipse was a [sign of] anxiety that
the emperor lacks successors and that the government risks falling into the
hands of another family. Your subject is an imperial clansman, and I believe
that the dynasty's succession should be settled quickly, so that the power of
the ministers may be curbed."[149] Since Liu Hsiang (79–8 B.C.E.) had been at
once a Han imperial clansman and one of that dynasty's great men of letters,
Shih-huan was in effect underlining the validity of a clan voice in discussing
the problem of heirs, an issue that, as we have seen, bedeviled the infertile
Southern Sung emperors. Whether his memorial had any impact is uncer-
tain. Li-tsung's nephew and successor, Chao Ch'i (1240–74, r. 1264–74) or
Tu-tsung, was not named crown prince until 1253, but the *Sung History* notes
that Li-tsung first became impressed with him and began thinking of him
as a possible heir in 1246.[150] Perhaps there was a connection.

As for Chao Shih-huan, his outspokenness made for a brief stay at court.
Although the memorial quoted above was not a problem, his frequent criticisms of those in power soon got him into trouble, and around 1247 he was
impeached and sent to the provinces, where he finished his career.[151] This
is hardly an inspiring example with which to conclude, but it is perhaps a
fitting one, for the abiding role of the clansmen-officials who rose to prominence in the Southern Sung was that of the loyal counselor rather than the
great or successful minister.

NINE

Maturity and Defeat

By the end of Ning-tsung's lengthy reign (1194–1224), dynasty and clan had been in the south for nearly a century. All those who could recall life in the north or the tumultuous events that had forged the Southern Sung had died. With the passing of generations, the Sung tree of Heaven had grown deep roots in southern soil. Scattered throughout the empire, imperial clansmen shared an institutional framework that was manifestly present for those who lived in one of the clan centers but less so for others, a status that was always reflected in their names and the privileges that they commanded, and a shared memory of past glory in the north. Clansmen were ubiquitous within the government, and although there were limits on the posts to which clansmen-officials could aspire, only the very highest positions were out of their grasp.

In a word, the imperial clan had matured. Overwhelmingly late Southern Sung sources speak not of bold or dramatic changes in the clan but of attempts to deal with opportunities and problems as they arose. Names, numbers, expenses, kinship, marriage, and issues of education and government service—such were the matters that occupied the thirteenth-century clan, at least until the 1260s. During the prolonged death throes of the dynasty, the imperial clan was once again caught up in dramatic events, some of them quite horrific. And for those who survived the transition to Yuan, there were new identities to be formed, since the clan, of course, was no longer imperial.

The Problems of Maturity

The core challenges that faced the late Southern Sung imperial clan—and the Sung government as it dealt with the clan—were demographic and fiscal. Although we have no figures for total clan membership at any point in the Southern Sung, Li Hsin-ch'uan's figures for clansmen in the civil and military services cited in Chapter 7 (see Table 7.6, p. 177) provide a benchmark.[1] His combined total of 3,947 contains no women and few if any boys; if we assume that virtually all clansmen held titular office, the total number of clan members must have been well over 8,000.

These numbers placed a considerable burden upon local governments, which were primarily responsible for payment of official stipends and orphan's allowances, which, along with dowries for clanswomen, constituted the main forms of clan support.[2] The problems that ensued from this support system seem to have been perceived in dramatically different terms by local officials on the one hand and members of the clan administration and court on the other.

Chu Hsi, who served as prefect of Chang-chou (Fu-chien) in 1190, was candid in conversations with disciples about the fiscal problem posed by the clansmen, especially since on the occasion of Kuang-tsung's accession in 1189, over sixty Chang-chou clansmen had been made officials in a single day, and the prefecture was expected to provide them with their stipends: "The court does not consider the future. Imperial clansmen daily increase and are becoming a burden for prefectures, as is now the case for one or two prefectures." He was particularly critical of the allowances for orphaned clansmen, not only because the large clan families increased the numbers of the needy, but also because many clansmen managed to get the allowances when they did not deserve them.

According to the law, only those without means of support may request an orphan's allowance (*ku-i ch'ien*); those with support may not ask. "To be with means of support" means that they have brothers or uncles who are officials and can support them, so they will not become impoverished. Now, there are those with brothers or uncles who are officials yet use their influence to apply for the orphan's allowance, while there are true orphans without any means of support yet who have difficulty with their requests because they lack influence and the prefectures obstruct them. . . . If a clansman is in mourning for his parents, according to the old [regulations] he may request an allowance; clansmen who are executory officials (*hsuan-jen*) awaiting vacancies may also have a stipend; the [imperial] grace is excessive. If the court again does not think of the future, in the future the damage to the prefectures will be without limit.[3]

Although Chu Hsi was sympathetic to the plight of clan members in genuine need, his central concern was the fiscal threat to the prefectures represented by the clan support system. By contrast, discussions at court focused on the reluctance of local officials to provide support payments to clan members. In a series of edicts and memorials dating from 1194 to 1217 in the *Sung hui-yao*, we find complaints that prefectures have not provided mandated increases in the orphan's allowance and that cunning local officials delay allowance payments.[4] Most remarkable is a memorial of 1217 from the Department of State Affairs alleging that certain local governments had halted orphan allowance payments for clansmen, clanswomen, and clan widows anywhere from a few months to one or two years. "The officials profit by reduced allowances, and by not releasing an individual's allowance from impoundment, whole families are helpless and dependent. Yet the prefectures and counties do not consider this to be perverse and violent. Through such means, the grace of the court's love of kinsmen is forfeited." In response, the emperor ordered the Great Office of Clan Affairs as well as the Western and Southern Offices to investigate prefectures and counties for instances of such impoundments.[5]

One cannot tell from the available records how many clan members were needy or how burdensome their support was to local governments (but see below for the special case of Ch'üan-chou). But both Chu Hsi's worries and the court's concerns suggest that the issue of clan support was contested in the late Southern Sung. More than that, they reflect a social reality in which the lines between the clan and other groups—elite and common—were increasingly varied and indistinct.

Although the clan members and families visible through biographies and histories display little of this blurring, it is apparent elsewhere. By the late twelfth century the elaborate system of generation names and registration in the Jade Register at the capital was in increasing disarray. In 1212 the Imperial Clan Court recorder Ch'en Cho (1190 *chin-shih*) observed from his study of the genealogies that "in the streams, branches, and leaves of the descendents of the three ancestors," there was an uneven striped pattern. Those in accord with the generation names (*hsun-ming*) constantly increased and were amply represented, whereas those not using them were not included.[6] These clansmen had not lost their clan status, for the bulk of Ch'en's memorial deals with providing them with orphans' allowances, but their failure to use the generational character must have weakened their claim to membership. The same problem appears again in a memorial dated 1223, which notes: "In recent times the branches of the imperial clan have flourished, with more than a tenfold increase over the past. The laws for [recording] births and generation names is not wanting, yet the wealthy [clansmen] are not more than one or two in ten, whereas the poor are no less than seven or eight." The standard naming procedures involved the submission of documents to county officials for forwarding to the prefecture and thence to the Court of the Imperial Clan; poor families lacked both the time and the necessary documents. The court's response to this memorial was to order respected elders (*tsun-chang*) to handle the matter, but given the problems involved that seems unlikely to have settled things.[7] This is an intriguing document, for it is one of the few places where an estimate is ventured as to the distribution of wealth within the clan, and although we have no way of telling what is meant by "wealthy" and "poor" (*fu, p'in*), the very perception that a majority of clansmen were "poor" suggests that economic differences were increasing within the clan.

Marriage legislation provides another measure of social changes within the imperial clan. Written in 1213, a memorial from the Great Office of Clan Affairs begins with a reiteration of the 1077 prohibition on marriages with families in which the fathers-in-law have been slaves, the sisters-in-law prostitutes, or where the parents have lived on the border under two regimes.[8] However, where the 1077 prohibition specified that these rules applied to mourning kin (*t'an-wen i-shang ch'in*), by 1213 they applied to non-mourning kin (*fei t'an-wen i-hsia ch'in*) as well. Following this preamble, the memorial goes on to describe the current problem, namely that "many cunning clerks" have engaged in illicit intercourse with registered clansmen,[9] and then have used that connection to bring suits that others dare not oppose. The proposed solution, accepted by the emperor, was to prohibit clan families from marriage with the families of clerks.

Although documents like the one just cited typically blame others for the woes of clansmen, legal sources offer quite a different perspective. Along with their allowances, stipends, and special access to office, clansmen had a special legal status. In the words of Brian McKnight, "Assaults and batteries against imperial relatives or officials were punished more heavily than were ordinary assaults and batteries if they were committed by status inferiors."[10] Moreover, as noted in Chapter 7, the punishment of clansmen was under the jurisdiction of clan authorities rather than local officials, and clansmen inclined to criminal activities had advantages over the commoner criminals. Even in the early Southern Sung, problems existed. In 1133 imperial clansmen in Lin-an were reportedly opening shops where they made liquor and robbed their customers.[11] The two most vivid examples of criminality in the imperial clan come from the collection of Sung and Yuan legal judgments, the *Ming-kung shu-p'an Ch'ing-ming chi* (Collection of enlightened judgment).[12]

Chao Jo-lou, a tenth-generation descendent of Wei-wang, was remarkable for his audaciousness.[13] Thanks to the cooperation of clerks in the Jao-chou (Chiang-hsi) government offices and the gang of thugs he gathered about him, he was able to act with impunity over the tenures of more than one prefect. Operating out of a fixed gang headquarters (*hua-chü*), Jo-lou ran prostitution and extortion rackets. Wu Yü-yen, the judge-author, wrote that "there is nothing he will not do." Such doings included causing the untimely death of a commoner he was harassing, beating a candidate at the prefectural examinations to death, and attacking people at a gambling hall. He repeatedly escaped either with a light punishment or by disappearing for a while. In the case of the examination candidate, the angry complaints of local scholars only got them in trouble, and Jo-lou emerged unscathed. Even in Wu Yü-yen's judgment, for the gambling hall incident, Jo-lou's punishment was to be remanded to the External Offices of the clan (probably the southern, Ch'üan-chou branch) for discipline, although his principal cronies were beaten and, in one case, exiled.

The second case involves not a clansman but a commoner impersonating one, but it is revealing of the place of the imperial clan in Southern Sung society. The chief culprit was a man originally named Jen Ju-hsi, who was characterized by the writer Ch'ien T'ing as "a disgraceful young man, the detritus of his village."[14] Jen fraudulently claimed the name of Chao Ju-hsi, the eldest son of the clansman Chao Shan-ts'ai. He fabricated a county birth certificate, secretly cut a seal for the household of the Prince of Jun, an imperial uncle, privately erected a yellow banner (denoting imperial clan status), and with iron bludgeons and staffs coerced itinerant merchants, seized ships, intimidated laborers, and beat people into acquiescence. Although discovered and convicted for these crimes, he was given a light sentence and soon was active again, this time using the name of Chao Shants'ai's second son. This time Ju-hsi fabricated not only a clan identity but also official rank and an official appointment. Having assembled a group of three to function as his assistants (as secretary, cook, and bodyguard), he would arrive in townships by sedan chair. He and his men would search and seize bronze goods from the common people, even to the point of taking Buddhist sacrificial bowls and babies' bells. Eventually they were caught and punished with heavy beatings, but only after multiple investigations by clan authorities and local officials.[15]

Whether real or fake, the criminal "clansmen" in both these cases were able to use their putative clan status as a screen for their activities, and the authorities clearly had trouble knowing how to handle them. In comparison with the Li Feng / Chao Shih-chü case of 1075 discussed in Chapter 4, Chao Jo-lou's punishment for blatantly criminal behavior, including manslaughter if not murder, was remarkably light. However, since Jo-lou had neither physical nor familial proximity to the emperor, his actions had none of the political overtones that underlay the Li Feng affair. Clan misbehavior had generally ceased to be an affair of state.

We have no way of estimating the extent of this kind of misbehavior; it seems reasonable to assume that these cases were included in the *Ch'ing-ming chi* because they were remarkable and thus perhaps not typical. At the same time, given the ease with which imperial clan status could translate into influence and power, it would be surprising if clansmen did not commonly used their status to prevail in disputes with others, whether over land, money, or people, as indeed was the case described in Chapter 7 of Southern Office administrators who illegally impounded the ships of commoners. One of the common refrains in epitaphs of Southern Sung clansmen and especially clanswomen is that *despite* being clan members they were friendly, modest, and the like.[16] Clearly there was a popular perception of clansmen as haughty and overbearing—problematic friends and dangerous enemies.

The Development of Family Identities

As clan families became settled longtime residents of their adopted locales throughout southern China, the clan ceased to be central in their social world, except for those living in the clan centers. Although clan status continued to be critically important for such matters as officeholding and marriage, clansmen increasingly adopted the values and practices of their landlord and *shih-ta-fu* acquaintances, especially values relating to family and kinship. The available evidence, though not abundant, points to the increasing importance of the individual family's identity and at least the initial steps in the creation of Chao lineages (as distinguished from the imperial clan); numerous post-Sung Chao lineages, for example, claimed a Southern Sung "founding ancestor" (*shih-tsu*). This is not to say that clan consciousness disappeared. Even as the histories and traditions of individual families were articulated, the imperial clan remained a constant referent, a source of pride that set the clan families off from their *shih-ta-fu* neighbors.

Chao Tzu-ssu (AAAACCI; 1089–1157) provides a good example of a founding ancestor. Having spent most of his first forty years at the Tun-tsung halls in the Southern Capital of Ying-t'ien fu, Tzu-ssu fled south in 1127, going first to the garrison town (*chen*) of Ching-k'ou, in Tan-t'u county (Jun-chou, Liang-che), and then in 1129 to Ta-kang, another garrison town in the same county located just south of the Yangtze River, where he settled with his family.[17] In 1132 his family became even more established when he received the titular office of grand master for closing court (*ch'ao-san ta-fu*, civil rank 6A) and was given a land grant of 100 *ch'ing* (approximately 1,600 acres) in honor of his designation as "palace master for T'ai-tsu's posterity" (T'ai-tsu *hou fu-chün*).[18] The land grant must have elevated his family instantly to the ranks of the large landowners in the county, and it cemented their connection to the locality. Indeed, the Ch'ing dynasty Chaos of Ta-kang recognized Tzu-ssu as their founding ancestor and counted the lineage's first generation from him, not T'ai-tsu.[19]

The Chao lineage of Hsiu-shui (Chia-hsing fu, Liang-che) traced its settlement there to the early Southern Sung, although in their case it happened with the second generation of Southern Sung clansmen. Chao Shih-k'o (BGBAKA; 1087–1174) took his family south and settled in Chin-hua county of Wu-chou. Then for reasons the genealogy does not explain, the second and third of his three sons moved elsewhere, one to the neighboring county of P'u-chiang, the other well north to Hsiu-shui.[20]

The family tradition of the descendents of Chao Tzu-shen (AADBFAB; n.d.) followed a slightly different pattern. Although he was later acknowledged as the founding ancestor of the lineage, in fact Tzu-hsien had followed the Southern Office to Ch'üan-chou and presumably lived in its residential quarters there, and at least some of his descendents stayed in the residences until the end of the dynasty.[21] But a grandson named Chao Shih-chiu (AADBFABGA) reportedly decided at an early age to avoid all misfortune, cultivate his person, and not serve in office. While out strolling one day, he came across a scenic spot that he thought would be appropriate for a life in retirement. According to the genealogist, "That spring morning he gazed at [the locale's] lush beauty and delighted in its fecundity. On this land they could have a profusion of descendents and secure continuous family possession." He moved his family there and there they stayed, creating an extensive lineage complex in the centuries that followed.[22]

Although all these stories had obvious importance for later lineage history, their significance for these lineages during the Southern Sung is debatable. However, the prefaces for two Southern Sung genealogies of imperial clan families demonstrate unmistakably the emergence of a new kind of kinship identity for clan families.

The earlier of these is the *P'o-yang Chao-shih hsu hsiu p'u* (Supplemental revised genealogy for the Chaos of P'o-yang), dated 1243, for which two prefaces survive, collected in the miscellaneous documents section of Chao Hsi-nien's *Chao-shih tsu-p'u*, a Kuang-tung lineage genealogy.[23] The first is by Ch'eng Kuei, the sheriff of P'ing-chiang county in Yueh-chou (Ching-hu-nan). According to Ch'eng, the genealogy was compiled by his brother-in-law, Garrison Commander Chao, who bemoaned the loss of kinship knowledge as his family dispersed; specifically his uncles had all left, and no longer lived with his family. The Jade Register was not incorrect in its listings, he stressed, but the commander was still concerned that in a society in which *shih-ta-fu* frequently gave no recognition to their more humble kinsmen, special attention needed to be paid to family relationships.[24] The second preface, by one Hsiung Ta-chang, not otherwise identified, also mentions the fear of losing genealogical knowledge, but places it in a moral context. The family's primary source of strength, said Hsiung, lies in the accumulation of good and illustrious ancestral names, and for that purpose the Jade Register is inadequate. In contrast to Ch'eng's focus on the dispersal of clansmen, Hsiung noted that many clansmen were living in their locality (*li*), and there was a need for clear records about them.[25]

With the broader imperial clan and the Jade Register ever present factors for these writers, there is some question as to whether this now-lost work was even a prototypical lineage genealogy. Although Ch'eng's essay does speak to the importance of ancestral temples (*miao*) for maintaining family identities, to my knowledge no later genealogies stem from this one, and while this genealogy suggests that there was a strong lineal identity for the Chaos of P'o-yang (a county in northern Chiang-hsi), that cannot be established from these prefaces.

In the preface for the 1263 *Genealogy of Auspicious Sources for the Chaos of Chün-i* by Chao Yü-tz'u (AADBDDCAFBA; n.d.), the issue of family identity was not in doubt.[26] The Hua-she lineage of Ming and Ch'ing times was descended from this line and accorded the title of founding ancestor to Yü-tz'u's son Meng-i (AADBDDCAFBAX; n.d.), who moved the family to what became its permanent location in the town of Hua-she in the early Yuan (see below for his actions in the Sung-Yuan transition).[27] But long before this, Chao Ling-ken (AADCBK; 1120 *chin-shih*) had been responsible for settling his family (including his brothers and their children) in Chu-chi county (in southwestern Shao-hsing fu), when he was serving as prefect of Shao-hsing around 1151; and for sending his nephew Chao Tzu-yueh (AADCBGB) north to K'ai-feng to retrieve the coffins of his parents, which were subsequently reburied in Chu-chi.[28] Ling-ken was not an ancestor of Yü-tz'u and Meng-i. When he and his family moved to Chu-chi, however, they were accompanied by a second cousin Chao Tzu-lin (AADBDDC; 1103 *chin-shih*), Yü-tz'u's great-great-grandfather, who during the troubles of the late 1120s had served with distinction as prefect of Hu-chou (Liang-che). It was from him that the Hua-she lineage was descended.

Chao Yü-tz'u begins his preface with the arboreal metaphor so common to much clan discourse: "Ever since our emperor-ancestors used humanity to establish the dynasty, the roots have flourished, and the branches proliferated." Initially, his focus is on his family's particular branch, and he traces its history through the generations, beginning with the Prince of Yen (Chao

Te-chao, AA; d. 979), and details in particular the accomplishments of Ling-ken and his nephew.

Although the common pattern in the formation of Southern Sung clan families (and later lineages) was to trace descent from an apical ancestor who lived during the early Southern Sung, in this case it seems likely that the descendents of both Ling-ken and his nephew and of Tzu-lin identified themselves as a broader family grouping within the imperial clan. They were "the Chaos of Chün-i," as the title of the 1263 genealogy stated, Chün-i being the original name of K'ai-feng's metropolitan county, which was renamed Hsiang-fu in 1009. We know Ling-ken to have been a K'ai-feng resident,[29] and so presumably was Tzu-lin, for his ancestors included Chao Shih-hsiung (AADBD), who was the Prince of Tzu, and that would have guaranteed K'ai-feng residency for his children and grandchildren. Since most of T'ai-tsu's descendents had moved to the Southern Capital when the Tun-tsung Halls were created, Ling-ken, Tzu-lin, and their families would have been distinguished by their K'ai-feng residency.

Having dealt with the family's establishment in Chu-chi, Yü-tz'u goes on to describe its Southern Sung fortunes: "Ever since arriving south of the Yangtze, [the family has been] frugal with its wealth and liberal in its use of people's labor. People's livelihoods have benefited, demonstrating humanity, friendliness, filiality, and complete loyalty. . . . As a result, over two hundred offspring now live in Shao-hsing." The family did not confine itself to Chu-chi, however. Yü-tz'u mentions branches in Yü-yao (also a county in Shao-hsing prefecture) and Hsi-an (in neighboring Ch'ü-chou), and a scattering of individuals throughout Wu-yueh, Che, and Min, that is, the southeastern coast from the Yangtze Delta to Fu-chien. Thanks to the depth and weight of the many offshoots sprung from Kung-hsien and An-ting,[30] "the accumulated good fortune has produced happiness, and the rich virtue has spread far."

Such a statement would have served as a fitting conclusion in most genealogical essays, but Yü-tz'u is not finished. Moving from branch to tree, he describes the imperial clan as a whole:

Loyalty and filiality are rooted in Heavenly nature; kindness and righteousness are ample among clan members. There is no division between far and near or between distant and close relations, and no differentiation among large and small or noble and mean. They meet using the rites, they are encouraged through learning, and they are instructed through loyalty and trust. This esteem and respect for clan righteousness did not exist even in antiquity. Thus the *Heng-chü* [commentary of the *I-ching*] says, "When the world is [well-]managed, the people's hearts are secured." The imperial clan has enriched customs and kept people from forgetting the root essentials.

This is a remarkable statement, echoing as it does the vision of a clan scattered, diverse yet united in amity, first articulated by T'ai-tsu some three centuries earlier,[31] and claiming its realization to be historically unique. By 1263 the threats to the dynasty's survival were very real, and one might expect clansmen to have stressed their local roots and autonomy. Yet here we see something quite different. Although the Chün-i Chaos had established roots in Chu-chi, they remained firmly attached to the great tree of the dynasty, and they repeatedly proclaimed its importance.

But what of the parts of that tree characterized by massed growth rather than discrete branches? How did the great clan centers of Lin-an, Shaohsing, Fu-chou, and Ch'üan-chou—and clan life within them—evolve as the Southern Sung progressed? Unfortunately, so poor are our sources for the first three of these centers that little can be said about them. It is to the better-documented Ch'üan-chou that we now turn.

The Southern Office in Ch'üan-chou

The Southern Office and its associated clan residences in Ch'üan-chou had two distinctive characteristics. First, they constituted by far the largest concentration of clansmen in the empire, and so functioned as the de facto center for all clan affairs even though they were far from the capital in Lin-an. Second, Ch'üan-chou was one of the greatest cities of the Southern Sung, one whose economic vibrancy depended primarily on its flourishing overseas trade.[32] Moreover, Ch'üan-chou—and Fu-chien generally—were at the height of their political influence, thanks to a highly developed academic culture that made Fu-chien the most successful circuit in the Southern Sung civil service examinations.[33] The section that follows is concerned not simply with the character of clan life and institutions in Ch'üan-chou, but also with the relationship of the clan to the city as an economic center.

During the century following the establishment of the Southern Office in Ch'üan-chou in 1131, the imperial clan presence there grew dramatically, from 339 clansmen, clanswomen, and clan wives to over 2,300 by the Shao-ting reign period (1228–33). As is apparent from Table 9.1, the most spectacular growth occurred during the twelfth century, but it continued throughout the period for which we have statistics. To put this in some perspective, the official population of Ch'üan-chou prefecture was 201,406 households in 1080 and 255,758 in 1241–52,[34] which, if one assumes an average of five people per household, translates into an overall population of one million for the earlier period, and 1.25 million for the later.

The 2,300 clan members represent only a fraction of 1 percent in a population of 1.25 million, but several factors served to give the clan a weight disproportionate to its numbers. First, they were clustered in and around the city of Ch'üan-chou, which had a population of perhaps 200,000 in the Southern Sung.[35] Second, since virtually all clan members received government support, through either official stipends or allowances, the fiscal implications of these numbers were considerable, an issue to which we will return. Third, given their wealth, the number of people whose livelihoods depended on the clan—whether as servants and attendants, craftsmen, merchants, and even monks—must have exceeded the number of clan members manyfold.

Two other aspects of Table 9.1 deserve consideration. One is the contrast between the over 400 percent growth in the sixty-odd years from 1131 to the 1190s, and the 33 percent growth from then until around 1230. Was there a thirteenth-century increase in the death rate or decrease in the birth rate that might explain the sharply reduced level of growth? Although such a question cannot be answered conclusively, I have seen no evidence of either of these in the historical records. There is another possible explanation, namely, that much of the large twelfth-century increase was the result of the in-migration of additional clan families. In support of this is the fact that a fivefold growth over two generations, while characteristic of the early clan in its K'ai-feng palaces, was not the case for the fourth through seventh generations, who largely constituted the imperial clan in the early Southern Sung (see Tables 2.2 and 2.3, pp. 31 and 32). Several factors point to the likelihood of migration as an explanation. First, conditions in 1131 were extremely unsettled, and there could have been an influx of refugee clan members in the next few years. Second, as mentioned in Chapter 7, there was a proposal in 1139 to have homeless or unsettled clan members sent to the clan

Table 9.1

Imperial Clan Members in Ch'üan-chou, 1131–1232

Date	Living in the residences	Living outside the residences	Total clan membership
1131			338
1195–1200	1,300	440	1,740+
1201–4			1,800+
1228–33	1,427	887	2,314

SOURCES: SHYCK, 20/37b–38a for 1131; Chen Te-hsiu, CWCKCC, 15/11a for 1195–1200; and *Wan-li Ch'üan-chou fu chih, chüan* 9 for 1201–4, cited in Li Tung-hua, *Ch'üan-chou yü wo-kuo chung-ku ti hai-shang chiao-t'ung,* pp. 186–87. Li cites the same gazetteer for a figure of 3,000-plus in 1228–32, but this must be a clerical error, since the figure is a thousand off Chen's figure for the same date. Li also dates Chen's second figure as 1217–19, but that is also mistaken (it is the date of Chen's first tour in Ch'üan-chou rather than the second, which is when he wrote the essay from which the figures are drawn.

centers.[36] Third, later Chao genealogies suggest that the geographical movement of clan families throughout the Southern Sung was quite common. Since the consensus among economic historians is that the twelfth century was a period of great prosperity for Ch'üan-chou,[37] it is plausible that it would have attracted clan families living elsewhere.

Another phenomenon apparent in Table 9.1 is the increasing proportion of clan members living outside the residential complexes. These complexes, together with the Southern Office buildings, were located in the western part of the city of Ch'üan-chou. The Mu-tsung Hall (Hall for a Friendly Clan, thus distinguished from Lin-an's Mu-ch'in-chai, or Hall for Friendly Kin), was built when the clan first established its presence there. By the Chia-t'ai era (1201–4), however, it was inadequate, and at the request of the prefect Ni Ssu (1166 *chin-shih*), a New Mu-tsung Hall was built near the old hall in the western part of the city.[38]

We know frustratingly little about these large residential complexes and life within them, for the vast majority of Southern Sung biographies are for clansmen who resided outside them. Some light is shed, however, by a record of the Southern Office clan allowances preserved in a later Chao

Table 9.2
*Allowances for the Southern Branch Clan Members
in Ch'üan-chou*

Residence and rank	Cash per month (strings)	Rice per month (*shih*)
Within the halls		
Virtuous (*tsun hsing*) or Great (*ta*)	13.0	1.0
Middle (*chung*): 20 *sui* and over	9.1	0.7
Small (*hsiao*): 10 *sui* and over	4.7	0.4
Pending (*wei*): 5 *sui* and over	1.0	0.4
Outside the halls		
Great (*da*): 10 *sui* and over	2.0	1.0
Small (*hsiao*): 5 *sui* and over	1.0	0.5

SOURCE: NWTYCSTP, pp. 694–95; from the *Pei-ch'i Chao-shih tsu-p'u*, which cites a Ch'üan-chou gazetteer.

genealogy (see Table 9.2). Clansmen-officials were specifically excluded, since they were entitled to stipends by virtue of their rank and office, but clanswomen over twenty *sui* could receive a dowry of 100 strings of cash if they lived in the residences, or one-third that if they lived outside.[39]

These allowances, for which we have no specific date, are remarkably generous, since, as noted earlier, the general allowance for orphans, first established in 1095, was two strings of cash and one *shih* (picul) of rice per person per month, which concurs with the allowance for those living outside in this case. It is unclear why those within the residences—who were already receiving their lodging for free—were entitled to so much more. Perhaps this was part of the government's policy of encouraging clan families to settle in the clan centers, but if so it was curiously unsuccessful, given the rapid increase in those living outside during the early thirteenth century. But whatever the explanation, the conclusion that clan members were maintained with considerable largesse is inescapable (we will be return to this issue when we consider the economic impact of the imperial clan in Ch'üan-chou).

We also have some intriguing evidence from the epitaph of Chao Ju-chieh (BCBPAMGA-d; 1199–1249), the wife of Ch'en Tseng (1200–66), for her natal *and* affinal families were both involved in the running of the halls.[40] Ju-chieh's great-grandfather was Chao Shih-wu (BCBPAM; 1108–53), a hero of the war against the Chin (see Chapter 6) and one of the early administrators of the Southern Office in Ch'üan-chou.[41] Shih-wu was from the prominent Prince of P'u branch of the T'ai-tsu line, descended from the brother of Ying-tsung, and as such he and his family were mourning kin of Kao-tsung and had the right to reside in Lin-an. However, they made their home in Ch'üan-chou, as we know from the tomb of Shih-wu's wife, Lady Ts'ai (BCBPAM-w; 1134–61), which was excavated in 1973.[42] Some years later, Shih-wu's son, Chao Pu-k'uang (BCBPAME; b. 1151), also served as administrator of the Southern Office. Neither Ju-chieh's grandfather nor her father, Chao Shan-lan (BCBPAMGA; n.d.), held such exalted positions, but her husband's grandfather, Ch'en Chün-ch'ing (1113–86), had served as teacher (*chiao-shou*) of the Mu-tsung Hall school before going on to an eminent career, culminating in the post of grand councilor, and in 1250 her husband was supervisor of the Mu-tsung Hall itself.[43] In this marriage tie between one of the most eminent families of Fu-chien (the Ch'ens were from P'u-t'ien county in the neighboring commandary of Hsing-hua) and one of the leading families of the imperial clan in Ch'üan-chou, governance of the clan appears to have brought them together.[44]

Although the clan residences seem destined to remain cloaked in obscurity, we know a good deal about the public face of the Ch'üan-chou clansmen, thanks to records for officeholding and the examinations. During the Southern Sung, in the two southern Fu-chien prefectures of Ch'üan-chou and Chang-chou alone, the imperial clan produced twelve prefects, 51 county magistrates, and ten superintendents of foreign trade.[45] So common were these postings that clansmen serving as local prefects and magistrates seem to have passed unremarked.

As for the examinations, an astounding 329 imperial clansmen from Fu-chien received *chin-shih* degrees during the Southern Sung; this represents roughly 7.3 percent of the 4,525 Southern Sung *chin-shih* from Fu-chien. As is apparent from Table 9.3, moreover, this percentage pales in comparison with those for the prefectures in which the clan was concentrated, particularly Fu-chou with its 210 *chin-shih* and the southern prefectures of Ch'üan-chou and Chang-chou (widely noted as a spillover locality for the Ch'üan-chou clan families), where roughly one-fifth of all *chin-shih* were imperial clansmen.

The record of clansmen from Fu-chou is quite startling. The paucity of sources makes it impossible to do more than speculate how the Western Office clansmen—by all accounts outnumbered by those from Ch'üan-chou—did so well in the examinations. However, given the enormous success of Fu-chou in the examinations generally, the 210 Fu-chou clans-men–*chin-shih* were probably not as prominent, locally, as those from Ch'üan-chou. As for that group, Table 9.4 is revealing in its details of the Ch'üan-chou examination record over time.

Two trends jump out from this table. The first is the dramatic rise in the clansmen's *chin-shih* numbers, peaking in the period 1225–47 at six degrees per triennial examination and almost 40 percent of the prefectural total. As in the other Fu-chien prefectures, it took the Ch'üan-chou clansmen over half a century before they began to appear in significant numbers, but thereafter their presence was almost constant.[46] As noted in Chapter 7, the clansmen were seldom in direct competition with the other candidates in the examinations; nevertheless, the great prestige that accrued to *chin-shih* and the power that they potentially represented must have contributed significantly to the visibility and influence of the clan in the life of the prefecture.

Second, there is a striking parallel between the large rise and smaller fall of both clan and non-clan prefectural *chin-shih* in the early and late Southern Sung. Whatever their differences, the two groups seem to have had a common fortune in the examinations. Why is open to speculation, but the timing of these trends strongly suggests the influence of the Ch'üan-chou economy. It is generally accepted by economic historians that the twelfth century was a period of unprecedented prosperity for the prefecture and the thirteenth century one of decline. Since success in the examinations involved investments in education that took decades to pay off, and the results of educational cutbacks took decades to become evident, one would expect a

Table 9.3
Imperial Clan Chin-shih *from Fu-chien*
During the Southern Sung

Prefecture	Imperial clan chin-shih	All Southern Sung chin-shih	Imperial clan as percentage of total
Chien-ning fu	6	509	1.2%
Fu-chou	210	2,249	9.3
Hsing-hua chün	20	558	3.6
Ch'üan-chou	122	582	21.0
Chang-chou	33	185	17.8

SOURCES: NWTYCSTP, pp. 647–77 (citing *Pei-ch'i Chao-shih tsu-p'u*) for the imperial clansmen; Chaffee, *Thorny Gates of Learning*, p. 197, for the prefectural totals. The other three prefectures in Fu-chien—Nan-chien chou, Shao-wu chün, and Ting-chou—had no imperial clan *chin-shih*.

Table 9.4
Imperial Clan Chin-shih *in Ch'üan-chou*
During the Southern Sung

Period	Imperial clan chin-shih	Total chin-shih	Clan as percentage of total	Clan *cs* per exam	Total *cs* per exam
1127–62	3	89	3.0%	0.3%	8.1%
1163–89	10	96	10.0	1.0	10.7
1190–1224	43	204	21.0	3.3	17.0
1225–47	54	139	39.0	6.1	17.4
1248–79	12	54	22.0	1.1	6.0
TOTAL	122	582	21.0	2.5	11.9

SOURCES: For the *chin-shih* totals, *Pa-min t'ung-chih* (1490), *chüan* 46ff; for the clansmen, *Ch'üan-chou fu chih* (1736–95 ed.), as cited in Yang Ch'ing-chiang, "Ch'üan-chou Nan-wai tsung-tzu chin-shih shih-hsi k'ao," *Ch'üan-chou Chao Sung Nan-wai tsung yen-chiu*, no. 1 (1991): 9–29. The NWTYCSTP, pp. 647–77, also has figures for all Fu-chien clansmen by year and by county. It lists 110 Ch'üan-chu clansmen rather than 122, thus lowering the percentages slightly, but not enough to modify my general findings.

lag in the *chin-shih* results, and that in fact is what we find in this table. Thus it is to the Ch'üan-chou economy, particularly its overseas trade, and the role in it played by the imperial clan that we now turn.

Overseas Trade and the Imperial Clan

One of the most distinctive features of Sung China was its orientation to maritime Asia. Cut off from the ready access to central Asia enjoyed by the Han, Northern Dynasties, and the T'ang, the Sung turned to the sea and thereby helped to spawn a vast trading system extending to the western reaches of the Indian Ocean.[47] And at the heart of that system lay Ch'üan-chou, which in 1087 was granted a Foreign Trade Superintendency (*Shih-po-ssu*) and by the early Southern Sung had supplanted Kuang-chou (Canton) as the primary Chinese port in the maritime trade. Through it passed the many luxury goods to which the Sung upper classes had become attached— spices, incense, cotton, yellow wax, rhinoceros horn, ivory, pearls, silver, gold, tortoise shells, and sulfur—in return for silk, silk brocade, porcelain, lacquerware, wine, rice, sugar, and illicit copper coins, to name just a few of the goods that were traded.[48]

Hugh Clark has suggested that the commercial wealth of Ch'üan-chou was a major reason for its selection as the Southern Office center,[49] and although there is no evidence to prove or disprove the suggestion, it is reasonable, for the imperial clan was an expensive burden. Moreover, since the Southern Office with its residential complexes and the Foreign Trade Superintendency were Ch'üan-chou's two extraordinary institutions, the connections between the two were complex. At least five deserve attention: the fiscal drain of the imperial clan on the Superintendency, the direct involvement of the clan (or clansmen) in the overseas trade, clansmen as superintendents of trade, religious aspects of the trade and clan involvement in them, and the role of the clan as consumers in the trade.

Around 1231, during his second tour as prefect of Ch'üan-chou, Chen Te-hsiu wrote a lengthy memorial concerning the costs of maintaining the Southern Office clan members; this memorial essentially set the terms for all subsequent discussions of the fiscal drain caused by the imperial clan.[50] In it he detailed the increasing burden of supporting the imperial clan that had been forced on the prefectural government. Although the initial arrangement had been a 50-50 split between prefecture and circuit in providing the funds for clan support, over time the circuit had managed to eliminate its obligations, and the prefecture had come to assume most of the burden. The prefecture paid 90,600 strings for cash stipends (out of a total 145,000-plus strings, the Foreign Trade Superintendency providing the remaining 54,400); 53,100 strings of the 60,600-string rice allowance (actually 20,200 *shih* at 3 strings per *shih*), with the Hsing-hua Commandary providing 7,500; and 15,600 strings for the educational support of clan youths.[51]

Chen then catalogued the social and economic woes of the prefecture over the past several decades. Until the Ch'ing-yuan period (1195–1201), the burden of supporting the imperial clan had not been a problem, thanks to an adequate tax base and a thriving maritime trade. However, the reduction of that base because of the encroachment by great families on farming lands and a precipitous decline in the trade had made the burden acute and had led the Ch'üan-chou government into such dubious practices as demanding taxes from the people a year or two in advance.[52]

Chen's proposed solution, it is interesting to note, was not to reduce the clan's allowances but rather to redistribute the burden of paying for them by increasing the funds contributed by the circuit fiscal office and the Superintendency.[53] The problem, as he addressed it, was one of cost-sharing, not the cost of the clan *per se*. For modern historians such as Li Tung-hua and Hugh Clark, however, the lesson to be drawn from Chen's memorial is that the support of the imperial clan with its ever-escalating demands was a primary cause in the economic decline of Ch'üan-chou in the thirteenth century.[54] However, in a cogently argued article on the causes of Ch'üan-chou's decline, Kee-long So disputes this view, noting that the major increases in the prefecture's clan numbers—and thus of expenditures for them—occurred in the twelfth century when their fiscal burden was manageable. Rather, So argues, the real culprit was an acute shortage of copper coinage, the result of a heavy drain of copper abroad combined with the government's introduction of paper money into the southeast beginning in the mid-twelfth century.[55]

Although the enormous expense of the imperial clan for not only the prefectural government but also the Superintendency should not be minimized, So's argument about the costs of clan support and the timing of

Ch'üan-chou's decline is persuasive. If anything, he concedes too much in stating that "expenses on this item [support for the increasing numbers of clan members] increase correspondingly,"[56] for in fact support per capita for clan members *decreased* over the first century of the Southern Sung. In 1131, the 339 members of the clan in Ch'üan-chou received 60,000 strings for their cash stipends, an average of 177 strings per person.[57] By contrast, the 145,000 strings for stipend support in 1231 came to just 63 strings per member. Far from the clan making growing demands on local authorities, there would appear to have been tight curbs on the support it received.

As for the clan's direct involvement in foreign trade, the available evidence is scanty but suggestive. The most direct evidence is related in Chapter 7, namely, the involvement of two senior clan administrators—Chao Shih-k'an and Shih-hsueh—not only in trade but in the illegal seizure and acquisition of ships belonging to merchants. The ensuing prohibition against the involvement of Western and Southern Office officials in foreign trade apparently applied only to those serving in clan offices.[58] Given the large number of clansmen resident in Ch'üan-chou, it seems highly likely that many of them were privately engaged in the trade, at least as investors, although we have no evidence to that effect.

From the year 1174, there is a suggestive report complaining that Southern Office officials had been involved in a private venture involving the production of wine and its sale to clan members, even while receiving their official stipends. This activity, thenceforth banned, had nothing to do with foreign trade but does reveal even more entrepreneurial activities on the part of clan officials.[59]

The most intriguing evidence for the clan's involvement in the overseas trade is a large oceangoing ship excavated in 1973 at Hou-chu, some ten kilometers outside the city of Ch'üan-chou (the ship was subsequently moved to the grounds of the K'ai-yuan Temple, where a museum was constructed for it; see Fig. 2). The ship, which can be dated precisely to the year 1277, measured 78 feet in length and 29.25 feet in beam (24 by 9 meters), was clearly designed for sea voyages, with a deep draft and twelve bulkheads. The cargo consisted of goods typical of Sung imports from abroad: over 5,060 pounds (2,300 kilograms) of fragrant wood from Southeast Asia, pepper, betel nut, cowries, tortoiseshell, cinnabar, and Somalian ambergris.[60]

Fig. 2 The great Sung ship in Ch'üan-chou. A Sung ship probably belonging to the Southern Office of the imperial clan that sank upon its return from the South Seas in 1279 and was excavated at Hou-chu, near Ch'üan-chou. The ship is now housed at the museum at K'ai-yuan Temple in Ch'üan-chou (photograph by Li Yü-k'un).

As one of the few major archaeological finds from the Sung in recent years, the "great ship," as it was called, elicited much interest from scholars and the public alike. But its full historical significance only became apparent in 1989 when the Fu-chien historian Fu Tsung-wen published an article demonstrating that the ship belonged to the Southern Office imperial clan. Of the 96 items aboard, 19 were labeled "Southern Family" (*nan-chia*), and one "Southern Family registry" (*nan-chia chi hao*). Moreover, other labels referred to clan princely houses, such as *An-chün* for the Prince of An-chün, and yet others to individuals serving as clan officials and to individual clan families.[61] Clearly this was an imperial clan ship, and its cargo of luxury goods from Southeast Asia is compelling proof of the clan's direct involvement in overseas trade in the late Southern Sung. Nor need we assume greed on the part of clan officials for engaging in it, although greed could well have been involved. In light of the fact that public support per capita for clan members had decreased drastically from the 1130s to the 1230s, and given the fiscal difficulties facing the Ch'üan-chou government in meeting those obligations, it would have made sense for the Southern Office officials to use the profits of trade to support clan members.

The third area of clan influence on foreign trade was bureaucratic, namely, the Superintendency of Foreign Trade, which was frequently headed by clansmen. Indeed, nine or ten of the 87 Southern Sung superintendents (10–11 percent) were clansmen.[62] These clansmen-officials had the opportunity to have a direct impact on the foreign trade, and several of them were noted for their activities. In one case, the record was notorious. In 1213 Chao Pu-hsi (BCBBDED; n.d.) was dismissed, demoted, and barred from future appointments as a prefect or director after being impeached for frequently commandeering foreign ships and then falsifying the records.[63]

By contrast, Chao Yen-hou (CDCKGACA; n.d.), who in 1228–33 served concurrently as superintendent and Southern Office administrator, was credited with dispersing a gluttonous and greedy atmosphere and with filling the coffers of the Superintendency.[64] Even more dramatic were the actions by Chao Ch'ung-tu (BAAKFBDAAE; 1175–1230), the fifth son of the former grand councilor Ju-yü, when he served as superintendent around 1217–19. Upon his arrival, he encountered a situation that had begun when a seafaring merchant, owing to a death, had changed his cargo. When he arrived, officials from the prefect on down took many of his goods in the name of "harmonious purchase" (*ho-mai*), including pearls, ivory, rhinoceros horn, blue kingfisher feathers, and scented wood. This practice then became customary, greatly upsetting the merchant community and resulting in a sharp decrease in the number of ships arriving in Ch'üan-chou. With the help of the new prefect Chen Te-hsiu (also the author of Ch'ung-tu's epitaph), Ch'ung-tu abolished these practices, and as a result, there was a threefold increase in the number of ships arriving over the next three years.[65]

Another official whose actions benefited commerce was Chao Ling-chin (AADBHF; d. 1158), whose bitter criticism of Ch'in Kuei was recounted in Chapter 6. Although he served as Ch'üan-chou prefect and not as superintendent, during his tenure in 1151–53 he was instrumental in the completion of the long An-p'ing Bridge, which because it connected the port area with the main market, was critical for the flourishing of commerce in the city. When it was finished, grateful townspeople built a sacrificial hall in his honor.[66]

In some ways the most lasting contributions to maritime commerce were made by Chao Ju-k'ua (BCBPAAACD; 1170–1231), who in 1224–25 served first as superintendent and then concurrently as Ch'üan-chou prefect *and* Southern Office administrator, the only person to hold all three posts at once.[67] His historical importance, however, is as a writer rather than an official, specifically as the author of the *Chu-fan chih* (Description of foreign peoples). From what we know of his upbringing, he was well prepared for this task, for his father, Shan-tai (BCBPAAAC; 1138–88), was a successful local official and a demanding teacher to his sons. His instruction in a variety of books was credited with making them all outstanding scholars.[68] The *Chu-fan chih*, however, is a uniquely important account of the Asian, African, and even Mediterranean maritime world as it was known to the Chinese in the thirteenth century, describing, first, countries and cultures, and second, the varieties of goods imported into China. Ju-k'ua used both the oral accounts of merchants and the records of the Superintendency in writing the book, and the result was a compendium that both expanded the Chinese literati's knowledge of foreign places and objects and has been an invaluable text for the history of maritime commerce ever since.[69]

The considerable role played by religion in the lives of the heterogeneous population engaged in the overseas trade is amply attested in the archaeological record of Islamic mosques and Hindu temples in addition to the numerous Buddhist and Taoist temples in Sung Ch'üan-chou. Indeed, Hugh Clark's account of the transformation of a lineage god into a protector for travelers venturing out to sea provides an excellent example of that role. In two instances that I have found, the imperial clan was also involved in this religious culture. The first comes from 1165, from the port of Ming-chou to the north. At that time, Chao Po-kuei (ABBACEAA; 1125–1202) was serving as prefect and engaged primarily in providing people with relief from a severe famine that had ravaged the region that year. When he learned that a foreign merchant had died outside the city walls, Po-kuei saw that a funeral was held with proper mourning arrangements. The following year, the merchant's countrymen thanked him profusely, praising "the humane government of the Central Kingdom" (Chung-kuo *jen-cheng*). The merchant's family established three Buddhist temples at which people prayed to images of Po-kuei, and the "island barbarians" (*tao-i*) were greatly moved. According to Lou Yueh, writing in the early thirteenth century, even in his own life-time Po-kuei was widely revered among the foreign traders.[70] To be sure, Po-kuei was no ordinary clansman. The fact that he was the younger brother of the emperor Hsiao-tsung undoubtedly contributed to the lavish response of the merchant's family to his act of generosity, as well as to his elevation to a position of reverence among the foreign community. At the same time, he was a clansman rather than a prince, for his brother had been adopted by the heirless Kao-tsung, and his example may well have helped establish a connection for clansmen and the public alike between the clan and the religious support of the maritime trade.

Whatever the impact of Po-kuei's action, by the late twelfth century the imperial clan in Ch'üan-chou had become firmly associated with frequent semiofficial sacrifices to the gods of the ocean (*hai-shen*). According to Li Yü-k'un, on eleven occasions day-long sacrifices organized by the Superinten-dency were performed on the top of Chiu-jih (Nine Day) Mountain in Nan-an county in the eastern suburbs of Ch'üan-chou city, during which prayers were offered to the ocean gods for the protection of the ships and a peaceful passage. Among those named as participants in the stone inscrip-tions on the mountain were invariably representatives of the Southern Of-fice.[71] None of the inscriptions—two of which are shown in the photograph in Fig. 3—speaks to the motivations of the clansmen and Southern Office officials for participating in such a public way in these ceremonies, but the very fact of their participation bespeaks an intimate and publicly acknowl-edged connection between the clan and the maritime trade.

The fifth and last way that the imperial clan influenced foreign trade is the most speculative but possibly the most important, namely, as consumers of that commerce. Obviously, the clan members with their official stipends (for those who were officials) and allowances would have been customers of the luxury commodities that made up the overseas trade, and some at least could have afforded a great many of them. We do not know how many of the goods carried by the great ship were intended for the clan rather than the open market, but presumably the clan authorities would have been able to keep choice items.

The most vivid example of clan members as consumers comes from the tomb of a thirteenth-century clan wife found virtually intact in Fu-chou in

Fig. 3 Chiu-jih Mountain rock inscription. An inscription commemorating sacrifices to the ocean gods dated 1201 at Chiu-jih Mountain west of Ch'üan-chou. Imperial clansmen were actively involved in these ceremonies organized by the Superintendency of Foreign Trade, and in fact three are mentioned in this inscription (photograph by Angela Schottenhammer).

the early 1980s.[72] Huang Sheng (1227–43) and her husband, Chao Yü-chün (AADEBCGBAXX, b. 1223), were from distinguished families. Her father, Huang P'u (1229 *chin-shih*), and his grandfather, Chao Shih-shu (AADEBC-GBA; n.d.), had met as students of Chu Hsi's disciple, Huang Kan (1152–1221), and this connection had led to the marriage. Although both families were from Fu-chou, they had important connections to Ch'üan-chou; Huang P'u served as the superintendent of foreign trade in 1234–36, and Chao Shih-shu (the author of Huang Sheng's epitaph) was administrator of the Southern Office around 1241. The tomb contained an abundance of silks of the highest quality—some 201 items of women's clothing and 153 pieces of cloth, mostly fine silks with beautiful designs—just the kind of textiles that were in demand for exports.[73]

This is not to argue that all clan members were like Huang Sheng; she and her husband were so highly placed in the clan hierarchy that they can hardly be considered typical. However, I would suggest that the sudden settlement of hundreds of clan members who were fully and—by the standards of commoners—lavishly supported by the government must have constituted a powerful impetus for the Ch'üan-chou economy, particularly the overseas trade. Throughout East Asian history, cities like Lin-an that became capitals subsequently grew and flourished thanks to the tax revenues that flowed into them and the wealthy who settled there, often supported by the revenues. Ch'üan-chou hardly constituted a capital, but the Southern Office clan establishment, while burdensome to the prefectural government, nevertheless accounted for an annual inflow of at least 30,000 strings of support money into the city for much of the twelfth century,[74] as well as the presence of those members and their servants as elite consumers.

But if the imperial clan contributed to Ch'üan-chou's era of greatest prosperity, they may have helped to account for its thirteenth-century decline. As stated above, this was not because clan members became too rapacious. Rather, the curtailment of the circuit's support cut off the inflow of capital from outside Ch'üan-chou even as shrinking levels of support made clan members less and less potent consumers. To revisit Table 9.4, although in the Sung the examination success of a locality was almost always the result of numerous factors, economics was clearly a crucial one. Thus in a variety of ways, the fortunes of Ch'üan-chou's clan members were inextricably linked to the city in which they had settled.

Politics and War in the Late Southern Sung

The final chapter of the Sung was marked by yet another problematic imperial succession, another dictatorial grand councilor, and war. Until very near the end, the imperial clan played little if any role, but as the dynasty collapsed in the face of the Mongol invasion, clansmen were caught up in a variety of ways as their privileged status and way of life came to an end.

Many were helpless victims, but we also find loyalists, turncoats, and just plain survivors.

Like most of his Southern Sung predecessors, Li-tsung found himself late in his reign without a direct heir, for his only sons had died early in childhood.[75] He turned to his nephew, the eldest son of his younger brother Chao Yü-jui (AABDEAEABBA), who was given the name Chao Ch'i, formally adopted as an imperial son in 1253, and made crown prince in 1260.[76] Chao Ch'i (1240–74) was a logical choice for adoption and was rigorously schooled by his tutors in history and the Classics under the personal supervision of Li-tsung, apparently to the emperor's satisfaction. Historians have been critical of his selection, however, partly because of congenital defects that required medication throughout his life and may have contributed to his early death at the age of 35 *sui*, but even more because as the emperor Tu-tsung (r. 1264–74), he proved passive and indecisive, interested mainly in the sensual pleasures afforded by palace life.[77] To cite the summary judgment of the *Sung History* historians:

> When the Sung reached [the reign of] Li-tsung, the frontier regions daily grew more troubled, and Chia Ssu-tao controlled the fortunes of the state. Tu-tsung succeeded him, and although he had no great moral failings, he folded his hands [in the face of] treasonous power, and decadence and corruption gradually increased. Examine the events of those times. Without the leadership of brave men and astute strategy, how could the declining remnants be roused and raised?[78]

Chia Ssu-tao (1213–75), the villain of this judgment, was without question the dominant figure in the Sung government from his rise to the grand councilorship in 1259 to his dismissal in early 1275, shortly before his death.[79] Like Han T'o-chou, Chia was an upstart in the world of scholar-officials and owed his rise to the imperial palace, for until her untimely death in 1247, his sister was Li-tsung's favorite consort and the mother of the emperor's only daughter. Also like Han, he lacked the *chin-shih* degree or other academic credentials that would have given him respectability among civil officials. Thanks to his connections, following his low-level entry to officialdom by the *yin* privilege, he advanced rapidly through increasingly important circuit-level positions, although his chief renown prior to assuming high office came from his lavish parties on pleasure boats and in the villas of Lin-an's West Lake.[80]

That said, during his sixteen-year tenure as a grand councilor, Chia proved to be adept at the use and maintenance of power, and although his faults were many, he was much more than the ogre who bewitched two emperors found in the portraits of many traditional historians. He moved against official profiteering and reinstituted the earlier practice of public petition boxes through which people could air their grievances. Most notably, in 1263 he undertook the Public Fields Program (*kung-t'ien fa*), an ambitious—some would say foolhardy—attempt to expropriate vast quantities of what were deemed excess landholdings from the landed classes of the dynasty. This was the first attempt at major reform in almost two centuries, and although carried out with considerable effectiveness, it guaranteed the bitter enmity of the *shih-ta-fu*, who were among those most affected, and further divided the dynasty when it could least afford it.[81]

For even as Chia's domestic programs progressed, accompanied by purges of his enemies, the long war against the Mongols was becoming a death struggle. In the years following the annihilation of the Chin in 1234, Sung-Mongol relations had waxed and waned, often in response to the internal politics of the Mongol leadership. Thus a major invasion by the Mongols under the Great Khan Mongke in 1258 resulted in the seizure of much of Ssu-ch'uan but came to a halt following his death. Over the following decade, the Sung was left in relative peace while Mongke's brother and successor, Khubilai, eliminated a third brother and consolidated his political position. But Khubilai was also busy creating a huge navy to challenge the Sung in the waterways of the Yangtze River and its many tributaries.[82]

In 1268, Khubilai moved against the city of Hsiang-yang on the Han River, which guarded the northwestern approach to the Yangtze River basin. Both sides recognized that this was a strategically crucial target. For five years it was the site of bitter fighting, with the Sung and Yuan courts devoting virtually unlimited resources to the siege. In 1273 the Mongols finally prevailed because of a massive artillery assault made possible by Muslim engineers. Hsiang-yang's fall left the weakened and shrunken Southern Sung empire open to invasion and was widely blamed on Chia Ssu-tao, who since 1269 had also been serving as special military commissioner.[83]

Following Hsiang-yang, the Mongol conquest of the Sung was completed in two phases. From 1273 to 1275, the Mongol armies under the leadership of the general Bayan—in the opinion of one historian, "probably the most gifted and successful military man of his generation"[84]—engaged the Sung across a wide front from the Yangtze Delta to Hunan and proved virtually unstoppable. By the end of 1275, the delta region had fallen, the city of Ch'ang-chou where the Sung armies had made a determined stand had been destroyed, and the situation in Lin-an appeared hopeless. The Sung court at this time was led by Li-tsung's widow, the Dowager Empress Hsieh (1210–83), and Tu-tsung's widow, the Empress Dowager Ch'üan (1241–1309), acting as a regent for the child-emperor Kung-tsung (1271–1323; r. 1274–76). Tu-tsung had unexpectedly died the preceding year, and Chia Ssu-tao had been dismissed and exiled (and then assassinated) in the summer of 1275. In late January and early February 1276, the court arranged a peaceful surrender to the Mongols, but not before the emperor's two brothers, Chao Shih (ca. 1268–78) and Chao Ping (1272–79), were surreptitiously sent from the capital in the company of the loyalist general Chang Shih-chieh (d. 1279). Like the K'ai-feng court in 1126, the Lin-an court was taken north, where its members lived out their days supported by the Mongols.[85]

The escape of the two princes, however, meant that the conquest was far from complete. Although the original plan of those in the princes' entourage had been to reconstitute the court in Wen-chou, where Kao-tsung had held court while fleeing the Jurchen almost 150 years earlier, it was decided to move south to Fu-chou, which was relatively more secure. There, on the first day of the fifth month (June 14), Chao Shih was installed as the emperor Tuan-tsung (r. 1276–78). This was a war with many theaters but few fronts. Large portions of Chiang-hsi, Fu-chien, and Kuang-tung—and even Ssu-ch'uan in the far west—were contested, with some cities taken and retaken on multiple occasions. For the imperial clan, disaster struck in late 1276, when some 3,000 clan members were massacred by a Sung official who had gone over to the Yuan, though the impact of this event on the war effort was minor.

From 1276 to 1279, the itinerant court moved further and further down the coast, from Fu-chou to Chang-chou (Fu-chien), then to Hui-chou in Kuang-tung, then to the island of Hsiu-shan (in the waterways of the West River), and finally to Yai-shan, an island further west along the Kuang-tung coast (see Fig. 4). In early 1279, eight months after the Sung court had

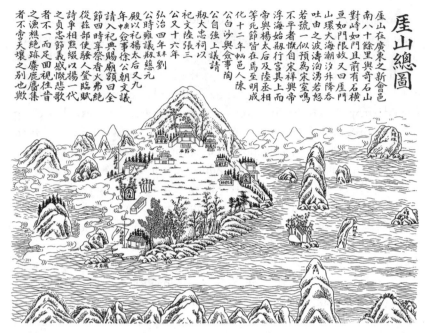

者之漁樵　者之貞相　之詩事義　從此忠節　節律時享　請年殿以　公時雍議　弘治四年　公又十六年　報文陸秀　公自強上　公白化十二年　帝與楊太　不平者一　若號一似　吐由之波　山環大海　旦如厓門　南八十餘里　厓山在廣東之新會邑

Fig. 4 Yai-shan and the later ancestral hall to the Sung; woodblock print. A map showing what was in the Sung the island of Yai-shan and the ancestral temple erected in memory of the Sung emperors. The temple was located close to the site of the temporary imperial quarters erected on the island in 1278–79, and the waterway in the foreground was the primary site of the naval battle with the Mongols. From Chao Hsi-nien, *Chao-shih tsu-p'u* (1901).

settled there—erecting a small city in what had been a rural backwater—the assembled forces of Sung and Yuan met. On the sixth day of the second month (March 19) of 1279, some 300,000 men in 2,000 ships engaged in a titanic struggle, and by the day's end some 100,000, including the Empress Dowager and the young emperor Ti-ping (r. 1278–79), who had succeeded his brother the year before, had perished. The dynasty was extinguished.

Clansmen and the Loyalist Cause

Throughout most of the events just described, clansmen-officials seem to have been noteworthy mainly by their absence, at least in comparison to their prominence through the early part of Li-tsung's reign. But this changed during the dynasty's last years. As the dynasty's mandate grew less and less secure and its supporters dwindled, its identity as the House of

Chao became increasingly central. In these circumstances, the imperial clan was naturally prominent, since they were a group whose service and loyalty were presumably beyond question.

The clansmen from these last days for whom there are records largely divide into two groups. One consists of those who are remembered chiefly for their relationship to the cause of Sung loyalism—whether as martyrs, recluses, or in some cases collaborators—and in fact we know of them mainly from collections of loyalist biographies. The other group is formed of those clansmen who survived the transition—some dramatically, others without fanfare—and became the ancestors of Ming and Ch'ing Chao lineages. Our sources for them are lineage genealogies.

The Sung loyalist movement was easily one of the most dramatic aspects of the Mongol conquest. In the writings of eleventh-century historians and even more in the thought of Ch'eng I and Chu Hsi, loyalty had come to be redefined as a moral obligation that an official owed not simply to the person of a ruler but to the dynasty as a whole. Sung loyalism in the 1270s and 1280s involved militia movements during the war and scattered rebellions afterward, but for individuals it was most commonly manifested through suicides, fights to the death, or the choice of eremitism by officials who survived the fall. Although it was far from universal—there were many who switched sides and served the Yuan—it has captured the attention of historians because it was a new phenomenon. No earlier dynastic change had inspired comparable demonstrations of loyalty. And it was to prove an influential precedent—the Ming loyalists of the seventeenth century looked to their Sung predecessors for models.[86]

We have no way of estimating how many clansmen were actively involved in resisting the Mongol invasion, but there are indications that they received the special attention of the court. In 1274, the court discussed a policy of gathering imperial clansmen into the inner prefectures (*nei-chün*) to serve as important officials, and at least one important appointment was made as a result.[87] Another source discussing the same year reports that the court's policy was to raise militias throughout the south, and "in every circuit many clansmen were providing their support."[88]

Whatever the numbers of loyalist clansmen, the histories portray them in a number of heroic guises. Chao Meng-chin (AADEAAAAEAAB; d. 1276) died during the battle for the Yangtze port of Chen-chou; during a daring strike on a Yuan flotilla under the cover of thick fog, the fog suddenly lifted and he was easily picked off.[89] Chao Meng-lei (ABBCCBAA-ABBC; 1259 *chin-shih*), who had been in the entourage of the young princes after the fall of Lin-an before being given a military command in Ming-chou, died there without submitting to the enemy.[90]

More elaborate stories have survived concerning two other battlefield deaths. In 1274 Chao Liang-ch'un (BAAKFBDAAEAA), then serving in the General Accounting Office in Lin-an, was appointed prefect of An-chi-chou (Hu-chou, Liang-che), an important prefecture in the Yangtze Delta. This was a large promotion for him and came in response to the court discussion of concentrating imperial clansmen in the inner prefectures described above. Liang-ch'un quickly proved his worth. He successfully relieved the famine from which the prefecture had been suffering at the time of his arrival, pacified a group of marauding soldiers, decapitated an envoy bringing an invitation to surrender from the turncoat Sung general Fan Wen-hu,[91] and marshaled the prefectural city's forces against the Yuan army when it arrived outside the city walls. However, he was betrayed by Wu Kuo-ting, a general who had been unable to reach his assigned post because it had fallen to the enemy, but who had so impressed Liang-ch'un by his air of nobility and fine talk that the latter had invited him to stay and assist in the fighting. After Wu opened the city's southern gate, thereby dooming it, Liang-ch'un retired to the governmental offices, sent his family away while refusing to flee himself, and finally hanged himself.[92]

In the case of Chao Yü-che (AABCDBADECE; n.d.), the Prince of Hsiu, an insistence upon martyrdom was linked to his status as an imperial clansman. In 1276, Yü-che was in the court of the two princes serving as investigating commissioner for the southeastern circuits (by this point virtually the whole empire) but made enemies by attacking what he saw as the dictatorial actions of Yang Liang-chieh, the brother of Empress Dowager Yang. When he was then ordered north to help defend the embattled city of Jui-an fu (Wen-chou, Liang-che), a minister praised his loyalty, arguing that he should be kept at court in order to "enhance the roots of the state," but he was sent anyway. Shortly after his arrival at Jui-an, the city was besieged, and together with the prefect, Yü-che vowed to fight to the death. As in An-chi, the city fell after a junior officer opened a gate, and after some street fighting Yü-che was captured. The Yuan commander asked him, "Are you the Prince of Hsiu? Can you now surrender?" Yü-che sternly replied, "I am a close relation of the dynasty. For me now to submit as I am about to die would be to separate [myself from it]. So why do you ask?" He was immediately killed.[93]

Like Yü-che, Chao Shih-shang (CXXXXXXXXX; 1265 *chin-shih*) was a clansman at the itinerant court in Fu-chien before being sent out to do battle, though unlike him he went willingly—he was a friend of the leading loyalist general Wen T'ien-hsiang (1236–83)—and distinguished himself in Chiang-hsi before being captured and killed. His heroism, however, did not blind him to the problems that beset the Sung cause. He is reported to have viewed the court in transit from one city to another—a vast convoy of baggage wagons with numberless ornamented consorts in attendance—and lamented: "This military campaign is like a spring outing. How can we save [the dynasty]?"[94]

These stories of martyrdom are, for the most part, strikingly similar to those from the war against the Jurchen that we saw in Chapter 6, but other accounts are very different. For Chao Hsi-chi (ABBBBGBBBA; d. 1278), a former minister of revenue and enemy of Chia Ssu-tao who led a military contingent under Wen T'ien-hsiang and who followed Wen in surrender to the Mongols in 1278, suicide was preferable to cooperation with his captors. He and his "nephew," Chao Pi-hsiang (d. 1278), refused the food that their family brought to their prison cell, dashed the crockery to pieces, and starved themselves to death.[95] Even more dramatic is the account of Chao Meng-kung (AABDEAEABACF; n.d.), the brother of Tu-tsung, who, with his father, Chao Yü-jui, worked to raise an army in Shao-hsing fu after the fall of Lin-an. Instead they were captured and Meng-kung was brought to Lin-an. There the turncoat general Fan Wen-hu questioned him concerning his "rebellion" (*ni*). Meng-kung furiously replied: "The bandit minister [i.e., Fan] has received the rich grace of the [Sung] state, yet has completely endangered the sacrifices to the Altar of Grain. I am a son in the emperor's house and wish to sweep away the shame of the ancestral temple. How could I be transformed into a rebel?" This infuriated Fan, who beheaded him. As he left the Sung ancestral temple, Fan declared in a loud voice, "The spirits of T'ai-tsu, T'ai-tsung, and the sages are in Heaven. How could they bring Meng-kung to this?" According to the *Sung History* historian, all the residents of the city were in tears, and the darkened skies echoed with thunder and lightning following Meng-kung's death.[96]

The most famous of the imperial clan loyalists was Chao Pi-hsiang (BCBQDCDDBAA; 1245–95), who ironically survived the fall of the Sung by sixteen years.[97] Pi-hsiang was born in Tung-kuan county in eastern Kuang-tung, where his grandfather had moved in the early 1240s, and as a youth his appearance greatly impressed a visiting scholar: "Without asking, he knew that [Pi-hsiang] was a royal youth."[98] He passed the *chin-shih* examinations in 1265 and held county-level positions in Kuang-tung before retiring to serve his elderly father. Between 1276 and the final defeat at Yaishan in 1279, Pi-hsiang played an important role in helping to keep the Kuang-tung region loyal to the Sung. Although Yuan forces had occupied Kuang-chou in 1276, Pi-hsiang convinced a local warlord, Hsiung Fei, to support the Sung cause against them. Hsiung retook the city and held it for much of the next two years, thus providing important security for the nearby Sung court.[99] It is not entirely clear what Pi-hsiang did during this period. On one occasion when Hsiung was about to commandeer large sums from the townspeople in order to pay his troops, Pi-hsiang donated 3,000 strings of cash and 500 piculs of rice from his family treasury and supervised a corvée program that he convinced Hsiung to employ in place of cash exactions.[100] Besides benefiting the people, this action is revealing of the kinds of resources a relatively unexceptional imperial clan family commanded. Pi-hsiang also impressed Wen T'ien-hsiang, the military hero and later grand councilor, who named him military supervisor of Hui-chou and a judicial intendant.[101] By the time of Yai-shan, however, Pi-hsiang was in retirement, and in retirement he remained. Refusing official appointment from the Yuan government, he lived out his life as a recluse, surrounded by a circle of loyalist friends, some of them fellow clansmen, bowing to a portrait of Wen T'ien-hsiang, prostrating himself in the direction of Yai-shan, and generally passing his time in poetry, song, and drink. By the time of his death, his family was reportedly impoverished—his largesse in Kuang-chou undoubtedly a contributing cause—but his sons, too, refused employment by the Yuan.[102]

In the large literature on Sung loyalism, these examples from the imperial clan do not stand out because they are so typical. The choices of martyrdom, suicide, and eremitism were made by dozens if not hundreds of others, often in more colorful ways. By contrast, the most prominent—and the most cited—example of collaboration was that of the imperial clansman Chao Meng-fu (ABBACEAACAAG; 1254–1322). From the county of Lan-ch'i in Wu-chou (Liang-che-tung) and the son of a clansman-official who had served as prefect of Hu-chou, Meng-fu was a young man when the Sung fell and in fact spent the first decade of Yuan rule in the south in the company of loyalist eremites.[103] However, in 1286 he was one of a group of noted scholars who were persuaded to enter the Yuan government, and over the course of a long and successful career he became president of the Han-lin Academy and a director in the Ministry of War. More than that, Meng-fu gained fame as a poet, calligrapher, and painter, indeed one of the greatest painters in Chinese history, in the view of many scholars.[104]

That a man of Chao Meng-fu's talents and accomplishments provided long and able service to the Mongols posed a problem for many of his loyalist contemporaries and even more so for many later historians. The Mongols clearly gained propaganda value from him; not only was he a Sung imperial clansman, but he was also the great-great-great-grandson of Hsiao-tsung's father, Chao Tzu-ch'eng (ABBACEA; d. 1144), which made him, in theory, a mourning kinsman of the last Sung emperors.[105] According to Frederick Mote, "some members of his own clan refused to recognize him as a clan member and wrote strong criticisms of him."[106] Meng-fu himself remained troubled throughout the rest of his life by his decision to serve the Yuan, praising past recluses and lamenting his official duties in his poems and letters. Indeed, such were the ambiguities of the loyalist movement that he was on good terms with some of its most prominent members.[107]

Chao Meng-fu's situation was so unique, so burdened with symbolic import, that one cannot take his collaboration or the responses to it as representative of the imperial clan at large. The genealogical records contain instances of clansmen-officials who quit government service after the fall of the Sung and lived out their lives in retirement.[108] But these are easily matched by the clan offspring who served as officials under the Yuan, including two who served in Ch'üan-chou.[109] Chao Jo-pei (CBADIA-CAAAA; n.d.), a military official from Ch'üan-chou, was especially noteworthy; both his son and his grandson served as Yuan officials, thanks to the exercise of the *yin* privilege, and a great-grandson served Ming T'ai-tsu.[110] Clearly, neither traditions of loyalism within the clan families nor the Yuan government deterred Chaos from serving.

The Imperial Clan in the Sung-Yuan Transition

As these examples suggest, the genealogical records provide invaluable information concerning the Sung-Yuan transition, especially since the clansmen detailed in them were the survivors—and thereafter the ancestors of the Chao lineages—rather than the heroes or villains of the loyalist cause. And nowhere are they more valuable than in the light they shed upon the two most traumatic events in this period for the clan: the massacre of the Ch'üan-chou clansmen in 1276, and the final defeat at Yai-shan.

Although the massacre of resisting populations was one of the hallmarks of the Mongol conquest in China and elsewhere, the Ch'üan-chou massacre was the act of P'u Shou-keng (d. ca. 1296), a Sung official of foreign—probably Arab—descent who had changed sides during the conflict. Many of the facts concerning P'u and the massacre are contested, owing to the widespread discrepancies among the sources, but the basic outline of events is clear.[111] In the eleventh month of 1276, the Mongol armies approached and then took Fu-chou, forcing the Sung court under the military command of Chang Shih-chieh to sail down the coast to Ch'üan-chou. Once there, P'u Shou-keng, the foreign trade superintendent who controlled Ch'üan-chou,[112] became angered when the suspicious court officials refused to disembark and instead sailed on to Chang-chou, and early the following month, with the support of the prefect T'ien Chen-tzu, he surrendered to the Mongols. Shortly thereafter he struck within the city, killing some 3,000 clansmen and, by some accounts, many *shih-ta-fu* and a Sung army unit from Huai-nan.[113]

There is little agreement among the accounts of the massacre concerning its details. These include the claim that the massacre followed the gathering of clan members at the Ch'üan-chou port to welcome the Sung admiral Chang Shih-chieh after a rumor circulated that he was returning to retake the city, another that P'u invited the clan to a banquet and then killed them in the midst of drinking, and yet another that the killing took three days.[114] A remarkable first-person account by Chao Yu-fu (AADBFABBAAAX;

b. 1270), from a genealogical preface written in 1300, provides the most reliable and vivid glimpse of the event:

I was born in a minor branch [of the imperial clan] in the Mu-tsung Hall in Ch'üan-chou, and my name was entered in the imperial genealogy. When in the Ching-yen period [1276–77] our [dynastic] house was extinguished and I was seven *sui*, the young emperor was forced by [pursuing Mongol] troops to approach the city walls [a reference to the Sung court's seaborne flight down the coast from Fu-chou]. The rebel official, bandit suppression commissioner P'u Shou-keng, closed the gates and barred any entry, and then massacred the clan members, young and old, over three thousand in all. I was also under the sword, but [a man who later] became a [Yuan] administrator—a compassionate and humane man with no sons—took pity on me. He alighted from his horse, clasped [me to him], remounted, and left. He led me to his home north of the river, where he raised me as his heir.[115]

Although Yu-fu thus escaped, the massacre effectively eliminated the vast majority of the clan members, or at least those residing within the clan residences. According to a mid-Ming genealogical preface, Ch'üan-chou had only eight or nine Chao branches descended from the imperial clan.[116] What remains a mystery is why P'u massacred the clan members, for none of the sources offer reasons.

Three possible reasons suggest themselves, however. First, to the extent that the massacre was motivated by P'u's anger at his treatment by the Sung court, it can be seen as a way of striking back at the court directly, for the imperial clan was associated with the dynasty rather than the government. Second, P'u may have received encouragement from Yuan commanders to move against the clan, for when the Mongol army occupied Fu-chou, the Western Office clansmen are reported to have "suffered disaster" and all their genealogies were destroyed.[117] Third, and perhaps most important, P'u Shou-keng could not have acted alone. This point is made persuasively by Kee-long So, who argues that the burden of supporting the imperial clan together with the clan's imperiousness had alienated important elements of the Ch'üan-chou elite and that their support must have been critical to P'u, who as superintendent would not have commanded the military resources to surrender to the Yuan unilaterally, let alone carry out the massacre. In support of this, he notes that T'ien Chen-tzu, the Ch'üan-chou prefect who was P'u's main confederate, was a Ch'üan-chou native and a first-class graduate of the 1256 *chin-shih* examinations.[118] Thus even though the fortunes of clan and prefecture may have waxed and waned together for a century and a half, in the end the clan was an artificial accretion, and P'u may well have had the support of significant portions of the local elite in moving against it.

One final detail regarding the Ch'üan-chou clan must be addressed, namely, the sinking of the great ship discussed above. In 1277, when it sank, Ch'üan-chou was already controlled by P'u, and there were no clan authorities to whom the crew could deliver the ship's valuable cargo. Since the location where the ship was found is sandy and the excavated ship itself shows no signs of having been wrecked, it seems likely that it was either scuttled, to avoid its falling into P'u's hands, or simply swamped. The fact that the cargo was not salvaged suggests that political conditions made it impossible for the cargo to be retrieved.[119]

Whereas the imperial clan was central to events in Ch'üan-chou, at Yai-shan it was peripheral. Although the clansmen in the imperial entourage and within the armed forces that had assembled in the months before the battle must have been numerous, their stories are lost. But as was the case for Ch'üan-chou, a remarkable eyewitness account has survived from the hand of a clansman: a brief autobiography written in 1316 by Chao Jo-ho (CGCBDCAAABX; 1267–1330).[120] Jo-ho's family, from the Wei-wang branch of the clan, had settled in Fu-chou in the early Southern Sung,[121] and when the court fled that city in late 1276, Jo-ho accompanied it as an attendant:

I was serving the emperor and assisted the [imperial] family in boarding the ships on which we fled south to Yai-shan in Hsin-hui county, Kuang-tung. Alas! At that time the loyal ministers, generals, and troops still numbered in the tens of thousands. We relied on the provisions of the household of the grand preceptor Wu [Lung-ch'i] (d. 1279) and had yet to be in need. I was possessed with great good fortune, and so was betrothed to the grand preceptor's daughter. Before a year was up, the Yuan forces arrived and in successive days a great battle was fought. When we knew the battle was lost, I went with Hsu Ta-fu, Minister Huang and others in sixteen ships, which broke out of the waterway. We encountered the ship of Ch'en I-chung in a shallow bay of Yai-shan. At a conference [people] wanted to go to Fu-chou to revive the dynasty's fortunes. But after we traveled seventy-odd *li* from Nan-ao in [eastern] Kuang-tung;[122] there was a typhoon and Ch'en's ship was wrecked, and they went ashore at Ho-p'u.

We had reached Wu-yü when our ship also lost its mast and crossbar; so we landed in P'u-hsi [i.e., western P'u-chang].[123]

There in the western corner of Chang-chou he settled, taking the surname Huang, and living a frugal but peaceful life. Only in this autobiography—a private essay intended exclusively for his descendents—did he air his feelings about the past:

I established a livelihood and passed the years. To the end of my life I have harbored hatred, but have never spoken of it to people. Within [the home] there have been no near relatives; outside I have had no servants. Lonely, I have only my form and shadow to console each other. On many nights I have wept in the cold while burning incense and praying to Heaven, thinking of our sons and grandsons adrift at Yai-shan.[124]

Despite this self-portrait of solitude and poverty, Chao Jo-ho had five sons and was considered by his descendents to be the founding ancestor of a lineage that has continued down to this century, although it was over a century before it returned to the use of the Chao surname.[125]

Although lacking the drama of Chao Jo-ho's story, the Chaos of San-chiang Island (just north of Yai-shan) had similar beginnings. Chao Pi-ying (BCBPCABCAAA; 1225–89) was also from Fu-chou, where his family had settled in the early Southern Sung. I Ie is described as a man of learning, profound thought, and few words, although outspoken in court on the subject of loyalist resistance to the Mongols. In 1274, in response to the court's policy—mentioned above—of encouraging clansmen throughout the empire to raise militias, he was enfeoffed as a prince and given a military post in Kuang-tung with the task of raising and leading a militia.[126] But after the death in 1275 of his father, who had accompanied him, he spent the last years of the Sung in mourning and was not present at Yai-shan. To the end of his life, he lamented not having died there, saying that he was neither loyal nor filial.[127]

The Yuan government seems not to have had a uniform policy concerning the Sung clansmen. The employment and promotion of Chao Meng-fu demonstrates that there was no blanket prohibition on their use in government. The government was quite prepared to stamp out attempts at a Sung revival, however. Shortly after the defeat at Yai-shan, Chao Pi-ying was approached with a proposal that he claim the emperorship and lead the Sung cause, but he is reported to have known that this was impossible and instead changed his name and went into hiding in the mountains.[128] Then in 1283, Chao Liang-ling (BCBPCABBBCBX; d. 1283), a third cousin of Pi-ying's whose father had died in the sea at Yai-shan, attempted a Sung restoration with a force of ten thousand. It quickly failed, and Liang-ling died in the process, but in response the Mongols instituted a fierce hunt for all Chaos, causing them to scatter and go into hiding.[129] Five years later, in 1288, a Chang-chou (Fu-chien) rebellion in the name of the Sung, though not involving clansmen, elicited a similar reaction from the government. Clansmen from Kuang-tung, Ch'üan-chou, and Fu-chou were rounded up and sent to the north as prisoners. Only after the rebellion had been settled were they allowed to return.[130]

Confronted by incidents like these, clan families were naturally fearful. Many families changed their surnames for the duration of the Yuan, and others went deep into the countryside to hide from the authorities.[131] The extant evidence comes almost exclusively from those that survived and gave rise to lineages in later times, of which I have found records of twenty-one. Since this certainly represents only a fraction of the families that survived the Sung-Yuan transition, even taking into account the Ch'üan-chou massacre, they can hardly be considered representative. However, we might usefully ask what it was that allowed them not only to survive but to maintain their identity as descendents of the Sung imperial clan? The answer seems to be land, records, and, in some cases, the acquiescence of the authorities.

Given the commonly acknowledged importance of landholding for the maintenance of elite status in premodern China, clan families, facing a future without allowances or privileges, needed land or the means to acquire land in order to provide security for themselves and their descendents. In the few cases where land is discussed rather than assumed, we find remarkable resources available for land purchases. Chao Pi-ying, while mourning his father in Kuang-tung at the time of Yai-shan, built a 120-step tomb for him with endowed mortuary fields. He also established a landed estate for his family and provided a total dowry for his three daughters of 24 *ch'ing* of land (over 360 acres). Following the death of his first wife, he remarried and decided to establish his family in a new location. He cast nine wooden geese into the water and after three days went looking for them. When one was found near the foundations of an old building on the island of Yai-shan, Pi-ying decided that this indicated the will of Heaven. He bought 47 *ch'ing* (ca. 720 acres) of fields. There was one further move in store for his family, for after Pi-ying's death his wife was forced to flee Yuan persecution, and she moved to neighboring San-chiang, where she eventually bought over 58 *ch'ing* of fields.[132] In another Kuang-tung case, after the 1283 rebellion that cost Chao Liang-ling his life, his brother Liang-ts'ung followed a loyalist ex-prefect, Lin Kuang-shan, into hiding. Lin, who had lost one of his sons in the rebellion, purchased over 220 *ch'ing* of land, which after his death was divided equally among his two sons and Liang-ts'ung.[133] In both these cases, large and successful lineages were the result of these initial land acquisitions.

While land provided security, genealogies conferred identity, and in the case of the imperial clan lineages, the proof of direct descent from Sung emperors was essential to claims of special distinction. In a genealogical preface written in 1300, Chao Yu-chüan (AABEABGCCCAXX; n.d.), who had served briefly as a Sung official and lived thereafter in retirement, describes the fate of the major clan genealogies at the end of the Sung. After the surrender of Lin-an, the genealogical archives were taken to the north. Following the loss of Fu-chou and the surrender and massacre in Ch'üan-chou, the genealogies of the Western and Southern offices were destroyed. He had been serving elsewhere at the time and thus avoided death, and after his return he had been able to obtain genealogical records for his branch of the clan that had been stored in a government strongbox. He had recompiled the fragementary genealogy, which he called the *Hsuan-yuan t'u-p'u* (Charts and genealogy for profound origins), for which he was now writing the preface.[134] Chao Yu-chieh (AADBFABGAXXXX; n.d.) had also been away serving in office at the time of the massacre and upon his return took his family into hiding with a different surname. By the end of the Yuan, his descendents would certainly have merged into the population at large had they not obtained a genealogy from another clan-descendent, which they then stored in a hall built specially for the purpose.[135] To cite one last example, even the family of Chao Pi-ying found itself without a genealogy in the early Yuan. In the view of later genealogists, Pi-ying's youngest son, Liang-shao (BCBPCABCAAAA; 1286–1332), contributed greatly to the lineage by obtaining a clan genealogy and editing it meticulously, adding documents and entries for relatives in Fu-chien. Indeed, his genealogy has proved one of the richest sources for this study.[136]

Finally, it must be noted that despite the fears of clan families and at times their very real persecution by the Yuan government, the authorities were not always hostile to the former clansmen. Chao Yu-fu, rescued as a child from the Ch'üan-chou massacre, is a fitting person with whom to end, for in his autobiography we see revealed many of the ambiguities of the post-Sung age. Raised as Sun Yu-fu in the household of his adoptive father, he attended the Imperial University in the capital, a rare occurrence for a southerner, not to mention a former clansman. Although grateful to Mr. Sun and filially mourning him after his death, he describes how he could not forget his past, pondering frequently on the source of water and the roots of trees. So he returned to his old neighborhood in Ch'üan-chou and, with his uncle, received an exemption from the service obligation, which was granted by a sympathetic assistant brigade commander, who also returned the family's tombsite.

Yu-fu then dealt with the dead, performing sacrifices for his ancestors. He lamented that because he did not know all the death dates for his uncles and aunts, he could not sacrifice to their spirits and had to be content with seasonal sacrifices. He then built a shrine, and neighbors from all around came to offer congratulations, and the elderly spoke and wept. Only the T'ien family did not come, for even though T'ien Chen-tzu had been the chief confederate of P'u Shou-keng in the surrender to the Mongols, he had later fallen out with P'u, who had killed his sons. This led Yu-fu to gloomy reflections: "Those who have taken our mansions, occupied our paddies and gardens, destroyed our graves, and seized our precious things, all are the sons and grandsons of this man [i.e., P'u]. I thought of how, in former dynasties, the sons and grandsons of the royal houses had been exterminated. Since antiquity it had been thus."[137] Although these musings seem to have been triggered by the thought of the deaths of the T'ien sons, clearly Yu-fu's larger concern was the death of the clan. Indeed, Yu-fu went on to describe the arrest and internment of clansmen in the north after the rebellion of 1289 and ended with a cautionary note to his descendents on the difficulties of avoiding calamity.

Yu-fu's essay is instructive in ways he probably did not intend. The fact that Yu-fu returned to Ch'üan-chou within a decade of the final defeat of the Sung (he apparently did so before the rebellion of 1289), built a shrine, and publicly sacrificed to the murdered clansmen and women is truly astounding. Even though it was made possible by a sympathetic official, the incident demonstrates that the Yuan was far from monolithic in its treatment of the Sung clan. As an artifact of emperorship that even in the Southern Sung had carried with it very tangible political, economic, and social attributes, the imperial clan was no more. Except in cases of rebellion, when the Chao name regained a glimmer of potency, ex-clansmen posed no threat to the Yuan state and could be accommodated, if local officials so chose.

Yu-fu's account also suggests new ways for the clan's descendents to speak about the imperial clan, which as a social and political entity was no more. The task left to the descendents was to find meaning in the past that would translate into the present. For Yu-fu—like Chao Jo-ho writing in the same year—it involved the telling of his own story, which linked the clan to the post-clan family and recounted his revival of the ancestral rites. For genealogists it lay in demonstrating a patriline extending to the Sung emperors. And for members of the huge Chao clan associations that exist today in China and abroad, special meaning is found in T'ai-tsu's vision of "generation upon generation all mourning kin."[138] Remarkably, over seven hundred years after the fall of the Sung, the imperial clan continues to be meaningful to many. The reasons for it lie outside this study. Our story ends with the Sung, and it is enough to recognize that for the clan's descendents, the story did not end at all.

TEN

Conclusion: The Sung Clan in Chinese History

Emperor, Society, and the Imperial Clan

Over three hundred years and a thousand miles separated Sung T'ai-tsu in his K'ai-feng palace enunciating his vision of a far-flung imperial clan and the massacre of clansmen at Ch'üan-chou and the subsequent defeat at Yai-shan that together marked the demise of the Chao clan, at least in its impe-rial guise. The preceding chapters have attempted to chronicle the complex and often dramatic changes that transpired in the interval and to make some sense of them. As we approach the end of this book, it might be helpful to think of these changes, broadly, in terms of their political, social, geographic, and institutional aspects.

The Sung imperial clan was, first and foremost, a political creation. The treatment of the monarch's children, whether in Sung China or elsewhere, necessarily involved decisions concerning succession and the allocation of power that were central to the monarchy. The creation of vast khanates for each of Chingghis Khan's sons in thirteenth-century central Asia offers an extreme example of perhaps the most common policy, the feudal investment of each prince with his own territory, a strategy followed in the early Han and Ming dynasties as well.

Sung policies toward princes varied over time, but territorial gestures of any kind were consistently avoided. T'ai-tsu's approach was bureaucratic; he named his younger brothers and sons to important prefectships, where they had significant power, albeit within the framework of the imperial government. T'ai-tsung was less trusting; his denial of substantive office to any imperial offspring, including those of Wei-wang (who might have been considered unlikely aspirants to the throne), even while maintaining them lavishly in imperial palaces, set the political and social parameters of the imperial clan for a century. Policies under Shen-tsung, Che-tsung, and Hui-tsung in the late Northern Sung were marked by ambiguity. Although the decision to allow non-mourning kin to take the examinations and hold regular office, even while reaffirming their status as clan members, was crucial for the future of the imperial clan, its political impact was initially insignificant. Large numbers of clansmen, especially those in the T'ai-tsung branch in which the emperorship resided, continued to hold the high military guard titles that kept them out of official service altogether. Among those pursuing official careers, only in the 1120s do we find the first of them entering the ranks of magistrates and prefects.

In the Southern Sung, the political status of clansmen evolved dramatically. Given the chance offered by the war against the Jurchen to play full roles in civil and military affairs, those clansmen who escaped to the south became fully integrated into the government and in many ways became indistinguishable from their non-imperial colleagues. In two important ways, however, the clansmen-officials remained a group apart. First, to the end of the dynasty their privileged status gave them an ease of entrée into the bureaucracy that was the envy of their contemporaries; through special tests in the *chin-shih* examinations, special degrees apart from the *chin-shih*, and widespread use of the *yin* privilege, the imperial clan came to account for over 3 percent of the civil service and 17 percent of the military service by 1213, a record dwarfing that of any other kin group.[1] Second, because clansmen in high office were more visible and vulnerable, they were subject to an evolving set of regulations and practices. These included virtual exclusion from ministerial positions throughout most of Kao-tsung's and Hsiao-tsung's reigns, the short-lived but remarkable tenure of Chao Ju-yü as grand councilor, and the thirteenth-century practice of allowing clansmen to hold high-level positions except for those at the level of councilor.

In light of this record, the historiographical silence concerning the political role of the imperial clan is noteworthy. With a few exceptions, such as Chao Ju-yü and the successions of Hsiao-tsung and Li-tsung—both clansmen-turned-emperor—few aspects of the clan receive more than a cursory mention, if that, from most Sung historians. This may simply reflect the insignificance of clansmen in Sung politics. That certainly was the case for the palace-bound clansmen of the Northern Sung, but it is questionable for the Southern Sung, as the evidence from Chapters 6 and 8 of their varied activities attests. However, the inattention of historians may also be taken as testimony to the success of the dynasty's policy toward the clan during the Southern Sung. In addition to providing successors to childless emperors, clansmen served their monarchs with remarkable loyalty. Thus for very different reasons, both the Northern and the Southern Sung avoided the political challenges from imperial kin so common to other dynasties and monarchial societies.

A sharp distinction between the Northern and the Southern Sung clan, as a social entity, is also in order. During the former, particularly prior to the reforms of the 1070s, the clan was characterized by a profligate waste of people. Secluded in their luxurious K'ai-feng residences and forbidden normal social intercourse with the city's elite society, clansmen, despite their noble titles and offices, had only minimal ceremonial functions at court. Moreover, their families functioned only partially as families, since they had neither an economic base in property nor control over the marriages of their members. In this they were hardly unique; the vast congregations of palace women and eunuchs, which have long been recognized as features of the Chinese imperium, shared many of these characteristics. But whereas palace women and eunuchs began as groups marginalized by virtue of their gender and sexual status, clansmen were male, fertile, affluent, and educated, differing from their *shih-ta-fu* contemporaries only by being "branches of Heaven." It is little wonder that their status was a cause for concern, as attested by Sung Ch'i's characterization of them as "discarded objects."

When in the late eleventh century the issue arose under Shen-tsung of how to deal with the emerging generation of clan members who had no mourning relationship to the emperor, a new social issue became central, namely, how to define the imperial clan. Confronted by the fiscal, demographic, and residential challenges posed by the remarkable fertility of the clan, the court had to decide between two competing models of clan definition. One, from the T'ang, held clan status to be defined by the five mourning relations (*wu-fu*); non-mourning kin were endowed with land and became commoners. The other harkened back to the royal lineage (*tsung*) of the Chou as well as to T'ai-tsu's vision of a far-flung and heterogeneous group of kinsmen united by common descent and a common genealogy. As we have seen, Shen-tsung's initial reforms pointed to the first model, but subsequent actions by him and Che-tsung dramatically expanded the definition of the clan to conform to the second model. It is intriguing that this discussion coincided with a broader debate—involving some of the same thinkers—about the possibility of reviving the *tsung* as an organizing principle for elite kin groups, a debate that played a critical role in the emergence of the common descent group or lineage (*tsu*) as a widespread form of kinship organization. Although I have found no explicit connections between the two debates, it is hard to believe that they were unrelated, especially since both resulted in groups that were unbounded in potential generational depth.

The imperial clan's social evolution in the Southern Sung involved different issues and processes. The visible clan, as seen in biographies, epitaphs, and genealogies, was scattered throughout southern China. Functioning as individual families that over time often took on the characteristics of lineages, these clan families were quite successful at assimilating into local *shih-ta-fu* society: settling on landed estates, intermarrying with elite families, participating in local culture, and entering official service. But there were limits to their assimilation, for they remained clan members, the recipients of stipends, allowances, and special recruitment privileges, often with broader marriage and social horizons than was common within the local elite. So even at their most dispersed, they remained in some crucial respects an extension of emperorship.

There was also what might be called the invisible clan, those about whom few records have survived, who were less well educated, and who tended to congregate in the less prestigious military service. We know from the *Hsien-yuan lei-p'u*, the extant fragment of the official genealogy, that they constituted a majority of all clansmen in the mid-twelfth century, and it seems likely that they congregated in the major clan centers of Fu-chou and Ch'üan-chou. But as with their non-imperial colleagues in the military service, we know little about their social standing, marriage ties, or lives in general. We might surmise, however, that their status as clansmen was even more central to their lives than was the case for those who had joined the ranks of the *shih-ta-fu*.

Although this book has ranged throughout the reaches of Sung China, it has focused on a rather small number of places central to the history of the imperial clan. Until the late Northern Sung, clan members were confined to the capital city of K'ai-feng and were rarely allowed to venture out, a restriction noted by the acquaintances of the acclaimed clansman-painter Chao Ling-jang (ABCBBA, active 1070–1100):

> Each time [Chao] made a painting, he tried to create some new ideas. But a friend would joke and say to him: "This must be the result of your having made another trip to the imperial tombs." This derisive remark referred to the fact that he was not able to make long-distance travel. All he ever saw was the scenery between K'ai-feng and Lo-yang, a distance of not more than five hundred *li*.[2]

Given the great costs of supporting the sprawling clan complexes in K'ai-feng, their role in the city's economy must have been substantial, even as the legally enforced segregation of clan members probably limited their social impact. When after 1102 the cities of Lo-yang and Ying-t'ien fu found themselves host to the Tun-tsung Halls for non-mourning clan members, the impact of clansmen on the local economy was probably greater than it was in K'ai-feng. Unfortunately no sources have survived to describe it.

Even with the satellite centers, the imperial clan was confined to just three locales at the end of the Northern Sung. But with the tumultuous events of the late 1120s, this changed dramatically. Although a majority of the clan was taken north into captivity and historical oblivion, hundreds of others—mainly from the satellite centers—escaped south and dispersed, so that in the Southern Sung every circuit had a clan presence. But the south, too, had its clan centers: minor centers at the capital of Lin-an and the nearby prefecture of Shao-hsing fu, and major centers in the Fu-chien prefectures of Fu-chou and Ch'üan-chou. Again, the documentation of their lives in these centers is often sorely wanting, but as we saw in Chapter 9, in Ch'üan-chou, the most important and best-documented of the centers, the clan occupied a central and highly visible place in the life of the city and came to play a complex role in its thriving overseas commerce.

One indisputable fact in the geographical evolution of the imperial clan is that the offspring of the Chao family of Ho-pei became southerners.

Indeed, those branches that survived the Sung-Yuan transition with their imperial pedigree intact were not just southerners but mainly southeasterners. Thus the clan today is represented primarily by Chaos in Fu-chien and Kuang-tung who claim descent from the Sung emperors.

Two points can be made regarding the institutional aspects of the imperial clan. First, over the course of the dynasty, the Sung demonstrated considerable institutional innovation with regard to the clan. In the early Sung creation of clan palace administrations, the genealogical Office of the Jade Register (Yü-tieh suo), and Court of the Imperial Clan (Tsung-cheng ssu), the dynasty was following T'ang precedent. The creation of the Great Office of Imperial Clan Affairs (Ta tsung-cheng ssu) in 1036 broke new ground, as did the later Offices of Imperial Clan Affairs in the Two Capitals (Liang-ching tsung-cheng ssu) at the end of the Northern Sung, and their successor institutions in Fu-chou and Ch'üan-chou in the Southern Sung.

Second, from the standpoint of historical consciousness, the Sung marks an important watershed in terms of the *idea* of imperial clans. Although with such innovations as the Court of the Imperial Clan the T'ang may be said to have had the first imperial clan (as distinct from imperial kin) in Chinese history, it was the Sung that initiated a discourse on imperial clans and created the imperial clan (*tsung-shih*) as a category of historical analysis. That discourse had its origins in T'ai-tsu's "Great Instructions" of 964 and was subsequently manifested in numerous court discussions on the history of imperial clans, assertions of the uniqueness of the Sung imperial clan in various essays and epitaphs, and in the unprecedented inclusion of sections on the imperial clan in the *New T'ang History* (*Hsin T'ang shu*), which was first published in 1060.[3] This was more than a passing development. The *New T'ang History* precedent established the imperial clan as a standard section of subsequent dynastic histories, and the discourse generally made the imperial clan a common unit of analysis, and one that often was portrayed as showing the dynasty at its best. Thus we have Chao Yü-tz'u in his genealogical preface of 1263 (cited in Chapter 9) asserting: "This esteem and respect for clan righteousness did not exist even in antiquity.... The imperial clan has enriched customs and kept people from forgetting the root essentials."[4] Whether one agrees with this generalization, the imperial clan as a social and institutional reality in the intellectual landscape of China seems to have been a Sung innovation and is unquestionably an important development.

High Culture and the Clan

The role of high culture in the life of the imperial clan has received uneven coverage in this book, with considerable attention given to it in Chapter 3, when discussing the clan under Jen-tsung, but little thereafter. The reason is that in the Northern Sung, cultural pursuits such as a classical education and the writing of poetry were essential to the self-definition of the clan, and therefore to our story. In the Southern Sung, it is clear that many clan members were highly cultured, both as consumers and producers of poetry, scholarship, and art and as participants in the examination system, which drew heavily on that culture. Yet because of their ready access to office, they had *less* need of cultural accomplishment in order to maintain their social positions than did non-clan *shih-ta-fu*. Indeed, among the majority of clansmen, who did not aspire to (or at least did not attain) *shih-ta-fu* status, cultural and educational levels were quite low. That said, the cultural accomplishments of Southern Sung clansmen were considerable and are worthy of at least brief consideration.

Few if any clansmen can be counted among the first rank of thinkers, scholars, or poets (at least as those canons have been historically defined), although this should not surprise us, since outstanding accomplishments seldom if ever are clustered in any given family. If any clansman has a claim to major intellectual importance, it is Chao Ju-yü (BAAKFBDAA; 1140–96), who in addition to serving as grand councilor was the author of the monumental *Huang-ch'ao chu-ch'en tsou-i* (Collected memorials of Northern Sung officials) in 150 *chüan* and the now-lost *T'ai-tsu shih-lu chü-yao* (Selected veritable records of T'ai-tsu) and a friend and correspondent to many of the major thinkers of the late twelfth century, particularly Chu Hsi.[5] In fact, the ties between Chu and Ju-yü's family were numerous. Chu wrote the epitaph for Ju-yü's father, Shan-ying (BAAKFBDA; 1118–77), describing among other things his writings, which included a 30-*chüan* history of the T'ang.[6] Chu is also reported to have acted as go-between in the marriage of Ju-yü's oldest son, Ch'ung-hsien (BAAKFBDAAA; 1160–1219), and to have given his fifth son, Ch'ung-tu (BAAKFBDAAE; 1175–1230), a copy of the *Great*

Learning.[7] Growing up in such a milieu, it is hardly a surprise that many in Ju-yü's family were themselves culturally prominent. Both Ch'ung-hsien and his oldest son, Pi-yuan (BAAKFBDAAAA; 1214 *chin-shih*; d. 1249), were active in the academy movement of the late twelfth and early thirteenth centuries, as was Ju-yü's nephew Ju-ching (BAAKFBDDA; n.d.).[8] And Ch'ung-tu, whom we encountered as an exemplary superintendent of foreign trade in Chapter 9, was the author of four books—two of them histories—and a poet praised by the grand councilor Tseng Ts'ung-lung (1195 *chin-shih*).[9]

Although Ju-yü's family was unique in its cluster of prominent individuals, it was hardly alone in its activities. In the early Southern Sung, Chao Shan-yü (BCABGHEB; 1143–89) was a prolific writer whose *I shuo* (Explanation of the *Book of Changes*) was honored with a preface by Ch'eng I's student Kuo Yung (1091–1187), who credited him with uniting several strands of thought, and was praised by Chu Hsi. Shan-yü also wrote four books of history, an explanation of the *Analects*, and 60 *chüan* of poetry.[10] Shan-yü's renown as a scholar of the *Book of Changes* was shared by Chao Yen-hsiao (CABDAAKA; 1166 *chin-shih*), whose work also received the praise of Chu Hsi; Chao Keng-fu (CCABHBACB; 1173–1219); and the minister Chao I-fu (CECBCCDAD; 1189–1256), who—as we saw in Chapter 8—greatly impressed Li-tsung with his interpretations of hexagrams.[11]

To cite just a few more examples of clan scholars, Chao Tzu-chou (AAEBFAE; 1089–1142), whose very prominent political role in the early Southern Sung was described in Chapter 6, was known as a classicist and his 27-*chüan* work on rites, the *T'ai-ch'ang yin-ko li*, was praised by Kao-tsung.[12] Chao Ju-t'an (BCBFAFAAA; d. 1237) was a renowned classicist who wrote books not only on virtually all the Classics but also on Hsun Tzu, Legalism (Han Fei Tzu), Taoism (Chuang Tzu), the T'ang poet Tu Fu, and the T'ang institutional compendium, the *T'ung-tien* (Comprehensive documents).[13] Finally, as noted in the preceding chapter, while serving as superintendent of foreign trade in Ch'üan-chou, Chao Ju-k'ua (BCBPA-AACD; 1170–1231) compiled the invaluable treatise on foreign places and trade, the *Chu-fan chih* (Description of foreign peoples).

The accomplishments of clansmen in poetry were also considerable. In the eighteenth-century collection of Sung poetry *Sung-shih chi-shih* (Recorded occasions in Sung poetry), all of *chüan* 82 is devoted to poems by imperial clansmen, 74 of whom are represented. They constitute just under 2 percent of the 3,812 authors whose work appear in the collection, a considerably lower figure than their representation in the Southern Sung bureaucracy, but impressive nevertheless.[14] Among the clansmen whose biographies were used in this study, thirteen were cited for their poetry, and in several of those cases admirers of their work are mentioned. An early example is Chao Te-wen (CG; 975–1046), nephew of both T'ai-tsu and T'ai-tsung, arguably one of the most talented of the first-generation clansmen, whose poetry and scholarship are said to have brought him a wide circle of scholarly friends and earned him the lavish praise of Jen-tsung.[15] In the Southern Sung, Chao Ch'ung-fu (CCAAAABAA; 1134–1218), although known primarily as a capable local and regional official, produced a volume of poetry and had as his closest friend one of the greatest Southern Sung poets, Yang Wan-li (1127–1206).[16] Yang is not quoted as commenting on Ch'ung-fu's work, but it is reasonable to assume that their common love of poetry played an important role in their friendship. The minister and philosopher Yeh Shih (1150–1223) is said to have admired the poetry of Chao Ju-tang (BCBFA-FAAB; 1208 chin-shih), the brother of Ju-t'an whose scholarship was discussed above.[17] And Yeh's student, Wu Tzu-liang (b. 1197), collected the poetry of Chao Pi-chien (BCABDAAAAAD; 1193–1262).[18] Finally, we might note two clansmen whose poetry was praised by their biographer, Liu K'o-chuang (1178–1279), himself a prolific author and a figure of considerable importance in Li-tsung's court. Liu noted that Chao Yen-hou (CDCK-GACA; fl. early thirteenth century) was an outstanding poet with over 50 chüan of poetry who had exchanged poems with Ch'en K'ung-shih (1172 chin-shih), a student of Chang Shih and Chu Hsi.[19] He similarly characterized Chao Ju-sui (BCBGNAGCC; 1172–1246) as a noted poet whose collection of poetry, the Yeh-ku chi, was quite popular.[20]

I am acutely aware of the limitations of the information and analysis presented above, for they do little more than demonstrate that clansmen were indeed active in the scholarly and literary activities of the shih-ta-fu. Unfortunately, it is beyond the scope of this study to attempt an evaluation of the impact of clansmen on Sung thought, scholarship, and poetry. Painting is a different matter, however, for the importance of the imperial clan in Sung painting has long been recognized.

Osvald Siren, in his monumental study of Chinese painting, states that "the imperial house of Sung had a more immediate influence on the evolution of painting than any other family in China."[21] This, in his view, was largely the result of the highly accomplished artistry and patronage of the Northern Sung emperors, most especially Hui-tsung, but he also mentions a dozen clansmen-painters of note, primarily from the Northern Sung. Moreover, the paintings of at least nine clansmen survive to the present, a remarkable 5 percent of the Sung painters with extant paintings.[22]

More important than these numbers is the fact that three clansmen-painters have been recognized as major artists. Chao Ling-jang (see above), who is more commonly known among art historians by his *tzu* of Ta-nien, grew up in the clan palaces of K'ai-feng and was active as a painter in the last decades of the eleventh century. He was a painter of intimate landscapes evoking the country of southern China, paintings that were both popular in his own day and extremely influential in the development of a non-monumental southern Chinese style of landscape painting.[23] As mentioned above, Ling-jang, as an imperial clansman, was confined to K'ai-feng and occasional trips to the imperial tombs in Ching-tung-hsi and so never had a chance to see the southern landscapes that he so often depicted. Thus in his painting, especially in his masterpiece *River Village in Clear Summer*, we see, to quote Wen Fong, "the romantic dreamworld of the citybound artist," an aesthetic perspective that was to flourish in the Southern Sung.[24]

The other two outstanding clan painters were both from the Southern Sung, but their circumstances and paintings were very different. Chao Po-chü (AADDFEBB, d. ca. 1162) and his brother Po-su (AADDFEBE; n.d.) were the grandsons of the painter Ling-chün (AADDFE). Thanks probably to his ducal title, they were raised in K'ai-feng, where Po-chü was a member of the Painting Academy under Hui-tsung.[25] In the early Southern Sung both made their way to Hang-chou, where they served as court painters under Kao-tsung. Po-chü, the more famous of the two, was highly regarded for his painterly skills, especially for those in the green and blue manner (*ch'ing-lü p'ai*) and illustrative picture-scrolls such as his famous *Han Palace*. Po-chü's vivid juxtaposition of consorts promenading behind the palace walls while commoners with their horses and carts gather in the street outside, although distant in time and space from his Han subject, suggests a first-hand knowledge of imperial palaces. But regardless of its accuracy, this is the only extant depiction of palace life from the hand of an imperial clansman.

In contrast to Chao Po-chü, Chao Meng-chien (AABCDBADBEAA, 1199–ca. 1267), living late in the Sung, was every bit the literati painter and poet. Although he passed the *chin-shih* examinations in 1226 and eventually served as prefect of Yen-chou (Liang-che) and a Han-lin academician, he is remembered as a man of great culture who traveled about on his houseboat, drinking with his friends, and singing Ch'ü Yuan's *Li Sao* (Encountering sorrow).[26] He is most famous for his *Narcissi*, a twelve-foot scroll consisting exclusively of intertwined narcissi, which according to Wen Fong "is highly valued by the Chinese as being expressive of the lofty and elegant nature of a scholar-painter."[27]

It is noteworthy that the differences between Ling-jang and Po-chü on the one hand, with their intimate ties to the palace and emperor, and Meng-chien on the other, socially and geographically removed from the court, can be seen to mirror the general transformation of the imperial clan from a capital-based institution to one with a high degree of literati identity. There is a broader question to be asked, however, and that is why clansmen were apparently so much more important in painting than they were in scholarship and poetry. The answer, I think, lies in the prominent imperial role in painting. Between the active patronage of emperors and the creation of the Painting Academy in the late Northern Sung—and its continuation in the south—Sung painting tended to be centered in the court and capital. Thus clansmen, so long as their connections to emperor and court remained close, were well situated to excel in painting. In this regard it is hardly coincidental that the great majority of noted clansmen-painters were from the Northern or early Southern Sung and were connected with court and capital. Only Meng-chien falls outside this pattern, and the very solitariness of his example, together with his clear identification as a literatus-poet, suggests that his case is simply an exception.[28]

The Legacy of the Sung Imperial Clan

The final question to be addressed concerns the post-Sung significance of the clan, both as a kinship group (or groups) and as a model for later imperial clans.

As discussed in Chapter 9, the transformation of Sung clan families into post-Sung lineages could be lengthy and complex. In some cases a kind of lineage consciousness began in the late Southern Sung; in others descendents had to wait until the early Ming to reclaim their Chao surname and create a formal lineage organization. The twenty-odd genealogies of clan offspring that I have tracked down represent only a tiny fraction of the clan families that flourished in the late Southern Sung. Nevertheless, it is to my mind remarkable that over twenty lineages survived into modern times, all claiming descent from the Sung emperors.

Even more striking has been the recent burst of interest and activity among Chaos around the world in their royal antecedents. To cite a few examples, a short bilingual history of the Sung imperial clan was published in San Francisco in 1965;[29] the Chao Clan Association (Chao-shih tsung-ch'in hui) of Taiwan published a volume of Sung portraits of emperors and empresses in 1971, which included a Chao clan song;[30] and most remarkably, an active Chao research association has been established in Ch'üan-chou and has, in the past decade, organized conferences and published newsletters, journals, and in 1994 a beautifully edited facsimile edition of a valuable early genealogy with a host of additional documents appended.[31] I will leave it to anthropologists to explain the significance of these many activities, which seem paralleled by a general resurgence of interest in surname organizations in China, but it is clear that considerable numbers of people today find great relevance in the thought that they are descendents of the Sung emperors and imperial clan.

The more historically relevant question concerns the impact of the Sung imperial clan model on subsequent dynasties. The brief answer is that it was negligible for the Yuan, considerable for the Ming, and of some importance for the Ch'ing. Mongol policies toward imperial kin were largely determined by nomadic customs in which social and political status depended upon the degree of consanguinity with the ruler and in which the ruler's sons were typically enfeoffed with their own lands. Thus the Yuan empire featured large appanages under imperial princes, and their control by the central government was highly contested.[32]

The Ming founder, T'ai-tsu (r. 1368–98), also looked to appanages as a way of handling his two dozen sons. They were enfeoffed in territories located primarily in the western and northern border regions of the empire.

With considerable autonomy and large guard units at their command, the princes were highly trusted by their father, who depended upon them as the first line of border defense, and on the whole this appanage system worked well through his death in 1398.[33] However, the civil war following the succession of T'ai-tsu's grandson, the Chien-wen emperor (r. 1398–1402), that resulted in the seizure of the throne by his son the Yung-lo emperor (r. 1402–24) revealed the inherent dangers of granting princes territorial power. The Yung-lo emperor severely curtailed their power, although it took another century and the revolts of two princes before the princely establishments were rendered truly powerless.[34]

Of more relevance for our purposes are the detailed provisions that guided the lives of the broader imperial clan. According to the *Ming History*, although princely titles were inherited according to a strict rule of primogeniture—thereby departing from the Sung practice of giving the title to the oldest living member of the oldest surviving generation among the descendents—other descendents received noble titles in a scale that decreased with each generation. But even princely descendents of the sixth generation *and beyond* received the title "supporter-commandant of the state" (*feng-kuo chung-wei*).[35] Thus in one critical respect the Ming followed Sung practice, namely, by considering all imperial descendents to be clan members regardless of their generational remove from the emperor.

In several other respects, the Ming clan differed from its Sung predecessor. First, like the Sung imperial clan until 1070 clansmen were excluded from the examinations and all public offices, but unlike the Sung this did not change when the Ming clansmen had gone beyond a mourning relationship to the emperor. In 1595—half a century before the dynasty's end—clansmen were permitted to take the *chin-shih* examinations, but few if any passed.[36] Second, because from the beginning the Ming government sent princes to their appanages in the countryside where they then stayed, those places became the residential centers for the clan, dispersed in dozens of locales about the empire. Indeed, such was the dynasty's concern with keeping the clansmen under control that they could not leave their residences without the explicit permission of the emperor.[37] Third, since the Ming were spared a catastrophe like the fall of the Northern Sung, the imperial clan grew without hindrance, until it reached the bloated size of 62,000 clansmen in 1594 and over 80,000 in the 1600s. The support of this vast group taxed the resources of the state, with a censor noting in 1562 that the princely establishments required 8.5 million piculs of grain per year, in contrast to 4 million piculs for the capital, although, as Frederic Wakeman notes, this did not stop large numbers of clansmen from becoming indebted and impoverished.[38]

The Ming imperial clan, which far more than the Sung tested the proposition of using the resources of the state to support virtually all members of the clan or *tsung*, was clearly wasteful of lives as well as money. This was the central point of Ku Yen-wu's essay on imperial clans in Chinese history ("Tsung-shih"), written in the early Ch'ing. Although the appellation of "discarded objects" came from Sung Ch'i of the Sung, for Ku it was particularly appropriate for the Ming clansmen, since they were so totally excluded from any role in government.[39]

In the Ch'ing, the role of the imperial clan—better known as the Aisin Gioro lineage—was complicated by the fact that it was part of the broader group of Manchus, whose Eight Banner forces constituted the military backbone of the dynasty (at least at its outset) and who constituted a political and social supra-stratum over the Chinese population at large. The Aisin Gioro, organized by the pre-conquest Manchu leader, Hung T'ai-chi (1592–1643), into "Three Superior Banners," was a privileged group among the privileged, the recipients of special schooling, trust, and support.[40] Like the Manchus generally, the imperial family and the broader lineage married only other Manchus.[41] In several important respects, however, the Aisin Gioro followed the precedents of earlier dynasties, especially the Sung. Like the Sung and Ming clans, the Ch'ing clan became segmented and highly stratified,[42] and all offspring were entered into the imperial genealogy. The number of clan members grew from 378 around 1660 to over 29,000 following the fall of the Ch'ing.[43] Like Sung clansmen, Ch'ing clansmen could participate in the examinations and were given limited access to a special "imperial clan metropolitan examination" (*tsung-shih hui-shih*) as early as 1697, although it was only after the introduction of special provincial examinations for imperial clansmen (*tsung-shih hsiang-shih*) in 1801 that their numbers became significant. The resulting 288 imperial clansmen who qualified for office through examinations, although a far smaller number than in the Sung, still greatly exceeded the handful of Ming clan graduates.[44] In addition, Aisin Gioro members had important military functions, and even the imperial princes, while kept in close check throughout the eighteenth and early nineteenth centuries, nevertheless played major roles in government in the late nineteenth century.[45]

From this brief historical survey, we can conclude that the primary legacy of the Sung imperial clan was definitional. The imperial clan had come to be viewed as a part of the broader polity, as noted early in this chapter, and a maximal definition of clans had been accepted, namely, that they included all the male descendents of the founding emperors plus their wives and daughters, regardless of their generational distance from the founder and the current emperor. Once this definition had been established, its consequences for the Ming and Ch'ing were major.

In the final analysis, however, it is the uniqueness of the Sung clan that stands out. In no other dynasty were the support, control, and use of the descendents of emperors managed so successfully and with so little in the way of intrigue, contested successions, and rebellion. This was partly the result of historical accident: the loss of the north and the consequent "weeding out" of large numbers of clansmen, which ensured that the clan would never grow to Ming or Ch'ing proportions. But of more importance were the Sung policies toward the clan and clansmen, and they merit the attention not only of Chinese historians but of anyone interested in the issue of how monarchial systems treat the kin of monarchs.

Appendixes

List of Clansmen with Biographies

The following chart lists the clansmen and clanswomen for whom I had biographical entries, listed according to their genealogical order, as explained in the Note on Genealogical Coding. Those whose entries could be considered actual biographies are indicated by a B in the fourth column. The sons of emperors are listed at the ends of the T'ai-tsu and T'ai-tsung branches. X, Y, and Z are used in cases in which the individual is not listed in the *Sung History* genealogy but those of some or all of his ancestors are. There is also a list at the end of clansmen I could not locate at all in the genealogy beyond their branch.

A question mark following a name indicates a character I have been unable to locate in any Chinese dictionary. A "-d" following a generational code indicates that the subject is the daughter of the individual designated by the code; a "-w" indicates that she is the wife of the individual designated. The following abbreviations are listed in the Sources column:

EL	Examination lists of 1148 and 1256
GEN	Genealogy, either the Sung *Hsien-yuan lei-p'u* or a Chao lineage genealogy
LH	Local history
MCM	*Mu-chih-ming* or epitaph
O	Other

Finally, it should be noted that the generation characters for the sixth and ninth generations of the Wei-wang (C) branch—respectively chih 之 and fu 夫—are used as the second, not first, character in their names.

SS Code/Name/Dates	Bio	Srcs	Author

T'ai-tsu Branch

SS Code/Name/Dates	Bio	Srcs	Author
AA　Te-chao 德昭 (d. 979)	B	SS	
AAA　Wei-cheng 惟正		SS	
AAAA　Ts'ung-tang 從讜	B	SS	
AAAACCI　Tzu-ssu 子祕 (1089–1157)	B	GEN	
AAAACCIACYX　Yü-ch'ui 與璽 (1237–1317)	B	GEN	
AAAACEBB　Po-lu 伯琭 (1135–1202)	B	MCM	Chou Pi-ta
AAAACJ　Ling-kang 令矼 (1066–1136)	B	SS	
AAAFUO　Ling-te 令德 (fl. 1132–65)	B	SS	

***

SS Code/Name/Dates	Bio	Srcs	Author
AAB　Wei-chi 惟吉 (966–1010)	B	SS	
AAB-d　Chao-shih 趙氏 (1009–68)	B	MCM	Cheng Hsieh
AABA　Shou-chieh 守節		SS	
AABAA　Shih-yung 世永 (1010–68)	B	MCM, SS	Cheng Hsieh
AABAACAAAAB　Yü-fang 與昉 (fl. 1235–62)	B	GEN	
AABAAEAAAAB　Yü-ch'iu 與薵 (1179–1260)	B	SS, LH	
AABAB　Shih-yen 世延 (1022–65)	B	MCM	Wang Kuei
AABACABC　Po-tse 伯澤 (fl. 1215)		SS	
AABACB　Ling-pang 令邦 (1051–69)	B	MCM	Ssu-ma Kuang
AABB　Shou-yueh 守約		SS	
AABBA　Shih-ching 世靜		SS	
AABBABDCA　Shih-lung 師龍 (1143–94)	B	MCM	Lou Yueh
AABBABE　Tzu-tung 子棟 (d. 1173)		SS	
AABBAX　Ling-x 令__ᵃ (1052–56)	B	MCM	Wang Kuei
AABBBDE　Tzu-ti 子覿 (fl. 1202)		SS	
AABBC　Shih-chang 世長		SS	
AABBCDABBC　Hsi-che 希哲 (fl. 1255)	B	O	
AABC　Shou-sun 守巽 (fl. 1044)		SS	
AABCA　Shih-ch'ing 世清 (fl. 1068–85)	B	SS	
AABCAB　Ling-k'uo 令廓 (fl. 1080)		SS	

SS Code/Name/Dates	Bio Srcs	Author
AABCAEAAB　Shih-meng 師孟 (1109–72)	EL, O	
AABCBBAAEABA　Meng-yen 孟儼 (1256 cs)	EL	
AABCDBADAAA　Yü-shih 與時 (1175–1231)	B　MCM	Chao Meng-chien
AABCDBADECE　Yü-che 與檡 (fl. 1276)	B　SS	
AABD　Shou-tu 守度	SS	
AABDCCABB　Shih-shih 師奭	O	
AABDDABAAA　Hsi-tan 希旦 (1190 cs)	LH	
AABDEAEABBAA　Meng-sung 孟朵 (fl. 1270s)	B　SS	
AABDEAEABBAX　Ch'i 祺 (1240–74)	B　SS	
(subsequently became the emperor Tu-tsung)		
AABDEAEABBX　Kuei-ch'eng 貴誠 [b] (1205–64)	B　SS	
(subsequently named Yün 昀; then became the emperor Li-tsung)		
AABDEFBA　Po-huai 伯淮 (1120–77)	B　MCM	Sun Ying-shih
AABDEFBAA　Shih-yuan 世淵 (1172 cs)	LH, O	
AABDEFBAA-d　Hsi-i 希怡 (1177–1235)	B　MCM	Yuan Fu
AABDEFBAD　Shih-hsia 師夏 (1190 cs)	LH, O	
AABDEFBADD　Hsi-ch'a 希怔 (fl. 1265)	B　LH	
AABDEFBADE　Hsi-yueh 希悅 (1211 cs)	LH, O	
AABDEFBBAD　Hsi-liang 希亮 (1211 cs)	LH	
AABDEFBBB　Shih-tuan 師端 (1184 cs)	B　LH, O	
AABDEFBBBD　Hsi-i 希廙 (1211 cs)	LH	
AABDEFBC　Po-chu 伯洙 (1157 cs)	B　LH	
AABDEFBCA　Shih-yung 師雍 (1187 cs)	B　LH, O	
AABDEFBD　Po-ch'ih 伯湹 (1157 cs)	LH	
AABDEFBDA　Shih-k'ai 師開 (1199 cs)	LH	
AABDEFBDB　Shih-yü 師羽 (1199 cs)	LH	
AABDEFBFB　Shih-keng 師耕 (1214 cs)	LH	
AABDEFBG　Po-hu 伯澔 (1190 cs)	LH	
AABE　Shou-lien 守廉	SS	
AABEABG　Tzu-liu 子鏐 (fl. 1130)	B　GEN	

SS Code/Name/Dates	Bio	Srcs	Author
AABEABGCCCA Yü-fan 與藩 (fl. 1276)	B	GEN	
AABEABGCCCAXX Yu-chüan 由瑑 (fl. 1270)	B	GEN	
AABEABGCCCAY Yu-t'eng 由騰	B	GEN	
AABF Shou-k'ang 守康		SS	
***			
AAC Wei-ku 惟固 (fl. 983)		SS	
***			
AAD Wei-chung 惟忠 (fl. 983–1015)		SS	
AADA Ts'ung-k'o 從恪		SS	
AADA-w Mi-shih 米氏		MCM	Ou-yang Hsiu
AADAAB-w P'an-shih 潘氏 (1046–69)		MCM	Ssu-ma Kuang
AADAB Shih-jung 世融 (1016–55)	B	MCM	Ou-yang Hsiu
AADAC Shih-ch'ang 世昌 (1020–61)	B	MCM	Wang Kuei
AADAD Shih-kuei 世規		SS	
AADAF Shih-heng 世衡 (1029–59)	B	MCM	Ou-yang Hsiu
AADB Ts'ung-ai 從藹 (fl. 1044)		SS	
AADBA Shih-feng 世豐		SS	
AADBB Shih-hsuan 世宣 (1023–58)	B	MCM	Ou-yang Hsiu
AADBBEEBBFCA Meng-tsuan 孟鑽 (1256 cs)		EL	
AADBBEFBCBA Yü-tung 與東 (1256 cs)		EL	
AADBBEGADA Hsi-kuan 希錧 (1176–1233)	B	MCM, SS	Wei Liao-weng
AADBC Shih-chun 世準 (fl. 1071)	B	SS	
AADBCCAAABAB Meng-hu 孟熩 (1256 cs)		EL	
AADBD Shih-hsiung 世雄 (1031–1105)	B	SS	
AADBDAD Tzu-ch'ih 子湞 (fl. 1127–31)	B	SS	
AADBDDBAAAA Yü-ling 與齡 (1214 cs)		LH	
AADBDDC Tzu-lin 子嶙 (1103 cs)	B	GEN	
AADBDDCAFBAX Meng-i 孟洢 (fl. 1280s)	B	GEN	
AADBDEB Tzu-ti 子砥 (d. 1128)	B	SS	

SS Code/Name/Dates	Bio	Srcs	Author
AADBDFA Tzu-sung 子崧 (d. 1132)	B	SS	
AADBEACABC Hsi-k'o 希恪 (1214 cs)		LH	
AADBFAB Tzu-shen 子侁 (fl. 1130s)	B	GEN	
AADBFABB Po-hsiang 伯詳	B	GEN	
AADBFABBA Shih-kung 師珙	B	GEN	
AADBFABBAA Hsi-i 希陳	B	GEN	
AADBFABBAAA Yü-yin 與音	B	GEN	
AADBFABBAAAA Meng-tai 孟隶	B	GEN	
AADBFABBAAAAX Yu-fu 由馥 (b. 1270)	B	GEN	
AADBFABGA Shih-chiu 師玖	B	GEN	
AADBFABGAXXXX Yu-chieh 由潔	B	GEN	
AADBG Shih-yueh 世岳 (1042–81)	B	MCM	Wang An-li
AADBHD Ling-ch'eng (?)ᶜ 令崴 (d. 1129)	B	SS	
AADBHF Ling-chin 令衿 (d. 1158)	B	SS	
AADBIABBAEA Yü-ts'en 與峇 (1256 cs)		EL	
AADC Ts'ung-ying 從穎		SS	
AADCBGB Tzu-yueh 子瀹 (fl. 1151)	B	GEN	
AADCBK Ling-ken 令誏 (fl. 1111–62)	B	SS	
AADD Ts'ung-chin 從謹		SS	
AADDA Shih-ch'ung 世崇 (1021–52)	B	MCM	Wang Kuei
AADDAA Ling-pin 令蠙 (1049–82)	B	MCM	Yang Chieh
AADDCIAA Po-hsu 伯栩 (fl. 1211)		SS	
AADDEC Ling-chih 令時 (1061–1134)	B	SS	
AADDECCA Po-chu 伯杙 (fl. 1208)		SS	
AADDFEBEA Shih-i 師羃 (1149–1217)	B	MCM, SS	Yeh Shih
AADDGADA Po-shu 伯擄 (1116–68)	B	MCM	Lou Yueh
AADE Ts'ung-chih 從質 (1010–52)	B	MCM, SS	Wang Kuei
AADEAAAAEAAB Meng-chin 孟錦 (d. 1276)	B	SS	
AADEAAACFA Hsi-yü 希瑀 (1217 cs)		LH	
AADEAAEAC Shih-hsin 師濤 (1148–99)	B	MCM	Lou Yueh

SS Code/Name/Dates	Bio	Srcs	Author
AADEBCGBAXX-w　Huang Sheng 黃昇 (1227–43)	B	MCM	Chao Shih-shu
AADEGABA　Po-chih 伯直 (1103–67)	B	MCM	Lou Yueh
AADEGABAD　Shih-ching 師邢 (1190 cs)		LH	
AADEHAF　Tzu-hsiao 子瀟 (1102–67)	B	MCM, SS	Hu Ch'üan
AADF　Ts'ung-hsin 從信 (1010–60)	B	MCM, SS	Wang Kuei
AADFABFB　Po-shu 伯術 (1121–88)	B	MCM, EL	Chao Shan-k'ao
AADFBAAAACX　Yü-t'e 與樗 (1256 cs)		EL	
AADFBAAAACY　Yü-ti 與楠 (1256 cs)		EL	
AADFCH　Ling-k'uang 令廛 (1069–1143)	B	SS	
AADFCHA　Tzu-yu 子游 (fl. 1162)	B	SS, SHY	
AADFCHAGBX　Hsi-yen 希言 (1164–1224)	B	SS	
AADFCHAGBXA　Yü-huan 與懽 (1214 cs)	B	SS	
AADFCHAHACAB　Meng-hsien 孟仚 (1256 cs)		EL	
AADFCHAIC　Shih-chao 師召 (fl. 1190s)		O	
AADFD　Shih-hu 世護 (fl. 1050s)	B	MCM	Hu Su
AADFFCDA　Po-chiu 伯玖—*see* Kao-B, Chü, at the end of the T'ai-tsung section			
AADFFDAB　Po-ch'ing 伯清 (1133–66)	B	MCM	Lu Tseng-hsiang
AADFFDBCA　Shih-yü 師雩 (fl. 1218)		O	
AADFK　Shih-fu 世福		SS	
AADFNA　Ling-hua 令話 (d. 1132)	B	SS	
AADFNAFAAAAA　Meng-fan 孟鐇 (1256 cs)		EL	
AADFNL　Ling-p'eng 令憉 (fl. 1172)	B	SS	
AADFNM　Ling-t'ai 令撞 (fl. 1172)		SS	
AADFOAAAA　Shih-yü 師譽 (1172 cs)		LH	
AADFOAAAB　Shih-hui 師劳 (1175 cs)		LH	
AADFOBA　Tzu-jung 子肜 (d. 1191)		SS	
AADFUGC　Tzu-kung 子恭 (d. 1209)		SS	
AADFUSD　Tzu-hsiu 子修 (1148 cs)		EL	
AADX　Ts'ung-ping 從秉		SS	

SS Code/Name/Dates	Bio Srcs		Author

***

AAE Wei-ho 惟和 (988–1013)	B	SS	
AAE-w Feng-shih 馮氏 (987–1053)	B	MCM	Ou-yang Hsiu
AAEA Ts'ung-hui 從誨		SS	
AAEAC Shih-k'ai 世開	B	SS	
AAEB Ts'ung-shen 從審 (1006–51)	B	MCM, SS	Wang Kuei
AAEBA Shih-ying 世英 (1028–63)	B	MCM	Wang Kuei
AAEBB Shih-chien 世堅 (d. 1048)	B	MCM	Hu Su
AAEBEACGBFA Yü-p'u 與溥 (1256 cs)		EL	
AAEBFAE Tzu-chou 子書 (1089–1142)	B	MCM, SS	Ch'eng Chü
AAEBFAECAB Hsi-ching 希瀞 (1194–1251)	B	MCM	Liu K'o-chuang
AAEBH Shih-jeng 世仍 (1047–68)	B	MCM	Wang An-shih

***

AB Te-fang 德芳 (959–81)	B	SS	
ABA Wei-hsu 惟敘 (977–1011)		SS	
ABAA Ts'ung-p'u 從溥		SS	

ABAAACBAAC Hsi-ch'ü 希瞿—see Hsiao-BBA, Chün, at the end of the T'ai-tsu section

ABAB Ts'ung-chao 從照		SS	
ABABADBAA Shih-tien 師蔵 (1205 cs)		LH	
ABABAHDA Po-shu 伯述		GEN	
ABABAHDAA Shih-kao 師誥	B	GEN	
ABABAHDAAD Hsi-hsiang 希庠 (1199 cs)	B	GEN	
ABABAHDAADC Yü-fang 與倣 (1219–92)	B	GEN	
ABABAHDAADCA Meng-ts'en 孟涔 (1256 cs)		EL	
ABABAHDAADCX Meng-mo 孟模 (1255–1302)	B	GEN	
ABABAIAB Po-hao 伯浩 (fl. 1140s)		SS	

SS Code/Name/Dates	Bio	Srcs	Author

***

SS Code/Name/Dates	Bio	Srcs	Author
ABB　Wei-hsien 惟憲 (979–1016)	B	SS	
ABBA　Ts'ung-yü 從郁 (998–1041)	B	MCM	Sung Ch'i
ABBAACCCEAB　Yü-ssu 與諰 (1256 cs)		EL	
ABBAACED　Po-mao 伯茂 (1148 cs)		EL	
ABBAB　Shih-pao 世褒 (1019–41)	B	MCM	Chang Fang-p'ing
ABBACEA　Tzu-ch'eng 子偁 (d. 1144)	B	SS	
ABBACEAA　Po-kuei 伯圭 (1125–1202)	B	MCM, SS	Lou Yüeh
ABBACEAAA　Shih-k'uei 師夔 (1142–1202)	B	SS	
(subsequently named Shen 慎, then became the emperor Hsiao-tsung)			
ABBACEAAB　Shih-k'uei 師揆 (d. 1214)	B	SS	
ABBACEAAD　Shih-yü 師禹		SS	
ABBACEAB　Po-ts'ung 伯琮 (1127–94)	B	SS	
ABBB　Ts'ung-shih 從式 (1007–71)	B	MCM, SS	Han Wei
ABBBBGBBBA　Hsi-chi 希泊 (d. 1278)	B	SS	
ABBBC　Shih-en 世恩		SS	
ABBBCDACA　Shih-chia 師榎 (fl. 1270s)	B	SS	
ABBC　Ts'ung-shih 從湜		SS	
ABBCCBAAABBC　Meng-lei 孟壘 (1259 cs)	B	SS	
ABBD　Ts'ung-pen 從賁 (fl. 1070s)	B	SS, HCP	
ABBX　Ts'ung-yen 從演		SS	
ABBY　Ts'ung-jung 從戎		SS	
ABBZ　Ts'ung-chieh 從戒		SS	

***

SS Code/Name/Dates	Bio	Srcs	Author
ABC　Wei-neng 惟能 (979–1008)		SS	
ABCA　Ts'ung-ku 從古 (fl. 1060)		SS	
ABCAA　Shih-mai 世邁 (1026–49)	B	MCM	Wang Kuei
ABCACAFBAAB　Yü-chung 與种 (1256 cs)		EL	
ABCC　Ts'ung-chih 從贄 (1007–50)	B	MCM, SS	Wang Kuei

SS Code/Name/Dates	Bio	Srcs	Author
ABCCDACB Po-ai 伯瑷 (1148 cs)		EL	
ABCCX Shih-chü 世居 (d. 1075)	B	HCP	
***			
Hsiao-A She 愭 (1144–67)	B	SS	
Hsiao-AA T'ing 挺 (d. 1169)		SS	
Hsiao-AB Chin 搢 (fl. 1206–15)		SS	
Hsiao-B K'ai 愷 (1146–80)	B	SS	
Hsiao-BA Shu 攄		SS	
Hsiao-BB Ping 抦 (d. 1206)		SS	
Hsiao-BBA Chün 均 *(originally ABAAACBAAC, Hsi-ch'ü)*		SS	
Hsiao-BBAA Kuei-ho 貴和—see Ning-I, Hung *(originally Yü-yuan AAXXXXXXXXX)*			
Ning-I Hung 竑 (d. 1225) *(originally Hsiao-BBAA, Kuei-ho)*	B	SS	
Ning-H Hsun 詢 (1192–1220)	B	SS	
T'ai-tsung Branch			
BA Yuan-tso 元佐 (962–1023)	B	SS	
BAA Yun-sheng 允升 (d. 1035)	B	SS	
BAAA Tsung-li 宗禮	B	SS	
BAABAAABA Ch'ung-li 崇禮 (1217 cs)		LH	
BAAC Tsung-tan 宗旦 (fl. 1064–80)	B	SS, SHY	
BAACAABAA Ju-i 汝翼 (1166 cs)		LH	
BAACACCAC Ju-chien 汝簡 (1190 cs)		LH	
BAACFCCACBC Pi-chiang 必䜶 (fl. 1279)	B	GEN	
BAADADA Pu-ch'i 不棄	B	SS	
BAADB Chung-mou 仲侔 (1039–81)	B	MCM,	Wang An-li
BAAF Tsung-hui 宗回 (1017–66)	B	MCM	Chang Fang-p'ing
BAAFBDADAC Ch'ung-yen 崇琰 (1211 cs)		LH	
BAAFBDAGBB Ch'ung-shih 崇湁 (1256 cs)		EL	

SS Code/Name/Dates	Bio	Srcs	Author
BAAG Tsung-t'i 宗悌	B	SS	
BAAH Tsung-mo 宗默 (1018–54)	B	MCM	Wang Kuei
BAAHBEAAC Ju-mo 汝謨 (fl. 1202)		O	
BAAJE Chung-k'ao 仲考 (1051–67)	B	MCM	Chang Fang-p'ing
BAAK Tsung-hui 宗惠 (fl. 1060–80s)		SS, SHY	
BAAKBCBCBDC Pi-ch'üan (?) 必珍 (1256 cs)		EL	
BAAKF Chung-ch'i 仲企 (1055–88)		MCM	Fan Tsu-yü
BAAKFBDA Shan-ying 善應 (1118–77)	B	MCM, SS	Chu Hsi
BAAKFBDAA Ju-yü 汝愚 (1140–96)	B	MCM, SS,	
		O	Liu Kuang-tsu
BAAKFBDAAA Ch'ung-hsien 崇憲 (1160–1219)	B	MCM, O	Chen Te-hsiu
BAAKFBDAAAA Pi-yuan 必愿 (d. 1249)	B	SS	
BAAKFBDAAD Ch'ung-mo 崇模	B	O	
BAAKFBDAAE Ch'ung-tu 崇度 (1175–1230)	B	MCM	Chen Te-hsiu
BAAKFBDAAEAA Liang-ch'un 良淳 (fl. 1270s)	B	SS	
BAAKFBDAAFA Pi-k'uei 必揆 (1256 cs)		EL	
BAAKFBDAAG Ch'ung-shih 崇實		SYHA	
BAAKFBDDA Ju-ching 汝靚	B	SYHA	
BAAKLCC Pu-shih 不試 (d. 1217)	B	SS	
BAAM Tsung-pien 宗辯 (1023–68)	B	MCM	Wang An-shih
BAAMBBGBBDB Pi-kun 必棍 (1256 cs)		EL	
BAAMBCBABCC Pi-hui 必瞦 (1256 cs)		EL	
BAAMHIABB Ju-hsiung 汝濷 (1256 cs)		EL	
BAANBE Shih-lung 士蘢 (1080–1131)	B	SS	
BAANDBABAAX Pi-ts'ung 必聰 (1256 cs)		EL	

***

BAB Yun-yen 允言 (d. 1029)	B	SS	
BABA Tsung-yueh 宗說 (fl. 1033–53)	B	SS	
BABAB Chung-ying 仲郢 (1025–47)	B	MCM	Chang Fang-p'ing

SS Code/Name/Dates	Bio	Srcs	Author
BABACEAD Shan-chueh 善珏 (1148 cs)		EL	
BABAFBAABBC Pi-fu 必玐 (1256 cs)		EL	
BABAFF Shih-ch'iu 士遒 (d. 1135)	B	SS	
BABAG Chung-k'uei 仲夔		MCM	Wang An-shih
BABAH Chung-min 仲旻	B	SS	
BABAJDFA Shan-shen 善屾 (1148 cs)		EL	
BABAKBBBCAAA Liang-yao 良玗 (1256 cs)		EL	
BABAVAABXX Ch'ung-ch'ih 崇墀 (1256 cs)		EL	
BABB Tsung-li 宗立	B	SS	
BABBBAB Pu-wu 不侮 (1074–1119)	B	MCM	Liu I-chih
BABBBAB-d Tzu-chen 趙紫眞 (1097–1140)	B	MCM	Sun Ti
BABBBACA-d Chao-shih 趙氏 (d. 1170)	B	MCM	Lo Yuan
BABBE Chung-lai 仲來		SS,	
		MCM	Wang An-li
BABBEAA Pu-t'ang 不儻		SS	
BABBEABDAA Ch'ung-hsi 崇悉 (1164–1228)	B	MCM, SHY	Liu Tsai
BABCE Chung-hsing 仲行 (d. 1067)		MCM	Wang An-shih
BABD Tsung-yü 宗育 (1012–41)	B	MCM	Chang Fang-p'ing

***

BAC Yun-ch'eng 允成		SS	
BACA Tsung-yen 宗顏 (1008–55)	B	MCM	Ou-yang Hsiu
BACAA Chung-lien 仲連 (1034–69)	B	MCM	Ssu-ma Kuang
BACB Tsung-na 宗訥 (1009–54)	B	MCM	Ou-yang Hsiu
BACDAA Shih-yen 士弇 (1060–63)	B	MCM	Wang Kuei
BACE Tsung-yen 宗嚴 (1013–65)	B	MCM	Wang Kuei
BACHDBBABEA Pi-tso 必澨 (1256 cs)		EL	
BACHFD-d Chao-shih 趙氏 (1121–58)	B	MCM	Hung Kua

***

BB Yuan-hsi 元僖 (d. 992)	B	SS	
BBAA Tsung-pao 宗保 (d. 1074)	B	SS	

SS Code/Name/Dates		Bio Srcs	Author
	***		
BC　Yuan-fen 元份 (968–1004)	B	SS, GEN	
BCA　Yun-ning 允寧 (d. 1034)	B	SS	
BCAA　Tsung-o 宗諤 (d. 1082)	B	SS	
BCAACDAABA　Ch'ung-yen 崇嵒 (1196 cs)		LH	
BCAACDABAF　Ch'ung-chung 崇中 (1214 cs)		LH	
BCAAEADBBA　Ch'ung-ko 崇鉻 (1256 cs)		EL	
BCAAEEB　Pu-shuai 不衰 (1107–79)	B	MCM	Chu Hsi
BCAAEEBA　Shan-chün 善俊 (1157 cs)	B	SS	
BCAAEEBB　Shan-i 善儀 (1134–85)	B	MCM	Chu Hsi
BCAAHA　Shih-tsan 士彩 (1095–1160)	B	MCM	Sun Ti
BCAB　Tsung-min 宗敏	B	SS	
BCABACA　Pu-yu 不尤 (fl. 1120s)	B	SS	
BCABACAA　Shan-hsi 善悉 (1141–98)	B	MCM	Yeh Shih
BCABCBACBCAX　Liang-ch'üan 良銓 (1256 cs)		EL	
BCABDAAAAAD　Pi-chien 必健 (1193–1262)	B	MCM	Liu K'o-chuang
BCABEADBAA　Ch'ung-shih 崇昰 (1199 cs)		LH	
BCABEAFA　Shan-chi 善濟		O	
BCABEBCCAEG　Pi-t'a 必逕 (1256 cs)		EL	
BCABEIB　Pu-ch'i 不攽 (1148 cs)		EL	
BCABGBEBACB　Pi-cheng 必錚 (1256 cs)		EL	
BCABGGAACCB　Pi-huan 必寰 (1256 cs)		EL	
BCABGGCCBAA　Pi-ch'üan 必佺 (1256 cs)		EL	
BCABGHEB　Shan-yü 善譽 (1143–89)	B	MCM, SS	Lou Yueh
BCABGLDA　Shan-tse 善擇 (1169 cs)	B	LH	
BCAD　Tsung-su 宗肅 (d. 1082)	B	SS	
BCADACBBB　Ju-kuan 汝鹽 (1172–1230)	B	MCM	Ch'en Mi
BCADE　Chung-na 仲肭 (1061–81)		MCM	Wang An-li
BCAEBCCDA　Ju-t'ing 汝斑 (1256 cs)		EL	

SS Code/Name/Dates		Bio Srcs	Author

***

SS Code/Name/Dates		Bio Srcs	Author
BCB　Yun-jang 允讓 (995–1059)	B	GEN, SS	Chao Hsi-nien
BCBA　Tsung-i 宗懿		SS	
BCBAAKA　Pu-ch'ün 不群 (fl. 1120s)	B	SS	
BCBAD　Chung-luan 仲鸞	B	SS	
BCBAEAADACB　Pi-ying 必膺 (1256 cs)		EL	
BCBAF　Chung-fen 仲汾	B	SS	
BCBAFGF　Pu-ling 不淩 (d. 1224)		SS	
BCBB　Tsung-p'u 宗樸 (fl. 1060s)	B	SS	
BCBBADABAB　Pi-liu 必沠 (1256 cs)		EL	
BCBBBFG-d　Chao-shih 趙氏 (1153–90)	B	MCM	Yang Wan-li
BCBBC　Chung-mang 仲厖 (1045–68)	B	MCM	Wang An-shih
BCBBDD　Shih-chien 士佺 (d. 1157)	B	SS	
BCBBDE　Shih-ko 士轕 (d. 1180)		SS	
BCBBDED　Pu-hsi 不熄 (fl. 1213)	B	SHY	
BCBC　Tsung-i 宗誼		SS	
BCBE　Tsung-shih 宗師 (1028–56)	B	MCM	Ou-yang Hsiu
BCBF　Tsung-hui 宗暉 (1024–94)	B	SS	
BCBFAFA　Pu-hsi 不息 (1121–87)	B	MCM, SS	Yeh Shih
BCBFAFAAA　Ju-t'an 汝談 (d. 1237)	B	LH, SS	
BCBFAFAAB　Ju-tang 汝譡 (1208 cs)	B	LH, SS	
BCBFB　Chung-yuan 仲爰 (1054–1123)		SS, SHY	
BCBFCBABAAA　Pi-ch'eng 必成 (1256 cs)		EL	
BCBFD　Chung-sui 仲璲 (fl. 1070s)	B	SS	
BCBFDBAAAX　Ch'ung-hui 崇回 (1256 cs)		EL	
BCBGCB　Shih-ch'i 士跂 (d. 1126)	B	SS	
BCBGF　Chung-shih 仲湜 (d. 1137)	B	SS	
BCBGFA　Shih-ts'ung 士從 (fl. 1126–34)	B	SS	
BCBGFC　Shih-chieh 士街 (d. 1160)	B	SS	
BCBGFCJA　Shan-hsiang 善湘 (d. 1242)	B	SS	

SS Code/Name/Dates	Bio	Srcs	Author
BCBGFE Shih-chien 士籛 (fl. 1163)	B	SS	
BCBGFF Shih-k'an 士衎 (fl. 1163–64)	B	SS	
BCBGFIB Pu-p'iao 不嫖 (d. 1219)		SS	
BCBGFJ Shih-hsin 士歆 (d. 1196)		SS	
BCBGL Chung-tseng 仲增 (d. 1115)		SS	
BCBGMCC Pu-ch'ü (?) 不秸 (d. 1199)	B	SS	
BCBGMDCCAA Ch'ung-t'ing 崇鋌 (1256 cs)		EL	
BCBGN Chung-li 仲理 (fl. 1126)		SS	
BCBGNAGC Shan-chien 善堅 (fl. 1190s)		O	
BCBGNAGCC Ju-sui 汝鐩 (1172–1246)	B	MCM	Liu K'o-chuang
BCBI Tsung-sheng 宗晟 (1031–95)	B	SS, SHY	
BCBIA Chung-yü 仲御 (1052–1122)	B	SS	
BCBIAG Shih-niao 士儠 (1084–1153)	B	SS	
BCBIAGA Pu-fan 不凡 (fl. 1120s)	B	SS	
BCBIAGBGAA Ch'ung-chü 崇詎 (1187 cs)		LH	
BCBIAGBHF Ju-yü 汝俞 (1187 cs)		LH	
BCBIAGBHGA Ch'ung-yü 崇禹 (1214 cs)		LH	
BCBIAGBIAB Ch'ung-hu 崇詁 (1220 cs)		LH	
BCBIAMDCEA Ch'ung-yu 崇珆 (1256 cs)		EL	
BCBIAMJ Pu-cho 不拙	B	O	
BCBIAMJ-d Chao-shih 趙氏 (1158–1213)	B	MCM	Yuan Hsieh
BCBIBH Shih-ch'iung 士嶇 (d. 1151)	B	SS	
BCBJAAAAAC Ch'ung-cheng 崇正 (1217 cs)		LH	
BCBKCKCBA Ju-pin 汝槼 (1193–1267)	B	MCM	Liu K'o-chuang
BCBL Tsung-yü 宗愈 (1031–95)	B	SS	
BCBLFD Shih-hsueh 士劄 (1108–62)	B	MCM	anon.
BCBLHE Shih-ch'ien 士晴 (fl. 1127)	B	SS	
BCBMAAA Pu-tu 不獨 (1106–76)	B	MCM	Yang Wan-li
BCBN Tsung-mien 宗沔 (d. 1050s)	B	MCM	Ou-yang Hsiu
BCBO Tsung-cho 宗綽 (d. 1096)		SS	

SS Code/Name/Dates	Bio Srcs		Author
BCBOBDACB Ju-li 汝歷 (fl. 1251)	B	LH	
BCBP Tsung-chih 宗治 (1036–91)		GEN	Chao Hsi-nien
BCBPAAAC Shan-tai 善待 (1138–88)	B	MCM	Yuan Hsieh
BCBPAAACA Ju-shu 汝述 (1184 cs)	B	SS	
BCBPAAACD Ju-k'ua 汝括 (1170–1231)	B	O	
BCBPAM Shih-wu 士珸 (1108–53)	B	SS	
BCBPAM-w Ts'ai-shih 蔡氏 (1134–61)	B	O	
BCBPAME Pu-k'uang 不懬 (b. 1151)		O	
BCBPAME-d Chao-shih 趙氏 (1216–43)	B	MCM	Liu K'o-chuang
BCBPAMF Pu-ch'ü 不劬 (1151–97)		O	
BCBPAMF-d Pi-shan 趙必善 (1188–1260)	B	MCM	Liu K'o-chuang
BCBPAMGA Shan-lan 善蘭		GEN	
BCBPAMGA-d Ju-chieh 趙汝借 (1199–1249)	B	MCM	Liu K'o-chuang
BCBPC Chung-chen 仲溱 (1070–1109)		GEN	Chao Hsi-nien
BCBPCA Shih-chen 士俤 (1090–1140)	B	GEN	Chao Hsi-nien
BCBPCAB Pu-tzu 不緇 (1110–57)		GEN	Chao Hsi-nien
BCBPCABBBCB Pi-t'ang 必樘 (1256 cs)		FL	
BCBPCABBBCBX Liang-ling 良駖 (fl. 1283)	B	GEN	Chao Hsi-nien
BCBPCABC Shan-pin 善賓 (1110–57)	B	GEN	Chao Hsi-nien
BCBPCABCA Ju-ku 汝固 (1181–1248)	B	GEN	Chao Hsi-nien
BCBPCABCAA Ch'ung-t'o 崇橐 (1200–76)	B	GEN	Chao Hsi-nien
BCBPCABCAAA Pi-ying 必迎 (1225–89)	B	GEN	Chao Hsi-nien
BCBPCABCAAAA Liang-shao 良韶 (1286–1332)	B	GEN	Chao Hsi-nien
BCBPCABCAAAAD Yu-shou 友壽d (1312–64)		GEN	Chao Hsi-nien
BCBPCABCAAAAE Yu-hsien 友賢 (1312–69)		GEN	Chao Hsi-nien
BCBQ Tsung-chin 宗薝 (1039–80)	B	MCM	Wang An-li
BCBQCABBC Ju-t'eng 汝縢 (d. 1261)	B	SS, O	
BCBQCABBCA Ch'ung-t'ang 崇堂 (1230–44)	B	MCM	Chao Ju-t'eng
BCBQCAE Pu-min 不泯 (12th c.)	B	MCM	Liu Kuang-ch'ao

SS Code/Name/Dates	Bio	Srcs	Author
BCBQDCDDBAA　Pi-hsiang 必瑺 (1245–95)	B	MCM	Ch'en Chi-chuang
BCBS　Tsung-ch'u 宗楚 (d. 1097)	B	SS	
BCBT　Tsung-yu 宗祐 (d. 1098)	B	SS	
BCBTGDA　Pu-t'ien 不浵 (1144–81)	B	MCM	Yang Hsing-tsung
BCBU　Tsung-han 宗漢 (d. 1109)	B	SS	
BCBUBCC　Pu-ch'ou 不儔 (d. 1217)		SS	
BCBUBDAABFX　Pi-keng 必畊 (1256 cs)		EL	
BCBUI　Chung-lei 仲儡 (d. 1139)	B	SS	
BCBX^e　Tsung-shih 宗實 (1032–67)	B	SS	
(*subsequently named Shu* 曙; *then became the emperor Ying-tsung*)			
BCBYYYY　Pu-wen 不璺 (fl. 1205–8)		SS	

***

BD　Yuan-chieh 元傑 (972–1003)	B	SS	
BDAA [b. BACF]　Tsung-wang 宗望 (1020–63)	B	MCM	Wang Kuei
BDAAAD　Shih-ch'iu 士蚪 (1058–69)	B	MCM	Ssu-ma Kuang

***

BE　Yuan-wo 元偓 (977–1018)	B	SS	
BEA　Yun-pi 允弼 (1008–70)	B	MCM, SS, SHY	Wang Kuei
BEAA　Tsung-shu 宗述 (1023–68)	B	MCM	Wang An-shih
BEAB　Tsung-i 宗藝 (1029–65)	B	MCM	Wang Kuei
BEABB　Chung-chin 仲頒 (1055–80)	B	MCM	Wang An-li
BEAC　Tsung-k'uei 宗續		SS	
BEACCEA　Pu-k'uei 不愧 (1148 cs)		EL	
BEACCEB　Pu-hui 不悔 (1148 cs)		EL	
BEAD　Tsung-ching 宗景 (1032–97)	B	SS	
BEAD-w　Li-shih 李氏 (1030–81)	B	MCM	Wang An-li
BEAGFEAC　Shan-kung 善恭 (1148–1217)	B	MCM	Wei Ching

SS Code/Name/Dates	Bio Srcs		Author
***			
BF Yuan-ch'eng 允偁 (981–1014)	B	SS	
***			
BG Yuan-yen 元儼 (987–1044)	B	MCM, SS	Sung Ch'i
BGB Yun-liang 允良 (1013–67)	B	SS, MCM	Chang Fang-p'ing
BGBAKA Shih-k'o 士開 (1087–1174)	B	GEN	
BGBAKAB Pu-tien 不玷 (1123–1214)	B	GEN	
BGBAKAC Pu-yü 不瑜	B	GEN	
BGBAKACX Shan-t'iao 善調 (1166 cs)	B	GEN	
BGBAKACXX Ju-pin 汝邠	B	GEN	
BGBAKACXY Ju-lin 汝鄰 (early Yuan)	B	GEN	
BGBBACDEAA Ch'ung-yü 崇譽 (1217 cs)		LH	
***			
BGC Yun-ti 允迪 (1014–48)	B	SS	
***			
BGD Yun-ch'u 允初 (d. 1064)	B	MCM, SS	Wang Kuei
***			
Chen-A Yu 祐 (995–1003)		MCM, SS	Yang I
Ying-A Hao 顥 (fl. 1060–86)	B	SS	
Ying-B Chün 頵 (1056–88)	B	SS, MCM	Fan Tsu-yü
Shen-A Pi 佖 (d. 1106)	B	SS	
Shen-B Wu 俣 (d. 1127)	B	SS	
Shen-C Ssu 似 (d. 1127)	B	SS	
Che-A Mao 茂 (d. 1101)	B	SS	
Hui-B K'ai 楷 (fl 1118–26)	B	SS	
Hui-D Shu 樞 (fl 1126)	B	SS	
Hui-E I 杞 (fl 1127)	B	SS	
Hui-F Hsu 栩 (fl 1127)	B	SS	

SS Code/Name/Dates	Bio	Srcs	Author
Hui-L Ti 棣 (fl. 1127)	B	SS	
Hui-M O 楞 (fl. 1127)	B	SS	
Hui-O Shih 杙 (fl. 1127)	B	SS	
Hui-P Chen 榛 (fl. 1127)	B	SS	
Ch'in-A Ch'en 諶 (b. 1117)	B	SS	
Ch'in-B Hsun 訓 (fl. 1140)	B	SS	
Kao-A Fu 旉 (b. 1127)	B	SS	
Kao-B Ch'ü 璩 (1130–88)	B	SS	
(originally AADFFCDA, Po-chiu)			

Wei-wang Branch

SS Code/Name/Dates	Bio	Srcs	Author
C T'ing-mei 廷美 (947–84)	B	SS	
CA Te-kung 德恭 (962–1006)	B	SS	
CAA Ch'eng-ch'ing 承慶 (d. 1039)	B	MCM	Yang Chieh
CAAB K'o-chi 克繼 (d. 1090)	B	SS	
CAABA Shu-tsao 叔藻 (d. 1074)	B	MCM	Shen Kou
CAABBB Hui-chih 徽之 (d. 1103)	B	MCM	Mu-jung Yen-feng
CAACD Shu-nai 叔鼐 (1051–55)		MCM	Liu Ch'ang
CAACE Shu-tsung 叔醜 (1055–59)	B	MCM	Liu Ch'ang
CAACF-w Weng-shih 翁氏 (1058–79)	B	MCM	Wang An-li
CAADAAGB Yen-hsun 彦恂 (1148 cs)		EL	
CAADAAGBBA Shih-k'an 時侃 (1196 cs)	B	LH	
CAADAAGBBAX Jo-kuei 若珪 (1214 cs)	B	LH, MCM	Liu Tsai
CAADAAGBBB Shih-tso 時佐 (1181–1233)	B	MCM	Liu Tsai
CAADAAGBBXX Jo-ch'i 若琪 (1214 cs)		LH	
CAADDBBMAA Shih-kuan 時貫 (1256 cs)		EL	
CAAE K'o-hsiao 克蕭 (1030–57)	B	MCM	Liu Ch'ang
CAAFA Shu-seng 叔僧 (1047–55)		MCM	Liu Ch'ang
CAAFBAAA-w Wang Hui-chen 王惠眞 (1150–1223)	B	MCM	Ch'en Mi
CAAFBAAAAEA Jo-peng 若玤 (1256 cs)		EL	

SS Code/Name/Dates		Bio Srcs	Author
CAAFBAAAAEB　Jo-p'ei 若㫵 (1256 cs)		EL	

***

CABA　K'o-chi 克己 (d. 1044)	B	MCM, SS	Sung Ch'i
CABA-w　Wu-shih 武氏 (1004–75)	B	MCM	Shen Kou
CABAA　Shu-shao 叔韶 (fl. 1046–55)	B	SS	
CABAAAX　Chi-p'ei 季培 (1059–59) *(never received an official name)*	B	MCM	Liu Ch'ang
CABABA　Hua-chih 化之[f] (1050–51)	B	MCM	Liu Ch'ang
CABBD　Shu-wei 叔壼 (1043–53)	B	MCM	Liu Ch'ang
CABBEBACAA　Shih-yü 時瑜 (1256 cs)		EL	
CABBFH　Hsun-chih 訓之 (d. 1129)	B	SS	
CABBFHBA　Yen-hsiao 彥㯞 (1148–1218)	B	MCM, SS	Yeh Shih
CABC　K'o-hsiu 克修	B	SS	
CABCA　Shu-ch'ung 叔充	B	SS	
CABCAA　Fu-chih 撫之	B	SS	
CABCAGC　Kung-mai 公邁 (1115–79)	B	MCM	Ch'en Mi
CABCAJAADD　Shih-t'ao 時洮 (1256 cs)		EL	
CABCBCCBE　Shen-fu 伸夫 (1162–1222)	B	MCM	Yuan Hsieh
CABDAAKA　Yen-hsiao 彥肅 (1166 cs)	B	LH	

***

CB　Te-lung 德隆 (964–86)	B	SS	
CBA　Ch'eng-hsun 承訓		SS	
CBA-w　Chang-shih 張氏 (994–1059)	B	MCM	Liu Ch'ang
CBAA　K'o-ch'in 克勤 (1030–79)	B	MCM	Wang An-li
CBAAAEBA　Yen-k'an 彥堪 (1119–61)	B	MCM	Han Yuan-chi
CBABBCAAAB　Shih-t'ung 時通 (1161–1221)	B	MCM	Chen Te-hsiu
CBABBCBACA　Shih-kung 時恭 (1223 cs)		LH	
CBADCB　T'ien-chih 田之 (1065–1106)	B	MCM	Mu-jung Yen-feng
CBADE　Shu-lo 叔樂 (1052–1102)	B	MCM	Mu-jung Yen-feng

SS Code/Name/Dates	Bio Srcs		Author
CBADIAAACBAX　Ssu-te 嗣德	B	GEN	
CBADIACAAAA　Jo-pei 若栝 (late S. Sung)	B	GEN	
CBAECAAA　Yen-tuan 彥端 (1121–75)	B	MCM	Han Yuan-chi
CBAECFB　Kung-t'ung 公迥 (1151 cs)	B	GEN	
CBAECGCD　Yen-min 彥敏 (1166 cs)		LH	

***

CC　Te-i 德彞 (967–1015)	B	SS	
CCA　Ch'eng-chü 承矩		SS	
CCAAAABAA　Ch'ung-fu 充夫 (1134–1218)	B	MCM	Yuan Hsieh
CCAAACBBBB　Shih-chu 時著 (1214 cs)		LH	
CCAAACBC　Yen-ling 彥齡 (1148 cs)		EL	
CCAADEAAADA　Jo-lu 若魯 (1256 cs)		EL	
CCAADEAACAA　Jo-hsien 若硂 (1256 cs)		EL	
CCAAF　Shu-chi 叔疾 (1049–53)		MCM	Liu Ch'ang
CCABF　Shu-tsun 叔尊 (1055–1103)		MCM	Mu-jung Yen-feng
CCABH　Shu-chih 叔峙 (1058–1104)	B	MCM	Mu-jung Yen-feng
CCABHBACB　Keng-fu 庚夫 (1173–1219)	B	MCM	Liu K'o-chuang
CCACCBAB　Yen-yü 彥逾 (1130–1225)	B	SS, LH, GEN	
CCADB　Shu-han 叔罕 (1045–50)	B	MCM	Liu Ch'ang
CCADECBBCAA　Jo-ch'i 若祺 (1256 cs)		EL	
CCADF　Shu-chih 叔趾 (1051–69)	B	MCM	Su Sung

***

CCBA　K'o-kou 克構 (1015–56)	B	MCM	Liu Ch'ang
CCBAAA　Ch'ih-chih 持之^g (1055–58)	B	MCM	Liu Ch'ang

***

CCC　Ch'eng-fan 承範		SS	
CCCAHABAAA　Shih-hsien 時賢 (1186–1225)	B	MCM	Tai Hsu
CCCAHFAA　Yen-ai 彥璦 (1163 cs)		LH	

SS Code/Name/Dates	Bio	Srcs	Author
CCCCCFAE Yen-na 彥呐 (d. 1238)	B	SS	
CCCCEBAA Yen-wu 彥俉 (1137–1201)	B	MCM	Chou Pi-ta
***			
CCD Ch'eng-kung 承拱		SS	
***			
CCE Ch'eng-k'an 承衎		SS	
CCEBA Shu-lü 叔閭[h] (1053–54)	B	MCM	Liu Ch'ang
CCECA Shu-cheng 叔鄭 (1064–1104)	B	MCM	Mu-jung Yen-feng
***			
CCF Ch'eng-hsi 承錫		SS	
CCFAE Shu-tang 叔璫 (1070–1103)	B	MCM	Mu-jung Yen-feng
CCFAFCB Kung-yü 公預 (1135–1212)	B	LH	
CCFAFCC Kung-sheng 公升 (1143–1216)	B	MCM	Yuan Hsieh
CCFB K'o-p'i 克闢 (1036–63)		MCM	Cheng Hsieh
CCFBA Shu-she 叔舍 (1056–59)	B	MCM	Liu Ch'ang
CCFDE Shu-chuan 叔篆 (1087–1106)		MCM	Mu-jung Yen-feng
CCFDFAACX Mu-fu 暮大 (1256 cs)		EL	
CCFGB Shu-pi 叔愊 (1085–1106)		MCM	Mu-jung Yen-feng
CCFHA Shu-kuan 叔官 (1086–1105)		MCM	Mu-jung Yen-feng
CCFHD Shu-kuei 叔珪 (1095–1103)		MCM	Mu-jung Yen-feng
CCFHIA Hsiang-chih 像之 (1128–1202)	B	MCM, EL	Yang Wan-li
CCFHIB Yen-chih 儼之 (1148 cs)		EL	
***			
CCX Ch'eng-hsu 承昫		SS	
***			
CD Te-yung 德雍		SS	
CDA Ch'eng-mu 承睦		MCM	Sung Ch'i
CDAB-w Li-shih 李氏 (1021–55)	B	MCM	Liu Ch'ang

SS Code/Name/Dates	Bio Srcs		Author
CDABG Shu-min 叔忞 (1068–1103)	B	MCM	Mu-jung Yen-feng
CDABGBABCAA Jo-shen (?) 若裧 (1256 cs)		EL	
CDAC K'o-hsieh 克協 (1022–48)	B	MCM	Liu Ch'ang
CDAD K'o-ning 克凝 (d. 1075)	B	MCM	Shen Kou
CDADA Shu-tan 叔澹 (1051–1103)	B	MCM	Mu-jung Yen-feng
CDADADBFBA Shih-huan 時煥 (1201–57)	B	MCM	Liu K'o-chuang
CDADAFA Kung-mao 公懋 (1148 cs)		EL	
CDADAFAB Yen-chen 彥眞 (1143–96)	B	MCM	Lu Yu
CDAFB Shu-na 叔納 (1053–1104)	B	MCM	Mu-jung Yen-feng

***

CDBBAFAAA Hsing-fu 性夫 (1176–1252)	B	MCM	Liu K'o-chuang
CDBCF Shu-i 叔佾 (ca. 1068–1100)	B	MCM	Mu-jung Yen-feng

***

CDCABA Shih-chih 矢之 (1063–1105)	B	MCM	Mu-jung Yen-feng
CDCABGCCAX Shih-sai 時賽 (1256 cs)		EL	
CDCABOABDX Shih-ch'i 時錡 (1210–68)	B	MCM	Liu K'o-chuang
CDCACA Sheng-chih 昇之 (1072–1105)	B	MCM	Mu-jung Yen-feng
CDCACJ Hsiang-chih 驫之 (1094–1105)		MCM	Mu-jung Yen-feng
CDCAEA I-chih 翊之 (1078–1105)	B	MCM	Mu-jung Yen-feng
CDCBE Shu-kan 叔紺 (1053–1106)	B	MCM	Mu-jung Yen-feng
CDCBEBADB Pi-fu 俾夫 (1179–1234)	B	MCM	Yuan Fu
CDCBGCACXX Shih-chui 時栚 (1256 cs)		EL	
CDCFIDB Kung-heng 公衡 (1138–96)	B	MCM	Chou Pi-ta
		MCM	Yang Wan-li
CDCG K'o-po 克播 (1038–56)	B	MCM	Liu Ch'ang
CDCHA Shu-yun 叔耘 (1058–1106)	B	MCM	Mu-jung Yen-feng
CDCI K'o-chuang 克壯 (1043–59)	B	MCM	Liu Ch'ang
CDCKG Shu-chin 叔近 (d. 1128)	B	SS	
CDCKGACA Yen-hou 彥侯 (fl. 1190s–1230s)	B	MCM	Liu K'o-chuang

SS Code/Name/Dates	Bio	Srcs	Author
***			
CDD Ch'eng-ts'ao 承操 (1022–58)	B	MCM	Liu Ch'ang
CDDBAX An-chih 安之 (1098–1106)		MCM	Mu-jung Yen-feng
***			
CDEEAAD Kung-pin 公斌 (1148 cs)		EL	
***			
CE Te-chün 德鈞 (d. 1007)	B	SS	
CEA Ch'eng-chen 承震		SS	
CEAAB Shu-chan 叔詹 (1034–58)	B	MCM	Liu Ch'ang
***			
CEB Ch'eng-chien 承簡		SS	
***			
CEC Ch'eng-kan 承幹		SS	
CECA K'o-tun 克敦 (1022–90)	B	SS	
CECBCCDAD I-fu 以夫 (1189–1256)	B	MCM, SS	Liu K'o-chuang
***			
CED Ch'eng-wei 承偉		SS	
CEDA K'o-wen 克溫 (1018–53)	B	MCM	Liu Ch'ang
CEDB-w Wang-shih 王氏 (1024–50)	B	MCM	Liu Ch'ang
CEDBBA Yü-chih 聿之 (fl. 1127–30)	B	SS	
CEDBBF Lei-chih 罍之 (d. ca. 1127)	B	SS	
***			
CEE Ch'eng-ya 承雅		SS	
CEEADCECAAX Jo-tsu 若祖 (d. 1276)	B	GEN	
***			
CEF Ch'eng-i 承裔 (997–1053)	B	SS, MCM	Liu Ch'ang
CEFCBCB Kung-yü 公育 (1136–1203)	B	MCM	Chou Pi-ta

SS Code/Name/Dates	Bio	Srcs	Author
CEFCBDBB　Yen-t'an 彦倓 (1155–1218)	B	MCM	Yeh Shih
CEFEACCXX　Ch'in-fu 寔夫 (1256 cs)		EL	
CEFX　Mr. Chao 趙公 (1030–34)	B	MCM	Sung Hsiang

***

CEG　Ch'eng-chien 承鑑		SS	
CEGX　K'o-wei 克威 (d. 1034)	B	MCM	Sung Hsiang

***

CEI　Ch'eng-yü 承裕		SS	
CEIAA-w　Wang-shih 王氏 (d. 1056)		MCM	Liu Ch'ang

***

CEJ　Ch'eng-i 承翊		SS	
CEJA-w　Li-shih 李氏 (1035–52)	B	MCM	Liu Ch'ang
CEJB　K'o-hsien 克賢 (1043–63)		MCM	Cheng Hsieh
CEJEAAAAAAAX　Ssu-ch'ang 嗣淐 (1256 cs)		EL	
CEJEAAAAAAAY　Ssu-en 嗣恩 (1256 cs)		EL	

***

CEX　Ching-hsu 苟承		SS	

***

CEY　Ch'eng-tse 承則		SS	

***

CF　Te-ch'in 德欽 (974–1004)		SS	
CFA　Ch'eng-tsun 承遵		SS	
CFAABB　Chüeh-chih 爵之 (1061–1105)	B	MCM	Mu-jung Yen-feng
CFABBDBAAXX　Jo-wu 若珸 (1256 cs)		EL	
CFABBDBAAXY　Jo-yü 若琟 (1256 cs)		EL	
CFABBDBBBB　Shih-kao 時杲 (1220 cs)		LH	
CFABBDBBBBX　Jo-cho 若焯 (1256 cs)		EL	
CFABBDBBC　Shu-fu 淑夫 (1202 cs)		LH	

SS Code/Name/Dates	Bio	Srcs	Author
CFACB Shu-ch'ien 叔前 (1054–1105)	B	MCM	Mu-jung Yen-feng
CFACBACB Yen-tzu 彦鼐 (1169 cs)		LH	
CFACBACBB Yun-fu 允夫 (1205 cs)		LH	
CFACBACBX Ch'ien-fu 潛夫 (1223 cs)		LH	

***

CG Te-wen 德文 (975–1046)	B	SS	
CGA Ch'eng-hsien 承顯		SS	
CGAAJBAEXX Shih-chen 時溱 (1256 cs)		EL	
CGABCAAABAXX Ssu-chang 嗣樟 (1256 cs)		EL	
CGBB-w Lu-shih 盧氏 (1027–55)		MCM	Liu Ch'ang
CGBBBA-d Chao-shih 趙氏 (1091–1166)	B	MCM	Wu Su
CGCBDCAAABX Jo-ho 若和 (1267–1330)	B	GEN	

***

CH Te-ts'un 德存 (982–1011)	B	SS	
CHA Ch'eng-yen 承衍		SS	
CHABEF Mu-chih 睦之 (1101–59)	B	MCM	Hu Hung
CHAECAAAXX Shih-k'en 時墾 (1256 cs)		EL	
CHAIDBEXX Ts'an-fu 瑑夫 (1256 cs)		EL	
CHAJB Shu-ch'u 叔濋 (1082–1106)	B	MCM	Mu-jung Yen-feng

Unlocated Clansmen

AAXXXXX Tzu-li 子櫟 (d. 1139)		SS	
AAXXXXXXXXX Hsi-i 希懌 (1155–1212)	B	MCM, SS	Chen Te-hsiu
AXXXXX Ling-tzu 令鼐 (1058–1100)	B	MCM	Hsu Ching-heng
AYYYYYYY Po-shen 伯深 (fl. 1128–51)	B	SS	
BX Yuan-i 元億 (fl. 1064–8)		SS	
BXXXXX Shih-i 士醫 (d. 1130)	B	SS	
BXXXXXX-d Chao-shih 趙氏 (12th c.)	B	MCM	Ch'en Liang
BXXXXXXXXX-d Ju-i 趙汝議 (1183–1221)	B	MCM	Yeh Shih
BXXXXXXXXXXX Pi-yeh 必嘩	B	GEN	

SS Code/Name/Dates	Bio	Srcs	Author
BYYYYYYYY Ch'ung-hsieh 崇槭		O	
BZZZZZZZZZ Ch'ung-hsueh 崇學 (1223 cs)		LH	
CX Te-jun 德潤 (965–1003)		SS	
CXXXX Shu-hsiang 叔向 (fl. 1120s)	B	SS	
CXXXXXXXXX Shih-shang 時賞 (1265 cs)	B	SS	
CXXXXXXXXXXX Ssu-chu 嗣助 (1265–ca. 1308)	B	LH	
CY Te-yuan 德愿 (976–99)		SS	
CYYYY Shu-chiao 叔皎 (d. 1128)	B	SS	
CZZZZ Shu-p'ing 叔憑 (d. 1127–30)	B	SS	

a. No name was given in the epitaph, but he was identified as coming from the *ling* generation.

b. Kuei-ch'eng is the name he received upon being brought into the palace, *kuei* being the generational character used by the grandsons (biological or adoptive) of Kuang-tsung. According to Ting (*A Compilation of Anecdotes of Sung Personalities*, p. 114), his original name was Yü-chü 與苣, but that fact is not mentioned in the *Sung History's* biographical section on him (SS 41:783–4).

c. In cases like this one, the dictionaries either do not have the character or give no pronunciation for it.

d. Living as they did in the Yuan, Yu-shou and his brother Yu-hsien are not in the *Sung History* genealogy. I have nevertheless given them a code because the lineage genealogy states clearly that they were the fourth and fifth sons of Liang-shao.

e. Tsung-shih was actually the thirteenth son of Yun-jang (BCB), but since he became emperor he is not listed as one of Yun-jang's sons in the *Sung History* genealogy.

f. Hua-chih was given name and office as an infant because he was an oldest son. KSC 54:652.

g. Ch'ih-chih was given name and office as an infant because he was an oldest son. KSC 54:651.

h. Following the precedent for giving eldest sons name and office as infants, Shu-lü received his when only ten days old, then died the following year.

The Imperial Clan Genealogy Offices

The compilation of the genealogy of the Sung imperial clan went through three distinct stages: the development of an array of constantly updated genealogical works through the Northern Sung; the reconstitution of records in southern China during the early years of the Southern Sung; and the appearance of specific branch or lineage genealogies during the last decades of the dynasty. This appendix briefly describes each of these.

Like the imperial clan whose records it kept, the genealogy office of the Sung imperial clan developed gradually over the course of the Northern Sung. As it did, it came to produce a bewildering variety of genealogical records for the clan. According to a preface dated 1123 by Yang Shih (1053–1135) to an imperial genealogy, the Office of the Jade Register (Yü-tieh suo), as the imperial genealogical office was called, maintained five categories of records, each with its own functions: *Yü-tieh* (Jade register); *Tsung-fan ch'ing-hsi lu* (Records of the auspicious branches of the princely houses); *Tsung-chih shu-chi* (Clan branch registry); *T'ien-yuan lei-p'u* (Classified genealogy of heavenly origins); and *Hsien-yuan chi-ch'ing t'u* (Chart of accumulated auspiciousness of immortal origins).[1]

The *Jade Register* contained the edicts and directives relating to all aspects of genealogy, including the naming of clansmen. It had its beginnings in 995, when the Office of the Jade Register was directed to compile a *Huang Sung yü-tieh* (Imperial Sung jade register), but whether it did so at that time we do not know.[2] In 1015, the office moved to new quarters, where the records for both the *Imperial Sung Jade Register* and the *Clan Branch Registry* were to be kept, although again we have no record of an actual publication.[3] However, in 1039 the *Huang-ti yü-tieh* (Emperor's jade register) in 2 *chüan* was published, and the following year the completion of the revisions of *Jade Registers* of the imperial ancestors was announced, as was a policy of annual updates and publication of a new edition of the *Jade Register* every ten years.[4] Although there was at least one complaint from the late eleventh century that the ten-year rule was not being followed, there are numerous references from the Northern Sung to publication of *yü-tieh*.[5]

The *Clan Branch Registry* was a genealogy for those clansmen within the five grades of imperial mourning, although this became a factor only after the mid-eleventh century when non-mourning-grade clan children began to appear.[6] Officials were first ordered to compile it in 998, and the result was a 33-*chüan Registry* presented to the emperor in 1001.[7] As with the *Jade Registers*, a new edition of the *Registry* was supposed to be produced every decade.[8]

The *Records of the Auspicious Branches of the Princely Houses* is described as providing an ordered list of imperial offspring, their names, and positions.[9] The work's original name was *Tsung-fan ch'ing-hsu lu*, but in 1091 an official noted that "*ch'ing-hsu*" was the name of the T'ang rebel An Lu-shan's son and opined that using it for an imperial genealogy was perverse in the extreme.[10] In response, the name was changed from *hsu* (thread) to *hsi* (connection, line).

The *Classified Genealogy of Heavenly Origins*, as the title is given in preface dated 1123, was more often known by the name *Hsien-yuan lei-p'u* (Classified genealogy of immortal origins). Described by the preface as recording the ranks and accomplishments and transgressions of male and female clan members,[11] it reportedly was begun by Chang Fang-p'ing (1007–91) in the 1040s but as of 1078 had not been completed.[12] Wang Sheng-to argues that the *Classified Genealogy* was poorly regarded, that during the Northern Sung it was not considered a proper imperial genealogy, and that there were no further revisions of it during the Southern Sung.[13] We will return to the issue below.

Finally, the *Chart of Accumulated Auspiciousness of Immortal Origins* is described as keeping clear the order of generations, branches, and subbranches within the imperial clan.[14] This was, in fact, one of the older genealogies, established in 1018 at the suggestion of the clan official Chao An-jen (958–1018; not a clansman), who cited the examples of T'ang branch genealogies for the imperial clan.[15] Although it is infrequently mentioned in subsequent records, in 1070 both *Chart* and the *Classified Genealogy* figured in legislation that was critical to the future of the imperial clan. In a memorial from the Court of the Imperial Clan in the sixth month of 1070, it was noted that on the first day of every year, updated copies of the *Chart* and *Classified Genealogy* were sent to three scholarly halls: the Dragon Diagram Hall (Lung-t'u ko) of the Imperial Archives, the Hall for Treasuring Culture (Pao-wen ko) of the Institute for Academicians, and the Hall of Heavenly Manifestations (T'ien-chang ko) within the Hanlin Academy. The memorial then raised a question: since it had just been decided that non-mourning kin would no longer receive names or official rank and would come under the rules for external officials, should they be included? After considerable discussion of the issue and of historical precedents relating to it, the decision was made to include them in both works.[16] Both works are mentioned again in an entry for 1104, when it was decided to update the *Chart* only once every three years, although the *Classified Genealogy* continued to be revised annually.[17]

Following the loss of northern China and the capture of the majority of the imperial clan by the Jurchen, clan officials at Kao-tsung's court in the south found themselves with none of the genealogies just described. This was a matter of the utmost seriousness, for without some means of verifying claims to clan membership, the imperial clan could not survive. The steps that were undertaken beginning in 1132 to reconstitute the genealogies are described in Chapter 6 and will not be revisited here. It is noteworthy, however, that the presentation of the first result of these efforts, the *Tsu-tsung ch'ing-hsi lu* (Records of the auspicious lineage of the imperial ancestors), was followed by an enumeration of the many lacunae in it (particularly the lack of information on empresses and clanswomen) and an offer of rewards for genealogical information.[18]

The critical event for the reconstitution of records occurred in 1140, when the Sung court acquired a copy of the *Records of the Auspicious Branches of the Princely Houses* from K'ai-feng. Made possible by Yueh Fei's drive to the outskirts of K'ai-feng that year, the acquisition gave the clan over 2,000 pages in fifteen volumes of information on clansmen, clanswomen, and clan wives and seems to have solved the clan's genealogical problems, for thereafter the issue of genealogical reconstitution largely disappears from the official records.[19]

Throughout the Southern Sung, an Office of the Jade Register was maintained in Lin-an and produced a variety of records for the imperial clan, much like its Northern Sung predecessor. In fact, in an autobiographical preface to the *Chien-yen i-lai Ch'ao-yeh tsa-chi*, the historian Li Hsin-ch'uan (1167–1244) recalls a glimpse of the "jade registers (*yü-tieh*) secretly stored in gold cupboards in a stone room," which he viewed as a boy when accompanying his father, the registrar of the Court of the Imperial Clan.[20]

More to the point, the Rare Book Room of the Peking National Library contains manuscript copies for portions of two of the official Sung genealogies, which I had the opportunity to study in 1991. These are 22 *chüan* of the *Records of Princely Houses* and 30 *chüan* of the *Hsien-yuan lei-p'u* (HYLP), a variant of the *Classified Records*. The first turned out to be difficult to date and of limited value, since it gives only the names, titular offices, and lineage positions of clansmen. By contrast, the HYLP contain clanswomen and wives in addition to clansmen, birth and death dates for many if not all of them, and the history of titular offices held by clansmen. It is definitely a Southern Sung work, with the editorship attributed to the statesman Shih Hao (1106–94), though since death dates as late as 1204 are given, he should be considered just one of the work's many editors. The work demonstrates the continuing care and attention given the clan genealogy during the Southern Sung. It also disproves Wang Sheng-to's assertion that the HYLP underwent no new revisions in the Southern Sung.

As for the development of separate genealogies for clan lineages during the late Southern Sung, I will not revisit the material treated in detail in Chapter 9. But I would note the assertion by Hsiung Ta-chang, who wrote, in his preface to the 1243 *Po-yang Chao-shih hsu hsiu p'u* (Supplemental revised genealogy for the Chaos of Po-yang), that the Jade Register was inadequate for the presentation of the good and illustrious ancestral names of the branch members.[21] So dispersed had the imperial clan with its many branches grown that the keeping of the genealogy had begun to become the responsibility of the local group.

Reference Matter

Notes

For complete author names, titles, and publication data on works cited here in short form, see the Bibliography, pp. 371–91. For the abbreviations used here, see pp. xix–xx in the front matter.

Chapter 1

1. SS, 485: 13994–4000, especially 13994–95. See also Ch'ang Pi-te et al., *Sung-jen ch'uan-chi*, 4: 3399. Yuan-hao was originally surnamed Li, but the Sung had given him the Chao name as a mark of favor.

2. YCC, 20/1a–3a, for Shih-yung; Han Wei, *Nan-yang chi*, 29/1a–3b, for Ts'ung-shih; and OYWCKWC, 37/3a–4a, for Shih-jung. I have conflated their accounts slightly, since in no case were other names mentioned (the figure of seven clansmen is given in Shih-jung's epitaph), but in each case the offers to take on Yuan-hao were politely rejected.

3. HTHSTCC, 142/10a–13a.

4. Ibid., 13a–b. So far as I know this is the only account of this attempted uprising. Chao Shan-hsiang's biography in SS (413: 12400–402) makes no mention of it.

5. Pan Ku, *Han shu*, 14: 391.

6. Hsu Cho-yun, *Ancient China in Transition*, p. 5.

7. See, e.g., Lewis, *Royal Succession in Capetian France*, an excellent study of the role of the family in the Capetian monarchy in tenth- to thirteenth-century France.

8. Hsu Cho-yun, *Social Mobility in Ancient China*, p. 54. See also Creel, *Origins of Statecraft in China*, pp. 380–81.

9. Kwang-chih Chang, *Early Chinese Civilization*, p. 187; see also pp. 53–54.

10. Wei Liao-weng, *Ch'ung-chiao Ho-shan hsien-sheng ta-ch'üan-chi*, 73/18a.

11. I follow the convention of Han historians in translating *wang* as king; but in dealing with those ennobled as *wang* in the Sung, I translate it as "prince," for the Sung *wang* had control over neither territory nor power.

12. See Loewe, "The Former Han Dynasty," pp. 139–44.

13. Ibid., pp. 157–59; Ch'ü T'ung-tsu, *Han Social Structure* (Seattle: University of Washington Press, 1972), pp. 165–67.

14. Chu Hsi, *Chu-tzu yü-lei*, III: 2720.

15. Bielenstein, "Wang Mang," p. 244.

16. Ibid., pp. 245–50. For greater detail, see Bielenstein's *Restoration of the Han Dynasty*.

17. Ku Yen-wu, *Jih-chih lu*, 9/23a–b, 24b–25a. To my knowledge, Ku's essay, "Imperial Clans" ("Tsung-shih"), despite its seventeenth-century date, remains the only general treatment of imperial clans in Chinese history.

18. Loewe, "Structure and Practice of Government," p. 469; Bielenstein, "The Institutions of Later Han," p. 497.

19. "The ruler tried, for example, to maintain a body of personal officials and advisors who were independent of the bureaucratic machinery and cliques (of course, the bureaucracy made efforts to penetrate and influence these circles); to make wide use of eunuchs and other 'independent' persons (e.g., priests), whose positions were highly ambivalent positions in the political struggle; and to create a core of officials of the 'inner court,' directly under his control, who would not be absorbed by the bureaucracy" (Eisenstadt, *Political Systems of Empires*, p. 160).

20. For example, in the succession struggle following the death of Chao-ti (r. 87–74 B.C.E.), who died mysteriously and without an heir at the age of 22, rivalry between two consort families led first to the succession of Liu Ho, King of Ch'ang-i, who was deposed after just 27 days, and then to the enthronement of Liu Ping-i, the grandson of a former heir apparent, who then reigned until 49 B.C.E. as Hsuan-ti. In the course of this struggle, some two hundred individuals were executed (Loewe, "Former Han Dynasty," pp. 183–84).

21. Holmgren, "Imperial Marriage," pp. 71–72.

22. Eisenberg, "Kingship," p. 231.

23. See, e.g., Twitchett, "T'ang Imperial Family," p. 20, *n*58.

24. Peirce, *Imperial Harem*, pp. 24–25, and chap. 2 generally.

25. Guisso, "Reigns of the Empress Wu, Chung-tsung and Jui-tsung," pp. 303–4.

26. Twitchett, "T'ang Imperial Family," pp. 44–46.

27. WHTK, 159: 2054. The entry describing this, which dates from the 740s, goes on to say that each princely house had over 400 people, and each hall for grandsons, some 30–40 inhabitants.

28. Ku Yen-wu, *Jih-chih lu*, 9/25a, citing Li Ch'ü of the late T'ang.

29. Wang P'u, *T'ang hui-yao*, 65: 1140. It was actually begun in 660 under the name Ssu-tsung ssu (Court of Clan Offices); the name change occurred in 670.

30. WHTK, 195: 2055.

31. The passage in WHTK (195: 2055) defining each of the five levels includes the relatives of empresses but for each level sets the requirements for empresses' relatives one mourning rank higher than for the emperors' kin. The levels for empresses' relatives are also spelled out in Wang P'u, *T'ang hui-yao*, 65: 1140–41.

32. Wang P'u, *T'ang hui-yao*, 65:1141, lists six instances of this from 619 and 620.

33. WHTK, 159: 2055.

34. Wang P'u, *T'ang hui-yao*, 65: 1141.

35. See Twitchett, "T'ang Imperial Family," pp. 35–36, 46, on the use of imperial princes in provincial posts. Richard Guisso ("Empress Wu, Chung-tsung, and Jui-tsung," p. 303) notes that in 690—on the eve of the clan's abortive rebellion against Empress Wu and less than 75 years into the dynasty—most clansmen "were serving as prefects in widely scattered parts of the country."

36. Ou-yang Hsiu, *Hsin T'ang-shu*. The Southern Sung historian Wang Ming-ch'ing argued that the correct number was actually thirteen (cited in WHTK, 159: 2055).

37. See Wang Ming-ch'ing's judgment of Li Lin-fu in WHTK, 259: 2055, which was also critical of two others: Li Ch'eng and Li Chih-jou. Despite its bad press, the early years, at least, of Li Lin-fu's nineteen-year tenure as grand councilor have received considerable praise from historians. It is also noteworthy that one of Lin-fu's bitterest opponents was another clansman–grand councilor, Li Shih-chih (d. 747). See Twitchett, "Hsüan-tsung," pp. 409–46.

38. Hurst, "Minamoto Family," pp. 176–77. According to Hurst, the intent was to create "strong noble lineages to offset the rising power of the Fujiwara family."

39. Crossley, "Rulerships of China," p. 1471.

40. Holmgren, "Imperial Marriage," p. 73.

41. See Chaffee, *Thorny Gates of Learning in Sung China*, pp. 47–51. The power that the expanded examinations gave to the emperor is an important part of the Japanese argument for the growth of autocracy during the Sung.

42. In Chinese, Wang Sheng-tuo has produced an excellent overview of the institutions of the imperial clan, "Sung-ch'ao tsung-shih chih-tu k'ao"; Chang Pang-wei devotes a section to the imperial clan in his book on Sung imperial relatives and governance, *Sung-tai huang-ch'in yü cheng-chih*; Chang Hsi-ch'ing has written a short but very useful article on the imperial clan examinations, "Sung-tai Sung-tai ying-chü chih-tu shu lun," Taipei Conference, December 1995; and a number of Fukienese scholars—most notably Fu Tsung-wen, Ch'en Tzu-ch'iang, Li Yü-k'un, and Wang Lien-mao (see citations in the Bibliography)—have been working on aspects of the Southern Sung imperial clan in Ch'üan-chou, which was its most important

center at that time. In Japanese, the primary article remains that of Moroto Tatsuo, "Sōdai no tai sōshitsu-saku ni tsuite." Finally, see the various articles that I have written in English over the past ten years.

43. SS, 164: 3887–91.

44. The first chapters (*chüan*) of both parts of CYTC have numerous entries devoted to imperial clansmen and their institutions.

45. Chapter 159 of WHTK is devoted to imperial clans throughout history; for the Sung, see pp. 2055–57.

46. See SHY:CK, chap. 20, for the Court and Great Office; SHY:CJ, chap. 1, for clan schools; SHY:HS, 18/21a–26a, for the examination of clansmen; and SHY:TH, chaps. 2–7, for the miscellaneous records. In addition, the newly compiled *Sung hui-yao chi-kao pu-pien* has important additional materials on pp. 7–18.

47. See SS, chaps. 244–47, for the clansmen; chap. 248, for the princesses.

48. Epitaphs were funerary inscriptions carved on stone, consisting of a biography (*mu-chih*) and poem (*ming*). Although they were placed in the tomb sites, it was common for the authors of epitaphs to keep copies. See the first section of the Bibliography for the specific epitaphs used and their sources, and Appendix A for a list of all clansmen with biographies.

49. Schottenhammer, "Characteristics of Song Epitaphs."

50. In many cases—the early generations in particular—noble titles and/or titular offices are provided, but there is no apparent consistency to the entries.

51. *Ho-lin yü-lu*, pt. 2, chap. 3; cited in Wang Sheng-to, "Sung-ch'ao tsung-shih chih-tu k'ao-lueh," p. 174.

52. For more discussion and information concerning the HYLP, see my "Two Sung Imperial Clan Genealogies."

53. The NWTYCSTP, in particular, is a beautifully edited edition containing a photocopy of the early Ch'ing manuscript and many other materials relating to the imperial clan in Ch'üan-chou.

Chapter 2

1. This was the claim made in some of the Heavenly Texts purportedly discovered in the years 1008–17, which led to Chen-tsung's (r. 997–1022) controversial enactment of the *feng* and *shan* ceremonies. See Cahill, "Taoism at the Sung Court," esp. pp. 33 and 40. At the beginning of the twentieth century, a Chao lineage genealogy from Kuang-tung offered a lengthy lineation for the family reaching back to the Yellow Emperor (CSTP, 1/7a–8b).

2. The following account draws mainly on TTSL, chap. 1, which the primary account of dynastic history in SS follows closely; and CSTP, 1/41b–43b. I have also made use of Miyazaki Ichisada, *Sō no Taiso to Taisō*, pp. 39–53, which remains the most balanced and informative treatment of the two first emperors.

3. See Miyazaki, *Sō no Taiso to Taisō*, p. 44. For an English-language account of this story, see Ting, *Compilation of Anecdotes of Sung Personalities*, p. 2.

4. Thanks to the family's imperial fortunes, both of the brothers underwent various name changes. K'uang-i's name was changed to Kuang-i after T'ai-tsu's accession to observe the taboo against using a character in the emperor's name, and then to Kuei, once he himself became emperor. K'uang-mei's name changed to Kuang-mei upon T'ai-tsu's accession, and then to T'ing-mei upon T'ai-tsung's accession, and he is known in many historical records as the Prince of Wei. See Sung Ch'ang-lien and Miyazaki Ichisada, Biography of T'ai-tsung; and Chikusa Masaaki, Biography of Chao T'ing-mei.

5. See Wang Gungwu, *Structure of Power in North China During the Five Dynasties*, chap. 7; and Worthy, "The Founding of Sung China."

6. This is a central point of Wang Gungwu's *Structure of Power*, although his argument is qualified in important ways by Worthy ("Founding of Sung China"), particularly insofar as the role of T'ai-tsu is concerned.

7. Chao T'iao had four sons, Chao T'ing two, Chao Ching three, and as mentioned above, Chao Hung-yin five, of whom three survived to maturity (CSTP, 1/8b).

8. "T'ai-tsu huang-ti yü-tieh ta-hsun," CSTP, 1/11a. It is also found in Chao Ssu-lin, *Hsu-hsiu Shan-yin Hua-she Chao-shih tsung-p'u* (1882). Although this document is found only in Chao genealogies and not in the *Sung History*, the *Sung hui-yao*, or other Sung sources, there are reasons for accepting it as authentic, for the Chao genealogies generally speak of treasuring all clan documents that might have been preserved through the years. Moreover, the quality of the CSTP is exceptionally good. As discussed below, the Chaos of San-chiang (Kuang-tung) traced themselves to a prominent branch of T'ai-tsung's descendents. Their common clansman ancestor from the end of the Sung, Chao Pi-ying (1225–89), had close ties with the Sung court in Kuang-tung during the 1270s, but was also able to establish his family there after 1279 with lavish landholdings (ibid., 2/10b–12a). It seems reasonable, then, that the family came into possession of an assortment of clan documents, which would in turn explain the wealth of documents in the lengthy (106 large folios) first chapter (*chüan*) of CSTP. Moreover, although many of these documents are unique and therefore cannot be independently verified, they employ Sung documentary forms and have proved reliable in their information that can be checked.

9. At the end of the document, Chao P'u is ordered to receive the document and store it in gold bindings.

10. "Yü-chih yü-tieh p'ai hsu," CSTP, 1/11b–12a.

11. Ibid., 11b.

12. The editors of CSTP note some later changes in generation names, but these

deal only with the thirteenth and fourteenth generations, names that were not used in the Sung. See Table 2.2 for the names used in the first ten generations.

13. TTSL, 3/1a–b; SS, 3: 40 and 4: 53; Franke, *Sung Biographies*, 3: 992.

14. SS, 244: 8666; and Franke, *Sung Biographies*, 1: 83.

15. SS, 244: 8676.

16. HCP, 17: 380–81. This story is also given in Ting, *Compilation of Anecdotes of Sung Personalities*, pp. 15–16. Both cite as their source Ssu-ma Kuang, *Su-shui chi-wen*. As Li T'ao noted in his commentary, neither the Empress Sung's nor Te-fang's biographies say that she was his mother. Nor, to my knowledge, is there any record of Te-fang's having been named crown prince; indeed such a development would have been unusual given the fact that his older brother, Te-chao, was in good standing with T'ai-tsu.

17. SS, 242: 8607; TTSL, 13/1b.

18. See Ting, *Compilation of Anecdotes of Sung Personalities*, pp. 17–18, and Chikusa, *Sō no Taiso to Taisō*, pp. 134–36. In addition to the anecdote cited in the text, Ssu-ma Kuang's account reveals two odd facts. First, when Wang Chi-lung arrived at Kuang-i's residence, he found a court doctor waiting outside, who said that he had been summoned to the prince's residence. Second, after learning of the emperor's death, Kuang-i insisted that he first needed to consult with family members and left for the palace only at the urgings of Wang, who said that time was of the essence.

19. See, e.g., Fang Hao, *Sung shih*, 1: 24–27.

20. This point is made in Sung Ch'ang-lien and Miyazaki Ichisada, Biography of T'ai-tsung, 3: 992.

21. SS, 244: 8669.

22. TTSL, 15/1b; SS, 244: 8666.

23. TTSL, 15/3b; SS, 244: 8676.

24. SS, 244: 8676. On T'ai-tsung's flight from Yu-chou, see Sung Ch'ang-lien and Miyazaki Ichisada, Biography of T'ai-tsung, 3: 992.

25. SS, 244: 8666–69.

26. SS, 244: 8669.

27. See the discussion of Han and T'ang succession disputes in Chapter 1.

28. SS, 245: 8697.

29. SS, 245: 8697; 6: 103–4. The one thing noted about Chao Heng's governance of K'ai-feng was that he was successful at keeping the capital's prisons relatively empty and was praised by T'ai-tsung for it.

30. SS, 245: 8671. For other examples, see Te-i (CC; 967–1015) and Te-ts'un (CH; 982–1011), SS, 245: 8673 and 8675, respectively.

31. SS, 245: 8703.

32. Ching Chung, *Palace Women*, p. 24.

33. SS, 245: 8697.

34. See Ching Chung, *Palace Women*, pp. 24–35, which points to the over-whelmingly military background of the husbands of imperial princesses; and also Chaffee, "Marriage of Sung Imperial Clanswomen," pp. 147–51.

35. SS, 245: 6895; CSTP, 2/6b.

36. SS, 245: 8697–98.

37. For examples, see SS, 244: 8678 and 245: 8693–94.

38. HCP, 43: 907–8.

39. SS, 244: 8678.

40. SS, 245: 8693–95.

41. SS, 277: 9418–19.

42. Ibid.

43. Ibid. This account is drawn mainly from Yao T'an's biography. Chao Yuan-chieh's biography (in SS, 245: 8700–701) also describes this incident (though not the earlier ones), albeit briefly. It quotes T'an as saying: "I have seen mountains of blood; how can this be an artificial mountain?" Yao T'an's biographer conveys a less than flattering portrait of the man. After Yuan-chieh's death, which was bitterly mourned by his brother Chen-tsung, T'an had an audience with the emperor in which he criticized the prince while praising his own boldness. After he departed, Chen-tsung commented that this was an example of problems arising because of a teacher's inability to instruct successfully according to proper principles. The biog-rapher's conclusion: "This is selling straightness to obtain a name."

Chapter 3

1. See Wang Gungwu, "The Rhetoric of Lesser Empire."

2. S. Cahill, "Taoism at the Heavenly Court." The lavish patronage of Taoism—the one lasting result of this affair—was largely reversed by Jen-tsung in the 1020s.

3. SS, 245: 8702–3.

4. Biography of Chao Yun-pi (BEA; 1008–70), in HYC, 39: 546.

5. KSC, 52: 627–28. Chao Shih-yung (AABAA; 1010–68) was also asked by Chen-tsung if he could recite books. He replied, "I can recite the *Classic of Filial Piety*." "What matters does it discuss?" "Loyalty and filiality." The emperor was pleased and gave him some rare fruit. Instead of eating it, however, Shih-yung asked if he could take it to his family. The emperor was impressed (YCC, 20/1a–b).

6. WWC, 12/3b–4a.

7. Ibid., 4a–b.

8. Ibid., 3a–b.

9. HYC, 39: 543–44. In response Shih-yen memorized several scores of T'ang poems—he later became famous for his knowledge of them—and was then given his name and titular office. (See below for a discussion of naming practices.)

10. Chao Tsung-li (BAAA; n.d.) once won one of Jen-tsung's poems in an archery contest during an imperial banquet at the T'ai-ch'ing Hall (SS, 245: 8695). The *Sung hui-yao* (SHY:TH 4/7b) also records a banquet held at the T'ai-ch'ing Hall on the seventeenth day of the second month of 1045 and notes that archery was held in the garden.

11. OYWCKWC, 37/1a–b. For other examples, see Chao Ts'ung-yü (ABBA; 998–1041), whom Jen-tsung singled out for praise for a poem composed at a clan literary gathering (Sung Ch'i, *Ching-wen chi*, 58: 770), and Chao K'o-chi (CABA; d. 1044), who at the emperor's request composed a poem at a banquet (ibid., 58: 770–71).

12. KSC, 52: 630–31.

13. For two examples, see the biographies of Chao Tsung-wang (BDAA; 1020–63) in HYC, 39: 540–41, and Chao K'o-hsiao (CAAE) in KSC, 52: 631, both of whom excelled in the examinations.

14. Chiang Shao-yü, *Sung-ch'ao shih-shih lei-yuan*, p. 422. Chiang, who lived in the late Northern Sung, had served in the Office of the Jade Register.

15. SHY:CK, 20/1a. The first dated entry for the Court of the Imperial Clan is found on 20/1b.

16. Ibid., 20/1b.

17. Ibid., 20/1b–4a.

18. SS, 164: 3887; SHY:CK, 20/6a.

19. One other group of kin to appear in the sources were the "imperial clansmen of Pao-chou" (*Pao-chou tsung-shih*) from the circuit of Ho-pei-hsi. These were descendents of Chao Ching, T'ai-tsu's grandfather, and in 1139 several score of them turned up at the Southern Sung court, four of them officials. The emperor welcomed them warmly and gave them imperial clan status, but with unique generation names (CYTC, pt. 1, 1:25).

20. SHY:CK, 20/1b–2a, for the 999 move; 3a–b, for that of 1015. HCP, 84: 1916, describes the fire that necessitated the move.

21. SHY:CK, 20/4b–5a.

22. Ibid., 20/4b, 5a.

23. According to Charles Hucker (*Dictionary of Official Titles*, p. 309), the two groups consisted of Hanlin Academicians and nominal members of the Secretariat.

24. Ibid., 20/1a–b.

25. SHY:TH, 4/4b.

26. SHY:CK, 20/16a.

27. Ibid., 20/16a–b. The officials were Chou Meng-yang and Li T'ien.

28. Yun-jang served in top positions of the Great Office from 1036 as least through 1044 (and quite likely until his death in 1059), and Yun-pi, whose initial appointment was as supervisor (*p'an*) of the Great Office, from 1036 to 1061. Shou-

chieh's dates of service are unclear—unfortunately we have no biography for him—but since the next T'ai-tsu-branch clansman to hold a top position in the Great Office was Chao Ts'ung-ku (ABCA) in 1060, it seems likely that Shou-chieh, too, had a long tenure.

29. See SS, 244: 2678–79 for Wei-chi; SS, 245: 8708, and CSTP, 2/6b–7a, for Yun-jang; and HYC, 39: 546–49 for Yun-pi.

30. HCP, 43: 907–8. According to Tsou Tao-yuan in *Hui-shu hsiang-chu*, the Southern Residence was for the offspring of T'ai-tsu and T'ai-tsung, and the Northern Residence for the Chao T'ing-mei's descendents (cited in Chou Ch'eng, *Sung Tung-ching k'ao*, p. 208).

31. SHY:TH, 4/3a.

32. HCP, 117: 2757–58; SHY:TH, 4/4a–b; WHTK, 259: 2055. The grounds used had been those of the Yü-ch'ing chao-ying Palace, one of three lavish imperial palaces built in the Ta–chung hsiang-fu period (1008–16) and criticized by various ministers as wasteful (Chou Ch'eng, *Sung Tung-ching k'ao*, p. 29, citing Hung Mai, *Jung-chai san-pi*).

33. HCP, 119: 2802; SHY:TH, 4/5a.

34. HCP, 161: 3887; SHY:TH, 4/8b. Presumably the Wang estate was adjacent to the Northern Residence.

35. HCP, 202: 4892; SHY:TH, 4/15b. The two clansmen who seem to have precipitated this development were Chao Tsung-tan (BAAC; fl. 1064–80) and Chao K'o-chieh (CDAB; n.d.). On the Fang-lin Park, which had been a favorite spot of T'ai-tsung's, see Chou Ch'eng, *Sung Tung-ching k'ao*, p. 188.

36. According to Li Hsin-ch'uan (CYTC, pt. 1, 2: 37), the residences later established were the Ch'in-hsien (Affection for worthies) for the two sons of Ying-tsung, Ti-hua (Plum blossom) for the five sons of Shen-tsung, and Fan-yen (Luxurious and abundant) for the many sons of Hui-tsung.

37. HYC, 39: 547–48. This is from Chao Yun-pi's epitaph.

38. Charles Hucker (*Dictionary of Official Titles*, p. 585) explains that this was a staff member "responsible for giving moral guidance as well as companionship."

39. SS, 162: 3826. For T'ai-tsung's act, see Chapter 2 in this book. In 1064 Ying-tsung appointed eight lecturers (*chiang-shu*) and thirteen preceptors to augment the existing six preceptors.

40. The practical implication of specifying Hsuan-tsu rather than Wei-wang was that it gave the Wei-wang clansmen a one-generation penalty vis-à-vis the other two branches. The reason for that is that the Wei-wang clansmen were one generation further removed from an emperor than were the others, since in Sung eyes Hsuan-tsu had imperial status.

41. HCP, 89: 2043; SHY:TH, 4/3a–4b; SS, 245: 8704. Throughout this section,

I have made extensive use of the excellent treatment of this sometimes confusing subject by Wang Sheng-to, "Sung-ch'ao tsung-shih chih-tu k'ao," pp. 178–80.

42. HCP, 117: 2763–64. According to the *Sung History* (SS, 169: 4033–44), the full sequence of offices from lowest to highest consisted of the following fourteen: vice-commander of the crown prince's right inner guard command (*t'ai-tzu yu-nei shuai-fu fu-shuai*); commander of the crown prince's right gate guard command (*t'ai-tzu yu-chien-men shuai-fu-shuai*); general of the right personal guard (*yu ch'ien-niu-wei chiang-chün*); general-in-chief of the right gate guard command (*yu-chien-men-wei ta-chiang-chün*); distant commandary prefect (*yao-chün tz'u-shih*); distant commandary military training commissioner (*yao-chün t'uan-lien shih*); prefect (*tz'u-shih*); military training commissioner (*t'uan-lien-shih*); defense commissioner (*fang-yü-shih*); surveillance commissioner (*kuan-ch'a shih*); deputy military and surveillance commissioner (*chieh-tu kuan-ch'a liu-hou*); left and right guard generalissimo–military commissioner (*tso-yu wei-shang chiang-chün chieh-tu-shih*); military commissioner and joint manager of affairs with the Secretariat-Chancellery (*chieh-tu-shih t'ung chung-shu men-hsia p'ing-chiang shih*); and military commissioner and concurrent palace attendant (*chieh-tu-shih chien shih-chung*).

43. HCP, 117: 2763.

44. See the 1053 edict to that effect in SHY:TH, 4/9a.

45. See the 1067 discussion of how frequently two of the most eminent and senior clansmen could attend court in SHY:TH, 4/16a–b.

46. SS, 245: 8705–6; Sung Ch'i, *Ching-wen chi*, 58: 767–69. Yuan-yen, whom Sung describes as an accomplished courtier and man of letters, got in trouble and was demoted in 1015 when his quarters caught on fire and damaged the palace. This was later forgiven, however.

47. SS, 171: 4103–5. See the useful tables in Wang Sheng-to, "Sung-ch'ao tsung-shih chih-tu k'ao," pp. 193–94, summarizing the schedules of salaries and gifts for various guard officials. These figures represent conditions in the Yuan-feng period, but are probably close to those that prevailed under Jen-tsung.

48. HYC, 39: 536. From the epitaph for Chao Ts'ung-hsin (AADF; 1012–62).

49. Hucker, *Dictionary of Official Titles*, p. 334.

50. See the three-*chüan* treatment of the Ming-t'ang in WHTK, ch. 73–75. The ceremony described below is found on 74: 674–75. For modern treatments of the Ming-t'ang, see James T. C. Liu, "The Sung Emperors and the *Ming-t'ang*"; and Howard Wechsler, *Offerings of Jade and Silk*.

51. James T. C. Liu, "The Sung Emperors and the *Ming-t'ang*," pp. 50–51.

52. HCP, 169: 4063. The promoted clansmen were specified as 17 from the second generation of the clan (the emperor's generation), 51 from the third, and 19 from the fourth.

53. KSC, 52: 629–30.

54. KSC, 54: 649–50. See also HYC, 39: 533–35.

55. SHY, *Li* section, 42/8b–9a, 10b; cited in Mark Robert Halperin, "Pieties and Responsibilities," p. 208.

56. See Patricia Ebrey's evocative description of this ceremony, which occurred in 1082, in "Portrait Sculptures in Imperial Ancestral Rites," pp. 42–45.

57. SHY:TH, 4/25b; SHY, *Li* section, 13/4b, cited in Halperin, "Pieties and Responsibilities," p. 245.

58. HYC, 39: 531–32. According to the epitaph, he told his wife and children at a feast that a figure in a dream had told him that his days were finished, and in fact, he died a few days later.

59. SS, 277: 9418.

60. SS, 244: 8670; CYTC, pt. 2, 13: 505–6.

61. SHY:TH, 4/2a–b.

62. For example, Chao Ts'ung-hsin (AADF; 1012–62) was credited with helping to reform clan education; he complained that noted teachers invited to the clan schools simply kept to their seats without lecturing, and that was then changed (HYC, 39: 536–38).

63. SHY:TH, 4/14a–15a.

64. LCC, 38/7b–8a.

65. CSTP, 2/6b–7a.

66. YCC, 20/3a. Lü, a palace teaching official, so greatly influenced Chao Shih-yung (AABAA; 1010–68) when teaching him the Classics that after Lü's death, Shih-yung had his tablet put up so his goodness could be honored.

67. HYC, 39: 538–39. Wang Lieh was a K'ai-feng scholar who had failed in the examinations but was recommended by Fan Chung-yen (989–1052) to be a clan school preceptor (Ch'ang Pi-te et al., *Sung-jen chuan-chi*, 1: 231).

68. HYC, 39: 535–36.

69. Ibid. His question was, briefly, how could the rulers of the state of Lu consider King Wen to be an ancestor when they refused to participate in the twelve-year sacrifices at the Chou ancestral temple? Chao Shih-ch'ang (AADAC; 1020–61) was the other clansman who studied with Sun (ibid., 39: 538–39).

70. WWC, 14/14b.

71. OYWCKWC, 37/5b–6a. Ou-yang explains that Shih-heng's father had died when he was young.

72. HYC, 39: 540–41. The printed set of books probably refers to the *Nine Classics* printed by the Directorate in the early Sung and distributed to various local schools (see SHY:CJ, 2/2b). I have been unable to identify Yü Ying-hsing.

73. SHY:TH, 4/6a–b.

74. See Chaffee, *Thorny Gates of Learning*, pp. 66–68.

75. The first such reward recorded by the *Sung hui-yao* (SHY:TH, 4/2b, 8a–12a *passim*) actually occurred in 1010 under Chen-tsung, but there had been no further rewards until 1047.

76. For example, Chao K'o-tun (CECA; 1022–90) was recommended by the Court of the Imperial Clan, selected in an examination and rewarded with 300 strings of cash. Similarly, Chao K'o-chi (CAAB; d. 1090) was recommended and tested on his accomplishments in calligraphy (SS, 244: 8674, 8671).

77. Examples include Chao Tsung-pien (BAAM; 1023–68), who with his three brothers placed at the top of an examination held at the Institute for Academicians (Hsueh-shih yuan) (Wang An-shih, *Lin-ch'uan hsien-sheng wen-chi*, 98/10b–11b), and Chao K'o-hsiao (CAAE)(KSC, 52: 631–2).

78. SS, 244: 8672 provides the fullest account. See also Wang Ying-lin, *Yü-hai*, 116/27b–28a.

79. Wang Ying-lin, *Yü-hai*, 116/27b–28a.

80. YCC, 20/1a–3a; Han Wei, *Nan-yang chi*, 29/1a–3b.

81. As the oldest boy of the fourth generation in his particular branch of the clan, he was given a name and office at two *sui*.

82. KSC, 54: 649.

83. Chaffee, "Two Sung Imperial Clan Genealogies," esp. table 3 on p. 105. The *Hsien-yuan lei-p'u* fragment is in the Rare Books Collection of the Peking National Library.

84. SHY:TH, 4/4/6a.

85. Ibid., 4/9b.

86. Ibid., 4/12a–b.

87. For example, Lady Li (1030–81), the wife of Chao Tsung-ching (BEAD; 1032–97) (Wang An-li, *Wang Wei-kung chi*, 7/4a–5a), and Lady Wang (1024–50), the wife of Chao K'o-chou (CEDB) (KSC, 52: 634).

88. SHY:CK 20/4b. For a more detailed treatment of this complex issue of marriage and marriage relationships, see my "Marriage of Sung Imperial Clanswomen"; my unpublished paper "Civil-izing the Emperor's Family"; and Chang Pang-wei, *Hun-yin yü she-hui*, pp. 114-20.

89. In 1058 this requirement was spelled out more precisely. To marry a clanswoman, a commoner (*pai-shen jen*) needed a family history of three generations of official service; if the groom was himself an official, then not all of his forebears for three generations needed to have been officials (SHY:CK, 20/5a; HCP, 187: 4511).

90. See Priscilla Ching Chung, *Palace Women in the Northern Sung*, pp. 24–35, on the marriages of empresses. As for the clan at large, Chaffee, "Marriage of Sung Imperial Clanswomen," pp. 147–51, and the discussion in Chapter 7 below, especially Tables 7.3–7.5, pp. 163 and 165.

91. Winston W. Lo, *An Introduction to the Civil Service of Sung China, with Emphasis on Its Personnel Administration*, pp. 27–28; and Lo, "New Perspective on the Sung Civil Service."

92. See Edward Kracke, *Civil Service in Early Sung China*, p. 56; and Umehara Kaoru, *Sōdai kanryō seido kenkyū*, pp. 99–101. Winston Lo (*Civil Service of Sung China*, p. 28) argues the military-rank officials constituted not a separate service but a section of the civil service. However, he does agree that there was a difference between them and the civil-rank officials. The former tended to fulfill the "bureaucratic-specific functions" of the civil service, and the latter "to serve as the political-cultural elite and generate support for the dynasty."

93. KSC, 52: 635–36.

94. See Chaffee, "The Marriage of Sung Imperial Clanswomen," pp. 142–44. Most of the documents spelling out dowry and recruitment privileges for the husbands date from the 1070s and later, but since the 1070s legislation was designed to limit the more generous provisions of the past, we can infer with confidence that at least the same level of benefits adhered under Jen-tsung.

95. See ibid., pp. 151–59.

96. For examples, see OYWCKWC, 37/2a–3a; Wang An-li, *Wang Wei kung chi*, 7/4a–5a; WWC, 12/6b; and KSC, 52: 634–35.

97. KSC, 52: 628–29.

98. Ibid., pp. 633–34.

99. Ibid., pp. 630–31.

100. Shen Kou et al., *Shen-shih san hsien-sheng wen-chi*, 37/51b–52b.

101. Wang An-li, *Wang Wei kung chi*, 7/5a–b.

102. KSC, 52: 633–34.

103. LCC, 38/9a–12a.

104. SS, 245: 8707. This incident—and the fact that it involved female slaves, which is not mentioned in the SS account—is also reported in SHY:TH, 4/7b.

105. HYC, 39: 536–38 for Ts'ung-hsin; LCC, 38/16a–17b for Tsung-yueh.

106. These and other related findings are analyzed in Chaffee, "Two Sung Imperial Clan Genealogies," but it should be noted that that article's labeling of generations is at variance with the numbering used in this book. What are numbered generations six and seven in the article should be four and five (the article was following the chapter numbering of the HYLP, which took Hsuan-tsu [T'ai-tsu's father] as the first generation). Also, the figure of 27 fathers does not match the 6 T'ai-tsu and 23 T'ai-tsung fathers given in table 1 of that article (p. 102). The reason is that I have excluded two fathers whose daughters clearly are not listed.

107. See ibid., pp. 104–9, for a fuller discussion of this issue. See also Li Chung-ch'i (James Lee) et al., "Liang chung pu-t'ung ti ssu-wang hsien-chih chi-chih,"

which argues that the large gender imbalances in the Ch'ing imperial clan were the result of intentional infanticide.

108. SS, 245: 8700. See also the epitaph for Chao Shih-yueh (AADBG; 1042–81), which mentions both his mother and his birth mother.

109. SS, 245: 8703–4.

110. One exception to this generalization is a 1071 edict denying clan status to children of maids within the clan residences (SHY:TH, 4/27b).

111. SS, 245: 8695. The account in the text is drawn from the biographies of father and son, both of which are on the same page. For the beatings and abuse that maids and concubines could receive in Sung upper-class households, see Ebrey, *Inner Quarters*, pp. 166–70; according to Ebrey, violence at the hands of the wife was most typical.

112. SS, 244: 8678.

113. Concerning the former, see SS, 245: 8700, for a fight between brothers in which one brother was accused of having stolen valuables belonging to the other brother. Concerning alcoholism, Wang An-shih (*Lin-ch'uan chi hsien-sheng*, 98/13b–14a) tells of how Chao Shih-jeng (AAEBH; 1047–68) died from drinking in his early twenties.

114. CWTC, 14/6b–7a, 9a–b.

115. WWC, 12/6a; YCC, 20/3a.

116. CWTC, 14/5a–b, 7a–b; SHY:TH, 4/3b–4a.

117. SHY:TH, 4/3b–4a. Ts'ung-chih's biography in HYC, 39: 533–35 also describes his action—which is credited with saving his brother—and the reward, but makes no mention of the debate.

118. YCC, 20/3a.

119. HCP, 65: 1443–44. The imperial clan burial ground is indicated in a map in Ho-nan sheng K'ai-feng ti-chü wen-wu kuan-li wei-yuan-hui and Ho-nan sheng Kung-hsien wen-wu kuan-li wei-yuan-hui, eds., *Sung ling* (Kung-hsien: Wen-wu ch'u-pan-she, 1982). During a visit to the Sung tombs in May 1996, however, I was told that no excavation work had been done on the imperial clan tombs and that getting there was very difficult.

120. The infant Chao Hua-chih (CABABA; 1050–51) died in 1051 but was not buried until 1060 (KSC, 54: 652). Nor was he unique; I have found well over a dozen other clansmen and wives whose coffins were stored for years before 1060.

121. WWC, 12/7a–b. Yang details the contents of this work, which included sections on the ordering of spirit tablets, quotations from the ancients to strengthen traditions of family life, encouragement of education and self-cultivation, and precepts from the *Analects*.

122. See esp. HCP, 117: 2757–58.

123. KSC, 52: 630–31. Wang Sheng-to ("Sung-ch'ao tsung-shih chih-tu k'ao," p. 175) also quotes the grand councilor Han Ch'i (1008–75), who, when asked by Jen-tsung to recommend clan youths who might be considered as his successor, said, "The imperial clansmen do not associate with people outside [their palaces]. How could we ministers know them personally?" Unfortunately, Wang's citation is for HCP 395, an obvious mistake, since that chapter is dated 1087, and I have been unable to locate the original passage.

124. SHY:TH, 4/18a.

125. See HYC, 39: 531–32, which describes a clan family's feast for their affinal relatives, and 39: 540–41, in which a clansman provided money to some poor affinal kin for funeral expenses.

126. LCC, 38/16a–17b.

127. KSC, 52: 632–33.

128. Ibid., pp. 628–29.

129. LCC, 38/15a–16a, in an epitaph for Chao Chung-k'ao (BAAJE; 1051–67), an outstanding student who died in his teens.

130. Sung Ch'i, *Ching-wen chi*, 58: 771–72.

131. Cited by the early Ch'ing scholar Ku Yen-wu in his *Jih-chih lu*, 9/24a–b. I have been unable to find the quotation in Sung's writings.

132. LCC, 38/17b–18b.

Chapter 4

1. HCP, 195: 4727–8.

2. Ibid., p. 4722. Similar suggestions were made by Han Ch'i, Pao Ch'eng, Lü Hui, and Fan Chen. For a lucid treatment of Ch'eng-ti's succession problems, see Loewe, "The Former Han Dynasty," pp. 213–15.

3. HCP, 195:4724.

4. Ibid., p. 4727. As noted in Chapter 3, note 123, on another occasion Han Ch'i gave a different answer to a similar query by Jen-tsung: "The imperial clansmen do not associate with people outside [their palaces]. How could we ministers know them personally?" (Wang Sheng-to, "Sung-ch'ao tsung-shih chih-tu k'ao," p. 175).

5. HCP, 195:4727.

6. For the role that Ying-tsung's older brother, Chao Tsung-p'u (BCBB; d. 1224), played in convincing him to enter the imperial palace to be groomed for possible succession, see SS, 245: 8711.

7. See Fisher, "The Ritual Dispute of Sung Ying-tsung," pp. 112–13.

8. CSTP, 2/6b–7a.

9. This account is drawn primarily from Fisher's excellent study of the controversy, "The Ritual Dispute of Ying-tsung."

10. Although Fisher (ibid.) interprets the dispute as a conflict between pragmatic and idealistic statesmen, Peter Bol (*"This Culture of Ours,"* p. 213) sees it as pitting "old allies of Fan Chung-yen who envisioned a government more responsive to the needs of the populace" against "men long associated with opposition to institutional change."

11. SHY:TH, 4/14a–15a; SHY:CK, 20/16b–17a.

12. His original name was Chung-chen, and his princely name was Hsu. For basic biographical information concerning Shen-tsung, see SS, 14: 263–65, 16: 314; and TTSL 8.

13. See Smith, "Shen-tsung's Reign (1068–1085)," pp. 2–8.

14. For a broad overview, see James T. C. Liu, *Reform in Sung China.* For a succinct and useful summary treatment of them, see Bol, *"This Culture of Ours,"* pp. 246–53. Also noteworthy is Paul Smith's outstanding study of Wang's economic policies toward the horse and tea industries, *Taxing Heaven's Storehouse,* and his draft chapter on Shen-tsung's reign for the *Cambridge History of China,* cited in the preceding note.

15. SHY:TH, 4/14a–15a.

16. Tseng Kung, *Nan-feng hsien-sheng Yuan-feng lei-kao* (SPTK ed.), 31/1b–2a; cited by Robert M. Hartwell, "The Imperial Treasuries," p. 45, who adds a figure of 870 for 1078. This figure, however, is mentioned at the beginning of Tseng's section dealing with the imperial clan rather than as a part of the series quoted; it is undated; and the reference is clearly to the number of clansmen among the lowest three ranks (*san-pan*) of court officials.

17. SHY:TH, 4/31b.

18. Ibid., 24a–b.

19. Ibid., 31b.

20. These discussions, which led to a lengthy joint memorial by the Secretariat and Bureau of Military Affairs, a preparatory edict discussing the need for change, and finally the edict of the twelfth month of 1069, which is quoted in full below, are all given in ibid., 31b–35b. The grouping of these discussions and the space devoted to them is unusual for the SHY and an indication of their importance. Unfortunately, the HCP is missing the chapters for 1068–69, depriving us of that valuable source of corroboration.

21. On one occasion, Shen-tsung asked Ch'en Sheng-chih and Wang An-shih where savings could be found, since the current tax revenues were not great. They pointed to the military and the imperial clan (SHY:TH, 4/32a).

22. Ibid., 32b. Wang Sheng-to ("Sung-ch'ao tsung-shih chih-tu k'ao," p. 180) also makes the point that reformers and anti-reformers alike supported the changes in the imperial clan.

23. See Bol, *"This Culture of Ours,"* pp. 247–48, for a list of the New Policies as they were enacted chronologically. The Wang An-li quotation, which is drawn from

a passage quoted more fully below, is from Wang An-li, *Wang Wei-kung chi*, 7/15a–16a.

24. See SHY:TH, 4/32b–34a for the memorial; 34a–b for the edict.

25. Ibid., 35a–b. Ch'en Chün, *Huang-ch'ao pien-nien kang-mu pei-yao*, 19/10a, also reports this action, but dates it in 1075.

26. See *Tz'u-hai* (Taipei: Chung-hua shu-chü, 1971), p. 2612.

27. Lu Yu, *Lao-hsueh yen pi-chi*, 2; cited in Wang Sheng-to, "Sung-ch'ao tsung-shih chih-tu k'ao lueh," p. 179.

28. See Ebrey, "Conceptions of the Family in the Sung Dynasty," pp. 229–32; Ebrey, *Family and Property in Sung China*, pp. 52–55; and a more recent publication, Birge, *Holding Her Own*, pp. 60–62, 191–96.

29. SHY:TH, 4/32b.

30. See ibid., 20b–23a, for the most substantial discussions of this issue.

31. See SS, 245: 8711–17, for the account of the specific transmission of the title, Prince of P'u, among the offspring of Chao Yun-jang.

32. SHY:TH, 4/35b–36a.

33. As the clan continued to grow, duplications in names were a continuing problem. Despite many attempts by the government to rectify them when discovered and the frequent use of extremely rare characters for the part of the name not the generation name, I know from hours of pouring through the *Sung History* genealogy that they remained a common problem for the rest of the dynasty.

34. SHY:TH, 20/6b–7b.

35. Since the idea was that they were to be treated as were other officials, appointment via *yin* remained an important if unmentioned route to office and played a crucial role for later generations of clansmen.

36. SHY:TH, 4/32b–34a.

37. Wang Sheng-to, "Sung-ch'ao tsung-shih chih-tu k'ao," pp. 181–83, provides an excellent history of the legislation concerning examinations and the imperial clan. See also Chaffee, *Thorny Gates of Learning*, pp. 106–8.

38. See SHY:TH, 4/28a, for an examination of four clansmen at the Bureau of Academicians in 1074; and 29a for a similar examination the next year involving eight clansmen. In the same vein, in 1077 clansmen of the guard rank general-in-chief and above were permitted to take an examination on one classic and either the *Analects* or the *Mencius* once every two years, and shortly thereafter two clansmen passed such an examination (ibid., 30b–31a).

39. HCP, 233: 5647.

40. SS, 157: 3676; WHTK, 31: 294. See Chaffee, *Thorny Gates of Learning*, pp. 98–105, for treatments of both the locked hall and the Directorate examinations. Although the sources do not address the issue, it seems highly likely that clansmen at

the locked hall examination were graded separately from officials and relatives of officials.

41. SHY:TH, 4/33a–b.

42. See Chang Hsi-ch'ing's excellent paper on the imperial clan examinations, "Sung-tai tsung-shih ying-chü chih-tu shu lun," presented at the International Conference on Sung History, Taipei, 1995.

43. For competition in the locked hall, Directorate, and departmental examinations, see Chaffee, *Thorny Gates of Learning*, pp. 231 *n*28, 103, and 106, respectively.

44. SHY:TH, 5/7b.

45. Wang Sheng-to, "Sung-tai tsung-shih chih-tu k'ao," p. 182, with figures drawn from the HCP.

46. Wang Sheng-to, "Sung-ch'ao tsung-shih chih-tu k'ao," p. 179. Taking into account the missing years, Wang calculates that the annual average was 54 for 1070–77 and 42 for 1086–98. He also cites comparable figures for 1130–60, during which 433 clansmen (or 20 per year) received name and office.

47. It is probably not coincidental that epitaph references to the success of clansmen in the examinations during this period are practically nonexistent. The only such reference I have found was in the Southern Sung epitaph for Chao Kung-mai (CABCAGC; 1115–79), which relates that three of his uncles received *chin-shih* degrees during the Yuan-feng era (1078–85), clearly a highly unusual accomplishment (Ch'en Mi, *Fu-chai hsien-sheng Lung-t'u Ch'en kung wen-chi*, 21/9a–12b).

48. To cite one example of the last, Chao Shu-ch'u (CHAJB; 1082–1106), who as a fourth-generation descendent of Wei-wang was a *t'an-wen* clansman, received a name and the office of *yu-pan tien-chih* in 1086. This was a signal honor for one of his status and probably occurred because of the high positions of his grandfather (the Prince of Ho-nan-tung) and father (a defense commissioner), but even so it is significant that he was not given a Southern Rank office (CWTC, 14/8a–b).

49. SHY:TH, 4/32b–33a. Wang Sheng-to ("Sung-ch'ao tsung-shih chih-tu k'ao," p. 184) presents these provisions lucidly. For the hierarchy of Southern Rank posts, see Chapter 3, note 42, to this book.

50. The *yin* privilege, which in later periods was the most common route into the bureaucracy for clansmen, was little used. I have found only one reference (from 1083) to non-mourning clansmen's use of *yin*, and it merely stipulated the allowances that such clansmen would receive (SHY:TH, 5/4a).

51. Wang Sheng-to, "Sung-ch'ao tsung-shih chih-tu k'ao," p. 185.

52. Wang An-li, *Wang Wei-kung chi*, 7/15a–16a. As a fourth-generation descendent of T'ai-tsu, Chung-mou was actually a mourning (*ssu-ma*) kinsman. But as we noted above, provisions were made for them to convert their Southern Rank office to *wai-kuan* offices.

53. SHY:CK, 20/6b.

54. See SHY:TH, 4/33b, for the 1069 memorial; and ibid., 4/20b, and SHY:CK, 20/6a, for the 1070 edict.

55. SHY:TH, 4/18b.

56. For examples of land grants, see ibid., 24b–25a, 27b, 5/1a, 1a–b, 1b. Most of these involved land in the Fang-lin Park, where, as noted in Chapter 3, the North Annex had been constructed in 1064. The cases of rentals date to 1077, when a *t'an-wen* clansman was allowed to live with his parents in a rented residence, and to 1081, when a mourning-degree clansman was permitted to rent a house outside the residential complex because his quarters had become too cramped (ibid., 30a, 5/2b).

57. Ibid., 24b.

58. Ibid., 31a.

59. Ibid., 5/2b.

60. Ibid., 5/3a.

61. SS, 246: 8720–1; Fan Tsu-yü, *Fan t'ai-shih chi*, 53/1a–3b.

62. SHY:TH, 5/8a–b.

63. Ibid., 5a.

64. Ibid., 7a.

65. Ibid., 7a–b.

66. Ibid., 8b–9a.

67. Ibid., 10a.

68. Ibid., 4/33b–34a.

69. This provision was not in the 1029 regulations and may have been a response to criticisms of Pao Cheng (998–1061) about the husband of a clanswoman who had acquired office through purchase (Chao Ju-yü, *Sung ming-ch'en tsou-i*, 33/10b–11a.

70. A note in the *Sung History* adds that a further category of criminal (*hsing-t'u jen*) was added later.

71. SS, 115: 2739.

72. HCP, 409/4b.

73. SHY:TH, 5/7b. The Great Office memorial successfully proposing this uses the term *tsung-shih*, imperial clan (members), without specifying whether this meant only mourning kin or something more than that. A memorial from 1098 concerning divorce, cited below in the text, speaks of clan members (*tsung-shih*) and non-mourning kin (*fei t'an-wen*), which suggests that in this period, at least, *tsung-shih* referred at most to mourning and *t'an-wen* kin.

74. SS, 115: 2739.

75. SHY:CK, 20/19b; SHY:TH, 5/8a–b.

76. SS, 115: 2739.

77. Ibid., p. 2740.

78. SHY:TH, 4/23b–24a; HCP, 213: 5172–73.

79. CYTC, pt. 1, 1: 25; WHTK, 259: 2057.

80. Ebrey (*Inner Quarters*, p. 100), in her brief discussion of cash dowries, cites several examples of dowries involving thousands of strings of cash, and even a dog butcher's wife who had brought a dowry of several dozen strings.

81. A comparison of these positions to those described in Chapter 3 shows that the sole difference is the addition of the aide (*ch'eng*). The ranks were a feature of the reorganization of the bureaucracy that occurred in 1080, which classified all executory officials into nine ranks and further divided them into upper (*cheng*) and lower (*ts'ung*). The most authoritative treatment of the 1080 reforms is that of Umehara, *Sōdai kanryō seido kenkyū*, chap. 1; his article "Civil and Military Officials in the Sung: The *Chi-lu-kuan* System" provides a very useful treatment in English.

82. SHY:CK, 20/5a–b. See Appendix B for a discussion of the genealogical records overseen by the Court of the Imperial Clan. The description of them in this passage is at variance with other sources in several particulars, and it would appear that this text is corrupt.

83. SS, 117: 3887–8; SHY:CK, 20/17a–b.

84. SHY:CK 20/17a.

85. SS, 117: 3888.

86. Ibid.; SHY:CK, 20/7a–b.

87. SS, 117: 3888.

88. Ibid.

89. SS, 245: 8696.

90. SHY:CK, 20/16b–17a.

91. His biography can be found in SS, 245: 8695, but most of the information about his officeholding must be gleaned from the SHY.

92. SS, 245: 8712; SHY:CK, 20/19a, 9b.

93. SS, 245: 8703–4. This is also described in Chapter 3, pp. 58–59 above. In 1095, shortly before his death, Tsung-ching himself was given an extraordinary promotion and a princely title to commemorate his ten years of service as vice-administrator of the Great Office. In honoring him, ministers extolled his virtue, and Che-tsung praised him for the great strictness of his family governance (SHY:CK, 20/19b).

94. Although other sources have references to the Li Feng affair, the HCP is the pre-eminent source for it, with ten separate entries in chapters 259–66, which cover the first seven months of 1075. Several of these entries—notably 259: 6317–18, 260: 6336–38, and 263: 6446–48—quote from other histories, give extended historiographical comments by Li T'ao, and frequently contain differing versions of the same events. What follows is an attempt at a coherent narrative, drawing from the varied accounts that Li T'ao provides.

95. According to another account, Wang found that there had been no serious plot and that people had falsely accused Li Feng in hopes of a reward (HCP, 261: 6356).

96. HCP, 259: 6317–18.

97. HCP, 261: 6356.

98. HCP, 263: 6446. This is the only entry in which information is provided concerning Chang and Ch'in.

99. HCP, 262: 6403.

100. Ssu-ma Kuang, *Su-shui chi-wen*, cited by Li T'ao, HCP, 259: 6318.

101. These were Liu Chin, the prefect of Ying-chou (Hopei), and T'eng Fu, prefect of Ming-chou. T'eng had the additional burden of being Li Feng's brother-in-law, although he was not charged on the grounds of being related (HCP, 260: 6334, 263: 6446–48).

102. A special edict absolved him of any knowledge of Liu's "sorcery," and he was allowed to keep his privilege of attending audiences (HCP, 263: 6448).

103. This is from the extended quote from Ssu-ma's essay provided by Li T'ao (HCP, 259: 6318).

104. In addition to Ssu-ma's essay, this allegation is also mentioned in HCP, 260: 6336–38.

105. See Anthony Sariti's excellent biography of Lü Hui-ch'ing in Herbert Franke, ed., *Sung Biographies*, 2: 707–12.

106. HCP, 263: 6447–48.

107. Ibid., p. 6446. It is noteworthy that the epitaph for Shih-chü's father, Ts'ung-chih (1007–50), was written by Wang Kuei (1019–85), who was an active court official at this time. Although it was written long before 1075, it contains no mention of Shih-chü, listing only Ts'ung-chih's five sons who are found in the SS genealogy. Shih-chü had, of course, been expunged (HYC, 39: 531–12).

108. HCP, 263: 6446.

109. HCP, 261: 6356.

110. HCP, 266: 6521; SHY:CK, 20/18b.

111. HCP, 262: 6403.

112. SS, 245: 8700. The accuser was one Chao Tsung-o (BCAA; d. 1082), whose accusations elicited this response from his brother, Tsung-su (BCAD; d. 1082): "Despite our honesty, you have such a dearth of trust for your brothers as this!" Tsung-su himself paid for the missing valuables, but his brother, shamed, refused to take the money, so they gave it to Buddhist monks. Later the objects were found, but Tsung-o said nothing more.

113. SS, 244: 8677. Flower and calyx are a literary metaphor for older and younger brothers.

114. Ibid., pp. 8677–78.

115. Chao Ju-yü, *Sung ming-ch'en tsou-i*, 33/11b–12a.

116. Chu Yü, *P'ing-chou k'o-t'an* (SKCS ed.), 2/10a; cited by Li Yü-k'un, *Ch'üan-chou hai-wai chiao-t'ung shih lueh*, p. 83.

117. Chao Ju-yü, *Sung ming-ch'en tsou-i*, 33/12b–13a.

118. Ibid., 13a.

Chapter 5

1. SS, 19: 357–58. The issues raised in the discussion between the empress dowager and the grand councilors concerned the identity of the mothers of the various princes, their ages, their health (the oldest, the Prince of Shen, was disqualified on the grounds of eye disease), and the sterling character of Hui-tsung. In fact, his character may have been the real reason he was opposed by Chang Tun, one of the grand councilors, for by some accounts the young prince was known for his delight in collecting rare plants and animals, and his fondness for gambling and prostitutes. See Ting, *Compilation of Anecdotes of Sung Personalities*, p. 60.

2. Her regency ended in the seventh month of 1100 (SS, 19: 359).

3. This case is forcefully made by Chou Pao-chu and Ch'en Chen in *Chien-ming Sung-shih*, pp. 215–16. On the significance of the changes in the service system, see McKnight, *Village and Bureaucracy in Southern Sung China*, pp. 35–37.

4. SS, 472: 13722. See also McKnight, biography of T'ung Kuan, in Herbert Franke, ed., *Sung Biographies*, 3: 1090–97.

5. Ch'en Pang-chan, *Sung-shih chi-shih pen-mo* (Ming; Peking: Chung-hua shu-chü, 1977), 2: 482–83. This occurred in the ninth month of 1102.

6. See Smith, *Taxing Heaven's Storehouse*, pp. 195–96.

7. See Worthy, "Regional Control in the Southern Sung Salt Administration," pp. 104–5.

8. Scogin, "Poor Relief in Northern Sung China," p. 34. In fact, as Scogin shows, the charity clinics were but a part of a broader relief program undertaken by Ts'ai Ching, which also included poorhouses and paupers' cemeteries.

9. The literature on this is large, but for useful treatments in English, see Lee, *Government Education and Examinations*, pp. 64–65, 77–80, 126–27, 256–57; and Chaffee, *Thorny Gates of Learning*, pp. 77–84.

10. The SHY editors split the memorial and placed it in two section. SHY:CK, 20/34a–b, contains the proposals for the residential complexes and the relief of stranded clan members; SHY:TH, 5/15b–18a, contains the rest.

11. SHY:CK, 20/34a.

12. Ibid.

13. SHY:TH, 5/16a. Unlike the locked hall and Directorate examinations for clansmen described in Chapter 4, the *liang-shih* had no formal connections with the examination system. As described by Ts'ai Ching, who wanted to refurbish it, it was open to non-mourning kin of 25 *sui* and above who had to answer two questions, either on the meaning of the Classics or on law. For its comparability to the facilitated examinations, see ibid., 18a–b.

14. Ibid., 15b–18a.

15. SHY:CK, 20/34a.

16. Ibid.

17. Ibid., 34b.

18. SHY:TH, 5/18b–19a; SHY:CK, 20/34b–35a. The former version of the report and edict is considerably more detailed than the latter.

19. SHY:CK, 20/35a–b.

20. See SHY, *Ch'ung-ju* section 2: 14b–17b.

21. SHY:CK, 20/35b–36a.

22. Ibid., 36a–b.

23. Ibid., 37a–b.

24. That the K'ai-feng clan residences continued to house large numbers of clansmen is indicated by the fact that, as we will see below, some 3,000 clansmen were taken north from K'ai-feng by the Jurchen in 1126.

25. This rough measure does not count clan boys who died before receiving their names, and it assumes that clanswomen who married out offset the women marrying into the clan. Minor adjustments in these estimates, however, would not change the general picture of imperial munificence toward these clan members.

26. Ko Sheng-chung, *Tan-yang chi*, 1/2a–b.

27. See SHY:CK, 20/36a, for actions taken in 1112 and 1113 providing residences for widows and clanswomen without close living relatives, and allowances for them, including remarriage allowances.

28. Ibid., 35a.

29. Ibid., 37a.

30. Ibid.

31. In addition to the 1109 and 1112 actions discussed above, the 1120 edict, which provided clan statistics but also announced cutbacks, was issued just two months after Ts'ai was removed from office again.

32. SHY:CK, 20/20a–21a.

33. This connection between ritual and examinations was a long-standing one; the Ministry of Rites housed and ran the department examination in the examination system.

34. SHY:TH 5/14a.

35. Ibid., 16b–17a. Punishments for nonparticipation ranged from a fine of one month's allowance for the first violation, to confinement in isolation rooms (*tzu-sung chai*) for the third. If two youths failed to enter the school, the official and clan elder (*pen-kuan pen-wei tsun-chang*) in charge were to be fined half a month's stipend; if three or more did not enter, the fine was one month's stipend; and if ten or more did not, then the fine was two months' stipend.

36. SHY:TH, 5/21a; SHY:CK, 20/35a.

37. SHY:TH, 5/22b.

38. For more detail, see the treatments in Lee and Chaffee cited above in note 9 to this chapter. The last statement should be qualified slightly, for in fact triennial departmental examinations continued to be held throughout Hui-tsung's reign. But they were restricted to prefectural school graduates and university students, for prefectural examinations were not held, and in the off years smaller numbers of *chin-shih* were produced by upper hall graduation. See Appendix 2 in Chaffee, *Thorny Gates of Learning*, pp. 193–94.

39. See Chaffee, *Thorny Gates of Learning*, p. 106.

40. Ch'eng Chü, *Pei-shan hsiao-chi*, 33/17b. See Chapter 6 in this book for Tzu-chou's career in the Southern Sung.

41. SHY:TH, 5/25a–b.

42. Ibid., 25b.

43. Ibid., 27b.

44. Ibid., 16a.

45. SS, 247: 8743–45.

46. SS, 244: 8683–84.

47. SS, 452: 13294.

48. SS, 244: 8686–87 for Tzu-ch'eng; Sun Ti, *Hung-ch'ing chü-shih wen-chi*, 38/23b, for Shih-ts'an.

49. SS, 244: 8683.

50. Hu Ch'üan, *Hu Tan-an hsien-sheng wen-chi*, 24/10b.

51. SS, 246: 8725. These were remarkable accomplishments for one so near the center of power, and not at all in keeping with the earlier dynastic policy of keeping power out of the hands of any potential rivals to the throne. According to the *Sung History*, he owed his official position—although not his examination success—to the support of his powerful mother, Empress Wang.

52. SHY:TH, 5/17b.

53. SS, 247: 8741–42.

54. CWTC, 14/2a–b.

55. SHY:TH, 5/14b. The edict added a total of 62 extra-quota positions in K'ai-feng and five circuits, most of them involving state monopoly (*chien-tang*) positions, but also including some governance (*ch'in-min*) positions. Specifically, K'ai-feng fu received four monopoly positions, Ching-tung ten monopoly positions, Ching-hsi ten governance positions, Huai-nan two governance and fourteen monopoly positions, Liang-che two governance and fourteen monopoly positions, and Hu-pei two governance and four monopoly positions. See W. Lo, *Introduction to the Civil Service of Sung China*, p. 120, concerning the extra-quota positions.

56. SHY:TH, 5/26a–b, 29a.

57. Ibid., 23b. The senior positions mentioned were those with responsibility for the military or civil positions down to the level of magistrate and assistant magistrate.

58. Ibid., 29b, 31b.

59. SS, 247: 8742.

60. These were Hsiao-tsung (r. 1162–89) and Li-tsung (r. 1224–64); their successions are discussed at length in Chapter 8.

Chapter 6

1. See Fang Hao, *Sung shih*, 1: 138–46. For a good English-language account of these events, see Hok-lam Chan, *Legitimation in Imperial China*, pp. 56–98.

2. Fang Hao, *Sung shih*, 1: 146.

3. John W. Haeger, "1126–27," pp. 144–48.

4. According to one Southern Sung account cited by Ting Ch'uan-ching (*Compilation of Anecdotes of Sung Personalities*, pp. 77–78), the leading eunuchs in the palace were fearful at the prospect of Chao Huan becoming emperor, since he had been outspoken in his criticism of them and attempted to have his brother Chao K'ai (Hui-B) (Hui-tsung's third son) installed in his stead. However, they were thwarted by Ho Kuan (1065–1126), the commander of the imperial guards. On the decline of eunuchs under Ch'in-tsung, see Haeger, "1126–27," pp. 149–52.

5. See below concerning the inner palace entourage. As for the number of clan members taken into captivity, the most commonly used figure—and one that I have cited in past writings—is 3,000 (Moroto, "Sōdai no tai sōshitsu-saku ni tsuite," p. 626; Chan, *Legitimation in Imperial China*, p. 58). Fang Hao (*Sung shih*, pp. 141–45) uses the 3,000 figure but includes in it the entire inner palace group. By contrast, James T. C. Liu (*China Turning Inward*, p. 57) writes of "nine hundred imperial clansmen and their families," although I have been unable to find that figure in the reference he cites. In an entry for the tenth day of the third month of 1127, Li Hsin-ch'uan (HNYL, 3: 69) describes how Chin soldiers took the imperial clan from K'ai-feng and says that "in all, there were over 3,000 people"; presumably at least half of them were women. Since the inner court entourage was not taken from K'ai-feng until the first day of the fourth month of 1127, the figure of 3,000 certainly does not include them.

6. Ting, *Compilation of Anecdotes of Sung Personalities*, pp. 82–83, citing a story from the Southern Sung *Nan-tu lu* by Hsin Ch'i-chi.

7. SS, 24: 439–43.

8. This paragraph, which condenses a great deal of extremely complicated history, is based mainly on James T. C. Liu, "China's Imperial Power in Mid-dynastic Crises."

9. For Yueh Fei, see M. Yamauchi's biography in Franke, *Sung Biographies*, 3: 1266–71; Helmut Wilhelm, "From Myth to Myth"; and Teng Kuang-ming, *Yueh Fei chuan*. For Ch'in Kuei, see Yamauchi's biography in Franke, *Sung Biographies*, 1: 241–47.

10. In fact, in 1138 the Chin threatened to make Ch'in-tsung emperor of a puppet-state in southern Honan (Ting, *Compilation of Anecdotes of Sung Personalities*, p. 603).

11. SS, 246: 8729. Unfortunately, nothing is known of his subsequent fate. Chu Hsi (*Chu Tzu yü-lei*, 7: 2721–22) ascribes responsibility for the prince's fate to Sun Fu, saying that Wu Ko had proposed the scheme, but that Sun was unwilling to take the responsibility for undertaking it.

12. The terms imperial sons, grandsons, daughters, and granddaughters refer to those of Hui-tsung, not to those of his son Ch'in-tsung.

13. From "K'ai-feng fu chuang chien-cheng," in Ch'üeh An and Nai An, *Ching-k'ang pai-shih chien-cheng*, pp. 92–119.

14. SS, 246: 8726. It also notes that when Ch'in-tsung wrote a prayer to Heaven requesting a mandate, he entrusted it to I.

15. Ibid., 8723.

16. Ibid., 8728.

17. SS, 247: 8755.

18. SS, 452: 13293. He was posthumously promoted by Kao-tsung.

19. Fang Hao, *Sung shih*, 1: 145.

20. James T. C. Liu, *China Turning Inward*, pp. 57–58.

21. SS, 246: 8727. According to SS 248, Ts'ai was the husband of Hui-tsung's fourth daughter, and Liu of his eighth, although Liu's name is given as Wen-yen rather than Yen-wen.

22. Hsu Meng-hsin, *San ch'ao pei meng hui-pien*, 98/11a, from a lengthy quotation (ibid., 98/8b–16a) from Chao Tzu-ti's *Yen-yün lu*, 98/8b–16a. Unfortunately, most of Tzu-ti's account deals with matters other than the fate of the imperial clan.

23. SHY:CK, 20/37a.

24. Ibid. Theoretically, Ling-k'uang was the administrator and Shih-ts'ung the vice-administrator.

25. Ibid., 21a–b.

26. Ibid., 21b–22a. According to the memorial, some thirty clansmen had made the trip to Kuang-chou. It also cites a hundredfold increase in grain prices in Hang-chou.

27. Ibid., 37b.

28. Ibid., 21a. This occurred in the fourth month of 1129.

29. Ibid., 22b.

30. Ibid., 22a–b. Their allowances came to over 3,000 strings of cash and 2,000 *shih* of rice per month, and the local resources they had been given were insufficient. The emperor directed the Kuang-tung fiscal intendant to help.

31. Ibid., 22b–23a. It also adds that the Southern Capital clan office was established in Ch'üan-chou, the Great Office was in Kuang-chou, and an office had also been established in the temporary capital.

32. Ibid., 37a–b.

33. SS, 456: 13410. So moved was the poet Tseng Ts'ao by the story that he wrote a poetic rhapsody (*fu*) about it. I have been unable to locate Po-shen and his father in the *Sung History* genealogy, and so have listed him in Appendix 1 as AYYYYYY.

34. SHY:CK, 20/37b–38a. HNYL, 30: 590, also has figures very close to these: 340-odd men and women for the Southern clan, 180 for the Western clan.

35. CYTC, pt. 1, 1: 26. Li provides figures only for the clan members in each branch: 349 for the Southern branch; 179 for the Western branch. Since the sum of the Southern clan members given in the SHY is 339, the 349 is most likely an arithmetical error. Writing a century later, Ma Tuan-lin (1254–1325; WHTK, 259: 2057) repeats Li's numbers for both clan members at the two branches and the amount of support given each center in 1131.

36. I have not found a precise date for the Western branch's move to Fu-chou, but by the sixth month of 1132 it had been made and the leaders of the two branches were proposing annual meetings for the discussion of mutual problems and the coordination of policy (SHY:CK, 20/33a).

37. On the Mu-ch'in Residence, see SHY:CK, 20/23b and 23b–24a. The issue of a residence for the Southern Rank clansmen was in fact contentious, for the clansmen objected to it while it was under construction and attempted, unsuccessfully, to obtain the buildings for the T'ung-wen Hall, which was also being built.

38. CYTC, pt. 1, 1: 25–26. In 1171, there were discussions about creating another center on the lines of the Ch'üan-chou and Fu-chou in Ssu-ch'uan, but nothing ever came of it.

39. SS, 247: 8755. Concerning the long-lived Li Ch'iung, who rebelled after the death of his patron, Tsung Tse (1059–1128), see Huang K'uan-chung, "Li Ch'iung ping-pien yü Nan-Sung ch'u-ch'i ti cheng-chü," p. 69.

40. SS, 247: 8745.

41. Ibid., 8752–53.

42. SS, 452: 13292. I have been unable to find Shu-chiao in the *Sung History* genealogy, and so have coded him CYYYY.

43. SS, 447: 13183.

44. SS, 452: 13291–92. The Sung court did recognize Shih-lung's valor with posthumous promotions and the granting of titular office to two of his grandsons.

45. Teng Kuang-ming, *Yueh Fei chuan*, p. 87; Ch'ang Pi-te et al., *Sung-jen ch'uan-chi tzu-liao suo-yin*, 2: 832.

46. Sun Ti, *Hung-ch'ing chü-shih wen-chi*, 38/23b–24a.

47. SS, 447: 13184.

48. Teng Kuang-ming, *Yueh Fei chuan*, p. 87.

49. One further clansman's death with at least an indirect connection to Li Ch'eng was Chao Shih-ch'iu (BABAFF), who in 1135 was killed while serving as prefect of Chiang prefecture (Chiang-nan-hsi) by Li's former lieutenant, Ma Chin (SS, 452: 13293).

50. SS, 447: 13184. It is also recorded that Ling-ch'eng was posthumously promoted for his loyalty and the people of Huang-chou built a temple (*miao*) in his honor.

51. SS, 452: 13295. Yü-chih was also honored with posthumous promotions and a temple (*miao*) in his honor, proposed by none other than Chu Hsi.

52. Ibid., 13293–94. Shu-p'ing, too, has proved unfindable in the *Sung History* genealogy. I have coded him CZZZZ.

53. SS, 246: 8728. In fact the intermediary, a certain Ma Kuang, was not very trustworthy, for he never even returned to join the prince, stopping rather in Ta-ming fu.

54. Ibid. One report following his defeat placed him in captivity with Ch'in-tsung in the north.

55. One of his actions was to dispatch another clansman, Chao Ling-piao (AADBHC), to Chang's native prefecture of Lu-chou with orders to kill Chang's mother.

56. SS, 247: 8743–45. The prediction, of course, was to prove true in another generation when Kao-tsung adopted a clansman from the T'ai-tsu line.

57. Ibid., p. 8765. This is another unlocatable clansman. I have coded him CXXXX.

58. The account that follows is found in Shu-chin's biography in ibid., p. 8764; and Wang Ming-ch'ing, *Hui-chu san lu*, 2: 797–801.

59. Specifically, that Yeh Meng-te (1077–1148) had insufficiently rewarded him. Yeh at this time was serving as minister of revenue (SS, 445: 13134).

60. HNYL, 5: 116; SHY:TH, 5/32a.

61. SHY:TH, 5/32b.

62. See Chaffee, *Thorny Gates of Learning*, p. 96, on the problem of lost examination records and the measures taken to remedy it.

63. See SHY:CK, 20/23b.

64. Ibid., 38b–39a, dated fourth month, 1134.

65. SHY:TH, 6/4b, dated eighth month, 1132.

66. SHY:CK, 20/10a–b, 10b.

67. Ibid., 10b–11a. In addition, in the ninth month of 1133, the assistant prefect in each prefecture was made responsible for collecting the pertinent records (ibid., 10/11a).

68. Ibid., 13a–14a.

69. SS, 25: 462–65; HNYL, ch. 32. For treatments of this coup, see John Haeger's biography of Miao Fu, in Franke, ed., *Sung Biographies*, 2: 787–90; and James T. C. Liu, "China's Imperial Power," pp. 23–27.

70. SS, 25: 462.

71. For the crucial role played by Chu, see James T. C. Liu, "China's Imperial Power," p. 23; and Y. Satake's biography of Chu in Franke, ed., *Sung Biographies*, 1: 295–97.

72. Hu Ch'üan, *Hu Tan-an hsien-sheng wen-chi*, 24/10b.

73. SS, 247: 8753.

74. Ibid., p. 8754.

75. The latter, which contain detailed accounts of the activities of each during the rebellion, are found in SS, 361: 11297–313 (Chang) and 362: 11319–24 (Lü).

76. SS, 247: 8753–4.

77. The biographical information that follows is drawn from Empress Meng's biography in SS, 243: 8632–38.

78. Chang Pang-ch'ang, installed by the Jurchen in K'ai-feng as a puppet sovereign, accorded Empress Meng great respect. He named her the Yuan-yu Empress (in reference to Che-tsung's Yuan-yu reign period), and in turn solicited her blessing for his short-lived regime (he never claimed to be emperor). Kao-tsung subsequently changed her title to the Lung-yu Empress (ibid., pp. 8634–35).

79. The go-between who arranged this was none other than Chao Shih-niao, whose role in quelling the Hang-chou coup was described above (ibid., p. 8635, 247: 8753).

80. This included personal service from the emperor, even though he had no relation to her by blood.

81. SS, 243: 8638; HNYL, 25: 506.

82. SS, 243: 8636; HNYL, 28: 566.

83. Chou Pi-ta, *Wen-chung chi*, 75/7a–b.

84. SS, 452: 13294; HNYL, 29: 577. The two received posthumous promotions for their valor, and the townspeople in Yung-feng erected a shrine to them.

85. The two "royal visages of the two emperors" (*erh-ti yü-jung*) were, with Empress Meng, key symbols of legitimacy that Kao-tsung's court was intent on protecting and the Chin were trying to seize. On the importance of imperial statues and portraits for the Sung emperors, see Ebrey, "Portrait Sculptures in Imperial Ancestral Rite."

86. SS, 247: 8755.

87. According to the HNYL (30: 603–4) account, the government granaries in Ch'ien-chou were empty even before the empress's party arrived. Then when her troops attempted to use the "sand money" (*sha-ch'ien*) with which they had been paid, the town merchants refused to accept it, which led to fighting. That in turn led to a militia of 300 being raised, and in the ensuing fighting much of the town burned down.

88. SS, 247: 8754–55. The HNYL makes no mention of the pardon or of Shih-ch'iung's role.

89. Sun Ti, *Hung-ch'ing chü-shih chi*, 38/22a–27b.

90. SS, 247: 8755.

91. Ibid., pp. 8741–42.

92. Ch'eng Chü, *Pei-shan hsiao-chi*, 33/17a–21a; SS, 247: 8746. On the subject of attendants (*shih-ts'ung*), see Li Hsin-ch'uan's note about the nineteen clansmen who achieved this rank (by ca. 1200 when he was writing) in CYTC, pt. 1, 1: 23; and Hucker, *Dictionary of Official Titles*, p. 431.

93. SS, 247: 8756. The enemy was the pacification commissioner of Ssu-ch'uan, Cheng Kang-chung (1088–1154), whose biography in SS, 370: 11512–14, also gives an account of Pu-ch'i's role.

94. Sun Ti, *Hung-ch'ing chü-shih wen-chi*, 38/22a–27b. His father-in-law was Wang I (1082–1153).

95. Liu K'o-chuang, *Hou-ts'un hsien-sheng ta-ch'üan chi*, 155/7b. This is from the epitaph of his great-grandson, Chao Hsi-ching (AAEBFAECAB).

96. SS, 247: 8757; Yeh Shih, *Shui-hsin wen-chi*, 21: 418–20 (from the epitaph for his son, Shan-hsi, BCABACAA).

97. SS, 244: 8683–84.

98. He was also given the exalted titles of junior preceptor and commander unequaled in honor.

99. SS, 247: 8754.

100. HNYL, 142: 2290; cited by Moroto, "Sōdai no tai sōshitsu-saku ni tsuite," p. 636.

101. HNYL, 142: 2290.

102. The ban would have been completely unenforceable for the clansmen scattered around the empire. It was conceivably enforceable for the clansmen in the clan centers at Fu-chou and Ch'üan-chou, but would have made little sense, since its intent was clearly to restrict the political influence of the clansmen among high-ranking officials. That leaves the Southern Rank clansmen in Lin-an, whom Shih-niao had gotten the court to define as all mourning and *t'an-wen* kinsmen (SS, 247: 8754), as the likely intended target of the restriction. But there is no reiteration of this ban in any subsequent memorial or edict.

103. HNYL, 152: 2456; SHY:TH, 6/17b.

104. Hu Ch'üan, *Hu Tan-an hsien-sheng wen-chi*, 24/12b.

Chapter 7

1. SHY:CK, 20/37a–b. See also Table 6.1 on p. 122.

2. See, e.g., SHY:TH 6/20a–b, for an attempt in 1150 to enforce time limits between instances of imperial grace bestowed on imperial clansmen, which distinguished between those from the distant circuits (Ssu-ch'uan, Kuang-tung, Kuang-hsi, Fu-chien, Hu-nan, and Hu-pei) and those nearer the capital.

3. The 1256 *chin-shih* are from one of two extant *chin-shih* lists for the Sung (the other being from 1148) and are taken from Hsu Nai-ch'ang, ed., *Sung Yuan k'o-chü san lu* (1923 ed.). Unfortunately, the 1148 list is of no help on this issue, for all of its imperial clansmen simply have the Jade Register (i.e., the imperial genealogy) listed as their place of residence. As indicated in Table 7.2, this was also the case for 28 of the 1256 clansmen.

4. That Fu-chien also hosted the Western and Southern clan establishments seems to have been only a minor factor for these clansmen. In each group, two of the eleven Fu-chien clansmen were from Ch'üan-chou and four were from Fu-chou, but most of them—especially those from Fu-chou—lived outside the metropolitan county and therefore could not have resided in the official clan residences.

5. In a book on the history of the Chao surname in Chinese history, Shen Ch'i-hsin (*Chung-hua hsing-shih t'ung-shu: Chao hsing*, pp. 126–38) has an intriguing chapter on the dispersion of the imperial clan in the Southern Sung. In it he distinguishes some 65 family shoots from the three branches of the imperial clan, according to the locale in which they settled. Because he makes clear neither his methodology nor his sources (except for citing some later genealogies), I have not included his findings in Table 7.2. Two of them are of interest, however. First, 20 (or 31 percent) of the 65 families were from Liang-che; and second, virtually all the Southern Sung circuits were represented, at least with one or two families.

6. SHY:TH, 6/5a.

7. Ibid., 12b–13a.

8. Ibid., 13b.

9. SHY:CK, 20/39b; SHY:TH, 6/8b; SS, 244: 8686–87.

10. SHY:TH, 6/12b–13a.

11. SHY:CK, 20/39b.

12. Ibid., 39a. This was from an 1132 memorial.

13. SHY:TH, 5/10a. See Chapter 4.

14. This follows CYTC, pt. 1, 1: 25. SHY:TH, 5/33b, and HNYL, 34: 661, both give this with some variants, but agree that the full allowances were restricted to wives of the mourning kin (alternatively identified as Nan-pan or *ssu-ma*—that is, the fourth degree of mourning) and partial allowances to wives of *t'an-wen* kin.

15. This occurred after a clansman died in Lin-an without assets (CYTC, pt. 1, 1: 25).

16. SHY:TH, 5/10a. The same phrase is used in a 1094 measure discussing clan allowances (ibid., 5/8b–9a).

17. See pp. 79–80. The per capita allowances in 1095 were 24 strings and two piculs per year.

18. See, e.g., SHY:TH, 6/30a for 1158; and 7/4b for 1165.

19. Ibid., 7/19b–20b.

20. Hung Mai, *Jung-chai san-pi*, 16/5a (p. 1270).

21. CYTC, pt. 2, 14: 534. See also Chaffee, "Marriage of Imperial Clanswomen," pp. 150–51, for examples of the use of this privilege by husbands of clanswomen with no mourning relationship to the emperor.

22. CYTC, pt. 1, 1: 25; WHTK, 259: 2057. Previously married clanswomen— presumably widowed and divorced—were to receive half these amounts.

23. Fang Ta-ts'ung, *T'ieh-an chi*, 26/7a. For a more comprehensive treatment of the official dowries, see Chaffee, "Marriage of Imperial Clanswomen," pp. 142–47.

24. CYTC, pt. 1, 6: 86.

25. The rules governing their attendance at court are spelled out in SHY:TH, 6/5b–6a.

26. SHY:CK, 20/21b–22a. See also p. 120 above.

27. SHY:TH, 6/16b–17a.

28. Ibid., 24b–25b.

29. SHY:CK, 20/23b, 23b–24a.

30. SHY:TH, 6/8b.

31. Ibid., 8b–9a.

32. Ibid., 9a. Kao-tsung responded that he had purposefully not gone through the Ministry of Revenue because he did not want to harm its fiscal balance.

33. For two examples from 1134 and 1165, see SHY:TH, 6/6a–b, 7/5a.

34. HCLAC, 6/4a–5b. The office was built on the site of what had been the Carriage Livery. In 1156 a ceremonial hall (*tien*) was added to the Office of the Jade Register.

35. From the map on government offices and military installations in Lin-an, appended to Umehara, *Chūgoku kinsei no toshi to bunka*.

36. SHY:CK, 20/27b–28a.

37. CYTC, pt. 1, 12: 150.

38. YSC, 26: 512–18. The others were Chao Shih-ko (BCBBDE; d. 1180), Chao Ling-ken (AADCBK; n.d.), and Chao Po-kuei (ABBACEAA; 1125–1202), who was most noteworthy for being Hsiao-tsung's brother.

39. Halperin, "Pieties and Responsibilities," pp. 251–55. All my information on the Hsing-sheng ssu is drawn from Halperin.

40. On Hsi-tao's relationship to Po-kuei, see KKC, 86: 1173.

41. See SS, 122: 2860–64, and 123: 2874–77, concerning these burials.

42. SHY:CK, 20/40b–41a; CYTC, pt. 1, 1: 26.

43. Ibid., 33a.

44. Ibid., 38b.

45. Halperin, "Pieties and Responsibilities," p. 250 *n*201. This apparently was the only site outside Lin-an at which the installation of imperial portraits was permitted by the Southern Sung court.

46. This is taken from an 1163 memorial cited in SHY:CK, 20/40b. For examples of individuals actually incarcerated in one of the Fu-chien clan offices, see the biography of Chao Ling-chin (AADBHF; d. 1156) in SS, 244: 8683–84, discussed in the preceding chapter, and CMC (the Sung collection of legal cases), 11: 398–99.

47. SHY:CK, 20/40a.

48. HNYL, 188: 3151. The same terminology is used in the brief reference to this affair in Shih-k'an's biographical entry in the *Sung History* (SS, 245: 8715).

49. SHY:CK, 20/30a–31a. Although the SHY does not name the memorialist, the HNYL identified him as the right grand master of remonstrance, Ho P'u (1099 *chin-shih*).

50. Chu Hsi, *Chu Tzu ch'üan-chi* 89; cited by Li Yü-k'un, *Ch'üan-chou hai-wai chiao-t'ung shih lueh*, p. 90.

51. *Min-chung chin-shih lueh*, 9/2b–3a. The epitaph was written by K'o Sung-ying, a teacher at the Shao-wu commandary school.

52. SS, 245: 8715. The SS chronicle for Hsiao-tsung's reign gives all the credit for this idea—which was then adopted by the rest of the Southern Rank clansmen—to Shih-chien, who was also the associate administrator of the Great Office.

53. That the prohibition was directed at the clan *officials* rather than *clansmen* may imply that Shih-k'an was acting in this affair in his official capacity, which would also make more sense of Shih-hsueh's culpability. On the other hand, in describing how the ship ended up in Shih-k'an's hands even after being returned to Wang Ch'iung, the *Sung hui-yao* (SHY:CK, 20/30b) says that it "entered the house of the administrator of the Western Office," which suggests a more personal interest.

54. HNYL, 188: 3151.

55. For example, the family of the grand councilor Chao Ju-yü (BAAKFBDAA; 1140–96)—who is discussed at length in Chapter 8—settled in Yü-kan county (Jao-chou; Chiang-nan-tung) in the early Southern Sung, and Ju-yü's biography in the *Sung History* (SS, 392: 11989) reports that he lived there together with his kinsmen, some 3,000 people in all. Presumably that figure included servants as well as kinsmen.

56. Wei Ching, *Hou-lo chi*, 18/6a–b.

57. WCC, 74/9b–11a. The WCC notes as another mark of Po-lu's success that three of his five sons became officials.

58. Ibid., 7b–9a.

59. KKC, 104: 1468–70. See also the case of Chao Po-shu (AADFABFB; 1121–88), whose family settled in Hung-chou (Chiang-hsi) but who—through a succession of judicial posts—had no settled residence himself, and at the time of his death was living in a rented house in Hunan (Chao Shan-k'uo, *Ying-chai tsa-chu*, 4/9b–11b).

60. YSC, 26: 517.

61. Hu Hung, *Wu-feng chi*, 3/41a–42b.

62. Ch'en Mi, *Fu-chai hsien-sheng Ch'en kung wen-chi*, 21/9a–12b.

63. KKC, 102: 1436–39.

64. Sun Ti, *Hung-ch'ing chü-shih wen-chi*, 38/22a–23a.

65. Yang Hsing-tsung, in Shang-yü Lo shih, ed., *Chiang-su chin-shih chih*, 13/16a–18a.

66. Sun Ying-shih, *Chu-hu chi*, 11/1b–2a.

67. Ch'eng Chü, *Pei-shan hsiao-chi*, 33/19b.

68. CCC, 122/4a–6b; WCC, 71/12b–14b.

69. The existence of family tombs in a locality was one of the ways in which examination candidates established their residence there.

70. It is, of course, possible that common burial sites were employed for the clan members in the Fu-chou and Ch'üan-chou residential complexes, but I have found no indication of such a practice.

71. Examples of different grave sites in the same county are: Kung-heng (CDC-FIDB; 1138–96), Kung-wu (CEFCBCB; 1136–1203), and Yen-wu (CCCCEBAA; 1137–1201) for Chi-chou; Shan-tai (BCBPAAAC; 1138–88) and Shih-hsin (AADE-AAEAC; 1148–99) for Ming-chou; Po-chih (AADEGABA; 1103–67) and Po-huai (AABDEFBA; 1120–77) for T'ai-chou; and Shih-i (AADDEFBEA; 1149–1217) and Hsi-i (AAXXXXXXXX—i.e., a descendent of T'ai-tsu's oldest son who is not included in the *Sung History* genealogy) for Su-chou. The exception occurred in Hu-chou, where Yen-t'an (CEFCBDBB; 1155–1218) was buried at the same site as Shih-yü (AADFFDBCA; fl. 1218), who is identified only as the administrative supervisor for Chen-chou, Huai-nan-tung (YSC, 23: 448). But since Yen-t'an's epitaph offers no reasons, and we have no independent information about Shih-yü, it is impossible to say why this was done.

72. Hymes, *Statesmen and Gentlemen*, chap. 3; and Hymes, "Marriage, Descent Groups and the Localist Strategy in Sung and Yuan Fu-chou." Hymes's thesis, which was first developed in his 1979 dissertation, is also reflected in Robert M. Hartwell, "Demographic, Political, and Social Transformations of China, 750–1550," *Harvard Journal of Asiatic Studies* 42 (1982): 365–442.

73. Bossler, *Powerful Relations.*

74. Yuan Hsieh, *Hsieh-chai chi,* 18: 306, 308.

75. YSC, 2: 418–20.

76. WCC, 75/6a–8b.

77. Since interregional marriages were likely to involve more prominent in-laws, these figures probably understate the percentages of local marriages, for I have only counted those cases in which the residency of the in-laws can be determined, a small proportion of the total.

78. In the epitaphs these individuals are simply named without any additional designation. Given the high quality of most of the epitaphs and their attention to the details of official status for the other in-laws, I believe it reasonable to assume that they were not officials.

79. SHY:CK, 20/38b.

80. SHY:CJ, 1/7a–b.

81. Ibid., 1/9b.

82. CCC, 119/36a.

83. This point is very well developed by Linda Walton in "The Institutional Context of Neo-Confucianism," pp. 464–68.

84. SHY:CJ, 1/11a–b.

85. Ibid., 13a.

86. YSC, 26: 516.

87. SHY:CJ, 1/4b; CYTC, pt. 2, 13: 505–6; HCLAC, 11/27a–32a.

88. SHY:CJ, 1/4b.

89. Ibid., 8a–b. Other provisions included setting daily food and drink allowances at the same amounts found in prefectural schools and mandating the establishment of school and dormitory rules.

90. Ibid., 10b.

91. HCLAC, 11/1a.

92. CYTC, pt. 2, 13: 505–6.

93. YSC, 26: 516.

94. SHY:CJ, 1/14a–b. Implicit in the emperor's rejection was an assumption that the clan schools would be subsumed by the University, a point made explicitly by the response of the Ministry and Directorate.

95. KKC, 86: 1172.

96. SHY:CJ, 1/15a.

97. SHY:CK, 20/39b; SHY:TH, 6/8b.

98. Chao Shan-k'uo, *Ying-chai tsa-chu,* 4/9b. His examination ranking is taken from the extant 1148 examination list (Hsu Nai-ch'ang, ed., *Sung Yuan k'o-chü san lu*).

99. SHY:TH, 6/26a–b.

100. KKC, 86: 1169. Lo Chün, *Pao-ch'ing Ssu-ming chih*, 2/4a, confirms a renovation of the Ming-chou prefectural school in 1170, although it provides no further details.

101. The literature on Southern Sung academies is huge, but Linda Walton's *Academies and Society in Southern Sung China* provides the best treatment of them.

102. Wei Liao-weng, *Ch'ung-chiao Ho-shan hsien-sheng ta-ch'ü-chi*, 73/15a.

103. WCC, 60/2b–4a. Reference to the academy and its unusual mission can also be found in the Ming geography, *Ta Ming i-t'ung chih* (1461 ed.), 57/6a, which is where I first learned of it.

104. KCC, 86: 1175.

105. KKC, 102: 1423. Shih-lung, who was already reading and discussing the *Spring and Autumn Annals*, could read a thousand characters a day, wrote in complete paragraphs, and, while studying with Shih Hao's sons, worked on poetical composition.

106. HTHSTCC, 152/4a.

107. CCC, 122/4b.

108. See Kracke, *Civil Service in Early Sung China*, pp. 70–72, 95–96; and Chaffee, *Thorny Gates of Learning*, pp. 22–24.

109. See, e.g., KKC, 103: 1451–42, about a special examination for clansmen in 1128; Lu Tseng-hsiang, *Pa-ch'iung chin-shih pu cheng*, 114/20a, about another in 1133; and CWKWC, 92/26b, for yet another.

110. SHY:HC, 18/21a–b.

111. Ibid., 21b–22a (from 1162).

112. It is worth noting that the section of the *Sung hui-yao* dealing with the measurement examinations (ibid., 21a–26a) is placed at the end of the chapter on the military examinations.

113. There were two deviations from this pattern in 1163: the top-ranked individual, one Chao Yen-huan, was given a regular *chin-shih* degree and accordingly civil official status; seven other individuals were given the title *ch'eng-hsin lang*, which was slightly lower than *ch'eng-chieh lang* (ibid., 22b–23a).

114. The figures for the other three examinations come from ibid., 8/10b–13a.

115. Ibid., 18/24a–b.

116. Ibid., 22b.

117. Ibid., 23a–b. According to its placement in the *Sung hui-yao*, the conferral of degrees occurred on 1166/2/17. However, I believe that this entry has been misplaced and should be dated 1163. The report of over 700 examinees with only 30 percent passing is dated 1163/22/11. The follow-up report of 216 degrees being given has no mention of the 30 percent passing rate, but in fact 30 percent of 700 is 210. Moreover, it is simply dated 2/11, but its placement follows another entry for 1166. Finally,

as I argue below, such largesse makes more sense at the outset of Hsiao-tsung's reign rather than four years into it.

118. Ibid., 22b.

119. Hung Mai, *Jung-chai san-pi*, 7; cited in Wang Sheng-to, "Sung-ch'ao tsung-shih chih-tu," p. 183.

120. SHY:TH, 6/12a.

121. This point is unclear in Chang Hsi-ch'ing's study, "Sung-tai tsung-shih ying-chü chih-tu shu lun," but in fact the point is self-evident, since the *t'an-wen* relationship applied only to a single generation of clansmen.

122. See SHY:HC, 16/11a–b.

123. SHY:TH, 6/18a–b.

124. I am much indebted to Chang Hsi-ch'ing, "Sung-tai tsung-shih ying-chü chih-tu shu lun," pp. 2–7, which does a masterful job of making sense of these often confusing categories. Concerning the *ch'ü-ying* examination, I would differ with him only in his assumption that this was limited to *t'an-wen* clansmen, for even the sources he cites do not bear this out.

125. SHY:HC, 16/11a–b.

126. CSTP, 1/15b–16a. The significance of this was primarily social, for Yen-yü's biographer reports that by mixing clansmen and commoners together at the examinations, many became friendly and established long-lasting ties.

127. See SHY:TH, 6/18a, for the edict permitting him to participate; and KKC, 102: 1436, for the account in his epitaph.

128. SHY:TH, 6/23a.

129. Ibid., 18a–b.

130. CYTC, pt. 1, 13: 179–80.

131. See Chaffee, *Thorny Gates of Learning*, pp. 35–36, 106.

132. CYTC, pt. 1, 13: 179–80.

133. Hsu Nai-ch'ang, *Sung Yuan k'o-chü san lu*. Following a practice begun in 1124 of keeping clansmen out of the fifth class—a class which that year included Chu Hsi—four were placed in the third class and the remaining twelve in the fourth. See CYTC, pt. 1, 1: 13, for their exclusion from the fifth class.

134. Chang Hao, *Yün-ku tsa-chi*, 3; cited by Yeh Te-hui, *Sung Chao Chung-ting Chou-wang pieh-lu*, 6/1b–2a.

135. CYTC, pt. 2, 14: 528. CYTC also includes an entry of 308 in the military executory category for husbands of clanswomen.

136. Among the Southern Sung clansmen listed in the *Hsien-yuan lei-p'u*, 73 (72 percent) of the 101 clansmen born in the years 1110–39 and 29 (94 percent) of the 33 clansmen born in 1140–79 are listed as military officials. This last figure probably overstates the representation of military officials, for many clansmen held military rank through exercise of the *yin* privilege before getting civil office through the

examinations, but because they were still young men when this version of the HYLP was compiled, that would not have been reflected in their entries.

137. Chang Hsi-ch'ing ("Sung-tai tsung-shih ying-chü chih-tu shu lun," pp. 9–10) estimates that over ten thousand clansmen passed one form of examination or another, thereby gaining official rank: 2,700 as *chin-shih*, the others as *ch'ü-ying* or graduates of the measurement examination.

138. Richard L. Davis, *Court and Family in Sung China*. By my own rough count of the genealogy list Davis provides in his Appendix 4, some 237 members held office during the Sung, a remarkable record for a single kin group but not comparable to the imperial clan.

139. Chu Hsi, *Chu-tzu yü-lei*, III: 2720.

Chapter 8

1. HNYL, 15: 310–11. Wang Ming-ch'ing, *Hui-chu san lu*, 1: 874–75.

2. HNYL, 45: 817–18.

3. HNYL, 15: 310; SS, 33: 615–16.

4. SS, 244: 8686–87.

5. Wang Ming-ch'ing, *Hui-chu san lu*, 1: 874. This story can also be found in Ting, *Compilation of Anecdotes of Sung Personalities*, pp. 94–95, citing Hsieh Wei-hsin, *Ku-chin Ho-pi shih-lei pei-yao*.

6. SS, 33: 616.

7. According to Chang Tuan-i's *Kuei-erh chi*, 1st chuan, after Kao-tsung gave both Shen and Chü personal copies of a work by the famous calligrapher Wang Hsi-chih (ca. 303–ca. 361) with instructions to copy it 500 times, Shen impressed him by copying it 700 times. I am indebted to Julia Murray for this information and the citation.

8. Chou Mi, *Ch'i-tung yeh-yü* (Peking: Chung-hua shu-chü, 1983), II: 201; cited in Ting, *Compilation of Anecdotes of Sung Personalities*, p. 96.

9. SS, 246: 8731.

10. Herbert Franke, "The Chin Dynasty," pp. 239–45.

11. Davis, *Court and Family in Sung China*, 56–57.

12. SHY:CK, 20/4a, 31a, 40b. See also the account in Chapter 7 of this book of Hsiao-tsung's praise for Chao Shih-k'an—the disgraced administrator of the Western Office—and his brother Shih-chien for offering to give back half their imperial rewards.

13. CYTC, pt. 1, 12: 151.

14. Yeh Te-hui, *Sung Chung-ting Chao Chou-wang pieh-lu*, 6/1b–2a.

15. CYTH, pt. 1, 13: 171–72.

16. SS, 246: 8731.

17. CYTC, pt. 1, 6: 86.

18. *Sung hui-yao chi-kao pu-pien*, p. 15 (12117a–18a).

19. The information about this action comes entirely from the epitaphs of clansmen recommended. The precise date is given in Han Yüan-chi, *Nan-chien chia-i kao*, 21: 427, and the details on who was to submit recommendations is from KKC, 104: 1469. SHY:TH, 7/4a, contains an edict dated the seventeenth day of the second month of 1164 ordering Chao Ling-ken (AADCBK; n.d.), the administrator of the Great Office, and Chao Tzu-hsiao (AADEHAF; 1102–67), the prefect of Mingchou, to recommend two clansmen-officials each. Although Tzu-hsiao was a highly valued and trusted official (see his epitaph in Hu Ch'üan, *Hu Tan-an hsien-sheng wenchi*, 24/9a–18b), the choice of just him and Ling-ken to make recommendations seems suspicious. I would suggest that, in fact, the edict asked for recommendations from a large number of ministers and that it was mutilated at some point in its transmission.

20. Lou begins the epitaph by describing the very favorable report that he had received on Shih-hsin and his family from the go-between prior to the marriage (KKC 104: 1468).

21. KKC, 104: 1469–70.

22. CCC, 119/37a–38b. The funeral essay (*chi-wen*) was supposed to have been written by Shih-hsin's recommender, Hsiao Sui, who was representing at the funeral the seven 1148 *chin-shih* (Shih-hsin among them) then serving at court. Sui, however, asked Shih-hsin to write the essay that proceeded to cause him trouble.

23. Han Yüan-chi, *Nan-chien chia-i kao*, 21: 428.

24. Hu Ch'üan, *Hu Tan-an hsien-sheng wen-chi*, 24/12b. Tzu-hsiao stepped on many toes during his career as an official, such as the prefect at his first post, with whom he had disagreements; a fellow clansman serving as prefect of Ming-chou, whom he impeached for tyrannical governance; wealthy families in Lin-an who had made a practice of forcing their indentured maids into concubinage; and powerful families in Ming-chou that had been conniving with coastal pirates (ibid., 24/9a–18b).

25. YSC, 26: 516. Pu-hsi's biography in the *Sung History* (SS, 247: 8757–60) is similar in its judgment.

26. SS, 247: 8762–63. Shan-yü was also among those recommended when the emperor again solicited recommendations for outstanding clansmen-officials. Shanyü was a prolific writer on both the Classics and history, and his classical scholarship was described by Hsiao-tsung at the time as outstanding even in the "forest of scholars" (KKC, 102: 1426).

27. Lu Yu, *Wei-nan chi*, 34: 304. Yen-chen's father had played an earlier role in the story. Prior to Yen-chen's taking the Fu-chou post, his father said to him that he would have responsibility over the lives and deaths of prisoners and that he should

not avoid it. Lu Yu further tells us that when Yen-chen was frustrated at being un-able to improve conditions in the prison, he lamented thus failing his father.

28. Wei Liao-weng, *Ho-shan hsien-sheng ta-ch'üan-chi*, 73/15b; Huang Tsung-hsi, *Sung Yuan hsüeh-an*, 61: 1971–72. The last quotation is found only in the *Sung Yuan hsüeh-an*. Wei Liao-weng says only, "The prefect deputed Hsi-kuan to take charge, and the people feared him."

29. HTHSTCC, 48/1a–b. This occurred in Hai-yen county of Chia-hsing fu (Hu-chou). Keng-fu's response was to lock himself away and immerse himself in the *Lao Tzu* and the *I-ching*.

30. HCC, 17: 286.

31. See Chapter 7, p. 138.

32. SS, 247: 8763.

33. Han Yuan-chi, *Nan-chien chia-i kao*, 21: 428.

34. SSWC, 21: 418–20.

35. Moroto Tatsuo, "Sōdai no tai sōshitsu-saku ni tsuite," pp. 632–33. The major exception to this, which Moroto implicitly accepts, is service at court as adminis-trator of the Great Office, which was the case with a number of these clansmen. For Li's list, see CYTC, pt. 1, 1: 23.

36. SSWC, 21: 419, 418.

37. See, e.g., Richard Davis's description of Hsiao-tsung's "autocratic drive" in *Court and Family in Sung China*, pp. 71–73.

38. For a broader study of Chao Ju-yü, which includes an analysis of his thought and connections with Chu Hsi and the other Learning of the Way (*tao-hsueh*) thinkers, see my "Chao Ju-yü, Spurious Learning, and Southern Sung Political Culture," from which much of this section is drawn. For a short but useful biogra-phy of Ju-yü in German by Herbert Franke, see Franke, ed., *Sung Biographies*, 1: 59–63.

39. Ch'ang Pi-teh et al., *Sung-jen chuan-chi tzu-liao suo-yin*, 4: 3461.

40. Liu Kuang-tsu, "Sung ch'eng-hsiang Chung-ting Chao kung mu-chih-ming," in SCGMCM, 71: 6b.

41. Shan-ying's funerary inscription was written by Chu Hsi (CWKWC, 92/6b–10a).

42. Shan-ying's mother (née Ch'ao) and wife (Li) were both from eminent southern families: his mother was from the Hang-chou family of Ch'ao Pu-chih (1053–1110), and his wife was the seventh-generation descendent of the early Sung minister Li Fang (925–96), a native of neighboring Shang-jao county (Yeh Teh-hui, *Pieh-lu*, 2/2b–3a, 6a; CWKWC, 92/9b). All his daughters are said to have been mar-ried into distant families, suggesting that the family maintained interregional social ties (ibid., 92/9a).

43. CWKWC, 92/8a; SS, 392: 11989; Yeh Teh-hui, *Pieh-lu*, 8: 3b; SCHMCM, 71/15a.

44. See Yeh Teh-hui, *Pieh-lu*, 6: 1b–2a, quoting from Chang Hao, *Yün-ku tsa-chi*, ch. 3.

45. While serving as commander (*shuai*) of Ssu-ch'uan in 1187, he was accused of underreporting the casualties of a fire that had devastated Ch'eng-tu and of mismanaging dike repairs in the Ch'eng-tu area, though eventually the charges were found to be groundless (SCHMCM, 71/11b; CYTC, pt. 1, 8: 450–52, which is also found in Yeh Teh-hui, *Pieh-lu*, 3: 13b–16a).

46. SS, 392: 11983; KKC, 86: 1172.

47. Two prominent examples are the brothers Chao Ju-t'an (1183 *chin-shih*) and Ju-tang (1208 *chin-shih*)—Ju-yü's seventh cousins, who strongly supported him at the height of Han T'o-chou's purges (Yeh Te-hui, *Pieh-lu*, 1/30a–b; Schirokauer, "Neo-Confucians Under Attack," p. 187).

48. Most sources describe Kuang-tsung's problem simply as mental illness, although alcoholism appears to have played a major role (Yeh Te-hui, *Pieh-lu*, 7/22a).

49. SCHMCM, 71/9a.

50. SS, 36: 693–94. See Ting, *Compilation of Anecdotes of Sung Personalities*, pp. 101–3, for stories about the impatience of the middle-aged crown prince. All previous Sung emperors had become emperor in their thirties or younger, the oldest having been T'ai-tsung, whose accession came in his thirty-eighth year.

51. See Schirokauer, "Neo-Confucians Under Attack," p. 175.

52. SS, 36: 701.

53. Ibid., p. 705; 392: 11983; SCHMCM, 71/2a.

54. SCHMCM, 71/2a. See also Schirokauer, "Neo-Confucians Under Attack," p. 178.

55. This involved another delicate problem, for K'uo had to be elevated ahead of his older brothers, especially the eldest, the Prince of Wu-hsing. K'uo, however, had earlier been his father's choice, only to have it vetoed by Hsiao-tsung, and was the popular choice of the court. See the account by Yeh Shao-weng from the *Ssu-ch'ao wen-chien lu* (ca. 1225), as found in Ting, *Compilation of Anecdotes of Sung Personalities*, pp. 109–10.

56. SS, 37: 714; 392: 11985. See, too, the account in Liu's biography in ibid., 391: 11975.

57. According to some sources, Ju-yü was already assured of Kuo's support and approached Yen-yü in part to test his intentions. Later Yen-yü was to turn against Ju-yü because of disappointment at being given a provincial appointment rather than the capital promotion that he felt was his due (SS, 392: 11985, 11987; SCHMCM, 71/4a).

58. SS, 392: 11986.

59. Ibid., p. 11987.

60. Ibid.

61. Ibid. See note 57 to this chapter concerning Yen-yü's change of heart.

62. SS, 400: 12149–51; Yeh Te-hui, *Pieh-lu*, 1: 28a–b.

63. SS, 392: 11988.

64. Not to be confused with the Hunanese philosopher Hu Hung (1106–1162).

65. SS, 392: 11988–89.

66. Ibid., p. 11989.

67. The literature on this is large. See, in particular, Tillman, *Confucian Discourse and Chu Hsi's Ascendency*. Important earlier studies include Schirokauer, "Neo-Confucians Under Attack," pp. 163–98; James T. C. Liu, "How Did a Neo-Confucian School Become the State Orthodoxy?"; and Liu's last book, *China Turning Inward*.

68. SS, 392: 11988.

69. See Kinugawa Tsuyoshi, "'Kaishi yōhei' o megutte," for a treatment of the war; and Richard Davis, *Court and Family in Sung China*, pp. 84–92, for a description of the events leading up to Han's assassination. Both events are also discussed in John Chaffee, "The Historian as Critic," pp. 330–35.

70. For a thoughtful and detailed treatment of Shih Mi-yuan, see Davis, *Court and Family in Sung China*, pp. 81–117.

71. For their biographies, see SS, 413: 12393–97; and HCLAC, 67/16b–19b. For their memorial, see Yeh Te-hui, *Pieh-lu*, 1/30a–b. They were the grandsons of Chao Pu-hsi, one of the prominent clansmen-officials under Hsiao-tsung discussed above.

72. CWCKCC, 45/2b, 7b.

73. Ibid., 1b–2a.

74. Ibid., 44/6b–14b. This was undoubtedly the result of his enforced retirement following his father's fall. Ch'ung-hsien had placed first in the *chin-shih* examinations of 1181 and had quite a successful early career until that point. He also made noteworthy contributions in Chiang-hsi, including the expansion and endowment of an academy in Chiu-chiang.

75. Ibid., 43/31b.

76. SS, 247: 8767–68. The specific charge was that after the death of Wu Hsi's father, Wu T'ing, in 1194, Yen-yü had opposed a proposal that would have collapsed the positions of military commissioner of Li-hsi and Li-tung circuits, thereby countering the power of the Wu family.

77. YSC, 24: 474.

78. These included serving as prefect of Chi-chou (Chiang-hsi) and Hsiu-chou (Liang-che), chief superintendent of mines, overseer-general in charge of military

provisions for Huai-tung, and vice–fiscal intendant for Huai-nan, where he was able to solve a local currency crisis (ibid., 475–76).

79. SS, 247: 8748–49.

80. YSC, 24: 476.

81. SS, 247: 8749. Using an account from Liu Shih-chü's *Hsu Sung chung-hsing pien-nien Tzu-chih t'ung-chien*, which I have been unable to consult, Thomas Lee (*Government Education and Examinations*, p. 193) recounts the incident with a few differences in detail, namely, that Han's original gift had been one large pearl each to the four concubines, and that Shih-i borrowed enough money to buy ten more.

82. Hargett, "The Pleasure Parks of Kaifeng and Lin'an," p. 24.

83. SS, 247: 8749.

84. This followed his impeachment by the attendant censor, Teng Yu-lung (1172 *chin-shih*), whose report on conditions in the Chin empire following an embassy that he had led gave critical support to the war plans (ibid.).

85. That Yeh Shih was the author of the epitaph is doubly ironic, for as one of those labeled a proponent of "spurious learning" in 1195, he had suffered at the hands of Han T'o-chou, yet he supported the war effort in 1206, just when Shih-i was opposing it.

86. These inflationary pressures are thoroughly and graphically documented in Ch'i Hsia, *Sung-tai ching-chi shih*, 2: 1072–86.

87. CWCKCC, 44/27a–28a. After living for some time in retirement in a house that he had built for himself on the slopes of Mt. Lu (Chiang-hsi), Shih-t'ung went on to serve with distinction as vice-prefect of Fu-chou (Chiang-hsi) and Shao-wu chün (Fu-chien).

88. SS, 247: 8749; HTCTC, 159: 4299. Yü Wen-pao's *Ch'ui-chien lu* offers a somewhat different account of this. In its version, four university students were discovered to have purchased property in Lin-an and were planning to lease it. When Shih-i discovered this, he arrested them and seized their money, even though they had already been disciplined by the university authorities, and it was this that led to the protests (cited in Thomas Lee, *Government Education and Examinations*, p. 184).

89. Namely, Chao Yen-hsiao (CABBFHBA, 1148–1218), Chao Shen-fu (CABC-BCCBE, 1162–1222), Ju-yü's son Chao Ch'ung-tu (BAAKFBDAAE, 1175–1230), and Chao Hsi-kuan, who is discussed below.

90. Wei Liao-weng, *Ho-shan hsien-sheng ta-ch'üan-chi*, 73/16a–18b.

91. SS, 172: 12398–99.

92. Wei Liao-weng, *Ho-shan hsien-sheng ta-ch'üan-chi*, 73/17a–18b; SS, 172: 12399.

93. According to Charles Peterson ("Old Illusions and New Realities," p. 209), virtually every spring from 1217 to 1222 the Chin launched attacks against the Sung.

94. See Liu Hsing-chün, *Nan-Sung Ching-hu-nan lu ti pien-luan chih yen-chiu*, on the history of banditry and rebellion in Hunan through the Southern Sung.

95. For the rebellion, which began as a revolt by the Yao people of southern Hunan and Chiang-hsi, see ibid., pp. 68–70 (see also the maps on pp. 116–17). For Hsi-i's role, see CWCKCC, 45/4b–5b.

96. CKWC, 22/31b.

97. HTHSTCC, 152/3a.

98. YSC, 24: 476.

99. HCC, 17: 288–91.

100. SS, 233: 7738.

101. SS, 246: 8734–35. The leading grand councilor Shih Mi-yuan had earlier been Hsün's "moral mentor," or tutor.

102. SS, 41: 783.

103. Hsün's biography can be found in SS, 246: 8734, Hung's in 246: 8735–38. Although Hung's date of birth is not given, he had a son in 1124.

104. Ibid., p. 8735. See also the account of this given by Ting, *Compilation of Anecdotes of Sung Personalities*, pp. 114–15. Empress Yang was also upset by Hung's coldness to his wife, Lady Wu, who was a grand-niece of the empress and had been selected by her (see Davis, *Court and Family in Sung China*, p. 100).

105. SS, 41: 784.

106. SS, 246: 8736. Hung's biography provides an evocative account of Mi-yuan's recruitment of Cheng Ch'ing-chih. One evening, after having taken Kuei-che'ng's father to dinner at the Ching-ts'u Monastery, Mi-yuan and Ch'ing-chih climbed the pagoda alone. Describing his dissatisfaction with Hung, he proposed that Ch'ing-chih tutor Kuei-ch'eng and "guide him toward the good" and swore him to secrecy. Protesting that he was not deserving, Ch'ing-chih accepted. Ch'ing-chih later served as grand councilor under his old student, Li-tsung.

107. SS, 41: 784.

108. HTCTC, 162: 4422. The HTCTC account also asserts that on the day that Ning-tsung became ill, Shih Mi-yuan and Cheng Ch'ing-chih went to Kuei-ch'eng and told him that they planned to make him emperor, to which Kuei-ch'eng responded with silence.

109. Ibid., p. 4423; SS, 246: 8736–37; Ting, *Compilations of Anecdotes of Sung Personalities*, p. 115.

110. Davis (*Court and Family in Sung China*, pp. 101–2), it should be noted, concludes that Ning-tsung probably knew and approved of the edict naming Yün imperial son.

111. HTCTC, 162: 4423–24; SS, 41: 784. Those receiving promotions included Chu Hsi's disciple Fu Po-ch'eng (1143–1226), Yang Chien (1169 *chin-shih*), Ch'ai Chung-hsing (1190 *chin-shih*), Ch'eng Pi (1164–1242), Chu Chu (1187 *chin-shih*), Ko Hung (1184 *chin-shih*), Ch'iao Hsing-chien (1156–1241), Li Tsung-cheng (n.d.), Ch'en

Kuei-i (1183–1234), Wang Chi (1199 *chin-shih*), Chen Te-hsiu (n.d.), and Wei Liao-weng (1178–1237).

112. HTCTC, 122: 4424.

113. SS, 246: 12394.

114. SS, 41: 785, 246: 8737; HTCTC, 123: 4426–27.

115. See Tillman, *Confucian Discourse and Chu Hsi's Ascendency*, pp. 232–50; and Wilson, *Genealogy of the Way*, pp. 39–47.

116. See James T. C. Liu, "How Did a Neo-Confucian School Become the State Orthodoxy?," pp. 502–4.

117. For the Shihs, see Davis, *Court and Family in Sung China*, chaps. 4 and 5. For Cheng Ch'ing-chih, see his biography by Peter Bodman in Franke, *Sung Biographies*, pp. 156–63.

118. In addition to those discussed below, Chao Ju-t'an (BCBFAFAAA, d. 1237) served as acting minister of justice, Chao Ju-t'eng (BCBQCABBC, d. 1261) as minister of rites, and Chao Hsing-fu (CDBBAFAAA, 1176–1252) first as minister of works and then of personnel. Chao Hsi-ching (AAEBFAECAB, 1194–1251) also served with distinction in the capital, first as director of the Bureau of General Accounts and then as vice-director of the Court of National Granaries.

119. SS, 413: 12407–12.

120. Ibid., p. 12408.

121. Ibid., p. 12410. This is clearly a reference to Shih Mi-yuan.

122. Ibid.

123. Ibid., p. 12412. One of the memorials dealt with the threatening military situation in Ssu-ch'uan.

124. Ibid., p. 12404.

125. Ibid., p. 12406. This was near the end of his career.

126. Ibid., p. 12404.

127. Protests were also signed by 144 students from the imperial university, 67 from the military academy (*wu-hsueh*), and 94 from the Lin-an prefectural school.

128. SS, 413: 12406.

129. The other two were the censor Liu Han-pi and Hsu Yuan-chieh (1194–1245), an official at the Ministry of War. For a full treatment of this affair, see Davis, "Ventures Foiled and Opportunities Missed."

130. SS, 413: 12406.

131. Ibid., 12400–401. Shan-hsiang's biography lists some thirteen books that he wrote, ample proof of his scholarship (ibid., p. 12402).

132. Ibid., p. 12401.

133. SS, 477: 13849. For the Chao brothers, see ibid., pp. 13845–50.

134. SS, 413: 12401.

135. Chang Tuan-i, *Kui-erh chi*, 1: 8–9.

136. SS, 413: 12401–2. He also happened to be the assistant administrator of the Chin Bureau of Military Affairs.

137. Chang Tuan-i, *Kuei-erh chi*, 1: 8–9.

138. SS, 413: 12402. His biography, however, does agree with Chao I-fu's in placing him in Ch'ing-yuan fu in 1238.

139. HTHSTCC, 142/10a–14b. Liu K'o-chuang's epitaph is our sole source for I-fu, who has no biography in the *Sung History*.

140. The "six affairs" are described in the *Ch'un-ch'iu Kung-yang chu shu* (*Kung-yang* commentary to the *Spring and Autumn Annals*), 4 (2: 2216a): "If the government is not united, there will be a loss of occupation by the people, ostentation in the palace, palace women taking political advantage of their position, bribery, slander, and rumor."

141. HTHSTCC, 142/14b–15a.

142. His analysis is quoted in his epitaph: "The Mongols do not speak Chinese. The arrival of their envoy means that they have come to pay respects, not to discuss peace. How many are engaged in this talk [i.e., the peace proposals]? We must not sell the country to other people. I asked Yueh-lü Mieh-ssu of his intentions and observed his unyielding demeanor. This left me deeply troubled, and I sent him away" (ibid., 142/15a).

143. Ibid., 15b.

144. Ibid., 15a–b. See Davis, *Court and Family in Sung China*, pp. 136–39, on Shih Chai-chih and his relations with the emperor.

145. Specifically, I-fu had (1) argued against creating and superintending the enclosure of fields; (2) used his interpretations of the *li* and *chieh* hexagrams in the *I-ching* to attack ministers for corruption; and (3) blamed the great ministers for governmental abuses (HTHSTCC 142/15b–16a).

146. Ibid., 16a–17b. The conferral of these prestige titles is described in ibid., 10a, at the beginning of the epitaph.

147. SS, 214: 5618 and 5620, state that Chao I-fu served as associate administrator of the Bureau of Military Affairs from the seventh month of 1238 to the third month of 1241, and Moroto Tatsuo ("Sōdai no tai sōshitsu-saku ni tsuite," p. 632) cites this in claiming I-fu as a second example of a clansman reaching the level of councilor. Since Liu K'o-chuang, I-fu's friend as well as biographer, does not mention this, I can only conclude that it is mistaken, especially since according to Liu, I-fu served as chief recipient of edicts for the Bureau of Military Affairs at that time. This more modest post makes sense in the context of I-fu's career, since his ministerial positions all came later.

148. See Charles O. Hucker's still classic treatment of the function of remonstrance for Confucian scholar-officials in "Confucianism and the Chinese Censorial System," pp. 193–207.

149. HTHSTCC, 158/2a–5a. The text is ambiguous as to the date, except to say that Shih-huan's memorial followed a solar eclipse in the first month. According to the record of solar eclipses in the *Sung History* (SS, 52: 1086), that must have been in 1246.

150. SS, 46: 891.

151. HTHSTCC, 158/2a–5a. His various memorials criticized the improprieties of the imperial concubines, the mishandling of the deaths of Tu Fan, Liu Han-pi, and Hsu Yuan-chieh (discussed above), and the grand councilors for mixing up age rankings at court. Like I-fu, he was also admired by the emperor for his interpretations of the *I-ching*.

Chapter 9

1. CYTC, pt. 2, 14: 528.

2. Although not explicitly stated in any document that I have found, most late Southern Sung documents, including those cited below, assume that most clan families were supported by the official stipends of their members. Thus the "orphan's allowance" (*ku-i ch'ien-mi*) for those without near relations serving as officials provided the safety net for the clan.

3. Chu Hsi, *Chu-tzu yü-lei*, III: 2720.

4. SHY:TH, 7/19b–21b.

5. Ibid., 20b–21a.

6. Ibid., 19b–20b.

7. Ibid., 26a–27a. They were to check on all clan members in their localities and to get all clan youths under five *sui* generation names within six months.

8. Ibid., 30a–b. For the 1077 edict, see SS, 115: 2739. See Table 4.1, p. 82, for a tabular representation of the history of marriage legislation.

9. An editor of the *Sung hui-yao* has added the character *wu* ("without") before "register" (*chi*), which would change the meaning to "unregistered" clansmen and suggest that clansmen not registered in the imperial genealogies were more vulnerable to manipulation. It seems more likely, however, that clerks would have targeted the registered clansmen, whose privileges were not open to challenge.

10. McKnight, *Law and Order in Sung China*, p. 90, citing various references from the *Sung hui-yao*.

11. SHY, *hsing-fa* section, 2/147a; cited in McKnight, *Law and Order in Sung China*, pp. 74, 286.

12. Until the 1980s, when a full version of this work was discovered at the Shanghai Municipal Library, only a portion was available. An annotated, punctuated edition of the complete work was published as *Ming-kung shu-p'an Ch'ing-ming chi* in 1987. Brian McKnight and James T. C. Liu have prepared a translation of roughly half the judgments in the work under the title *Ch'ing-ming chi, the Sung Dynasty Work:*

A Collection of Enlightened Judgments. Bettine Birge has also discussed this work at length and made extensive use of its judgments relating to women and marriage in *Holding Her Own.*

13. CMC, ii: 398–99. This is translated in Liu and McKnight, *Ch'ing-ming chi,* chap. ii. I have been unable to find Chao Jo-lou in the SS genealogy. It is possible that he was removed from the imperial genealogy because of his crimes.

14. CMC, ii: 400–402.

15. Investigations must have been especially problematic for prefectural officials, since without the clan genealogy at their disposal—and there is no evidence that would suggest that copies of the genealogy were distributed—proving or disproving the clan status of individuals would have been difficult.

16. See the examples given in Chaffee, "Marriage of Sung Imperial Clanswomen," p. 158.

17. This account is from the 1809 genealogy, *Ta-kang Chao-shih tsung-p'u,* 1/5a–b, 7/1a–b, which was edited by Chao T'ing-chih. Although relatively late in date, the earliest of the several prefaces in this work is dated 1400.

18. This presumably honored his genealogical position (AAAACCI), since his line stemmed from the successively first-born son, grandson, and great-grandson of T'ai-tsu. In my research, I have found no Southern Sung individuals with a "higher" genealogical position than Tzu-ssu.

19. *Ta-kang Chao-shih tsung-p'u,* 7/10a–11b.

20. Chao I-ch'in, *Chao-shih chia sheng,* 1/27a–28b.

21. For example, Chao Yu-chieh (AADBFABGAXXXX; n.d.), who was serving elsewhere when P'u Shou-king massacred the Ch'üan-chou clan (*Chao-shi tsu-pu,* p, 11).

22. Chao-shih tsu-p'u pien-tsuan wei-yuan-hui, *Chao-shih tsu-p'u,* pp. 11–12.

23. CSTP, 1/89a–b.

24. Ibid., 89a.

25. Ibid., 89a–b.

26. Chao Ssu-lien, *Hsu-hsiu Shan-yin Hua-she Chao-shih tsung-p'u,* 1/1a–b. This title is unusual. "Auspicious origins" (*ch'ing yuan*) may well be a shorthand reference to two of the basic imperial genealogies maintained by the Office of the Jade Register: the *Tsung-fan ch'ing-hsi lu* (Records of the auspicious branches of the princely houses) and the *Hsien-yuan lei-p'u* (Classified genealogy of immortal origins). For the "Chaos of Chün-i," see the discussion below.

27. Ibid., ch. 1, "Li-shih chih lueh." Meng-i was known to his descendents as Wan-i.

28. The move made by Meng-i was a small one, for Hua-she was also in Chu-chi county. Chao Ling-ken's biography in the *Sung History* (SS 244: 8683) makes no mention of his family-related activities.

29. This is stated in Chao Yü-tz'u's preface.

30. Kung-hsien is the posthumous title given to Chao Shih-hsiung, and An-ting refers to Ling-ken, who at the end of his life was the Prince of An-ting.

31. For T'ai-tsu's "Great Instructions," see Chapter 2 above. The text of the "Great Instructions" can be found in CSTP, 1/12a.

32. The literature on Ch'üan-chou is large, but special notice should be taken of three recent treatments of it: Li Tung-hua, *Ch'üan-chou yü wo kuo chung-ku ti hai-shang chiao-t'ung*; Su Chi-lang, *T'ang Sung shih-tai Min-nan Ch'üan-chou shih ti lun kao*; and Clark, *Community, Trade, and Networks: Southern Fujian Province from the Third to the Thirteenth Century*.

33. See Chaffee, *Thorny Gates of Learning*, pp. 149–53 and Appendix 3.

34. Clark, *Community, Trade, and Networks*, p. 77.

35. See ibid., pp. 139 and 230 *n*71, and Appendix 2.

36. See pp. 144–45 above. For the memorial in question, see SHY:TH, 6/12b–13a.

37. See Clark, *Community, Trade, and Networks*, chap. 6.

38. NWTYCSTP, pp. 694–95. Ni Ssu, it is interesting to note, had been a prominent opponent of Chao Ju-yü.

39. Ibid. This is part of a group of documents drawn from the *Pei-ch'i Chao-shih tsu-p'u*, but the text on allowances cites its source as a Ch'üan-chou gazetteer.

40. For her epitaph, see HTHSTCC, 154/4b–5b.

41. For Shih-wu's biography, see SS 247: 8752–53.

42. NWTYCSTP, p. 578. The excavation is noteworthy for containing a land purchase deed (*shih-ti chuan*) for a plot of land to support the upkeep of her grave site. The purchase price was a ritually pleasing 99,999 strings of cash, which should not be taken literally, but the geographical features used to describe and thus iden-tify the land are quite believable.

43. For Ch'en Chün-ch'ing, see Ch'ang Pi-te et al., *Sung-jen chuan-chi tzu-liao suo-yin*, pp. 2601–2; and for Ch'en Tseng, see HTHSTCC, 165/12, as well as Ch'ang Pi-te et al., pp. 2510–11.

44. The two families also shared a marriage connection with a third family, the Niehs. Liu K'o-chuang (HTHSTCC, 154/4b–5b) notes that the Ch'en tie with the Niehs had been established with Ch'en Chün-ch'ing, and indeed his wife as well as the wife of his son Ch'en Shu (Tseng's father) were both Niehs. So, too, was the mother of Chao Ju-chieh.

45. NWTYCSTP, pp. 637–46. This list actually gives thirteen prefects, seven for Chang-chou and six for Ch'üan-chou. However, one of the latter is Chao Pi-yuan (BAAKFBDAAAA; 1214 *chin-shih*; d. 1249), who is said to have served as pre-fect during the Ch'un-hsi period (1174–89). Since NWTYCSTP acknowledges that only later (Ch'ing) gazetteers list him, and his lengthy *Sung History* biography—used in the account of his career in Chapter 8—does not mention service in Ch'üan-chou,

it seems safe to conclude that the Ch'ing sources were mistaken. Since Pi-yuan did serve with distinction as prefect of Fu-chou at the end of his career, that may be the source of the later error.

46. Clansmen first appear on the *chin-shih* lists in 1168 in Chang-chou, 1171 in Chien-ning fu, 1190 in Fu-chou, and 1196 in Hsing-hua (NWTYCSTP, pp. 647–77).

47. The literature on this topic is vast. For China's turn to the sea, see Lo Jung-pang's classic "The Emergence of China as a Seapower." China's role in the broader maritime trading system is admirably treated in Abu-Lughod, *Before European Hegemony*.

48. Yoshinobu Shiba, "Sung Foreign Trade," pp. 107–8.

49. Clark, *Community, Trade, and Networks*, p. 140.

50. Chen Te-hsiu, *Hsi-shan hsien-sheng Chen wen-chung kung ch'üan-chi*, 15/10b–16a. For a detailed treatment of this essay, with several extended quotations, see Clark, *Community, Trade, and Networks*, pp. 174–76.

51. Chen Te-hsiu, *Ch'üan-chi*, 15/12b–13a.

52. Ibid., 13a–14a.

53. Ibid., 15a–b.

54. Li Tung-hua, *Ch'üan-chou*, pp. 186–87; Clark, *Community, Trade, and Networks*, pp. 174–75. Neither author claims that the clan was the sole cause of Ch'üan-chou's decline; Clark also points to corruption and pirates.

55. So, "Financial Crisis and Local Economy."

56. Ibid., p. 123.

57. The figure of 60,000 strings is found both in CYTC, pt. 1, 1: 25–26; and in WHTK, 259: 2057.

58. SHY:CK, 20/30b.

59. *Sung hui-yao chi-kao pu-pien*, p. 8.

60. Green, "The Song Dynasty Shipwreck at Quanzhou"; Chieh Ch'in-mi and Ko Lin, "Ch'üan-chou Sung-tai ku-ch'uan."

61. Fu Tsung-wen, "Hou-chu ku-ch'uan."

62. Li Yü-k'un, *Ch'üan-chou hai-wai chiao-t'ung shih lueh*, p. 87. The ten were Ju-huo, ca. 1190–94; Ju-tang (BCBFAFAAB) and Liang-fu (CAADAAGBB), ca. 1205–7; Pu-hsi (BCBBDED) in 1213; Ch'ung-tu (BAAKFBDAAE), ca. 1217–19; Ju-k'ua (BCBPAAACD) in 1224–25; Yen-hou (CDCKGACA), ca. 1228–33; Hsi-mou and Shih-keng (AABDEFBFB) in 1247; and Meng-ch'uan in 1262. This is Li's list, for which he does not provide sources (the genealogical identifications are mine). I am skeptical of Ju-tang's service as superintendent, however, for it is mentioned in neither of his biographies (see SS, 413: 12397; and Ch'ien Yüeh-yu, *Hsien-ch'un Lin-an chih*, 67/18b–19b). The *Sung History* biography does mention an early posting at the Superintendency of Foreign Trade, but certainly not as the superintendent.

63. SHY:CK, 75/2a–b. Hugh Clark (*Community, Trade, and Networks*, p. 173) notes that it was one of five cases in a 28-year period (1186–1214) in which superintendents were dismissed for corruption. Pu-hsi was the only clansman in the group, however.

64. HTHSTCC, 169/12a.

65. CWCKCC, 43/33a–b. According to Li Yü-k'un (*Ch'üan-chou hai-wai chiao-t'ung shih lueh*, p. 87), the number of ships increased from 18 in the first year to 24 in the second and 36 in the third, but he does not cite his source.

66. Ling-chin also managed to upset some of the local scholars by granting permission to the city's Muslim community to build a mosque in front of the prefectural school, and indeed their complaints may have been a factor in his subsequent imprisonment by Ch'in. This information comes from Li Yü-k'un, *Ch'üan-chou hai-wai chiao-t'ung shih lueh*, pp. 87–88, citing the biography of Fu Tzu-te in Chu Hsi, *Chu-tzu ch'uan-chi*, 98/1. It is not mentioned in Ling-chin's biography in the *Sung History*.

67. Fu Chin-hsing, "Chao Ju-kua."

68. HCC, 17: 284.

69. See the English translation by Friedrich Hirth and W. W. Rockhill, *Chau Ju-kua*.

70. KKC, 86: 1172.

71. Li Yü-k'un, *Ch'üan-chou hai-wai chiao-tung shih lueh*, p. 89. Li's account, which does not cite sources, lists eleven different clansmen who participated in one or another of these sacrifices. NWTYCSTP (p. 716) provides photographs of some of the stone inscriptions on Chiu-jih Mountain detailing the participants, although that text refers only to ceremonies performed in the fourth and tenth months of 1188 and mentions three clansmen-officials, Chao Kung-chiung, the administrator of the Southern Office during the first ceremony, Chao Pu-t'i, who held the same post by the time of the later ceremony, and Chao Shan-shen, whose position is not identified.

72. Fu-chien Provincial Museum, ed., *Fu-chou Nan-Sung Huang Sheng mu* (1982). The text of Huang Sheng's epitaph and discussion of her, her husband, and their families can be found on pp. 82–83.

73. Ibid., pp. 81–82. Fu Chin-hsing ("Lueh-t'an Nan-wai-tsung tui Ch'üan-chou ti ying-hsiang," p. 43) notes that one silk bundle was even labeled "officially registered as gold thread spun and dyed by the imperial clan" (*tsung-cheng fang-jan chin-ssu kuan chi*). See also Angela Yu-yun Sheng, "Textile Use, Technology, and Change in Rural Textile Production in Song China," pp. 109–12.

74. This was half the allowance of 60,000 strings set in 1131, the amount provided by the circuit for much of the early Southern Sung, according to Chen Te-hsiu.

These figures do not include the official stipends paid clansmen-officials; undoubtedly a portion of that money found its way to Ch'üan-chou as well.

75. SS, 42: 817 and 820, record the death of two sons in 1239. CSTP, 1/69a, lists four sons of Li-tsung, one of whom was supposedly named "imperial son" before he died prematurely. I have found no verification of these sons in SS or any Sung sources, however.

76. SS, 46: 891–2.

77. See Davis, *Wind Against the Mountain*, pp. 28–29. Davis cites "credible informants" who asserted that Chao Ch'i's defects stemmed from his mother's unsuccessful attempt at an abortion.

78. SS, 46: 919.

79. Biographical accounts of Chia begin with his SS biography (474: 13779–87), although there and virtually everywhere else there are severe historiographical problems since he was almost from the outset considered a treasonous minister. These issues are discussed in Franke, "Chia Ssu-tao." The best recent treatment of Chia in English is Davis, *Wind Against the Mountain*, esp. pp. 42–49.

80. See SS, 474: 13780. Davis (*Wind Against the Mountain*, pp. 42–46) makes much of Chia's lifestyle, drawing heavily from contemporary anecdotal accounts about it.

81. Davis, *Wind Against the Mountain*, pp. 46–48; SS, 474: 13782–83.

82. Rossabi, *Khubilai Khan*, pp. 44–50, 77–78.

83. See ibid., pp. 82–87; and Davis, *Wind Against the Mountain*, pp. 49–58, for contrasting treatments of the siege of Hsiang-yang. For an analysis in depth of the military aspects of the siege, see Franke, "Siege and Defense of Towns in Medieval China."

84. Rossabi, *Khubilai Khan*, p. 87.

85. Ibid., pp. 87–90; Jay, *Change in Dynasties*, pp. 36–40.

86. The literature on Sung loyalism is large. For studies in English, special mention should be made of Frederick W. Mote's influential article, "Confucian Eremitism in the Yuan Period"; Wang Gungwu's "Feng Tao: An Essay on Confucian Loyalty"; and of the two recent books on the subject already cited in this chapter: Richard Davis's *Wind Against the Mountain*, and Jennifer Jay's *Change in Dynasties*.

87. SS, 451: 13266. Unfortunately I have found no other references to this tantalizing item, which demonstrates a sense of the imperial clan as a resource to be husbanded.

88. CSTP, 2/11b.

89. SS, 450: 13262. Meng-chin is also noteworthy for the biographer's description of him as "unrestrained" when young and of having chosen a military career from his youth.

90. SS, 454: 13356. NWTYCSTP, p. 544, also asserts that Chao Jo-tsu (CEE-ADCECAAX; 1235–76) died while defending Ch'ih-chou (Chiang-nan-tung) as vice-prefect in 1276. The problem with this is that the vice-prefect was a well-documented martyr, but SS, 450: 13259–60, identifies him as Chao Mao-fa (a non-clansman). See Davis's vivid description of Mao-fa's death in *Wind Against the Mountain*, pp. 76–77.

91. Fan was one of the more controversial figures of the late Southern Sung. His refusal to commit his troops at Hsiang-yang contributed to that city's fall in 1274. Subsequently pardoned for that act by Chia Ssu-tao, he was given command of the central Yangtze city of An-ch'ing (Huai-nan-hsi), which he then surrendered to the Yuan. He subsequently had considerable success in the service of the Yuan in getting other Sung commanders to surrender. See Davis, *Wind Against the Mountain*, pp. 52–54, 77.

92. SS, 451: 13266.

93. SS, 450: 13262.

94. SS, 454: 13341–2.

95. Ibid. Although Pi-hsiang is called Hsi-chi's nephew (*ts'ung-tzu*), this cannot be taken literally, for *pi* was the tenth-generation name character of the T'ai-tsung branch, whereas Hsi-chi was in the ninth generation of the T'ai-tsu branch. It is noteworthy that two distantly related clansmen formed such a close bond, suggesting the continued importance of clan identity.

96. Ibid., p. 13357.

97. The following account is taken from Ch'en Chi-chuang's biography (*hsing-chuang*) of Pi-hsiang in Chao Pi-hsiang, *Ch'iu-hsiao hsien-sheng fu-p'ou chi*, 6/2b–7a. See also Jay's treatment of him in *Change in Dynasties*.

98. Ch'en Chi-chuang, 6/3a.

99. Ibid., 4a–b.

100. Ibid., 4b–5a.

101. Ibid., 5a. According to Jay (*Change in Dynasties*, p. 191), Chao Pi-hsiang had offered his support to WenT'ien-hsiang's brother, Wen Pi, but soon thereafter left because of his family responsibilities.

102. Ch'en Chi-chuang, 6/5a–6a. The details about Wen T'ien-hsiang and Yai-shan are from Jay, *Change in Dynasties*.

103. Jay, *Change in Dynasties*, p. 222. See Li E and Ma Yueh-kuan, *Sung-shih chi-shih* (Wen-yuan ko edition), 85/10a (p. 1898) for Meng-fu's father, Yü-yin.

104. Rossabi, *Khubilai Khan*, pp. 166–68.

105. SS, 222: 6411. As Tzu-ch'eng's fifth-generation offspring, Meng-fu was at the outer limits of mourning obligation to his fellow descendents. Of course, Li-tsung was from a different branch of the clan altogether, although as an adopted son of Ning-tsung, he was ritually in the same branch.

106. Mote, "Confucian Eremitism in the Yuan Era," p. 286.

107. Jennifer Jay (*Change of Dynasties*, pp. 222–25) provides a perceptive account of Meng-fu's responses to his situation.

108. For example, Yü-fan (AABEABGCCC), Pi-chiang (BAACFCCACBC), Yü-fang (AABAACAAAAB), and Ssu-chu, whose biographies are found in NW-TYCSTP, pp. 333, 615, 689, and 616, respectively. Ssu-chu, a clansman from the Wei-wang (C) branch whom I have been unable to locate in the SS, provided service to Wen T'ien-hsiang when the latter was headquartered in Ch'ao-yang (Chang-chou), and for the rest of his life maintained a shrine to Wen and Chang Shih-chieh.

109. Wang Lien-mao, "P'u Shou-keng t'u-sha Nan-wai tsung-tzu k'ao," p. 82. Wang, drawing from the NWTYCSTP, cites six examples of clansmen who served as officials during the Yuan.

110. NWTYCSTP, p. 509. This information is understandably presented without editorial comment, for filial principles would have dictated against criticism of an ancestor in a genealogical biography.

111. See Yoshinobu Shiba's biography of P'u in Franke, ed., *Sung Biographies*, pp. 839–42, which has an excellent summary of the historiography prior to the 1970s. For an excellent revisionist article concerning P'u's service in Ch'üan-chou and surrender to the Mongols, see Su Chi-lang, *T'ang Sung shih-tai Min-nan Ch'üan-chou shih ti lun kao*, chap. 1. As to the massacre itself, Wang Lien-mao ("P'u Shou-keng t'u-sha Nan-wai tsung-tzu k'ao") does a masterful job of comparing and evaluating the various sources describing it.

112. According to SS, 47: 942, P'u had served as superintendent for thirty years, but Su Chi-lang (*T'ang Sung shih-tai Min-nan Ch'üan-chou shih ti lun kao*, pp. 4–12) argues persuasively that the period was only a year or so.

113. I am following Wang Lien-mao ("P'u Shou-keng t'u-sha Nan-wai tsung-tzu k'ao," pp. 75–80) on two points here: first, that the massacre occurred around the end of 1276 and not the seventh month of 1277, as some accounts (all of them Ming or Ch'ing) have suggested; and that the number of clan members killed was 3,000 (accounts range from 1,000 to several tens of thousands).

114. See ibid., p. 76, which provides the texts of five versions of the massacre.

115. NWTYCSTP, 50. He was also known as Sun Yu-fu, after his adopted father. Another anecdote relating tangentially to the massacre is given in NWTYC-STP, pp. 614–15, but since the earliest extant version of it is in an eighteenth-century Ch'üan-chou prefectural gazeteer, I have not included it in the main text. Briefly, it concerns Chao Pi-yeh (BXXXXXXXXXX), a minor official who at the time of P'u Shou-keng's surrender fled to the countryside, where he was captured by troops sent by T'ien Chen-tzu, although only after beheading seven of his attackers. He was brought back to Ch'üan-chou, where he had a tearful farewell from Chao

Chi-fu, the administrator of the Southern Office. At the time of the massacre, P'u had him bound and was preparing to kill him when a Yuan commander ordered him spared, and he subsequently lived out his days quietly in eastern Ch'üan-chou.

116. Wang Lien-mao, "P'u Shou-keng t'u-sha Nan-wai tsung-tzu k'ao," p. 80.

117. NWTYCSTP, p. 48. This was from the genealogical preface by Chao Yu-chüan dated 1300, the earliest extant account of the clan during the Mongol conquest.

118. Su Chi-lang, *T'ang Sung shih-tai Min-nan Ch'üan-chou shih ti lun kao*, pp. 13–24.

119. I am indebted to Dr. Janice Stargardt of the University of Cambridge for providing me with much of this corroborating detail concerning the wreck.

120. NWTYCSTP, pp. 56–62.

121. Jo-ho's genealogy is given in *Chao Chia pao tzu-liao hui pien*, pp. 18–19.

122. Nan-ao (Southern Bay) is an island in Ch'ao-chou, virtually on the border between Kuang-tung and Fu-chien.

123. NWTYCSTP, p. 57.

124. Ibid., p. 59.

125. *Chao Chia Pao tzu-liao hui pien*, p. 1. One factor adding much of the later prominence of the lineage was the building ca. 1620 of the Chao Family Walled Village (Chao Chia Pao), which survives to this day.

126. CSTP, 2/11b.

127. Ibid., 12a.

128. Ibid., 10b.

129. Ibid., 1/78a–b, 2/11a.

130. NWTYCSTP, p. 51. This is from the 1300 essay by Chao Yu-fu that also relates his rescue at the time of the massacre, quoted above.

131. As an example of the latter, Chao Yü-fang (ABABAHDAADA), according to the genealogy of the lineage descended from him, fled to his family home deep in the mountains of western Chang-chou, and there his family lived in peace throughout the Yuan (*Chao Te-mao Ch'ing-chang Ch'i-pei Yin-t'ang Chao-shih tsu-p'u*, p. 3). NWTYCSTP, p. 689, provides a parallel account for Chao I-ch'un (AABA-ACAAAABA), the son of a former Ch'üan-chou prefect, who fled the Yuan and lived as a retired scholar in the mountains.

132. CSTP, 2/10a–b, 10b–11a. When Pi-ying arrived in Kuang-tung in 1274, he was accompanied by over a hundred people, who scattered to neighboring villages after the fall of the Sung. The modern genealogist who compiled CSTP noted that the Fu-chien dialect is still spoken in these villages (ibid., 2/12b).

133. Ibid., 1/78b.

134. NWTYCSTP, pp. 48–49.

135. Chao-shih tsu-p'u pien-ts'uan wei-yuan-hui, *Chao-shih tsu-p'u*, p. 11.

136. CSTP, 2/12b.

137. NWTYCSTP, 50–1.

138. See the essay to that effect in *Nan-wai tsung hui hsun,* no. 1 (1995): 21.

Chapter 10

1. CYTC, pt. 2, 14: 528. See Table 7.6, p. 177.

2. Teng Ch'un in *Hua-chi,* trans. Fong, *Sung and Yuan Paintings,* p. 59.

3. On the last point, see Ou-yang Hsiu, *Hsin T'ang shu,* specifically *chüan* 70A and 70B, which contain genealogical tables for the imperial clan, and 131, a chapter on imperial clansmen–grand councilors. I developed this argument at much greater length in "Sung Discourse on the History of Chinese Imperial Kin and Clans."

4. Chao Ssu-lien, *Shan-yin Hua-she Chao-shih tsung-p'u,* 1/1a–b.

5. See Chaffee, "Chao Ju-yü, Spurious Learning, and Southern Sung Political Culture," pp. 36–54. For his writings, see SS, 392: 11989; and SCHMCM, 71/14a–b.

6. This was the *T'ang-shu lu i.* For the epitaph, see CWCKCC, 92/6b–10a. Shan-ying's biography in the *Sung History* also cites the scholar Yu Mou's (1127–93) praise of him as a "gentleman of antiquity" (*ku chün-tzu*) and mentions that his tomb inscription was written by the minister Ch'en Chün-ch'ing (1113–86).

7. CWCKCC, 44/13a–b, 43/30b–31a.

8. Pi-yuan was most famous as an important official (see SS, 413: 12407–12, for details of his career). His academy activities occurred in Hu-nan and are described in the Ming geography *Ta Ming i-t'ung chih,* 83/10a; for the Ju-ching's academy activities in Chiang-hsi, see the latter, 49/20b.

9. CWCKCC, 43/36a. The fact that Chen Te-hsiu wrote the epitaphs for both Ch'ung-hsien and Ch'ung-tu, and in fact married his daughter to Ch'ung-tu's son, provides additional evidence for the prominence of the family.

10. KKC, 102: 1428.

11. Fang Jen-jung, *Ching-ting Yen-chou hsu-chih* (1262), 3/18b–19a; HTHSTCC, 148/1a–3a, 142/10a–19b. I-fu, it should be noted, also played an important if controversial role as a historian in the Bureau of History.

12. SS, 247: 8746.

13. SS, 413: 12396. Ju-t'an's biography in Ch'ien Yueh-yu, *Hsien-ch'un Lin-an chih,* 67/16b–18b, also lists as his friends and intellectual companions an impressive group of men: Chu Hsi, Ts'ai Yuan-ting (1135–98), Lü Tsu-chien (d. 1196), Ch'ai Chung-hsing (1190 *chin-shih*), Hsiang An-shih (d. 1208), Ch'en K'ung-shih (1172 *chin-shih*), and Huang Kan (1152–1221).

14. *Sung-shih chi-shih.* The figure on the overall number of authors is from Nienhauser, *Indiana Companion to Traditional Chinese Literature,* p. 738.

15. SS, 244: 8674–75. Specifically mentioned among Te-wen's friends was the noted scholar and minister Yang I (974–1020).

16. HCC, 18: 308.

17. Ch'ien Yueh-yu, *Hsien-ch'un Lin-an chih*, 67/19a–b.

18. HTHSTCC, 160/21a.

19. Ibid., 169/14a.

20. Ibid., 152/4a.

21. Siren, *Chinese Painting*, p. 69.

22. Siren (ibid., pp. 35–36) lists 174 Sung painters with surviving paintings; the nine clansmen constitute 5.2 percent of the group. James Cahill's (*Index*, chap. 4) more comprehensive list also lists nine clansmen (one of them differing from Siren's clansmen) out of a total of 205 artists, for 4.4 percent. In addition, both mention that paintings by Hui-tsung and Kao-tsung survive.

23. For evaluations of Ling-jang's art, see Siren, *Chinese Painting*, pp. 71–74; Loehr, *Great Painters of China*, pp. 151–58; and Fong, *Sung and Yuan Paintings*, pp. 59–61. Concerning his popularity, Siren (p. 72) writes that he was honored by Che-tsung for his painting and also driven to distraction by people asking for his pictures.

24. Fong, *Sung and Yuan Paintings*, p. 61.

25. Siren, *Chinese Paintings*, p. 106; James Cahill, *Index*, pp. 65–68. Cahill misidentifies Ling-chün as Chao Ling-jang's brother. However, both the *Sung History* genealogy and the epitaph of Po-su's son Chao Shih-i (AADDFEBEA; 1149–1217) in YSC, 24: 474–77, make it clear that he was the father of Po-chü and Po-su and only very distantly related to Ling-jang.

26. *Sung-shih chi-shih*, 72/12a–b (pp. 1900–901). See also Siren, *Chinese Painting*, pp. 158–59; and Fong, *Sung and Yuan Paintings*, p. 70.

27. Fong, *Sung and Yuan Paintings*, p. 68.

28. I would add that in all the Southern Sung biographies of clansmen that I read, only one, Chao Pi-chien, is cited as having been talented at painting, and even that is mentioned as a youthful activity rather than an adult achievement (HTHSTCC, 160/16a).

29. Chao Ying-jung, *Brief History of the Chiu Clan*. See also Jennifer Jay's (*Change in Dynasties*, pp. 86–87) account of her interactions with Chao descendents and her information concerning Chao clan activities in Vancouver and Hong Kong.

30. Chao Heng-t'i, ed., *Chao-shih Ta-Sung huang-ti huang-hou hsiang-chi*.

31. The organization is the Research Committee on the Southern External Office of Clan Affairs for the Chao Sung in Ch'üan-chou (Ch'üan-chou Chao Sung nan-wai tsung-cheng-ssu yen-chiu hui). Their publications have appeared under a variety of names, but the genealogy is the work cited here as NWTYCSTP.

32. Endicott-West, *Mongolian Rule in China*.

33. See Farmer, *Early Ming Government*, pp. 73–79.

34. Dreyer, *Early Ming China*, pp. 148–52, 186–87; Wakeman, *Great Enterprise*, 1: 335.

35. Chang T'ing-yü et al., *Ming shih* (Peking: Chung-hua shu-chü, 1974), 116: 3557.

36. Wakeman, *Great Enterprise*, 1: 334.

37. Ray Huang, *1587, A Year of No Significance*, p. 18.

38. Wakeman, *Great Enterprise*, 1: 332–33. One more probable difference has to do with clan marriages. Ellen Soulliere ("Imperial Marriages") has amply documented the Ming policy of selecting the marriage partners of imperial princes and princesses from "families of no social consequence" in order to ensure that they would not be able to become rivals for political power. Although I know of no studies of the marriages of Ming clan members (Soulliere's focus being the emperors' immediate families), it would be surprising if the same restrictions did not pertain to them as well.

39. Ku Yen-wu, *Jih-chih lu*, 9/24a–b.

40. Crossley, *The Manchus*, pp. 30–31, 55, 79.

41. Rawski, *The Last Emperors*, pp. 130–31.

42. See Kuo Sung-i, "Ch'ing tsung-shih ti teng-chi chieh-kou chi ching-chi ti-wei"; Kuo's essay is found in the excellent collection on the demography of the Ch'ing imperial clan edited by Li Chung-ch'ing (James Lee) and Kuo Sung-i, *Ch'ing-tai huang-tsu jen-k'ou hsing-wei ho she-hui huan-ching*.

43. Rawski, "Ch'ing Imperial Marriage and Problems of Rulership," pp. 172–73.

44. Lai Hui-min, "Ch'ing-tai huang-tsu ti feng-chueh yü jen-kuan yen-chiu," pp. 138–39. Specifically, 228 were provincial graduates (*chü-jen*), 104 were *chin-shih*, and another 44 and 14 had passed special *chü-jen* and *chin-shih* examinations in translation (*fan-i hsiang-shih, fan-i hui-shih*) respectively, held specifically for imperial clansmen.

45. Evelyn Rawski, "Ch'ing Imperial Marriage and Problems of Rulership," p. 197.

Appendix B

1. "Yü-tieh tsuan-hsiu hsu," CSTP, 1/12a–b. With a few differences in nomenclature, this listing agrees with that given in SS, 164: 3890–91, which forms the basis of analysis for Wang Sheng-to, "Sung-ch'ao tsung-shih chih-tu k'ao," pp. 174–75.

2. SS, 164: 3890.

3. SHY:CK, 20/3b.

4. HCP, 124: 2935, 127: 3006.

5. For the complaint that no *yü-tieh* had been compiled for Shen-tsung's reign, see SS, 164: 3890. Wang Sheng-to ("Sung-tai tsung-shih chih-tu k'ao," p. 174) also mentions the publication of *yü-tieh* for Jen-tsung's and Ying-tsung's reigns in 1068.

6. CSTP, 1/12b.

7. See SS, 164: 3890, for the order to begin work in 998; and HCP, 48: 1044, for the announcement of the work's completion.

8. SHY:CK, 20/56a.

9. CSTP, 1/12b.

10. SHY:CK, 20/6b.

11. CSTP, 1/12b.

12. Wang Sheng-to, "Sung-tai tsung-shih chih-tu k'ao," p. 175, citing SHY:CK, 20/6. I was unable to find the cited passage there, however.

13. Wang Sheng-to, "Sung-tai tsung-shih chih-tu k'ao," p. 175.

14. CSTP, 1/12b.

15. HCP, 86: 1980.

16. HCP, 212: 5153–54. The names and descriptions of the three halls are from Hucker, *Dictionary of Official Titles*, pp. 325, 370, and 509.

17. SHY:CK, 20/8a.

18. Ibid., 12b–13a.

19. Ibid., 13b–14a. One curious feature of the reported acquisition is that the pre-1091 form of the name was used, the *Tsung-fan ch'ing-hsu lu*.

20. CYTC, 1: 1.

21. CSTP, 1/89a–b.

Bibliography

The following abbreviations are used in the Bibliography:

SKCS	Ssu-k'u ch'üan-shu 四庫全書
SKCSCP	Ssu-k'u ch'üan-shu chen-pen 四庫全書珍本
SPTK	Ssu-pu ts'ung-k'an 四倍叢刊
TSCC	Ts'ung-shu chi-ch'eng 叢書集成

Sources and Locations of Epitaphs (*mu-chih-ming*)

Anonymous. *Min-chung chin-shih lueh* 閩中金石略. Shanghai: Chung-hua shu-
chü, 1934.
  9/1a 4a: Shih-hsueh, BCBLFD
Chang Fang-p'ing 張方平. *Lo-ch'uan chi* 樂全集. SKCSCP, ch'u-chi.
  38/17b–18b: Shih-pao, ABBAB
  38/12a–14a: Tsung-hui, BAAF
  38/15a–16a: Chung-k'ao, BAAJE
  38/16a–17b: Chung-ying, BABAB
  38/14a–15a: Tsung-yü, BABD
  38/5a–9a: Yun-liang, BGB
Chao Hsi-nien 趙錫年. *Chao-shih tsu-p'u* 趙氏族譜. Kuang-tung, 1902.
  2/6a–7a: Yun-jang, BCB
  2/7b: Tsung-chih, BCBP
  2/7b: Chung-chen, BCBPC
  2/8a–b: Shih-chen, BCBPCA
  2/8b–9a: Pu-tzu, BCBPCAB
  2/9b: Shan-pin, BCBPCABC
  2/11a: Liang-ling, BCBPCABBBCBX
  2/9b–10a: Ju-ku, BCBPCABCA

2/10a–b: Ch'ung-t'o, BCBPCABCAA

2/10b–12a: Pi-ying, BCBPCABCAAA

2/12a–13a: Liang-shao, BCBPCABCAAAA

2/13a: Yu-shou, Yuan-D

2/13a–b: Yu-hsien, Yuan-E

Chao Ju-t'eng 趙汝滕. *Yung-chai chi* 庸齋集. SKCSCP, ch'u-chi.

6/20b–22a: Ch'ung-t'ang, BCBQCABBCA

Chao Meng-chien 趙孟堅. *I-chai wen-pien* 彝齋文編. SKCS.

4/43a–44b: Yü-shih, AABCDBADAAA

Chao Shan-k'uo 趙善括. *Ying-chai tsa-chu* 應齋雜著. SKCSCP.

4/9b–11b: Po-shu, AADFABFB

Chao Shih-shu 趙師恕. In Fukien Provincial Museum, *Fu-chou Nan-Sung Huang Sheng mu* 福州南宋黃升墓. 1982.

pp. 82–83: Huang Sheng, wife of Yü-chün, AADEBCGBAXX

Chao Te-mao 趙德懋, *Ch'ing-chang Ch'i-pei yin-t'ang Chao-shih tsu-p'u* 清漳銀塘趙氏族譜. Photocopy of manuscript supplied by Hugh Clark.

p. 34: Po-shu, ABABAHDA

p. 34: Shih-kao, ABABAHDAA

p. 34: Hsi-hsiang, ABABAHDAAD

p. 34: Yü-fang, ABABAHDAADC

p. 34: Meng-mo, ABABAHDAADCX

Chen Te-hsiu 眞德修. *Hsi-shan hsien-sheng Chen wen-chung kung ch'üan-chi* 西山先生眞文忠公全集. SPTK.

45/1a–9b: Hsi-i, AAXXXXXXXX

44/6b–14b: Ch'ung-hsien, BAAKFBDAAA

43/30b–36b: Ch'ung-tu, BAAKFBDAAE

44/26a–29b: Shih-t'ung, CBABBCAAAB

Ch'en Chi-chuang 陳紀狀. In Chao Pi-hsiang 趙必琭. *Ch'iu-hsiao hsien-sheng fu-p'ou chi* 秋曉先生覆瓿集. SKCSCP, 8.

6/2b–7a: Pi-hsiang, BCBQDCDDBAA

Ch'en Liang 陳亮. *Ch'en Liang chi* 陳亮集. Peking: Chung-hua shu-chü, n.d.

29: 431: daughter of anonymous seventh-generation descendent of T'ai-tsung

Ch'en Mi 陳宓. *Fu-chai hsien-sheng Lung-t'u Ch'en kung wen-chi* 復齋先生龍圖陳公文集. Ching-chia-t'ang wen-k'u.

22/31b–35b: Ju-kuan, BCADACBBB

21/25b–27b: Wang Hui-chen, wife of Yen-lai 彥駥, CAAFBAAA

21/9a–12b: Kung-mai, CABCAGC

Cheng Hsieh 鄭獬. *Yun-ch'i chi* 郧溪集. SKCSCP, 3.

21/16a–18a: daughter of Wei-chi, AAB

20/1a–3b: Shih-yung, AABAA

21/15b–16a: K'o-p'i, CCFB

21/15a–b: K'o-hisen, CEJB

Ch'eng Chü 程俱. *Pei-shan hsiao chi* 北山小集. SPTK.

33/17a–21a: Tzu-chou, AAEBFAE

Chou Pi-ta 周必大. *Wen-chung chi* 文忠集. SKCSCP, 2.

74/9b–11a: Po-lu, AAAACEBB

74/7b–9a: Yen-wu, CCCCEBAA

71/12b–14b: Kung-heng, CDCFIDB

75/6a–8b: Kung-yü, CEFCBCB

Chu Hsi 朱熹. *Chu Wen-kung wen-chi* 朱文公文集. SPTK.

92/6b–10a (pp. 1627–29): Shan-ying, BAAKFBDA

91/24a–25b (pp. 1616–17): Pu-shuai, BCAAEEB

92/25b–28a (pp. 1632–34): Shan-i, BCAAEEBB

Fan Tsu-yü 范祖禹. *Fan t'ai-shih chi* 范太史集. SKCSCP, ch'u-chi.

51/11b: Chung-ch'i, BAAKF

53/1a–3b: Chün, Ying-B

Han Wei 韓維. *Nan-yang chi* 南陽集. SKCH.

29/1a–3b: Ts'ung-shih, ABBB

Han Yuan-chi 韓元吉. *Nan-chien chia-i kao* 南澗甲乙稿. TSCC.

22: 465–67: Yen-k'an, CBAΛΛEBA

21: 426–29: Yen-tuan, CBAECAAA

Hsu Ching-heng 許景衡. *Heng-t'ang chi* 衡塘集. SKCS.

20/6a–8a: Ling-tzu, AXXXXX

Hu Ch'üan 胡銓. *Hu Tan-an hsien-sheng wen-chi* 胡澹庵先生文集. Facsimile reproduction of Tao-kuang edition; Taipei: Han-hua wen-hua shih-yeh kung-ssu, 1970.

24/9a–18b: Tzu-hsiao, AADEHAF

Hu Hung 胡宏. *Wu-feng chi* 五峰集. SKCSCP, ch'u-chi.

3/41a–42b: Mu-chih, CHABEF

Hu Su 胡宿. *Wen-kung chi* 文恭集. TSCC.

35: 429: Shih-hu, AADFD

38: 457–58: Shih-chien, AAEBB

Hung Kua 洪适. *P'an-chou wen-chi* 盤洲文集. SPTK.

75/6a–7b: daughter of Shih-ts'e, BACHFD

Lin Kuang-ch'ao 林光朝. *Ai-hsien chi* 艾軒集. SKCSCP, ch'u-chi.

9/10b–12a: Pu-min, BCBQCAE

Liu Ch'ang 劉敞. *Kung-shih chi* 公是集. TSCC.

54: 653: Shu-nai, CAACD

54: 651–52: Shu-tsung, CAACE

52: 631: K'o-hsiao, CAAE

54: 654: Shu-seng, CAAFA

54: 651: Chi-pei, CABAAAX

54: 652: Hua–chih, CABABA

54: 652–53: Shu-wei, CABBD

52: 633–34: wife of Ch'eng-hsun, CBA

54: 650: Shu-chi, CCAAF

54: 650: Shu-han, CCADB

52: 630–31: K'o-kou, CCBA

54: 651: Ch'ih-chih, CCBAAA

54: 653: Shu-lü, CCEBA

54: 649: Shu-she, CCFBA

52: 634–35: wife of K'o-chieh, CDAB

52: 632: K'o-hsieh, CDAC

54: 652: K'o-po, CDCG

54: 649–50: K'o-chuang, CDCI

52: 629–30: Ch'eng-ts'ao, CDD

52: 632–33: Shu-chan, CEAAB

52: 628–29: K'o-wen, CEDA

52: 634: wife of K'o-chou, CEDB

52: 627–28: Ch'eng-i, CEF

54: 654: wife of Shu-ts'e, CEIAA

52: 635: wife of K'o-ch'un, CEJA

52: 635–36: wife of K'o-ch'ang, CGBB

Liu I-chih 劉一止. *T'iao-hsi chi* 苕溪集. SKCSCP, 2.

    51/15b–18b: Pu-wu, BABBBAB

Liu K'o-chuang 劉克莊. *Hou-ts'un hsien-sheng ta-ch'üan-chi* 後村先生大全集.
SPTK.

    155/7b–13b: Hsi-ching, AAEBFAECAB

    160/15b–22a: Pi-chien, BCABDAAAAAD

    152/1b–5a: Ju-sui, BCBGNAGCC

    165/14a–16a: Ju-pin, BCBKCKCBA

    150/17b–19a: daughter of Pu-k'uang, BCBPAME

    158/13b–15a: daughter of Pu-ch'ü, BCBPAMF

    154/4b–5b: daughter of Shan-lan, BCBPAMGA

    148/1a–3a: Keng-fu, CCABHBACB

    158/1a–5a: Shih-huan, CDADADBFBA

    142/1a–4b: Hsing-fu, CDBBAFAAA

    165/16a–17a: Shih-ch'i, CDCABOABDX

    169/11b–14b: Yen-hou, CDCKGACA

    142/10a–19b: I-fu, CECBCCDAD

Liu Kuang-tsu 劉光祖. "Sung ch'eng-hsiang Chung-ting Chao kung mu-chih-ming." In Fu Tseng-hsiang 傅增湘, ed., *Sung-tai Shu-wen chi-ts'un* 宋代蜀文輯存. 1943.

    71/1a–15b: Ju-yü, BAAKFBDAA

Liu Tsai 劉宰. *Man-t'ang wen-chi* 漫塘文集. SKCSCP, 9.

    31/1a–3b: Ch'ung-hsi, BABBEABDAA

    31/3b–6b: Jo-kuei, CAADAAGBBAX

    32/1a–3b: Shih-tso, CAADAAGBBB

Lo Yuan 羅願. *E-chou hsiao chi* 鄂州小集. SKCSCP, 12.

    4/5b–6b: daughter of Shan-liang, BABBBACA

Lou Yueh 樓鑰. *Kung-k'uei chi* 攻媿集. TSCC

    102: 1423–26: Shih-lung, AABBABDCA

    102: 1436–39: Po-shu, AADDGADA

    104: 1468–70: Shih-hsin, AADEAAEAC

    103: 1451–53: Po-chih, AADEGABA

    86: 1167–76: Po-kuei, ABBACEAA

    102: 1425–29: Shan-yü, BCABGHEB

Lu Tseng-hsiang 陸增祥. *Pa-ch'iung chin-shih pu cheng* 八瓊金石補正. 1925; re-printed—Taipei: Wen-hai, 1967.

    114/20a–b: Po-ch'ing, AADFFDAB

Lu Yu 陸游. *Wei-nan chi* 渭南集. SPTK

    34: 304–6: Yen-chen, CDADAFAB

Mu-jung Yen-feng 慕容彥逢. *Ch'ih-wen t'ang-chi* 摛文堂集. Ch'ang-chou hsien-che i-shu, 1.

    14/3a: Hui-chih, CAABBB

    14/8b–9a: T'ien-chih, CBADCB

    14/1b–2a: Shu-lo, CBADE

    14/3a–b: Shu-tsun, CCABF

    14/5a–b: Shu-chih, CCABH

    14/14a–b: Shu-cheng, CCECA

    14/3b–4a: Shu-tang, CCFAE

    14/8b: Shu-chuan, CCFDE

    14/9b–10a: Shu-pi, CCFGB

    14/6a: Shu-kuan, CCFHA

    14/4a: Shu-kuei, CCFHD

    14/2b: Shu-min, CDABG

    14/2a–b: Shu-tan, CDADA

    14/4b–5a: Shu-na, CDAFB

    14/9a–b: Shu-i, CDBCF

    14/8a: Shih-chih, CDCABA

14/5b–6a: Sheng-chih, CDCACA

14/5b: Hsiang-chih, CDCACJ

14/7a–b: I-chih, CDCAEA

14/10a–b: Shu-kan, CDCBE

14/6b–7a: Shu-yun, CDCHA

14/9a: An-chih, CDDBAX

14/6a–b: Chüeh-chih, CFAABB

14/7a–b: Shu-ch'ien, CFACB

14/8a–b: Shu-ch'u, CHAJB

Ou-yang Hsiu 歐陽修. *Ou-yang wen-chung wen-chi* 歐陽文忠文集. SPTK.

37/8b–9a (pp. 285–86): wife of Ts'ung-k'o, AADA

37/3a–4a (p. 283): Shih-jung, AADAB

37/5b–6a (p. 284): Shih-heng, AADAF

37/6b–7a (pp. 284–85): Shih-hsuan, AADBB

37/7a–8a (p. 285): wife of Wei-ho, AAE

37/1a–2a (p. 282): Tsung-yen, BACA

37/2a–3a (pp. 282–83): Tsung-na, BACB

37/4a–b (p. 283): Tsung-shih, BCBE

37/5a–b (p. 284): Tsung-mien, BCBN

Shen Kou 沈遘, Shen Kua 沈括, and Shen Liao 沈遼. *Shen-shih san hsien-sheng wen-chi* 沈氏先生文集. SPTK.

37/50b–51b: Shu-tsao, CAABA

37/51b–52b: wife of K'o-chi, CABA

37/52b–54a: K'o-ning, CDAD

Ssu-ma Kuang 司馬光. *Wen-kuo wen-cheng Ssu-ma kung wen-chi* 溫國文正司馬公文集. SPTK.

78/2a–b (p. 561): Ling-pang, AABACB

78/2b–3a (pp. 561–62): wife of Ling-chao, AADAAB

78/1a–2a (p. 561): Chung-lien, BACAA

78/3a–b (p. 562): Shih-ch'iu, BDAAAD

Su Sung 蘇頌. *Su wei-kung wen-chi* 蘇魏公文集. SKCS.

60/21b–22b: Shu-chih, CCADF

Sun Ti 孫覿. *Hung-ch'ing chü-shih wen-chi* 鴻慶居士文集. SKCSCP, 12.

41/1a–6b: daughter of Pu-wu, BABBBAB

38/22a–27b: Shih-tsan, BCAAHA

Sun Ying-shih 孫應時. *Chu-hu chi* 燭湖集. SKCSCP, 4.

11/1a–5a: Po-huai, AABDEFBA

Sung Ch'i 宋祁. *Ching-wen chi* 景文集. TSCC.

58: 770: Ts'ung-yü, ABBA

58: 767–69: Yuan-yen, BG

58: 770–71: K'o-chi, CABA

58: 771–72: Ch'eng-mu, CDA

Sung Hsiang 宋庠. *Yuan-hsien chi* 元憲集. TSCC.

34: 362: Mr. Chao, CEFX

34: 361–62: K'o-wei, CEGX

Tai Hsu 戴栩. *Huan-ch'uan chi* 浣川集. Ching-hsiang-lou ts'ung-shu 敬鄉樓叢書.

10/4b–5b: Shih-hsien, CCCAHABAAA

Wang An-li 王安禮. *Wang Wei-kung chi* 王魏公集. Yü-chang ts'ung-shu 豫章叢書. Taipei: Shang-we shu-tien, 1975.

7/17a–18a: Shih-yueh, AADBG

7/15a–16a: Chung-mou, BAADB

7/16a–b: Chung-lai, BABBE

7/14b–15a: Chung-na, BCADE

7/12b–14a: Tsung-chin, BCBQ

7/14a–b: Chung-chin, BEABB

7/4a–5a: wife of Tsung-ching, BEAD

7/5a–b: wife of Shu-chi, CAACF

7/10b–12b: K'o-ch'in, CBAA

Wang An-shih 王安石. *Lin-ch'uan hsien-sheng chi* 臨川先生集. SPTK.

98/13b–14a (pp. 617–18): Shih-jeng, AAEBH

98/10b–11b (p. 616): Tsung-pien, BAAM

98/13a–b (p. 617): Chung-k'uei, BABAG

98/11b–12a (pp. 616–17): Chung-hsing, BABCE

98/12a–b (p. 617): Chung-mang, BCBBC

98/12b–13a (p. 617): Tsung-shu, BEAA

Wang Kuei 王珪. *Hua-yang chi* 華陽集. TSCC.

39: 543–44: Shih-yen, AABAB

39: 549–50: Ling-x, AABBAX

39: 538–39: Shih-ch'ang, AADAC

39: 645–46: Shih-ch'ung, AADDA

39: 533–35: Ts'ung-chih, AADE

39: 536–38: Ts'ung-hsin, AADF

39: 532–33: Ts'ung-shen, AAEB

39: 539–40: Shih-ying, AAEBA

39: 529–30: Shih-mai, ABCAA

39: 531–32: Ts'ung-chih, ABCC

39: 530: Tsung-mo, BAAH

39: 550–51: Shih-yen, BACDAA

39: 544–45: Tsung-yen, BACE

    39: 540–41: Tsung-wang, BDAA

    39: 546–49: Yun-pi, BEA

    39: 543: Tsung-i, BEAB

    39: 541–43: Yun-ch'u, BGD

Wei Ching 衛涇. *Hou-lo chi* 後樂集. SKCSCP, ch'u-chi.

    18/5b–10a: Shan-kung, BEAGFEAC

Wei Liao-weng 魏了翁. *Ch'ung-chiao Ho-shan hsien-sheng ta-ch'üan-chi* 重校鶴山先生大全集. SPTK.

    73/14b–20a (pp. 597–600): Hsi-kuan, AADBBEGADA

Wu Su 吳愬. In Lo Chen-yü 羅振玉, *Mang-lo chung-mu i-wen ssu-pien* 芒洛冢墓遺四編. Shih-k'o shih-liao hsin-pien 石刻史料新編, no. 19. Hsin-wen feng ch'u-pan-she.

    6/47a: daughter of Shu-chih, CGBBBA

Yang Chieh 楊傑. *Wu-wei chi* 無爲集. SKCSCP, 5.

    14/14a–16a: Ling-pin, AADDAA

    12/1a–8a: Ch'eng-ch'ing, CAA

Yang Hsing-tsung 楊興宗. In *Chiang-su chin-shih chih* 江蘇金石誌. 1927 ed.

    13/16a–18a: Pu-t'ien, BCBTGDA

Yang I 楊億. *Wu-i hsin chi* 武夷新集. SKCSCP, 8.

    11/12a–14b: Yu, Chen-A

Yang Wan-li 楊萬里. *Ch'eng-chai chi* 誠齋集. SPTK.

    129/10b–12a: daughter of Pu-?, BCBBBFG

    128/1a–3a: Pu-tu, BCBMAAA

    119/33a–40a: Hsiang-chih, CCFHIA

    122/4a–6b: Kung-heng, CDCFIDB

Yeh Shih 葉適. *Yeh Shih chi* 葉適集. Peking: Chung-hua shu-chü, 1961.

    24: 474–77: Shih-i, AADDFEBEA

    21: 418–20: Shan-hsi, BCABACAA

    26: 512–18: Pu-hsi, BCBFAFA

    23: 449–53: Yen-hsiao, CABBFHBA

    23: 446–49: Yen-t'an, CEFCBDBB

    25/500–501: daughter of BXXXXXXXX

Yuan Fu 袁甫. *Meng-chai chi* 蒙齋集. TSCC.

    18: 256–57: daughter of Shih-tuan, AABDEFBAA

    17: 251–52: Pi-fu, CDCBEBADB

Yuan Hsieh 袁燮. *Hsieh-chai chi* 絜齋集. TSCC ed.

    21/17b–18b: daughter of Pu-cho, BCBIAMJ (Wu-ying-tien ts'ung-shu 武英殿叢書 ed.)

    17: 284–87: Shan-tai, BCBPAAAC

    17: 287–92: Shen-fu, CABCBCCBE

18: 306–9: Ch'ung-fu, CCAAAABAA
17: 292–94: Kung-sheng, CCFAFCC

Other Sources

Abu-Lughod, Janet. *Before European Hegemony: The World System, AD 1250–1350*. Oxford: Oxford University Press, 1989.

Bielenstein, Hans. "The Institutions of Later Han." In Denis Twitchett and Michael Loewe, eds., *The Cambridge History of China*, vol. 1, *The Ch'in and Han Empires, 221 B.C.–A.D. 220*, pp. 491–519. Cambridge, Eng.: Cambridge University Press, 1986.

———. *The Restoration of the Han Dynasty, with Prolegomena on the Historiography of the "Hou Han Shu."* Stockholm: Göteborg, 1953.

———. "Wang Mang, the Restoration of the Han Dynasty, and Later Han." In Denis Twitchett and Michael Loewe, eds., *The Cambridge History of China*, vol. 1, *The Ch'in and Han Empires, 221 B.C.–A.D. 220*, pp. 223–90. Cambridge, Eng.: Cambridge University Press, 1986.

Birge, Bettine. *Holding Her Own: Women, Property, and Confucian Reaction in Sung and Yüan China (960–1368)*. Cambridge, Eng.: Cambridge University Press, forthcoming.

Bodman, Peter. Biography of Cheng Ch'ing-chih. In Herbert Franke, *Sung Biographies*, pp. 156–63. Wiesbaden: Franz Stein Verlag, 1976.

Bol, Peter. *"This Culture of Ours": Intellectual Transitions in T'ang and Sung China*. Stanford: Stanford University Press, 1992.

Bossler, Beverly Jo. *Powerful Relations: Kinship, Status, and the State in Sung China (960–1279)*. Cambridge, Mass.: Harvard University, Council on East Asian Studies, 1998.

Cahill, James. *An Index of Early Chinese Painters and Paintings: T'ang, Sung, and Yuan*. Berkeley: University of California Press, 1980.

Cahill, Suzanne E. "Taoism at the Sung Court: The Heavenly Text Affair of 1008." *Bulletin of Sung Yuan Studies* 16 (1980): 23–44.

Chaffee, John. "Chao Jü-yü, Spurious Learning, and Southern Sung Political Culture." *Journal of Sung Yuan Studies* 22 (1990–92): 23–61.

———. "Civil-izing the Emperor's Family: Marriage and the Sung Imperial Clan." Paper presented at the annual meeting of the Association for Asian Studies, Boston, 1994.

———. "From Capital to Countryside: Changing Residency Patterns of the Sung Imperial Clan." In *Proceedings of the International Symposium on Sung History*, pp. 986–97. Taipei: Chinese Culture University, 1988; also published in *Chinese Culture* 30 (1989): 23–24.

————. "The Historian as Critic: Li Hsin-ch'uan and the Dilemmas of Statecraft in Southern Sung China." In Robert Hymes and Conrad Schirokauer, eds., *Ordering the World: Approaches to State and Society in Sung Dynasty China*, pp. 310–35. Berkeley: University of California Press, 1993.

————. "The Marriage of Sung Imperial Clanswomen." In Rubie Watson and Patricia Ebrey, eds., *Marriage and Inequality in Chinese Society*, pp. 133–69. Berkeley: University of California Press, 1991.

————. "The Political Roles of the Sung Imperial Clan." Paper presented at the annual meeting of the New York Conference on Asian Studies, New Paltz, 1993.

————. "Sung Discourse on the History of Chinese Imperial Kin and Clans." Paper presented at the Conference on Sung Historical Thinking. Bahamas, Jan. 1997.

————. *The Thorny Gates of Learning in Sung China: A Social History of Examinations*. Cambridge, Eng.: Cambridge University Press, 1985; reprinted—State University of New York Press, 1994.

————. "Two Sung Imperial Clan Genealogies: Preliminary Findings and Questions." *Journal of Sung Yuan Studies* 23 (1993): 99–109.

Chan, Hok-lam. *Legitimation in Imperial China: Discussions Under the Jurchen-Chin Dynasty (1115–1234)*. Seattle: University of Washington Press, 1984.

Chan, Wing-tsit. Biography of Chu Hsi. In Herbert Franke, ed., *Sung Biographies*, 1: 287. Wiesbaden: Franz Stein Verlag, 1976.

Chan, Wing-tsit, trans. *Reflections on Things at Hand: The Neo-Confucian Anthology Compiled by Chu Hsi and Lü Tsu-ch'ien*. New York: Columbia University Press, 1967.

Chang, Kwang-chih. *Early Chinese Civilization: Anthropological Perspectives*. Cambridge, Mass., Harvard University Press, 1976.

Chang Pang-wei (Zhang Bangwei) 張邦緯. *Hun-yin yü she-hui (Sung-tai)* 婚姻與社會(宋代). Ch'eng-tu: Ssu-ch'uan jen-min ch'u-pan-she, 1989.

————. *Sung-tai huang-ch'in yü cheng-chih* 宋代皇親與政治. Ch'eng-tu: Ssu-ch'uan jen-min ch'u-pan-she, 1993.

Chang Tuan-i 張端義. *Kuei-erh chi* 貴耳集. TSCC.

Ch'ang Pi-te 昌彼得, Wang Te-i 王德毅, Ch'eng Yuan-min 程元敏, and Hou Chün-te 侯俊德. *Sung-jen chuan-chi tzu-liao suo-yin* 宋人傳記資料索引. 6 vols. Taipei: Ting-wen shu-chu, 1974–76.

Chao Chia Pao tzu-liao hui pien 趙家保資料匯編. Fu-chien sheng Chang-p'u hsien wen-hua chü 福建省漳浦縣文化局, 1988.

Chao Heng-t'i 趙恆忿, ed. *Chao-shih Ta Sung huang-ti huang-hou hsiang-chi* 趙氏大宋皇帝皇后像紀. Ch'in-ho t'ang ts'ung-shu 琴鶴堂叢書. Taipei: Chao-shih ts'ung-ch'in hui, 1971.

Chao I-ch'in 趙詒沿. *Chao-shih chia sheng* 趙氏家乘. 1919 (copy at Columbia University).

Chao Ju-yü 趙汝愚. *Sung ming-ch'en tsou-i* 宋明臣奏議 (originally titled *Kuo-ch'ao ming-ch'en tsou-i* 國朝明臣奏議). Compiled in 1186. SPTK.

Chao-shih ts'u-p'u pien-tsuan wei-yuan-hui 趙氏族譜編纂委員會. *Chao-shih tsu-p'u* 趙氏族譜. Chang-hua: Hsin-sheng ch'u-pan-she, 1973.

Chao Shih-t'ung 趙世通, ed. *Nan-wai t'ien-yuan Chao-shih tsu-p'u* 南外天源趙氏族譜. Compiled in 1724. Ch'üan-chou: Ch'üan-chou yin-shua kuang-kao kung-ssu, 1994.

Chao Ssu-lien 趙思濂. *Hsu-hsiu Shan-yin Hua-she Chao-shih tsung-p'u* 續修山陰華舍趙氏宗譜. Alternative titles: *Shan-yin Hua-she Chao-shih tsung-p'u* or *Hua-she Chao-shih tsung-p'u*. N.P.: Ts'ui-huan t'ang, 1916.

Chao T'ing-chih 趙廷芝. *Ta-kang Chao-shih tsung-p'u* 大港趙氏宗譜. 1809 ed.

Chao Ying-jung 趙英榮. *Chao-tsu chien-shih* 趙族簡史 Additional title in English: *A Brief History of the Chiu Clan*. San Francisco: Chao chia kung suo, 1965.

Ch'en Chün 陳均. *Huang-ch'ao pien-nien kang-mu pei-yao* 皇朝編年綱目備要. Taipei: Ch'eng-wen ch'u-pan she, 1966.

Chen Te-hsiu 眞德秀. *Chen wen-chung kung wen-chi* 眞文忠公文集. SPTK.

Ch'i Hsia (Qi Xia) 漆俠. *Sung-tai ching-chi shih* 宋代經濟史. 2 vols. Shanghai: Shanghai jen-min ta-pan-she, 1988.

Chiang Shao-yü 江少虞. *Sung-ch'ao shih-shih lei-yuan* 宋朝事實類苑. Taipei: Yuan-liu ch'u-pan-she, 1982.

Chieh Ch'in-mi 杰勤米 and Ko Lin 格林. "Ch'üan-chou Sung-tai ku-ch'uan" 泉州宋代古船. *Hai chiao-shih yen-chiu* 海交史研究 2 (1989): 84–87.

Ch'ien Yueh-yu 潛說友. *Hsien-ch'un Lin-an chih* 咸淳臨安志. 1268 ed.

Chikusa Masaaki. Biography of Chao T'ing-mei. In Herbert Franke, ed., *Sung Biographies*, 1: 83–84. Wiesbaden: Franz Steiner Verlag, 1976.

Ching Chung, Priscilla. *Palace Women in the Northern Sung, 960–1126*. Leiden: E. J. Brill, 1981.

Chou Ch'eng 周城 (Ch'ing). *Sung Tung-ching k'ao* 宋東京考. Peking: Chung-hua shu-chü, 1988.

Chou Pao-chu 周寶珠 and Ch'en Chen 陳振. *Chien-ming Sung-shih*. Peking: Jen-min, 1985.

Chu Hsi 朱熹. *Chu-tzu yü-lei* 朱子語類. Ed. Li Ching-te 黎靖德. Peking: Chung-hua shu-chü, 1986.

Chu Yü 朱彧. *P'ing-chou k'o-t'an* 萍洲可談. SKCS.

Ch'üeh An 確庵 and Nai An 耐庵. *Ching-k'ang pai-shih chien-cheng* 靖康稗史箋證. Peking: Chung-hua shu-chü, 1988.

Clark, Hugh R. *Community, Trade, and Networks: Southern Fujian Province from the Third to the Thirteenth Century.* Cambridge, Eng.: Cambridge University Press, 1991.

Creel, Herlee. *The Origins of Statecraft in China,* vol. 1, *The Western Chou Empire.* Chicago: University of Chicago Press, 1970.

Crossley, Pamela Kyle. *The Manchus.* Oxford: Blackwell Publishers, 1997.

———. "The Rulerships of China." *American Historical Review* 97 (1992): 1468–83.

Davis, Richard L. *Court and Family in Sung China, 960–1279: Bureaucratic Success and Kinship Fortunes for the Shih of Ming-chou.* Durham, N.C.: Duke University Press, 1986.

———. "Ventures Foiled and Opportunities Missed: The Times of Li-tsung (1224–1264)." Draft chapter for the *Cambridge History of China.*

———. *Wind Against the Mountain: The Crisis of Politics and Culture in Thirteenth-Century China.* Cambridge, Mass.: Harvard University, Council on East Asian Studies, 1996.

de Bary, Wm. Theodore, and John Chaffee, eds. *Neo-Confucian Education: The Formative Stage.* Berkeley: University of California Press, 1989.

de Pee, Christian. "Negotiating Marriage: Weddings, Text, and Ritual in Song and Yuan China." Ph.D. diss., Columbia University, 1997.

Dreyer, Edward L. *Early Ming China: A Political History, 1355–1435.* Stanford: Stanford University Press, 1982.

Ebrey, Patricia. "Conceptions of the Family in the Sung Dynasty." *Journal of Asian Studies* 43 (1984): 219–45.

———. *Family and Property in Sung China: Yüan Ts'ai's Precepts for Social Life.* Princeton: Princeton University Press, 1984.

———. *The Inner Quarters: Marriage and the Lives of Chinese Women in the Sung Period.* Berkeley: University of California Press, 1993.

———. "Portrait Sculptures in Imperial Ancestral Rites in Song China." *T'oung Pao* 83 (1997): 42–92.

Eisenberg, Andrew. "Kingship, Power and the Hsuan-wu Men Incident of the T'ang." *T'oung Pao* 80 (1994): 223–59.

Eisenstadt, S. N. *The Political Systems of Empires: The Rise and Fall of the Historical Bureaucratic Societies.* New York: Free Press, 1963.

Endicott-West, Elizabeth. *Mongolian Rule in China: Local Administration in the Yuan Dynasty.* Cambridge, Mass.: Harvard University, Council on East Asian Studies, 1989.

Fan Chen 范鎮. *Tung-chai chi-shih* 東齋記事. Peking: Chung-hua shu-chü, 1980.

Fang Hao 方豪. *Sung shih* 宋史. Taipei: Hua-kang shu-chü, 1968.

Fang Jen-jung 方仁榮. *Ching-ting Yen-chou hsu-chih* 景定嚴州續志. 1262 ed.

Fang Ta-ts'ung 方大琮. *T'ieh-an chi* 鐵菴集. SKCS ed.

Farmer, Edward L. *Early Ming Government: The Evolution of Dual Capitals.* Cambridge, Mass.: Harvard University, Council on East Asian Studies, 1976.

Fisher, Carney T. "The Ritual Dispute of Sung Ying-tsung." *Papers on Far Eastern History* 36 (1987): 109–38.

Fong, Wen. *Sung and Yuan Paintings.* New York: Metropolitan Museum of Art, 1973.

Franke, Herbert. Biography of Chao Ju-yü. In Herbert Franke, ed., *Sung Biographies*, 1: 59–63. Wiesbaden: Fritz Stein Verlag, 1976.

———. "Chia Ssu-tao (1213–1275): A 'Bad Last Minister'?" In Arthur F. Wright and Denis Twitchett, eds., *Confucian Personalities*, pp. 217–34. Stanford: Stanford University Press, 1962.

———. "The Chin Dynasty." In Herbert Franke and Denis Twitchett, eds., *The Cambridge History of China*, vol. 6, *Alien Regimes and Border States, 907–1368*, pp. 215–320. Cambridge, Eng.: Cambridge University Press, 1994.

———. "Seige and Defense of Towns in Medieval China." In Frank A. Kierman, Jr., and John K. Fairbank, eds., *Chinese Ways in Warfare*, pp. 151–201. Cambridge, Mass.: Harvard University Press, 1974.

Franke, Herbert, ed. *Sung Biographies.* 3 vols. Wiesbaden: Fritz Stein Verlag, 1976.

Fu Chin-hsing 傅金星. "Chao Ju-kua" 趙汝适. *Ch'üan-chou shih chih t'ung-hsun* 泉州史之通訊 1992, no. 1: 36.

———. "Lueh-t'an Nan-wai tsung tui Ch'üan-chou ti ying-hsiang" 略談南外宗對泉州的影響. *Ch'üan-chou Chao Sung Nan-wai-tsung yen-chiu* 泉州趙宋南外宗研究 1993, no. 1: 41–46.

Fu Tsung-wen 傅宗文. "Hou-chu ku-ch'uan: Sung chi nan-wai tsung-shih hai-wai ching-shang ti wu-cheng" 后渚古船: 宋季南外宗室海外經商的物證. *Hai-wai chiao-t'ung yen-chiu* 海外交通研究 2 (1989): 77–83.

Green, Jeremy. "The Song Dynasty Shipwreck at Quanzhou, Fujian Province, People's Republic of China." *International Journal of Nautical Archaeology and Underwater Exploration* 12, no. 3 (1983): 253-61.

Guisso, Richard W. L. "The Reigns of the Empress Wu, Chung-tsung and Jui-tsung (684–712)." In Denis Twitchett and Michael Loewe, eds., *The Cambridge History of China*, vol. 3, *Sui and T'ang China, 589–906, Part I*, pp. 290–332. Cambridge, Eng.: Cambridge University Press, 1979.

Haeger, John W. "1126-27: Political Crises and the Integrity of Culture." In Haeger, ed., *Crises and Prosperity in Sung China*, pp. 143–62. Tucson: University of Arizona Press, 1975.

Halperin, Mark Robert. "Pieties and Responsibilities: Buddhism and the Chinese Literati, 780–1280." Ph.D. diss., University of California, Berkeley, 1997.

Han-ou Chao-shih tsung-p'u 韓區趙氏宗譜. 1908.

Hargett, James M. "The Pleasure Parks of Kaifeng and Lin'an During the Sung Dynasty (960–1279)." In *Proceedings of the International Symposium on Sung History*, pp. 17–36. Taipei: Chinese Culture University, 1988.

Hartwell, Robert M. "The Imperial Treasuries: Finance and Power in Song China." *Bulletin of Sung Yuan Studies* 20 (1988): 18–89.

Hirth, Friederich, and W. W. Rockhill, trans. *Chau Ju-kua: His Work on the Chinese and Arab Trade in the Twelfth and Thirteenth Centuries, Entitled "Chu-fan-chi."* St. Petersburg: Imperial Academy of Sciences, 1911; reprinted—Taipei: Ch'eng-wen, 1970.

Holmgren, Jennifer. "Imperial Marriage in the Native Chinese and Non-Han State, Han to Ming." In Rubie S. Watson and Patricia Buckley Ebrey, eds., *Marriage and Inequality in Chinese Society*, pp. 58–96. Berkeley: University of California Press, 1991.

Hsu, Cho-yun. *Ancient China in Transition: An Analysis of Social Mobility, 722–222 B.C.* Stanford: Stanford University Press, 1965.

Hsu Meng-hsin 徐夢莘. *San-ch'ao pei-meng hui-pien* 三朝北盟會編. Taipei: Wen-hai ch'u-pan she, 1962.

Hsu Nai-ch'ang 徐乃昌, ed. *Sung Yuan k'o-chü san lu* 宋元科舉三錄. 1929.

Huang K'uan-chung 黃寬重. "Li Ch'iung ping-pien yü Nan-Sung ch'u-ch'i ti cheng-chü" 酈瓊兵變與南宋初期的政局. In idem, *Nan-Sung chün-cheng yü wen-hsien t'an-suo* 南宋軍政與文獻, pp. 51–104. Taipei: Hsin wen-feng, 1990.

Huang, Ray. *1587, a Year of No Significance: The Ming Dynasty in Decline*. New Haven: Yale University Press, 1981.

Huang Tsung-hsi 黃宗羲. *Sung Yuan hsüeh-an* 宋元學案. Peking: Chung-hua shu-chü, 1989.

Hucker, Charles O. "Confucianism and the Chinese Censorial System." In David S. Nivison and Arthur F. Wright, eds., *Confucianism in Action*, pp. 182–208. Stanford: Stanford University Press, 1959.

————. *A Dictionary of Official Titles in Imperial China*. Stanford: Stanford University Press, 1985.

Hung Mai 洪邁. *Jung-chai san-pi* 容齋三筆. Pi-chi hsiao-shuo ed.

Hurst, G. Cameron. "Minamoto Family." In *Kodansha Encyclopedia of Japan*, 5: 176–78. Tokyo: Kodansha, 1983.

Hymes, Robert P. "Marriage, Descent Groups and the Localist Strategy in Sung and Yuan Fu-chou." In Patricia Buckley Ebrey and James L. Watson, eds., *Kinship Organization in Late Imperial China*, pp. 95–136. Berkeley: University of California Press, 1986.

————. *Statesmen and Gentlemen: The Elite of Fu-chou, Chiang-Hsi, in Northern and Southern Sung*. Cambridge, Eng.: Cambridge University Press, 1986.

Ihara Hiroshi 伊原弘. "Nan Sō Shisen ni okeru Go Gi no rango no seiji dōkō" 南宋四川における呉曦の乱後の政治動向. *Shigaku* 史學 5 (1980): 105–28.

Jay, Jennifer W. *A Change in Dynasties: Loyalism in Thirteenth-Century China*. Bellingham, Wash.: Western Washington University, Center for East Asian Studies, 1991.

Kinugawa Tsuyoshi 衣川強. "Kaishi yōhei' o megutte" 開禧用兵をめぐって. *Tōyōshi kenkyū* 東洋研究 36, no. 3 (1977): 128–51.

Kracke, Edward. *Civil Service in Early Sung China, 960–1067*. Cambridge, Mass.: Harvard University Press, 1953.

Ko Sheng-chung 葛勝仲. *Tan-yang chi* 丹陽集. Ch'ang-chou hsien-che i-shu ed.

Ku Yen-wu 顧炎武. *Jih-chih lu* 日知錄. Taipei: Ming-lin, 1970.

Kuo Sung-i 郭松義. "Ch'ing tsung-shih ti teng-chi chieh-kou chi ching-chi ti-wei" 清宗室的等級結構及經濟地位. In Li Chung-ch'ing 李中清 (James Lee) and Kuo Sung-i, *Ch'ing-tai huang-tsu jen-k'ou hsing-wei ho she-hui huan-ching* 清代皇族人口行爲和社會環境, pp. 116–33. Peking: Pei-ching ta-hsueh ch'u-pan-she, 1994.

Lai Hui-min 賴惠民. "Ch'ing-tai huang-tsu ti feng-chueh yü jen-kuan yen-chiu" 清代皇族的封爵與任官研究. In Li Chung-ch'ing 李中清 (James Lee) and Kuo Sung-i 郭松義, eds., *Ch'ing-tai huang-tsu jen-k'ou hsing-wei ho she-hui huan-ching* 清代皇族人口行爲和社會環境, pp. 134–53. Peking: Pei-ching ta-hsueh ch'u-pan-she, 1994.

Lam, Joseph S. C. "Musical Relics and Cultural Expressions: State Sacrificial Songs from the Southern Song Court." *Journal of Sung Yuan Studies* 25 (1995): 1–27.

Lee, Thomas H. C. *Government Education and Examinations in Sung China*. Hong Kong: Chinese University Press, 1986.

Lewis, Andrew W. *Royal Succession in Capetian France: Studies on Familial Order and the State*. Cambridge, Mass.: Harvard University Press, 1981.

Li Chung-ch'ing 李中清 (James Lee), Wang Feng 王豐, and Cameron Campbell. "Liang chung pu-t'ung ti ssu-wang hsien-chih kou-chih: huang-tsu jen-k'ou chung ti ying-erh ho erh-t'ung ssu-wang shuai" 兩忠不同的死亡限制機制: 皇族人口中的嬰兒和兒童的死亡率. In Li Chung-ch'ing and Kuo Sung-i 郭松義, eds., *Ch'ing-tai huang-tsu jen-k'ou hsing-wei ho she-hui huan-ching* 清代皇族人口行爲和社會環境, pp. 39–59. Peking: Pei-ching ta-hsueh ch'u-pan-she, 1994.

Li Hsin-ch'uan 李心傳. *Chien-yen i-lai ch'ao-yeh tsa-chi* 建炎以來朝野雜記. Compiled early 13th century. Taipei: Wen-hai, 1968.

———. *Chien-yen i-lai Hsi-nien yao-lu* 建炎以來繫年要錄. Taiwan: Wen-hai, 1968.

———. *Tao-ming lu* 道命錄. Chih-pu-tsu chai ts'ung-shu.

Li T'ao 李燾. *Hsu Tzu-chih t'ung-chien ch'ang-pien* 續資治通鑒長編. Peking: Chung-hua shu-chü.

Li Tung-hua 李東華. *Ch'üan-chou yü wo kuo chung-ku ti hai-shang chiao-t'ung* 泉州與我國中古的海上交通. Taipei: Hsueh-sheng shu-chü, 1986.

Li Yü-k'un 李與昆. *Ch'üan-chou hai-wai chiao-t'ung shih lueh* 泉州海外交通史略. Hsia-men: Hsia-men ta-hsueh ch'u-pan-she, 1992. Chapter 13, "Chao Sung Nan-wai tsung-tzu yü Ch'üan-chou hai-wai chiao-t'ung" 趙宋南外宗子與泉州海外交通," is reprinted in *Ch'üan-chou Chao Sung Nan-wai-tsung yen-chiu* 泉州趙宋南外宗研究 1993, no. 1: 48–55.

Liu Hsing-chün 劉馨珺. *Nan-Sung Ching-hu-nan lu ti pien-luan chih yen-chiu* 南宋荊湖南陸的變亂之研究. Taipei: T'ai-wan ta-hsueh wen-hsueh yuan, 1994.

Liu I-ch'ing 劉一清. *Ch'ien-t'ang i-shih* 錢塘遺史. Nanking: Chiang-su kuang-ling ku-chi k'o yin she, 1990.

Liu, James T. C. "China's Imperial Power in Mid-dynastic Crises: The Case in 1127–30." Paper presented to the Columbia University Traditional China Seminar, 1982.

———. *China Turning Inward: Intellectual Changes in the Early Twelfth Century.* Cambridge, Mass.: Harvard University, Council on East Asian Studies, 1988.

———. "How Did a Neo-Confucian School Become the State Orthodoxy?" *Philosophy East and West* 23 (1973): 483–505.

———. *Reform in Sung China: Wang An-shih (1021–1086) and His New Policies.* Cambridge, Mass.: Harvard University Press, 1959.

———. "The Sung Emperors and the *Ming-t'ang* or Hall of Enlightenment." In Françoise Aubin, ed., *Etudes in memorium Etienne Balazs*, Série II, pp. 45–58. Paris: Mouton, 1973.

Lo Chün 羅濬. *Pao-ch'ing Ssu-ming chih* 寶慶四明志. 1227. Sung Yuan Ssu-ming liu chih ed.

Lo Jung-pang. "The Emergence of China as a Seapower During the Late Sung and Early Yuan Periods. *Far Eastern Quarterly* 11 (1952). Republished in John A. Harrison, ed., *Enduring Scholarship Selected from the "Far Eastern Quarterly"—the "Journal of Asian Studies," 1941–1971*, pp. 91–105. Tucson: University of Arizona Press, 1972.

Lo, Winston W. *An Introduction to the Civil Service of Sung China, with Emphasis on Its Personnel Administration.* Honolulu: University of Hawaii Press, 1987.

———. "A New Perspective on the Sung Civil Service." *Journal of Asian Studies* 17 (1982): 121–35.

Loehr, Max. *The Great Painters of China.* Oxford: Phaidon Press, 1980.

Loewe, Michael. "The Former Han Dynasty." In Denis Twitchett and Michael Loewe, eds., *The Cambridge History of China*, vol. 1, *The Ch'in and Han Empires, 221 B.C.–A.D. 220*, pp. 103–222. Cambridge, Eng.: Cambridge University Press, 1986.

————. "The Structure and Practice of Government." *The Cambridge History of China*, vol. 1, *The Ch'in and Han Empires, 221 B.C.–A.D. 220*, pp. 463–90. Cambridge, Eng.: Cambridge University Press, 1986.

Ma Tuan-lin 馬端臨. *Wen-hsien t'ung-k'ao* 文獻統考. Taipei: Hsin-hsing shu-chü, 1964.

McKnight, Brian E. *Law and Order in Sung China*. Cambridge, Eng.: Cambridge University Press, 1992.

————. *Village and Bureaucracy in Southern Sung China*. Chicago: University of Chicago Press, 1971.

McKnight, Brian, and James T. C. Liu. *Ch'ing-ming chi, the Sung Dynasty Work: A Collection*. Albany: State University of New York Press, 1999.

Min-chung chin-shih lueh 閩中金石略. Shanghai: Chung-hua shu-chü, 1934.

Ming-kung shu-k'an Ch'ing-ming chi 名公書判清明集. Peking: Chung-hua shu-chü, 1987.

Miyazaki Ichisada 竺沙雅章. *Sō no Taiso to Taisō* 宋の太祖と太宗. Tokyo: Shimizu shoin, 1975.

Moroto Tatsuo 諸戸立雄. "Sōdai no tai sōshitsu-saku ni tsuite" 宋代の對宗室策について. *Bungaku* 文學 22 (1958): 623–40.

Mote, Frederick. "Confucian Eremitism in the Yuan Period." In Arthur Wright, ed., *Confucianism and Chinese Civilization*, pp. 252–90. Stanford: Stanford University Press, 1964.

Murray, Julia. "Sung Kao-tsung, Ma Ho-chih, and the *Mao-shih* Scrolls." Ph.D. diss., Princeton University, 1981.

Nienhauser, William H., Jr., ed. *The Indiana Companion to Traditional Chinese Literature*. Bloomington: Indiana University Press, 1986.

Ou-yang Hsiu 歐陽修. *Hsin T'ang-shu* 新唐書 (also called *T'ang-shu*). Peking: Chung-hua shu-chü, 1987.

Pan Ku 班固. *Han shu* 漢書. Chung-hua shu-chü, 1962.

Peirce, Leslie P. *The Imperial Harem: Women and Sovereignty in the Ottoman Empire*. Oxford: Oxford University Press, 1993.

Peterson, Charles A. "Old Illusions and New Realities: Sung Foreign Policy, 1217–1234." In Morris Rossabi, ed., *China Among Equals: The Middle Kingdom and Its Neighbors, 10th–14th Centuries*, pp. 204–39. Berkeley: University of California Press, 1983.

Pi Yuan 畢沅. *Hsu Tzu-chih t'ung-chien* 續資治通鑒. Peking: Chung-hua shu-chü, 1988.

Rawski, Evelyn Sakakida, "Ch'ing Imperial Marriage and Problems of Rulership." In Rubie Watson and Patricia Ebrey, eds., *Marriage and Inequality in Chinese Society*, pp. 170–203. Berkeley: University of California Press, 1991.

————. *The Last Emperors: A Social History of Qing Imperial Institutions*. Berkeley: University of California Press, 1998.

Rossabi, Morris. *Khubilai Khan: His Life and Times*. Berkeley: University of California Press, 1988.

Sariti, Anthony. Biography of Lü Hui-ch'ing. In Herbert Franke, ed., *Sung Biographies*, 2: 707-12. Wiesbaden: Fritz Stein Verlag, 1976.

Schirokauer, Conrad. "Neo-Confucians Under Attack: The Condemnation of *Wei-hsueh*." In John Haeger, ed., *Crisis and Prosperity in Sung China*. Tucson: University of Arizona Press, 1975.

Schneider, Laurence A. *A Madman of Ch'u: The Chinese Myth of Loyalty and Dissent*. Berkeley: University of California Press, 1980.

Schottenhammer, Angela. "Characteristics of Song Epitaphs." In Dieter Kuhn, ed., *Burial in Song China*, pp. 253–306. Ed. Forum. Würzburg: Würzburger Sinologische Schriften, 1994.

Scogin, Hugh. "Poor Relief in Northern Sung China." *Oriens Extremus* 25, no. 1 (1978): 30-46.

Shen Ch'i-hsin (Shen Qixin). *Chung-hua hsing-shih t'ung-shu: Chao-hsing* 中華姓氏通書：趙姓. Ch'ang-sha: San-huan, 1991.

Sheng, Angela Yu-yun. "Textile Use, Technology, and Change in Rural Textile Production in Song China (960-1279)." Ph.D. diss., University of Pennsylvania, 1990.

Shiba Yoshinobu. Biography of P'u Shou-keng. In Herbert Franke, ed., *Sung Biographies*, 2: 839–42. Wiesbaden: Fritz Stein Verlag, 1976.

————. "Sung Foreign Trade: Its Scope and Organization." In Morris Rossabi, ed., *China Among Equals: The Middle Kingdom and Its Neighbors, 10th–14th Centuries*, pp. 89–115. Berkeley: University of California Press, 1983.

Shih Hao 史浩, ed. *Hsien-yuan lei-p'u* 僊淵類譜. 30 *chuan* extant. 12th c. Surviving fragment in the Beijing National Library rare books collection.

Siren, Osvald, *Chinese Painting: Leading Masters and Principles*, Part I, *The First Millennium*, vol. 2, *The Sung Period*. London: Percy Lund, Humphries & Co., 1956.

Smith, Paul. "Shen-tsung's Reign (1068–1085)." Draft chapter for the *Cambridge History of China*, vol. 5, *The Sung*.

————. "State Power and Economic Activism During the New Policies, 1068–1085: The Tea and Horse Trade and the 'Green Sprouts' Loan Policy." In Robert Hymes and Conrad Schirokauer, eds., *Ordering the World: Views of State and Society in Sung China*, pp. 76–127. Berkeley: University of California Press, 1993.

————. *Taxing Heaven's Storehouse: Horses, Bureaucrats, and the Destruction of the Sichuan Tea Industry, 1074–1224*. Cambridge, Mass.: Harvard University, Council on East Asian Studies, 1991.

So, Kee-long (see also Su Chi-lang). "Financial Crisis and Local Economy: Ch'üan-chou in the Thirteenth Century." *T'oung Pao* 77 (1991): 119–37.

Soulliere, Ellen. "The Imperial Marriages of the Ming Dynasty." *Papers on Far Eastern History* 37 (1988): 15–42.

————. "Palace Women in the Ming Dynasty." Ph.D. diss., Princeton University, 1987.

————. "Reflections on Chinese Despotism and the Power of the Inner Court." *Asian Profile* 12, no. 2 (1984): 129–45.

Su Chi-lang (Billy Kee-long So) 蘇基朗. *T'ang Sung shih-tai Min-nan Ch'üan-chou shih ti lun kao* 唐宋時代閩南泉州史地論稿. Taipei: Shang-wu, 1992.

Sun Yen-min 孫彥民. *Sung-tai shu-yüan chih-tu chih yen-chiu* 宋代書院制度之研究. Taipei: Kuo-li Cheng-chih ta-hsüeh, 1963.

Sung Ch'ang-lien and Miyazaki Ichisada. Biography of T'ai-tsung. In Herbert Franke, ed., *Sung Biographies*, 3: 992–95. Wiesbaden: Franz Steiner Verlag, 1976.

Sung hui-yao chi-kao 宋會要輯稿: "Chih-kuan" 治官, "Ch'ung-ju" 崇儒, "Hsuan-chü" 選舉, and "Ti-hsi" 帝繫 sections. Taipei: Shih-chieh shu-chü, 1964.

Sung hui-yao chi-kao pu-pien 宋會要輯稿補編. Peking: Ch'üan-kuo t'u-shu-kuan wen-hsien su-wei fu-chih chung-hsin, 1988.

Sung-shih chi-shih 宋史紀實. 17+6 ed. Reprinted—Taipei, 1968.

Ta Ming i-t'ung chih 大明一統誌. 1461 ed.

Teng Kuang-ming 鄧廣銘. *Yueh Fei chuan* 岳飛傳. Peking: Hsin-hua shu-chü, 1963.

Tillman, Hoyt Cleveland. *Confucian Discourse and Chu Hsi's Ascendency*. Honolulu: University of Hawaii Press, 1992.

————. "Southern Sung Confucianism: The *Tao-hsüeh* Fellowship." Draft chapter for the *Cambridge History of China*, vol. 5.

————. *Utilitarian Confucianism: Ch'en Liang's Challenge to Chu Hsi*. Cambridge, Mass.: Harvard University, Council on East Asian Studies, 1982.

Ting Ch'uan-ching. *A Compilation of Anecdotes of Sung Personalities*. Selected and trans. by Chu Djang and Jane C. Djang. New York: St. John's University Press, 1989.

T'o T'o 脫脫. *Sung shih* 宋史. 495 *chuan*. Peking: Chung-hua shu-chü, 1977.

Twitchett, Denis. "The Fan Clan's Charitable Estate, 1050–1760." In David S. Nivison, ed., *Confucianism in Action*, pp. 97–133. Stanford: Stanford University Press, 1959.

————. "Hsüan-tsung (reign 712–56)." In Denis Twitchett, ed., *The Cambridge History of China*, vol. 3, *Sui and T'ang China, 589–906*, Part I, pp. 333–463. Cambridge, Eng.: Cambridge University Press, 1979.

————. "The T'ang Imperial Family." *Asia Major*, 3d series, 7, no. 2 (1994): 1–61.

Umehara Kaoru 梅原郁. *Chūgoku kinsei no toshi to bunka* 中國近世の都市と文化. Kyoto: Kyōto daigaku Jinbunka kenkyūsha, 1984.

————. "Civil and Military Officials in the Sung: The *Chi-lu-kuan* System." *Acta Asiatica* 50 (1986): 1–30.

Wakeman, Frederic, Jr. *The Great Enterprise: The Manchu Reconstruction of Imperial Order in Seventeenth Century China*. 2 vols. Berkeley: University of California Press, 1985.

Walton, Linda A. *Academies and Society in Southern Sung China*. Honolulu: University of Hawaii Press, 1999.

————. "The Institutional Context of Neo-Confucianism: Scholars, Schools, and *Shu-yüan* in Sung-Yüan China." In Wm. Theodore de Bary and John Chaffee, eds., *Neo-Confucian Education: The Formative Stage*, pp. 457–92. Berkeley: University of California Press, 1989.

Wang Ch'eng 王稱. *Tung-tu shih-lueh* 東都史略. Taipei: Wenhai, 1967.

Wang Gungwu. "Feng Tao: An Essay on Confucian Loyalty." In Arthur Wright, ed., *Confucianism and Chinese Civilization*, pp. 188–210. Stanford: Stanford University Press, 1964.

————. "The Rhetoric of Lesser Empire: Early Sung Relations with Its Neighbors." In Morris Rossabi, ed., *China Among Equals: The Middle Kingdom and Its Neighbors, 10th-14th Centuries*, pp. 47–65. Berkeley: University of California Press, 1983.

————. *The Structure of Power in North China During the Five Dynasties*. Stanford: Stanford University Press, 1963.

Wang Lien-mao 王濂茂. "P'u Shou-keng t'u-sha Nan-wai tsung-tzu k'ao" 蒲壽庚屠殺南外宗子考. *Ch'üan-chou wen shih* 泉州文史 12, no. 4 (1980): 75–82.

Wang Ming-ch'ing 王明清. *Hui-chu san lu* 揮麈三錄. TSCC.

Wang P'u 王溥. *T'ang hui-yao* 唐會要. Taipei: Shih-chieh shu-chü, 1968.

Wang Sheng-to 汪聖鐸. "Sung-ch'ao tsung-shih chih-tu k'ao" 宋朝宗室制度考. *Wen-shih* 文史 33 (1990): 171–200.

Wang Ying-lin 土應麟. *Yü-hai* 玉海. Taipei: Hua-wen shu-chü, 1967.

Wechsler, Howard. *Offerings of Jade and Silk: Ritual and Symbol in the Legitimation of the T'ang Dynasty*. New Haven: Yale University Press, 1985.

Wilhelm, Helmut. "From Myth to Myth: The Case of Yüeh Fei's Biography." In Arthur F. Wright, ed., *Confucianism and Chinese Civilization*, pp. 211–26. Stanford: Stanford University Press, 1975.

Wilson, Thomas A. *Genealogy of the Way: The Construction and Uses of the Confucian Tradition in Late Imperial China*. Stanford: Stanford University Press, 1995.

Worthy, Edmund H. "The Founding of Sung China, 950–1000: Integrative Changes in Military and Political Institutions." Ph.D. diss., Princeton University, 1975.

———. "Regional Control in the Southern Sung Salt Administration." In John Haeger, ed., *Crisis and Prosperity in Sung China*, pp. 101–42. Tucson: University of Arizona Press, 1975.

Yeh Te-hui 葉德輝, ed. *Sung Chung-ting Chao Chou-wang pieh-lu* 宋忠定趙周王別錄. 8 *chuan*. Ch'ang-sha, 1908.

———. *Sung Chao Chung-ting tsou-i* 宋趙忠定奏議. 3 *chuan*. Ch'ang-sha, 1910.

Glossary

an 案
An-chi chou (Liang-che) 安吉州
An-chün, Prince of 安郡王
an-hsi 案系
An Lu-shan 安祿山
An-p'ing Bridge 安平橋
An-ting 安定

ch'a-k'ou 茶寇
Ch'ai Chung-hsing 柴中行
ch'ai-i fa 差役法
Chang, Lady 張氏
Chang Ching 張靖
Chang-ch'iu county (Chi-nan fu) 章丘縣
Chang-chou (Fu-chien) 漳州
Chang Chün (1097–1164) 張俊
Chang Chün (1086–1154) 張浚
Chang Fang-p'ing 張方平
Chang Hao 張澔
Chang-hsien Empress 章獻太后
Chang Pang-ch'ang 張邦昌
chang-shih 長史
Chang Shih 張栻
Chang Shih-chieh 張世傑
Chang Tuan-i 張端義
Chang Tun 章惇

Ch'ang-an Gate 長安門
Ch'ang-chou (Liang-che) 常州
Ch'ang-shan county (Ch'u-chou, Liang-che) 常山縣
Ch'ang-shou county (Su-chou) 常熟縣
Chao An-jen 趙安仁
Chao Chen 趙禎
Chao Chi 趙佶
Chao Ch'i (Hui-tsung) 趙祺
Chao Ch'i (Li-tsung's 2d son) 趙緝
Chao Chia Pao 趙家堡
Chao Ch'ien-fu 趙灊夫
Chao Ching 趙敬
Chao Chung-tsung 趙仲琮
Chao Ch'ung-chi 趙崇濟
Chao Fan 趙范
Chao Fen 趙汾
Chao Heng 趙恆
Chao Hsi-ch'ü 趙希瞿
Chao Hsi-lu 趙希瓐
Chao Hsi-tao 趙希道
Chao Hsu 趙頊
Chao Hsu 趙煦
Chao Huan 趙桓
Chao Hung-yin 趙弘殷
Chao I-ch'un 趙宜春

Chao K'o-chieh 趙克戒
Chao Kou 趙構
Chao Kuang-i 趙光義
Chao K'uang-i 趙匡義
Chao Kuang-mei 趙光美
Chao K'uang-mei 趙匡美
Chao K'uang-yin 趙匡胤
Chao Kuei 趙炅
Chao Kuei-ch'eng 趙貴誠
Chao Kuei-ho 趙貴和
Chao K'uei 趙葵
Chao Kung-chiung 趙公迵
Chao K'uo 趙擴
Chao Ling-chün 趙令畯
Chao Ling-jang 趙令穰
Chao Mao-fu 趙卯發
Chao Meng-chien 趙孟堅
Chao Meng-fu 趙孟頫
Chao Pi-hsiang 趙必向
Chao Pi-ying 趙必迎
Chao Ping 趙昺
Chao Po-chü 趙伯駒
Chao Po-su 趙伯驌
Chao Pu-ch'en 趙不塵
Chao Pu-lou 趙不塵
Chao Pu-t'i 趙不逖
Chao P'u 趙普
Chao Shan-shen 趙善慎
Chao Shan-shih 趙善時
Chao Shen 趙慎
Chao Shih 趙是
Chao Shih-ku 趙時詁
Chao-shih tsu-p'u 趙氏族譜
Chao-shih tsung-ch'in hui 趙氏宗親會
Chao Shu 趙曙
Chao Ta-nien 趙大年
Chao-ti 昭帝
Chao T'iao 趙眺
Chao Ting 趙鼎

Chao T'ing 趙珽
Chao T'ing-mei 趙挺美
Chao Tun 趙盾
Chao Wan 趙萬
Chao Yen 趙曦
Chao Yen-huan 趙彥瑗
Chao Yü-jui 趙與芮
Chao Yü-yuan 趙與愿
Chao Yuan-hao 趙元昊
Ch'ao Pu-chih 超補之
ch'ao-san ta-fu 朝散大夫
Ch'ao-yang 潮陽
Che 浙
Che-tsung 哲宗
chen 鎮
Chen-chiang fu (Liang-che) 眞江府
Chen-chou (Huai-nan-tung) 眞州
Chen-chou (in Liao) 鎮州
chen-fu-shih 鎮撫使
Chen Te-hsiu 眞德修
Chen-ting fu (Ho-pei-hsi) 眞定府
Chen-tsung 眞宗
Chen wen-chung kung wen-chi 眞文忠公文集
Ch'en, Empress Dowager 皇太后陳氏
Ch'en Cho 陳卓
Ch'en-chou (Ching-hsi-pei) 陳州
Ch'en-chou (Ching-hu-nan) 郴州
Ch'en Chün-ch'ing 陳俊卿
Ch'en Fu-liang 陳傅良
Ch'en I-chung 陳宜中
Ch'en Kai 陳晐
Ch'en Kuei-i 陳貴誼
Ch'en K'ung-shih 陳孔碩
Ch'en Sheng-chih 陳升之
Ch'en Su 陳宿
Ch'en T'ang 陳棠
Ch'en Tseng 陳增
Ch'en T'ung 陳通

Ch'en Tzu-jen 陳自仁
cheng-ch'i 正氣
Cheng Ch'ing-chih 鄭清之
cheng-feng ta-fu 正奉大夫
Cheng Kang-chung 鄭剛中
Cheng-shih t'ang 政事堂
cheng-shuai 正帥
ch'eng 丞
ch'eng-chieh-lang 承節郎
ch'eng-hsin-lang 承信郎
Ch'eng I 程頤
Ch'eng Kuei 程桂
Ch'eng Pi 程珌
Ch'eng-ti 成帝
Ch'eng-tu fu 成都府
Chi 季
Chi, Prince of 濟王
Chi-chou (Chiang-nan-hsi) 吉州
Chi-nan fu (Ching-tung-tung)
　濟南府
chi-shih 計室
chi-shih ts'an-chün 計室參軍
Chi-shui county (Chi-chou) 吉水縣
chi-wen 祭文
Ch'i 濟
Ch'i, Prince of 濟王
Ch'i-chou (Huai-nan-hsi) 蘄州
ch'i-min 齊民
chia 家
Chia, Prince of 嘉王
Chia-hsun 家訓
Chia Hu 賈胡
chia-jen kua 家人卦
chia-shan 假山
Chia-shu 家塾
Chia Ssu-tao 賈似道
Chia-t'ai 嘉泰
Chiang Che 江澤
Chiang-chou (Chiang-nan-hsi) 江州
chiang-chün 將軍

Chiang-ning fu (Chiang-nan-tung)
　江寧府
chiang-shih-lang 將仕郎
chiang-shu 講書
chiang-shu chiao-shou 講書教授
Chiang-tu county (Yang-chou)
　興都縣
Chiang-yin chün (Liang-che) 江陰軍
chiao-shou 教授
Ch'iao Hsing-chien 喬行簡
chieh (hexagram) 節
chieh-tu kuan-ch'a liu-hou 節度觀察
　留後
chieh-tu-shih 節度使
chieh-tu-shih chien shih-chung 節度
　使兼侍中
chieh-tu-shih t'ung chung-shu men-
　hsia p'ing-chang shih 節度使同
　中書門下平章事
chien (room) 間
Chien-chou (Fu-chien) 建州
Chien Chou-fu 蹇周輔
Chien-k'ang fu (Chiang-nan-tung)
　建康府
Chien-ning fu (Fu-chien) 建寧府
chien-tang 監當
chien-tang kuan 監當官
Chien-wen 文建
Chien-yen i-lai ch'ao-yeh tsa-chi 建炎以
　來朝野雜記
Chien-yen i-lai hsi-nien yao-lu 建炎以來
　繫年要錄
Ch'ien, Lady 錢氏
Ch'ien-chou (Chiang-nan-hsi) 虔州
Ch'ien-shan county (Hsin-chou)
　鉛山縣
Ch'ien Ting 僉廳
chih 知
chih-cheng 執政
chih-ssu suo 置司所

chih Ta-tsung-cheng shih
　知大宗正事
Ch'ih-chou (Chiang-nan-tung) 池州
Chin, Prince of 晉王
Chin-hua 金華
Chin-ling 金陵
chin-shen 搢紳
ch'in 親
Ch'in, Prince of 秦王
Ch'in-hsien 親賢
Ch'in Kuei 秦檜
ch'in-min 親民
Ch'in Piao 秦彪
ch'in-tao 親道
Ch'in-tsung 欽宗
Ch'in-wang chün 勤王軍
ch'in-wang-fu 親王府
Ching, Prince of 景王
Ching-chao fu (Yung-hsing) 京兆府
Ching-k'ou 京口
ching-ling kung 景靈宮
Ching-tz'u Monastery 淨慈寺
Ching-yen 景炎
ch'ing 頃
ch'ing-lü p'ai 青綠派
ching yuan 慶源
Ch'ing-yuan fu (Ho-pei-hsi) 慶源府
Ch'ing-yuan fu (Liang-che) 慶元府
Chiu-chiang 九江
Chiu-jih Mountain 九日山
Cho-chou 涿州
Chou, Lady 周氏
Chou Meng-yang 周孟陽
Chou Pi-ta 周必大
Chou Shih-tsung 周世宗
Chu-chi 諸暨
Chu Chu 朱著
Chu-fan chih 諸藩志
Chu Fei 朱芾
Chu Hsi 朱熹

chu-hun tsung-shih 主婚宗室
chu-pu 主簿
Chu Sheng-fei 朱勝非
chu-ssu fu-shih 諸司副使
Chu T'ang 朱唐
chu-ying fu-sheng 燭影斧聲
Chu Yü 朱彧
chü-jen 舉人
Ch'u-chou (Huai-nan-tung) 楚州
Ch'u ming 除名
Ch'ü-chou (Liang-che) 衢州
ch'ü-ying 取應
Ch'ü Yuan 屈原
Ch'üan, Empress 全皇后
Ch'üan-chou (Fu-chien) 泉州
*Ch'üan-chou Chao Sung Nan-wai tsung-
　cheng-ssu yen-chiu hui pien* 泉州趙
　宋南外宗政司研究會編
chuang-yuan 狀院
Ch'ui-chien lu 吹劍錄
Chün-i Chao-shih ch'ing yuan p'u 浚儀趙
　氏慶源譜
ch'un 純
Ch'un-ch'iu 春秋
Ch'un-hsi 淳熙
Chung-chen 仲鍼
Chung-kuo jen-cheng 中國仁政
Ch'ung-ning 崇寧
ch'ung-wen chien-wu 崇文賤武

erh-ti yü-jung 二帝御容

Fan Chung-yen 范仲淹
fan-i hsiang-shih 翻譯鄉試
fan-i hui-shih 翻譯會試
Fan Ju-kuei 范如圭
Fan Wen-hu 范文虎
Fan-yen 蕃衍
Fang-lin yuan 芳林院
Fang Ta-ts'ung 方大琮

fang-yü-shih 防藥使

fei-jen 匪人

fei shih-tsu chih chia 非士族之家

fei t'an-wen i-hsia ch'in 非免文
以下親

feng 封

feng-kuo chung-wei 奉國仲尉

fo-tzu 佛子

fu (mentor) 傅

fu (rhapsody) 賦

fu, p'in 富，貧

fu-ch'en 輔臣

Fu Chin-hsing 傅金星

fu chin-shih 附進士

Fu-chou (Chiang-nan-hsi) 撫州

Fu-chou (Fu-chien) 福州

Fu Pi 富弼

Fu Po-ch'eng 傅伯成

Fu-shan quarter 福善坊

fu-shih 副使

fu-shuai 副率

Fu-tzu miao 夫子廟

Hai-ling, Prince of 海陵王

hai-shen 海神

Han Ch'i 韓琦

Han Chiang 漢絳

Han Kao-ti 漢高帝

Han T'o-chou 韓侂冑

Hang-chou (Liang-che) 杭州

Heng-chou (Ching-hu-nan) 衡州

Heng-ch'ü 橫渠

Heng-shan county (T'an-chou)
衡山縣

ho-mai 和買

Ho Kuan 何瓘

Ho-nan fu (Ching-hsi-pei) 河南府

Ho P'u 何溥

hou 侯

Hou-chu 后渚

hou-miao 后廟

hsi 系

Hsi-an 西安

Hsi-chai 西宅

Hsi-, Nan-wai tsung-cheng-ssu 西，
南外宗政司

Hsi-nien yao-lu 繫年要錄

hsi-t'ou kung-feng kuan 西頭供奉官

Hsiang An-shih 項安世

Hsiang-chou (Ho-pei-tung) 相州

Hsiang Tzu-yin 向子諲

Hsiang-yang 襄陽

hsiao 絹

hsiao-hsueh 小學

hsiao-hsueh chiao-shou 小學教授

hsiao-shih-ch'en 小使臣

Hsiao Sui 蕭燧

Hsiao-tsung 孝宗

Hsieh, Empress Dowager 謝太后

Hsieh K'o-chia 謝克家

Hsieh Shen-fu 謝深甫

Hsien-lu Temple 仙露寺

hsien-wang shu 祆妄書

Hsien-yuan chi-ch'ing t'u 僊(or 仙)源積
慶圖

Hsien-yuan lei-p'u 僊(or 仙)源類譜

hsin 心

Hsin, Prince of 信王

Hsin-an 新安

Hsin-an, Commandary Duke of 信安
郡公

hsin-ch'eng 新城

Hsin-chou (Chiang-nan-tung) 信州

Hsin-fa 新法

Hsin-hui county (Kuang-chou, Kuang-
nan-tung) 新會縣

Hsin mu-tsung-yuan 新睦宗院

Hsin T'ang-shu 新唐書

Hsin Tao-tsung 辛道宗

hsing an-hsi 刑案係

"Hsing-ch'en hsing-tu t'u" 星辰行
　度圖
Hsing-chou (Ho-pei-hsi) 邢州
Hsing-hua chün (Fu-chien) 興化軍
hsing-pien 星變
Hsing-sheng ssu 興聖寺
hsing-ssu 行司
hsing-t'u jen 刑徒人
Hsing-yuan fu (Li-chou circuit)
　興元府
hsiu-chih-lang 修職郎
Hsiu, Prince of 秀王
Hsiu-chou (Liang-che) 秀州
Hsiu-shan 秀山
Hsiu-shui 秀水
Hsiung Fei 熊飛
Hsiung Ta-chang 熊大章
hsu 緒
Hsu 項
Hsu-chou (Ching-tung-hsi) 徐州
Hsu I 徐誼
Hsu Ta-fu 許達甫
Hsu Tzu-chih t'ung-chien ch'ang-pien
　續資治通鑑長編
Hsu Yuan-chieh 徐元杰
Hsuan-chou (Chiang-nan-tung) 宣州
Hsuan-ho 宣和
hsuan-jen 選人
Hsuan-ti 宣帝
Hsuan-yuan t'u-p'u 璿源圖譜
Hsueh-shih yuan 學士院
hsun-ming 訓名
hu an-hsi 戶案係
Hu Chia 胡賈
Hu-chou (Liang-che) 湖州
Hu Hung 胡紘
Hu Mao-lao 胡茂老
Hu Wen-hsiu 胡文修
hua-chü 譁局
Hua-she 華舍

Huai-ning fu (Ching-hsi-pei) 淮寧府
Huai River 淮河
huan-wei kuan 環衛官
Huang, Minister 黃侍臣
Huang-ch'ao chu-ch'en tsou-i 皇朝諸臣
　奏議
Huang-ch'eng ssu 皇城司
Huang-chou (Huai-nan-hsi) 黃州
Huang Hsia 黃洽
Huang Kan 黃榦
huang-po 皇伯
Huang P'u 黃朴
Huang Sheng 黃昇
Huang Shih-shu 黃師恕
Huang Sung yü-tieh 皇宋玉牒
Huang-ti yü-tieh 皇帝玉牒
Huang-yen county (T'ai-chou, Liang-
　che) 黃巖縣
hui 慧
Hui-chou (Chiang-nan-tung) 徽州
Hui-chou (Kuang-nan-tung) 惠州
Hui-tsung 徽宗
Hung-chou (Chiang-nan-hsi) 洪州
Hung Mai 洪邁
Hung T'ai-chi 洪台吉

i an-hsi 儀案係
I-chou (Ching-tung-tung) 沂州
I-hsing county (Ch'ang-chou)
　宜興縣
i-kuan shih-tsu 衣冠士族
I-shuo 易說
i-tz'u 益辭
i-yü 意欲

Jao-chou (Chiang-nan-tung) 饒州
Jen Ju-hsi 任汝昔
Jen-tsung 仁宗
Ju-chou (Ching-hsi-pei) 汝州
ju-mu 乳母

Jui-an fu (Liang-che) 瑞安府

k'ai-fu i-t'ung san-ssu 開府儀同 三司
K'ai-yuan hamlet 開元鄉
K'ai-yuan Temple 開元寺
K'ang, Prince of 康王
Kao-tsung 高宗
Kao-yu chün (Huai-nan-tung) 高郵軍
k'ao-hsuan fa 考選法
Ko Hung 葛洪
k'o 刻
k'o-chü 科舉
K'o Sung-ying 柯宋英
ku chün-tzu 古君子
ku-i ch'ien 孤遺錢
ku-i ch'ien mi 孤遺錢米
Ku-shih county (Kuang-chou, Kuang-tung) 固始縣
kuan 貫
kuan-ch'a-shih 觀察使
kuan-hu 官戶
Kuan Li 關禮
kuan-t'ien 官田
Kuang-ch'in-chai 廣親宅
Kuang-chou (Huai-nan-hsi) 光州
Kuang-chou (Kuang-nan-tung) 廣州
kuang-lu ta-fu 光祿大夫
Kuang Ning erh-ch'ao pao hsun 光寧 二朝寶訓
Kuang-tsung 光宗
Kuang-wu 光武
kung 宮
kung an-hsi 工案係
Kung hsien (Ho-nan fu) 鞏縣
kung-hsien 恭憲
Kung-shou t'u-shu 功守圖書
kung-t'ien fa 公田法
kung-tsu 公族

kung-tsung 恭宗
kung-yuan (clan residence) 宮院
kuo 國
Kuo Kao 郭杲
kuo-t'i 國體
Kuo-tzu hsueh 國子學
kuo yü wu teng che pu wei ch'in 過于 五等者不爲親
Kuo Yung 郭雍

Lan-ch'i 藍溪
li (clerk) 吏
li (hexagram) 離
li (locality) 里
li (ritual) 禮
Li, Lady 李氏
Li Ch'eng 李成
li-chiao 禮教
Li Chien-p'u 李謙溥
Li Ch'iung 麗瓊
Li Ch'üan 李全
Li Fang 李昉
Li Feng 李逢
Li Han-pin 李漢斌
Li Hsin-ch'uan 李心傳
Li Kang 李綱
Li Lin-fu 李林甫
Li Mu 李沐
Li Sao 離騷
Li Shih-chih 李適之
Li Shih-min 李世民
Li Shih-ning 李士寧
Li Shou 李綬
Li T'ao 李燾
Li T'ien 李田
Li-tsung 理宗
Li Tsung-cheng 李宗政
Li Tung-hua 李東華
Li Yü-k'un 李玉昆
Li Yuan 李淵

Li Yuan-li 李元礪
liang 兩
liang-chia nü 良家女
liang-chih kuan 兩制官
Liang-ching tsung-cheng-ssu 兩京宗
　政司
Liang hsien (Ju-chou) 梁縣
liang-shih 量試
lien 奩
Lin-an fu (Liang-che) 臨安府
Lin Kuang-shan 林光山
ling 綾
Liu Cheng 留正
Liu Cheng-yen 劉正彥
Liu Chin 劉瑾
Liu Ch'ing-fu 劉慶福
Liu Ch'ü-li 劉屈氂
Liu Han-pi 劉漢弼
Liu Ho 劉賀
Liu Hsiang 劉向
Liu Hsiu 劉秀
Liu Hsuan 劉玄
liu-i 六藝
Liu K'o-chuang 劉克莊
Liu Kuang-tsu 劉光祖
Liu Pang 劉邦
Liu Ping-i 劉病已
Liu Shu 劉述
Liu Te-hsiu 劉德修
Liu Yen-wen 劉彥文
Liu Yü 劉育 (1073–1146)
Liu Yü 劉預 (fl. 1120s)
lo 羅
Lo-shan shu-yuan 樂善書院
Lo-yang 洛陽
Lou Yueh 樓鑰
Lu, Mount 廬山
Lu-chou (Huai-nan-hsi) 廬州
Lu-ling county (Chi-chou) 廬陵縣
lu-shih ts'an-chün 錄事參軍

Lu Tuo-hsun 盧多遜
Lu Yu 陸游
Lü Hui 呂誨
Lü Hui-ch'ing 呂惠卿
Lü I-hao 呂頤浩
Lü Meng-cheng 呂蒙正
Lü Tsao 呂造
Lü Tsu-chien 呂祖儉
Lü Tsu-ch'ien 呂祖謙
lun 論
lung-tao 龍刀
Lung-hsing 隆興
Lung-t'u ko 龍圖閣
Lung-yu Empress Dowager 隆祐
　太后

Ma Chin 馬進
Ma Kuang 馬廣
Ma Tuan-lin 馬端臨
Meng, Empress 孟太后
Meng Keng 孟庚
Mi-chou (Ching-tung-tung) 密州
miao 廟
Miao Ch'ang-i 苗昌裔
Miao Fu 苗傅
mien 綿
Min 閩
Ming-ch'ing Temple 明慶寺
Ming-chou (Ho-pei-hsi) 洺州
Ming-chou (Liang-che) 明州
Ming-t'ang 明堂
Moroto Tatsuo 諸戶立雄
mu-chih-ming 墓誌銘
Mu-ch'in-chai 睦親宅
Mu-ch'in kuang-ch'in pei-chai
　睦親廣親北宅
Mu-ch'in yuan 睦親院
Mu-jung Yen-feng 幕容
　彥逢
Mu-tsung yuan 睦宗院

Na-ho Mai-chu 納合買住
Nan-an county 南安縣
Nan-ao 南澳
Nan-chai 南宅
Nan-chia 南家
Nan-chia chi-hao 南家記號
Nan-hsiung-chou (Kuang-nan-tung) 南雄州
Nan-kung 南宮
nan-pan 南班
nan-pan-kuan 南班管
Nan-pan shu 南班書
Nan-wai t'ien-yuan Chao-shih tsu-p'u 南外天源趙氏族譜
Nan-yang Liu 南陽劉
nei-ch'en chih chia 內臣之家
nei-chün 內郡
Nei-shih sheng 內侍省
nei-tien ch'ung-pan 內殿崇班
ni 逆
Ni Ssu 倪思
Ning-kuo fu (Chiang-nan-tung) 寧國府
Ning-tsung 寧宗
nu-nü 奴女

o-ni 惡逆
Ou-yang Hsiu 歐陽修

pai-shen-jen 白身人
p'an 判
P'an Chih 潘時
Pao Cheng 包拯
Pao-chou tsung-shih 保州宗室
pao-i-lang 保義郎
Pao-wen ko 寶文閣
Pei-chai 北宅
Pei-ch'i Chao-shih tsu-p'u 北溪趙氏族譜

pen-kuan pen-wei tsun-chang 本官本位尊長
P'eng Ju-li 彭汝礪
P'eng Kuei-nien 彭龜年
p'i 匹
ping an-hsi 兵安係
ping-ma tu-chien 兵馬都監
P'ing-chiang fu (Liang-che) 平江府
po 伯
po-shih 博士
P'o-yang Chao-shih hsu hsiu p'u 鄱陽趙氏續修譜
pu 簿
pu ch'eng wen-li che 不成文理者
pu chi feng 不及封
pu chi ming 不及名
pu hsien shih-shu 不限世數
pu li-wu 不釐務
P'u, Prince of 普王
P'u, Prince of (Ying-tsung's family) 僕工
P'u-chiang 浦江
P'u-chou (Ching-tung-hsi) 濮州
P'u-hsi 浦西
P'u Shou-keng 簿壽庚
P'u-t'ien county 浦田縣

San-chiang 三江
san-pan 三班
san-pan feng-chih 三班奉職
San-she fa 三舍法
sha-ch'ien 沙錢
Shan-chou (Yung-hsing) 陝州
Shan-yin county (Shao-hsing fu) 山陰縣
Shan-yuan 澶淵
Shang-ch'ing Palace 上清宮
Shang-jao county (Hsin-chou) 上饒縣
shao-ch'ing 少卿

Shao-hsing fu (Liang-che) 紹興府
Shao-ting 紹定
Shao-wu chün (Fu-chien) 邵武軍
Shen, Prince 申王
Shen Ch'i-hsin 沈其新
Shen Hui 沈晦
Shen Kua 沈括
Shen-tsung 神宗
shen-yü k'u 神御庫
sheng 升
shih (house) 室
shih (picul) 石
shih an-hsi 士案係
Shih Chai-chih 史宅之
Shih Ching-ch'ing 史璟卿
shih-fu 詩賦
Shih Hao 史浩
Shih-ku shu-yuan 石鼓書院
Shih Mi-yuan 史彌遠
Shih-po-ssu 市舶司
Shih Sung-chih 史嵩之
shih-ta-fu 士大夫
shih-tsu 士族
Shih-tsung 世宗
Shih-ts'ung 侍從
shu-chi 屬籍
Shu-chou (Huai-nan-hsi) 舒州
shu-hsing fa 庶姓法
shu-yuan 書院
shuai 帥
Shuai-fu fu-shai 率府副率
ssu-ma (assistant administrator) 司馬
ssu-ma (degree of mourning) 緦麻
Ssu-ma Kuang 司馬光
Ssu-tsung-ssu 司宗寺
Su-chou (Liang-che) 蘇州
Su Hsun 蘇洵
Su Shih 蘇軾
Su-shui chi-wen 涑水記聞
Sun Fu (992–1057) 孫復

Sun Fu (1078–1128) 孫傅
Sun Ti 孫覿
Sun Yu-fu 孫由馥
sun-yuan 孫院
Sung Ch'i 宋琪
Sung hui-yao 宋會要
Sung hui-yao chi-kao 宋會要輯稿
sung-jan 悚然
Sung-shih chi-shih 宋詩紀事
suo 所
suo-t'ing shih 鎖廳試
suo-tsai kuan-ssu 所在官司

Ta-ch'ing-tien 大慶殿
ta-hsueh 大學
Ta-kuan 大觀
ta-li 大禮
Ta-ming fu (Ho-pei-tung) 大名府
Ta-ning chien (K'uei-chou lu) 大寧監
ta-shih-ch'en 大使臣
Ta tsung-cheng ssu 大宗正司
ta yuan-shuai 大元帥
T'ai, Mount 泰山
T'ai-ch'ang ch'eng 太常丞
T'ai-ch'ang yin-ko li 太常因革禮
t'ai-chien 臺諫
T'ai-ch'ing Hall 太清樓
T'ai-chou (Huai-nan-tung) 泰州
T'ai-chou (Liang-che) 台州
T'ai-ho Palace 太和殿
T'ai-miao 太廟
T'ai-tsu 太祖
T'ai-tsu hou fu-chün 太祖後府君
"T'ai-tsu huang-ti yü-tieh ta-hsun"
     太祖皇帝玉牒大訓
T'ai-tsu shih-lu chü-yao 太祖實錄舉要
T'ai-tsung 太宗
t'ai-tzu chung-yun 太子中允
t'ai-tzu yu-chien-men shuai-fu-shuai
     太子右監門率府副率

t'ai-tzu yu-nei shuai-fu fu-shuai
太子右內率府副率

T'ai-yuan fu (Ho-tung) 太原府

t'an-chi 禮祭

T'an-chou (Ching-hu-nan) 潭州

t'an-wen 祖免

t'an-wen i-shang ch'in 祖免以上親

T'ang, King 湯王

T'ang Hsuan-tsung 唐玄宗

T'ang-shu lu i 唐書錄遺

tao-hsueh 道學

tao-i 島夷

Te-chou (Ho-pei-tung) 德州

Teng Wan 鄧綰

Teng Yu-lung 鄧友龍

T'eng Fu 滕甫

Ti-chou (Ho-pei-tung) 棣州

Ti-hua 棣華

Ti-o hui 棣萼會

Ti-ping 帝昺

tien 殿

tien-chih 殿直

t'ien-ch'ai 添差

T'ien-chang ko 天章閣

T'ien Chen-tzu 田眞子

T'ien-yuan lei-p'u 天源類譜

ting-chih 定制

Ting Chin 丁進

Ting-chou (Ching-hu-pei) 鼎州

T'ing-chou (Fu-chien) 汀州

tsa-fan 雜犯

tsa-lei 雜類

Ts'ai, Lady 蔡氏

Ts'ai Ching 蔡京

Ts'ai River 蔡河

Ts'ai T'iao 蔡條

Ts'ai Yuan-ting 蔡元定

ts'e 策

Tseng Kung 曾鞏

Tseng Kung-liang 曾公亮

Tseng Tsao 曾慥

Tseng Ts'ung-lung 曾從龍

tso-yu wei-shang chiang-chün chieh-
tu-shih 左右衛上將軍節度使

tsu 族

Tsu-tsung ch'ing-hsi lu 祖宗慶系錄

tsun-chang 尊長

tsung 宗

tsung-cheng 宗正

Tsung-cheng ch'ing 宗正卿

tsung-cheng fang-jan chin-ssu kuan chi
宗正紡染金絲官記

Tsung-cheng shao-ch'ing 宗正少卿

Tsung-cheng ssu 宗正寺

Tsung-chih shu-chi 宗枝屬籍

tsung-fa 宗法

Tsung-fan ch'ing-hsi lu 宗藩慶系錄

tsung-hsing 宗姓

tsung-hsueh 宗學

tsung-ling 宗令

tsung-p'u 宗譜

tsung-shih 宗室

tsung-shih hsiang-shih 宗室鄉試

tsung-shih hui-shih 宗室會試

tsung-shih kuan-chuang 宗室官莊

tsung-tzu kai-en 宗子該恩

tsung-tzu kuo-li pu-kuan 宗子過禮
補官

tsung-tzu shih-fa 宗子試法

Tu 杜

Tu, Empress 杜太后

Tu Fan 杜範

Tu I t'ung chung p'ien 讀易通終篇

Tu Jang 杜讓

Tu-tsung 度宗

t'u-ch'en 圖

t'u-chen wen-shu 圖讖文書

Tuan, Prince of 端王

Tuan-p'ing 端平

Tuan-tsung 端宗

t'uan-lien-shih 團練使
Tun-tsung yuan 敦宗院
Tung-kung 東宮
Tung Ling-sheng 董令升
t'ung-chih 同知
t'ung-chih Ta-tsung-cheng ssu 同知大宗正司
T'ung Kuan 童貫
T'ung-tien 通典
T'ung-wen Hall 同文館
Tzu-chou (Ching-tung-tung) 淄州
tzu-fa 字法
tzu-i 諮議
tzu-i ts'an-chün 諮議參軍
Tzu-shan tien 自善殿
tzu-sung chai 自訟宅
tz'u-ch'en 詞臣
Tz'u-fu, Empress 慈福太后
tz'u-ming shou-kuan 賜名受官
tz'u-shih 刺史

wai-kuan 外官
wai-kuan fa 外官法
Wai tsung-cheng ssu 外宗正司
Wan-i 萬一
wang 王
Wang, Empress 王太后
Wang, Lady 王氏
Wang An-shih 王安石
wang-chai 王宅
Wang Chi 王墅
Wang Chi-en 王繼恩
Wang Chi-lung 王繼隆
Wang Ch'in-jo 王欽若
Wang Ch'iung 王瓊
wang-fu 王府
wang-fu chiao-shou 王府教授
Wang Hsi-chih 王羲之
Wang I 王誼
Wang I-tuan 王義端

Wang Huai 王淮
Wang Jung 王鎔
Wang Kuei 王桂
Wang Kung 王鞏
wang-kung ta hsiao hsueh 王宮大小學
Wang Lieh 王獵
Wang Mang 王莽
Wang Ming-ch'ing 王明清
Wang Sheng-to 王聖鐸
Wang Shih 王爽
Wang Tan 王旦
Wang T'ing-yun 王庭筠
Wang Tseng 王曾
Wang Yen 王淹
Wang Yen-ch'ao 王彥超
Wang Yuan 王淵
Wei, Lady 韋氏
Wei, Prince of 魏王
wei-ch'i 圍棋
wei-chiang-chün 衛將軍
wei-hsueh 偽學
wei-hsueh mi-tang 偽學逆黨
Wei Liao-weng 魏了翁
wei-po pu hsiu 惟薄不修
wen-chi 文集
Wen-chou (Liang-che) 溫州
Wen-hsien t'ung-k'ao 文獻通考
Wen Pi 文璧
Wen T'ien-hsiang 文天祥
wen-tzu 文字
Wen Yen-po 文彥博
Wu, Emperor 武帝
Wu, Senior Empress Dowager 吳憲聖太后
wu-chi 無耤
Wu-chou (Liang-che) 婺州
Wu Chü 吳琚
wu-chü chin-shih 武舉進士
wu fen 五分

wu-fu 五服
Wu Hsi 吳曦
Wu-hsing, Prince of 吳興王
wu-hsueh 武學
Wu Ko 吳革
Wu-kung, Commandary Prince of
　武功郡王
Wu Kuo-ting 武國定
Wu Lieh 吳獵
Wu Lung-ch'i 伍隆起
wu teng 五等
Wu T'ing 吳挺
Wu Tzu-liang 吳子良
Wu Yü 吳嶼
Wu Yü-yen 吳雨巖
Wu-yüeh 吳越

Yai-shan 崖山
Yang, Empress Dowager 楊皇后
Yang Chien 楊簡
Yang-chou (Huai-nan-tung) 楊州
Yang Chung-ho 楊中和
Yang I 楊億
Yang Liang-chieh 楊亮節
Yang Shih 楊時
Yang Wan-li 楊萬理
yao-chün t'uan-lien-shih 遙郡
　團練使
yao-chün tz'u-shih 遙郡刺史
Yao people 傜民
Yao T'an 姚坦
Yeh-ku chi 野谷集
Yeh Meng-te 葉夢得
Yeh Shih 葉適
Yen-ching (Liao) 燕京
Yen-chou (Liang-che) 嚴州
Yen-i, Prince of 燕懿王
Yen-ning Palace 延寧宮
Yen-shan 燕山

Yen-yün lu 燕雲錄
yin 陰
Yin county (Ch'ing-yuan fu) 鄞縣
ying 楹
Ying-chou (Ching-hsi-nan) 郢州
ying-chü 應舉
Ying-t'ien fu (Ching-tung-hsi) 應天府
Ying-tsung 英宗
yu 友
yu-chien-men-wei ta-chiang-chün
　右監門衛大將軍
yu ch'ien-niu-wei chiang-chün
　右千牛衛將軍
Yu-chou 幽州
Yu Chung-hung 游仲鴻
Yu Mao 尤袤
yu pan-tien-chih 右班殿直
yu-shih-chin 右侍禁
Yü 與
Yü Huan 于渙
Yü-kan county (Hsin-chou) 餘干縣
yü-shan 翊善
Yü-shan county (Shao-hsing fu) 玉山
　縣
Yü-tieh 玉牒
Yü-tieh suo 玉牒所
Yü Wen-pao 俞文豹
Yü-yao county 餘姚縣
Yü Yung-hsing 虞永興
Yuan-yu 元祐
Yueh-chou (Liang-che) 越州
Yueh Fei 岳飛
Yueh-lü Mieh-ssu 月呂篾思
Yun-chou (Chiang-nan-hsi) 筠州
Yung-an hsien (Ho-nan fu) 永安縣
Yung-chou (Ching-hu-nan) 永州
Yung-feng hsien (Chi-chou) 永豐縣
Yung-lo 永樂
yung-yeh t'ien 永業田

Index

Harvard East Asian Monographs
(* out-of-print)

Harvard East Asian Monographs

Harvard East Asian Monographs

Harvard East Asian Monographs

Harvard East Asian Monographs

Harvard East Asian Monographs